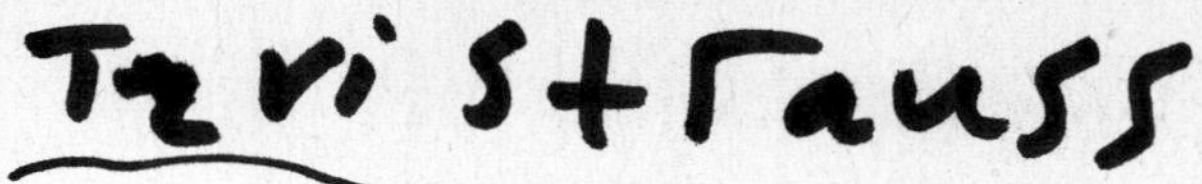

# CliffsTestPrep®

## Regents Living Environment Workbook

*An American BookWorks Corporation Project*


*Contributing Authors*

Vincent Amodeo
*Albany High School,*
*Albany, NY*

Kevin DiBitetto
*Garden City High School,*
*Garden City, NY*

Sandra Slusar
*Guilderland High School,*
*Guilderland, NY*

Carolyn Wilczynski
*Binghamton High School,*
*Binghamton, NY*


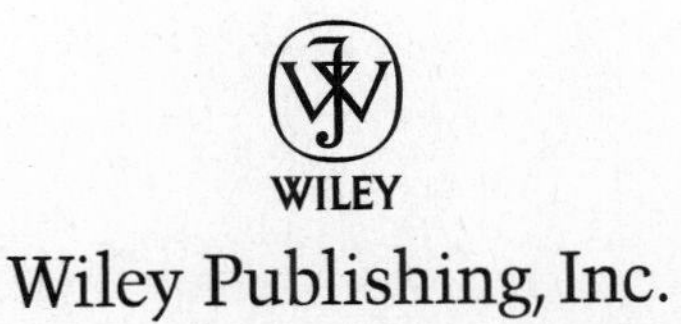

Wiley Publishing, Inc.

*Publisher's Acknowledgments*

*Editorial*

**Acquisitions Editor:** Greg Tubach

**Project Editor:** Elizabeth Kuball

**Copy Editor:** Elizabeth Kuball

**Technical Editor:** Irene Kasai

*Composition*

**Proofreader:** Melissa D. Buddendeck

Wiley Publishing, Inc. Composition Services

*CliffsTestPrep® Regents Living Environment Workbook*

Published by:
**Wiley Publishing, Inc.**
111 River Street
Hoboken, NJ 07030-5774
www.wiley.com



Published by Wiley, Hoboken, NJ
Published simultaneously in Canada

Library of Congress Cataloging-in-Publication data is available from the publisher upon request.

**ISBN:** 978-0-470-16783-0

Printed in the United States of America

10 9 8 7 6 5 4 3 2

# Table of Contents

# Introduction

## About This Book

The New York State Regents living environment examination is not an easy one, but we've tried to create a unique book that will help you prepare for this exam in a logical manner. Why is it unique? Instead of presenting pages and pages of review material, like most other test-preparation books, this book focuses solely on the test questions themselves. The more you practice answering the types of questions that will appear on the actual examination, the better you will do on the final test. Therefore, what we've done for you in this book is present you with hundreds of questions and answers—all from previous Regents exams.

To present these questions in a logical manner, we've divided the book into chapters based on the *types* of questions that you will find on the actual living environment exam. You will find all the same types of questions in a chapter together so you can practice answering them as you go along. We provide the answer explanations right after each question to help reinforce your knowledge. Read the question, answer it to the best of your ability, and then *immediately* check the answer to see if it's correct. We have focused on the correct answers here, although when a question may be somewhat confusing, we also explain why the other answers are incorrect. In most instances, the correct answers are factual, so if you get the correct answer, there is no need to explain why the other answers are incorrect. In the open-response questions, we explain the answers in clear, understandable terms.

We have divided the book into eight major sections based on the requirements of the actual exam:

- Organization of Life
- Genetics
- Evolution: Change over Time
- Reproduction and Development
- Homeostasis
- Ecology
- Human Impact on the Environment
- Laboratory Skills: Scientific Inquiry and Technique

Within each topic, we've also included the subtopics that are normally covered on the exam and you find each answer coded by this subtopic. By using these subtopics, you can quickly determine where you need additional help. These topics include the following:

- The Characteristics of Life
- Cell Structure
- Cells and Their Environment

- Single-Cell and Multicellular Organisms
- Heredity
- The Structure of DNA/RNA
- How a Gene Becomes a Protein
- Genetic Engineering
- The Theory of Evolution
- Mechanisms of Evolution
- Patterns of Evolution
- Types of Reproduction
- Cell Division
- Human Reproduction
- Technology of Reproduction
- Biochemistry
- Feedback
- Human Body Systems
- Disease
- Biodiversity
- Organisms in Their Environment
- The Structure of Ecosystems
- Energy Flow in Ecosystems
- Positive Effects of Humans on the Environment
- Negative Effects of Humans on the Environment
- Microscopes
- Lab Safety
- Scientific Method
- Interpreting Graphs
- Diffusion/Osmosis
- Biodiversity
- Making Connections
- Beaks of Finches

As you work through the book, it's up to you to answer the questions before you look at the answers. You're "on your honor" to test yourself. There's no grade at the end, of course, so if you look at the answers first, you're only cheating yourself. You will want to practice answering as many of the test questions as possible.

# The Multiple-Choice Format

Most of the standardized tests that you've probably taken throughout your educational career have contained multiple-choice questions. For some reason, these types of questions give a large percentage of test-takers a difficult time. If you approach these questions carefully, they're easier than you think.

Let's analyze the concept of the multiple-choice question. Keep in mind that these questions are created to test your ability to recognize the correct answer from four choices, at least on this specific exam. Other tests may have more or fewer choices.

Questions are comprised of several parts:

- The question stem
- The correct choice
- Distracters

As test-item writers create questions, they normally approach it as follows:

- One choice is absolutely correct.
- One or two choices are absolutely incorrect (distracters).
- One or two choices may be similar to the correct answer, but may contain some information that is not quite accurate or on target, or even may not answer the specific question (distracters).

How do you approach these questions? First, read the question and see whether you know the answer. If you know it automatically, then you can look at the choices and select the correct one. But keep in mind that the answers to the multiple-choice questions on the living environment exam are based on specific material that you may have read or listened to, so keep this in mind as you go through the passages. Do not bring in any outside knowledge. Just focus on the question and the material on which it is based.

The easiest way to answer a multiple-choice question is the time-honored approach of *process of elimination*—especially if you don't know the answer right from the start.

You start by eliminating choices that do not seem logical, or those that you know immediately are incorrect. If you can start by eliminating one of those choices, you now have only three choices left. You've increased your odds of selecting the correct answer from one out of four (25 percent) to one out of three (33⅓ percent), which is a lot better.

Can you eliminate another answer choice? Perhaps one doesn't sound quite right, or it doesn't seem to pertain to the passage you just read. If you can eliminate another choice, you've increased your odds to one out of two (50 percent).

Now, unless you know the correct answer, you can guess.

Pay attention to words like *always, never,* or *not.* Most things in the world are not *always* or *never,* and you should be careful if a question asks you to choose which of the choices is *not.* Watch the wording also on questions that state "All are correct *except. . . .*"

# The Open-Response Format

The open-response (or constructed-response) questions appear in many forms throughout parts B, C, and D, and these formats vary throughout the years. We present a wide-range of these questions so that you'll be prepared for any eventuality.

You may be asked to read a passage and interpret it. The question will likely ask you to base your answers on the passage *as well as your knowledge of biology.* You will also be given graphs or charts and asked to interpret them, organize and/or plot data, and answer questions based on the reorganized data. Other questions will present illustrations and ask you several questions so that you can demonstrate your understanding of the illustration presented, and utilize your knowledge of the subject in order to correctly answer the questions. Unlike the multiple-choice questions in Part A, these are *not* fact-based questions, and will include the material that you've covered throughout the course.

The living environment exam can be difficult, but as long as you read carefully, follow the instructions, and, most important, understand the material, you should be able to do well on the exam. Practice answering all the questions in the book to become familiar with the style and approach that you'll find on the actual exam. Check your answers as you go through the material. Try to determine what needs further study. The wealth of questions and answers presented here represent almost all the material that you've studied throughout the year and should serve as an ideal review of the subject.

Finally, take the practice test at the end of the book and, again, check your answers. It's the best way to evaluate how far you've come and how prepared you are for the actual test. Don't panic if you had problems with this test. Go back to the subjects and reread the earlier questions in the appropriate chapters. If you still don't understand the material, check your textbook, or ask your teacher.

Remember that the more you practice, the better you will do on your actual test. But now it's time to start working. Good luck!

# Organization of Life

**Directions:** For each statement or question, choose the *number* of the word or expression that best completes the statement or answers the question. Then check your answer against the one that immediately follows the question. Try not to look at the answer before making your selection.

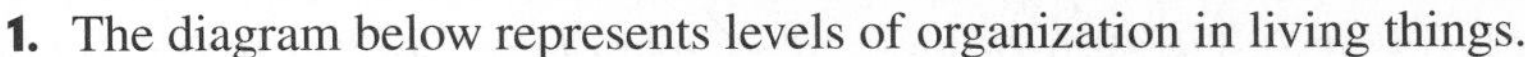

**1.** The diagram below represents levels of organization in living things.

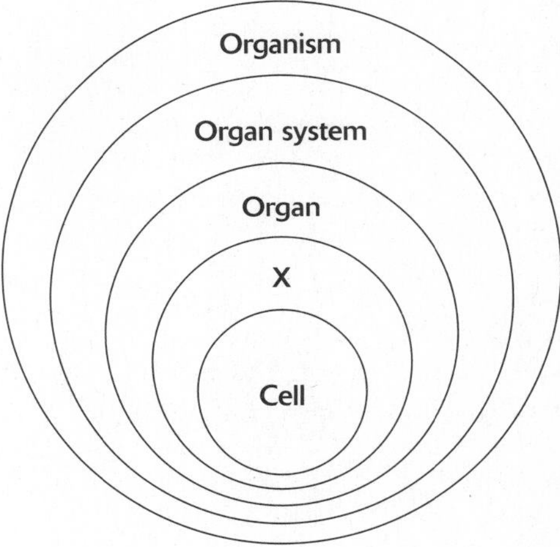


Which term would best represent X?

**(1)** human
**(2)** tissue
**(3)** stomach
**(4)** organelle

**Correct Answer: (2)** Cells are the basic unit of life. In other words, all living things are made of cells. A group of cells that work together to perform a function are called tissues. Tissues that work together to perform a function are called an organ. Several organs that work together to perform a function are called a system. All together these make the whole organism. So, for example, in a human (organism), there are many systems (digestive, circulatory, reproductive, and so on). Within each system, there are several organs (the digestive system is made up of a stomach, small intestine, colon, pancreas, and so on). The colon is made of tissue, which is made of cells. *(Single-Cell and Multicellular Organisms)*

**2.** Which sequence illustrates the increasing complexity of levels of organization in multicellular organisms?

**(1)** organelle → cell → tissue → organ → organ system → organism
**(2)** cell → organelle → tissue → organ → organ system → organism
**(3)** organelle → tissue → cell → organ → organ system → organism
**(4)** cell → organism → organ system → organ → tissue → organelle

**Correct Answer: (1)** This is the correct order for placing the terms in an increasing level of complexity. Most times you can answer this kind of question if you know what the first and last terms should be. Using this strategy you can get rid of choices (2) and (4), leaving you with (1) and (3). The only difference between (1) and (3) is with the second and third terms of each choice. To answer the question correctly, you need to know the order of how living things become more complex. *(The Characteristics of Life)*

**3.** Which structures in diagram I and diagram II carry out a similar life function?

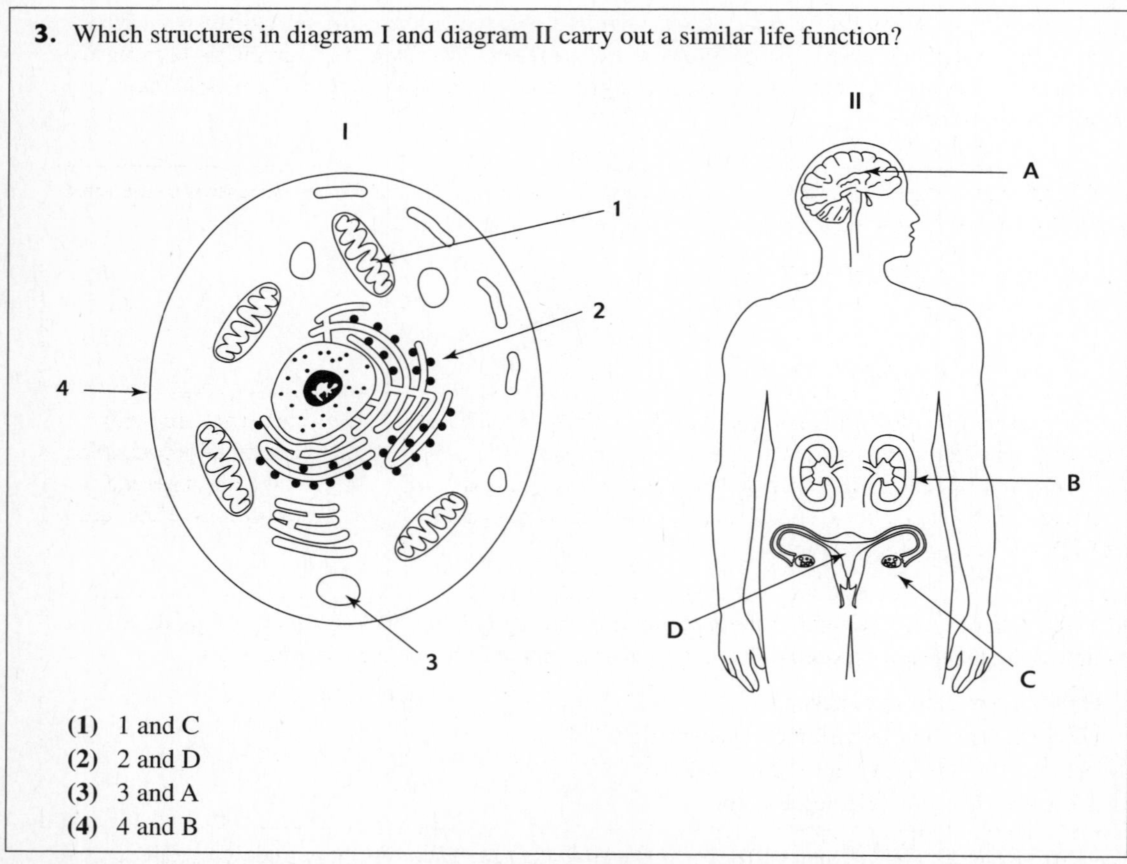


**(1)** 1 and C
**(2)** 2 and D
**(3)** 3 and A
**(4)** 4 and B

**Correct Answer: (4)** In choice (1), 1 is the mitochondrion, noted as the site of cellular respiration and the production of energy. Its match, C, is an ovary, which produces eggs and female hormones—not a match. In choice (2), organelle 2 is the rough ER, which is used to transport materials through the cytoplasm. It is paired with D, the uterus. The uterus is where the embryo develops—not a match. In choice (3), organelle 3 is the vacuole, a storage site for food, water, and wastes. It is paired with A, the brain—not a match. The best answer is choice (4), the cell membrane, which is paired with B, the kidney. The cell membrane performs several important functions: It provides the cell with shape and some protection; it has protein receptors in it to receive information and cell identity, and it is paired with B, the kidney, because of the cell membranes' ability to regulate or filter what passes into and out of the cell, a characteristic known as *selective permeability.* The kidneys perform a similar function by filtering the blood, removing impurities that need to be excreted, and reabsorbing water and essential molecules. *(The Characteristics of Life)*

**4.** Which sequence represents the correct order of organization in complex organisms?

**(1)** tissues → organs → systems → cells
**(2)** organs → tissues → systems → cells
**(3)** systems → organs → cells → tissues
**(4)** cells → tissues → organs → systems

**Correct Answer: (4)** Cells are the smallest unit of life. In complex organisms, cells of the same type make up tissue, which helps the organ to function in each system. Muscle cells combine to form muscle tissue. Muscle tissue makes the heart, which is an organ in the circulatory system. *(Single-Cell and Multicellular Organisms)*

**5.** Which sequence of terms represents a *decrease* from the greatest number of structures to the least number of structures present in a cell?

**(1)** nucleus → gene → chromosome
**(2)** gene → nucleus → chromosome
**(3)** gene → chromosome → nucleus
**(4)** chromosome → gene → nucleus

**Correct Answer: (3)** Most students would answer this question based on size of the structure, with nucleus being the largest then decreasing in size to the gene. You have to know the level of organization (genes make up chromosomes, which are found in the nucleus), and you must read the question and answers carefully. In cells, there is only one nucleus. In humans, there are 46 chromosomes. There are about 40,000 genes. *(Cell Structure)*

**6.** Plants inherit genes that enable them to produce chlorophyll, but this pigment is not produced unless the plants are exposed to light. This is an example of how the environment can

**(1)** cause mutations to occur
**(2)** influence the expression of a genetic trait
**(3)** result in the appearance of a new species
**(4)** affect one plant species, but not another

**Correct Answer: (2)** Genes can be affected by the environment. What makes this question hard are the words *the expression of a genetic trait.* You probably know that genes control what traits you have, but you may not be sure what *the expression of a genetic trait* means. Most of the time, *the expression of a genetic trait* means what we see on or about an organism: hair color, eye color, attached ear lobes, and so on. Even though we can't see chlorophyll, it is still a trait that is "expressed." *(Cells and Their Environment)*

**7.** Which organelle is correctly paired with its specific function?

**(1)** cell membrane—storage of hereditary information
**(2)** chloroplast—transport of materials
**(3)** ribosome—synthesis of proteins
**(4)** vacuole—production of ATP

**Correct Answer: (3)** Ribosomes are the sites of protein synthesis. mRNA brings the information from the DNA code to the ribosome, where a protein is produced. *(Cell Structure)*

**8.** Hereditary information is stored inside the

**(1)** ribosomes, which have chromosomes that contain many genes
**(2)** ribosomes, which have genes that contain many chromosomes
**(3)** nucleus, which has chromosomes that contain many genes
**(4)** nucleus, which has genes that contain many chromosomes

**Correct Answer: (3)** DNA makes up chromosomes. A section of DNA that codes for a particular trait is known as a gene. There are many genes found on each chromosome. The chromosomes hold the genetic information of the cell. Chromosomes are found in the nucleus. Ribosomes are used by the cell to help translate the DNA and build proteins that the cell can use. *(Cell Structure)*

**9.** Which statements best describe the relationship between the terms *chromosomes, genes,* and *nuclei?*

**(1)** Chromosomes are found on genes. Genes are found in nuclei.
**(2)** Chromosomes are found in nuclei. Nuclei are found in genes.
**(3)** Genes are found on chromosomes. Chromosomes are found in nuclei.
**(4)** Genes are found in nuclei. Nuclei are found in chromosomes.

**Correct Answer: (3)** Genes are segments of chromosomes and chromosomes are found in the nuclei of cells. *(Cell Structure)*

**10.** Homeostasis in unicellular organisms depends on the proper functioning of

**(1)** organelles
**(2)** insulin
**(3)** guard cells
**(4)** antibodies

**Correct Answer: (1)** Homeostasis is the ability to maintain a stable internal environment (equilibrium). The organelles are the working parts of a cell the way the organs are the working parts of a body system. Because a unicellular organism doesn't have systems, the organelles are responsible for maintaining homeostasis in the cell. *(Single-Cell and Multicellular Organisms)*

**11.** A human liver cell is very different in structure and function from a nerve cell in the same person. This is best explained by the fact that

(1) different genes function in each type of cell
(2) liver cells can reproduce while the nerve cells cannot
(3) liver cells contain fewer chromosomes than nerve cells
(4) different DNA is present in each type of cell

**Correct Answer: (1)** Each cell in a human body has a complete set of identical DNA (except for the gametes). Each cell, however, uses only a portion of the DNA in order to function. An analogy is an instruction manual for a video gaming system. The manual may contain the complete instruction manual in different languages. You ignore the instructions in Japanese or French, because you don't use those languages. Similarly, a liver cell would ignore the portion of DNA that pertains to a nerve cell, and vice versa. *(Single-Cell and Multicellular Organisms)*

**12.** Which statement best compares a multicellular organism to a single-celled organism?

(1) A multicellular organism has organ systems that interact to carry out life functions, while a single-celled organism carries out life functions without using organ systems.
(2) A single-celled organism carries out fewer life functions than each cell of a multicellular organism.
(3) A multicellular organism always obtains energy through a process that is different from that used by a single-celled organism.
(4) The cell of a single-celled organism is always much larger than an individual cell of a multicellular organism.

**Correct Answer: (1)** All cells are relatively small because diffusion must occur efficiently in order for the cell to stay alive. All cells utilize cellular respiration to obtain energy from their food source. All organisms carry out the same life functions. However, multicellular organisms have organ systems to carry out life functions, while single-cell organisms accomplish the same goal without using organ systems. *(Single-Cell and Multicellular Organisms)*

**13.** Some human body cells are shown in the diagrams below.

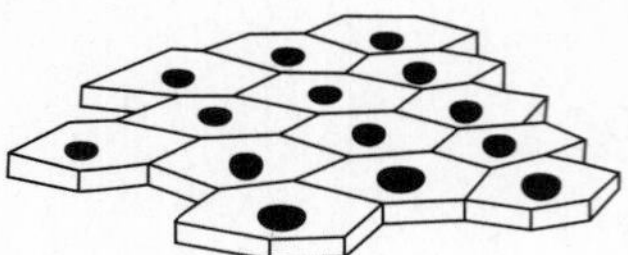

Cells from skin

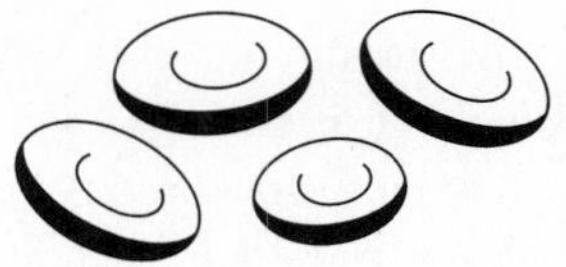

Blood cells

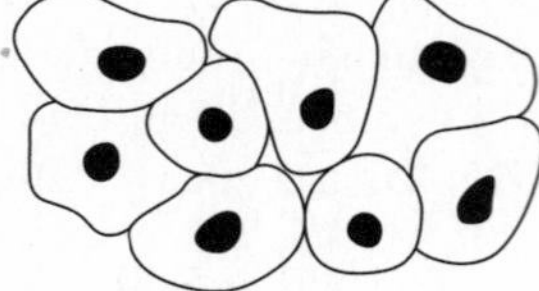

Cells from lining of bladder

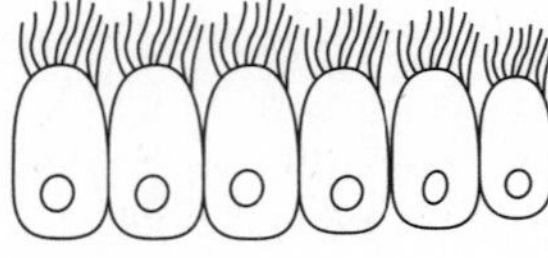

Cells from lining of trachea

These groups of cells represent different

**(1)** tissues in which similar cells function together
**(2)** organs that help to carry out a specific life activity
**(3)** systems that are responsible for a specific life activity
**(4)** organelles that carry out different functions

**Correct Answer: (1)** By definition, tissue is a group of similar cells that work together to perform one function. So, in the diagram, a group of skin cells act together to form a barrier. Red blood cells work together to carry oxygen. Bladder cells line the bladder and the trachea cells trap foreign particles like dust, pollen, and so on from entering the lungs. The rest of the choices are all true statements, but they are not represented in the diagram. *(Single-Cell and Multicellular Organisms)*

**14.** The arrows in the diagram below indicate the movement of materials into and out of a single-celled organism.

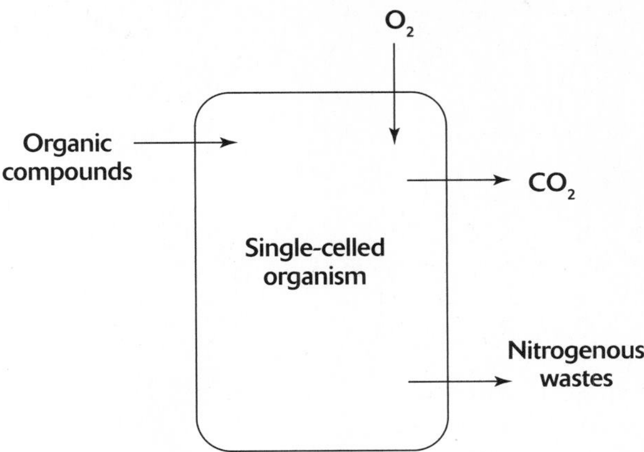


The movements indicated by all the arrows are directly involved in

**(1)** the maintenance of homeostasis
**(2)** photosynthesis only
**(3)** excretion only
**(4)** the digestion of minerals

**Correct Answer: (1)** The cell membrane is selectively permeable—it allows some substances to pass through it in either direction and does not allow other substances to do the same. Cells take in materials needed to perform life functions, and release materials that are considered waste products and potentially dangerous to maintain homeostasis—a stable internal environment. *(Cells and Their Environment)*

**15.** In the human pancreas, acinar cells produce digestive enzymes and beta cells produce insulin. The best explanation for this is that

**(1)** a mutation occurs in the beta cells to produce insulin when the sugar level increases in the blood
**(2)** different parts of an individual's DNA are used to direct the synthesis of different proteins in different types of cells
**(3)** lowered sugar levels cause the production of insulin in acinar cells to help maintain homeostasis
**(4)** the genes in acinar cells came from one parent while the genes in beta cells came from the other parent

**Correct Answer: (2)** In multicellular organisms, groups of cells that perform the same functions make up tissues, and groups of tissues make up organs. Although every cell in these tissues and organs has the same genetic information, different cells perform different functions and produce different proteins because only some of the genes are expressed, or "turned on," at a given time. In this case, the human pancreas is an organ made up of different tissues. Some of those tissues contain acinar cells in which the genes that produce digestive enzymes are "turned on" and some tissues contain beta cells in which the genes that produce insulin are "turned on." *(Single-Cell and Multicellular Organisms)*

**16.** The cells that make up the skin of an individual have some functions different from the cells that make up the liver because

(1) all cells have a common ancestor
(2) different cells have different genetic material
(3) environment and past history have no influence on cell function
(4) different parts of genetic instructions are used in different types of cells

**Correct Answer: (4)** Every cell in an organism has the same genetic information, but different cells perform different functions. Genes, which are responsible for the production of particular proteins, are turned "on" or "off" depending on the needs of the particular cell. *(Single-Cell and Multicellular Organisms)*

**17.** The organism represented below is multicellular, heterotrophic, and completely aquatic.

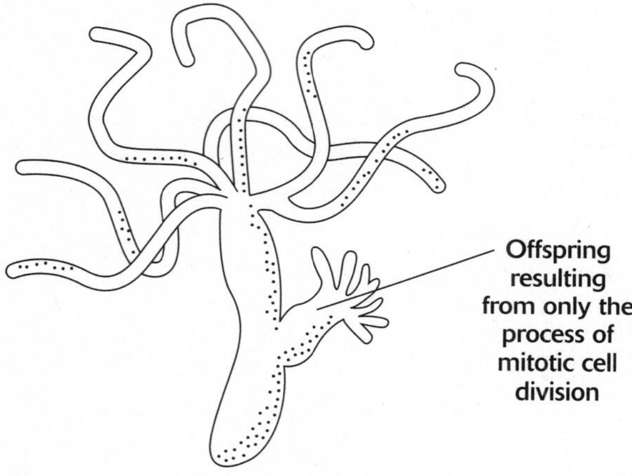


Which other characteristics could be used to describe this organism?

(1) carries out photosynthesis and needs oxygen
(2) deposits cellular wastes on land and decomposes dead organisms
(3) reproduces asexually and is a consumer
(4) reproduces in a water habitat and is a producer

**Correct Answer: (3)** The description of the organism provides a lot of information. It tells you that the organism is made up of more than one cell (multicellular), it relies on other organisms for its nutrition (heterotrophic), and it lives in the water (aquatic). Choice (3) tells you that the organism is a consumer. This meshes with the information given that it is a heterotroph. The diagram shows a new offspring budding off from the organism, and the diagram states that it is going through mitotic cell division, which is another way to say it is asexual. The organism cannot be a heterotroph and carry on photosynthesis at the same time, as in choice (1). If it lives in the water, it cannot deposit wastes on land, as in choice (2). And it cannot be a producer (which is the realm of plants) if it is described as a heterotroph, as in choice (4). *(Single-Cell and Multicellular Organisms)*

**18.** Which group contains only molecules that are each assembled from smaller organic compounds?

**(1)** proteins, water, DNA, fats
**(2)** proteins, starch, carbon dioxide, water
**(3)** proteins, DNA, fats, starch
**(4)** proteins, carbon dioxide, DNA, starch

**Correct Answer: (3)** The key here is knowing that, in this choice, all the compounds are organic and that if you're going to assemble molecules from smaller organic compounds, then the compound you make must also be organic. So, even if you don't know what smaller organic compounds the compounds in this choice are made from, you can eliminate the other choice on the basis that each one has an inorganic compound among them: In choice (1), the inorganic compound is water; in choice (2), there are two inorganic compounds, water and carbon dioxide; and in choice (4), the inorganic compound is carbon dioxide. *(The Characteristics of Life)*

**19.** Plants in areas with short growing seasons often have more chloroplasts in their cells than plants in areas with longer growing seasons. Compared to plants in areas with longer growing seasons, plants in areas with shorter growing seasons most likely

**(1)** make and store food more quickly
**(2)** have a higher rate of protein metabolism
**(3)** grow taller
**(4)** have a different method of respiration

**Correct Answer: (1)** Chloroplasts are the site of photosynthesis, and photosynthesis is the process of making food. In areas with shorter growing seasons, plants have more chloroplasts to make the food they need to survive the shorter season. *(The Characteristics of Life)*

**20.** An enzyme known as rubisco enables plants to use large amounts of carbon dioxide. This enzyme is most likely active in the

**(1)** nucleus
**(2)** vacuoles
**(3)** mitochondria
**(4)** chloroplasts

**Correct Answer: (4)** Plants use carbon dioxide during photosynthesis to produce sugar. Photosynthesis occurs within the chloroplasts, so this is where the carbon dioxide is used. The enzyme rubisco is involved in photosynthesis and would be active in the chloroplast. *(Cell Structure)*

**21.** Which process provides the initial energy to support all the levels in the energy pyramid shown below?

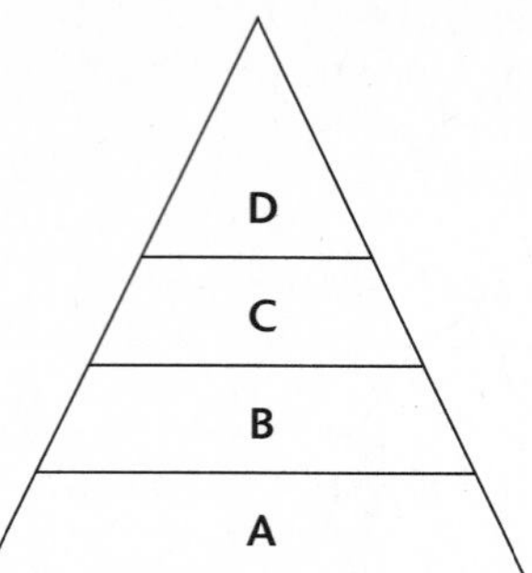


(1) circulation
(2) photosynthesis
(3) active transport
(4) digestion

**Correct Answer: (2)** Photosynthesis in plants and algae provides energy in the form of glucose that all other forms of life depend on. Choice (1), circulation, is not an energy-producing process. Choice (3), active transport, is a process that needs energy—it does not supply it. Choice (4), digestion, does provide energy, but it does not begin in the bottom level, A—it only takes place above level A by consumers. *(The Characteristics of Life)*

**22.** Starch molecules present in a maple tree are made from materials that originally entered the tree from the external environment as

(1) enzymes
(2) simple sugars
(3) amino acids
(4) inorganic compounds

**Correct Answer: (4)** Starch is an organic molecule that contains carbon and hydrogen. The molecules that enter the plant that are involved in producing the starch during photosynthesis are water and carbon dioxide. Both water and carbon dioxide are considered inorganic compounds because neither contains carbon and hydrogen together. *(Cell Structure)*

**23.** Which statement best describes cellular respiration?

(1) It occurs in animal cells but not in plant cells.
(2) It converts energy in food into a more usable form.
(3) It uses carbon dioxide and produces oxygen.
(4) It stores energy in food molecules.

**Correct Answer: (2)** Whenever you see the words *respiration, oxygen, energy, glucose,* and *mitochondria,* you must realize that they are connected to each other. You may not know exactly how they are connected, but you should realize that they are. The mitochondria takes food in the form of glucose and uses oxygen to "burn it," to release the energy stored in the bonds of the glucose molecule. When you burn a piece of wood and get heat (and light) that is stored in the bonds of the wood, you know that in order to burn anything you need oxygen. The same is true with respiration and glucose: You need oxygen to burn to release the energy. *(The Characteristics of Life)*

Base your answer to question 24 on the chart below and on your knowledge of biology.

| *A* | *B* | *C* |
|---|---|---|
| The diversity of multicellular organisms increases. | Simple, single-celled organisms appear. | Multicellular organisms begin to evolve. |

**24.** According to most scientists, which sequence best represents the order of biological evolution on Earth?

(1) A → B → C
(2) B → C → A
(3) B → A → C
(4) C → A → B

**Correct Answer: (2)** Because the atmosphere of early Earth contained little or no oxygen, the first organisms thought to have appeared on Earth were single-celled anaerobic prokaryotes, most likely taking in organic molecules from their environment. Over time, complex autotrophic and heterotrophic multicellular organisms began to develop as oxygen was added to the environment. Finally, organisms would continue to grow and develop until many different species existed on Earth. *(Single-Cell and Multicellular Organisms)*

**25.** Which change in a sample of pond water could indicate that heterotrophic microbes were active?

(1) increase in ozone level
(2) increase in glucose level
(3) decrease in oxygen level
(4) decrease in carbon dioxide level

**Correct Answer: (3)** Heterotrophic organisms are those that do not produce their own food. Heterotrophs, also known as consumers, utilize oxygen while producing carbon dioxide during cellular respiration. A water sample in which heterotrophs were present would have a decrease in oxygen levels over time because these organisms were using oxygen for cellular respiration. *(Cell Structure)*

**26.** The diagram below represents a cell organelle involved in the transfer of energy from organic compounds.

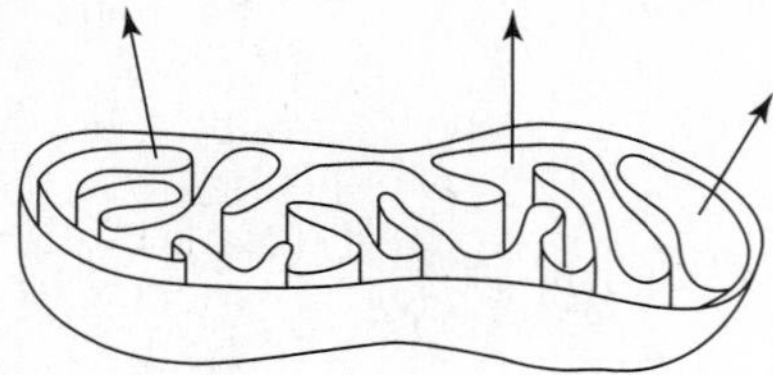

The arrows in the diagram could represent the release of

(1) ATP from a chloroplast carrying out photosynthesis
(2) oxygen from a mitochondrion carrying out photosynthesis
(3) glucose from a chloroplast carrying out respiration
(4) carbon dioxide from a mitochondrion carrying out respiration

**Correct Answer: (4)** The diagram shows a mitochondrion, the organelle in which cell respiration occurs. Cell respiration uses oxygen and glucose to produce ATP, an energy-rich molecule that the cell utilizes, and carbon dioxide a waste product. *(Cell Structure)*

**27.** Antibody molecules and receptor molecules are similar in that they both

(1) control transport through the cell membrane
(2) have a specific shape related to their specific function
(3) remove wastes from the body
(4) speed up chemical reactions in cells

**Correct Answer: (2)** Antibodies and receptor molecules (the latter of which are found in the cell membrane) function because of their unique shape. They have a unique shape because they are proteins, and all proteins (including all different kinds of molecules) have a three-dimensional shape. Each one is different from the next. This unique shape is key to the function of a protein. If the molecules are antibodies, their shape must match up with the antigens that they are made to fight. If the molecules are receptor molecules, they must match up to receive the correct molecules. *(The Characteristics of Life)*

**28.** The diagram below illustrates the movement of materials involved in a process that is vital for the energy needs of an organism.

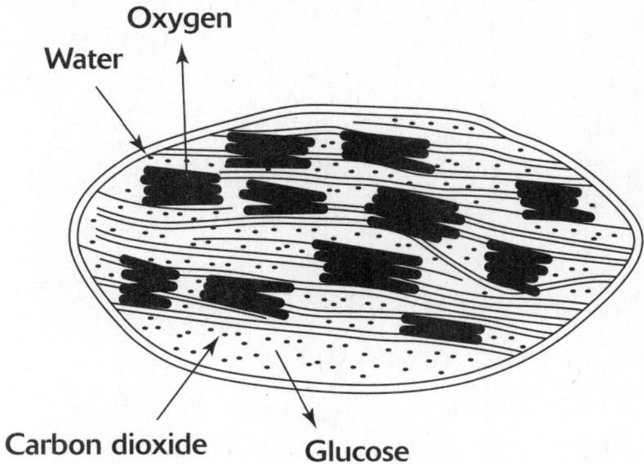


The process illustrated occurs within

**(1)** chloroplasts
**(2)** mitochondria
**(3)** ribosomes
**(4)** vacuoles

**Correct Answer: (1)** Everything in the diagram is involved in both respiration and photosynthesis. This is one of the few times when you need to be able to tell the difference between a mitochondrion and a chloroplast based solely on what they look like. This is a diagram of a chloroplast. The inside of a chloroplast has those small stacks that look a little bit like a small stack of coins. The inside of a mitochondrion—choice (2)—has a wavy appearance. If it were a ribosome—choice (3)—you would expect to find amino acids and proteins inside. *Remember:* The ribosome is the site of protein synthesis. Inside a vacuole—choice (4)—you would most likely find water or wastes, not essential molecules like those in the diagram. *(Cell Structure)*

**29.** The green aquatic plant represented in the diagram below was exposed to light for several hours.

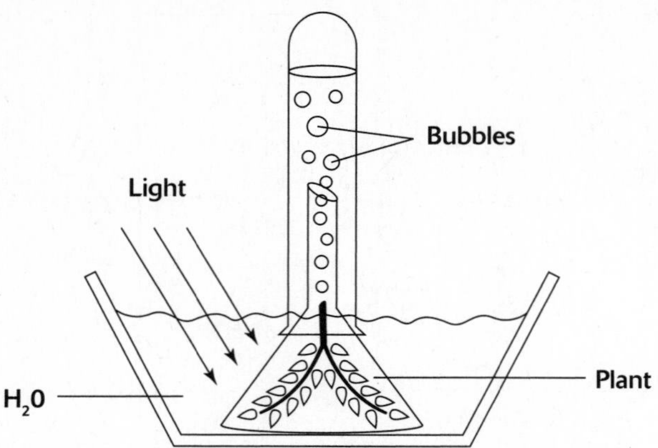


Which gas would most likely be found in the greatest amount in the bubbles?

**(1)** oxygen
**(2)** nitrogen
**(3)** ozone
**(4)** carbon dioxide

**Correct Answer: (1)** The key to this question is the light. It means that the plant is going to be going through photosynthesis, and photosynthesis produces oxygen. *(Cells and Their Environment)*

**30.** Which process usually uses carbon dioxide molecules?

**(1)** cellular respiration
**(2)** asexual reproduction
**(3)** active transport
**(4)** autotrophic nutrition

**Correct Answer: (4)** The process of photosynthesis carried out by autotrophs requires carbon dioxide, water, and solar energy. Oxygen gas is a product of photosynthesis and is used in the process of aerobic cellular respiration. *(The Characteristics of Life)*

**31.** Which set of terms best identifies the letters in the diagram below?

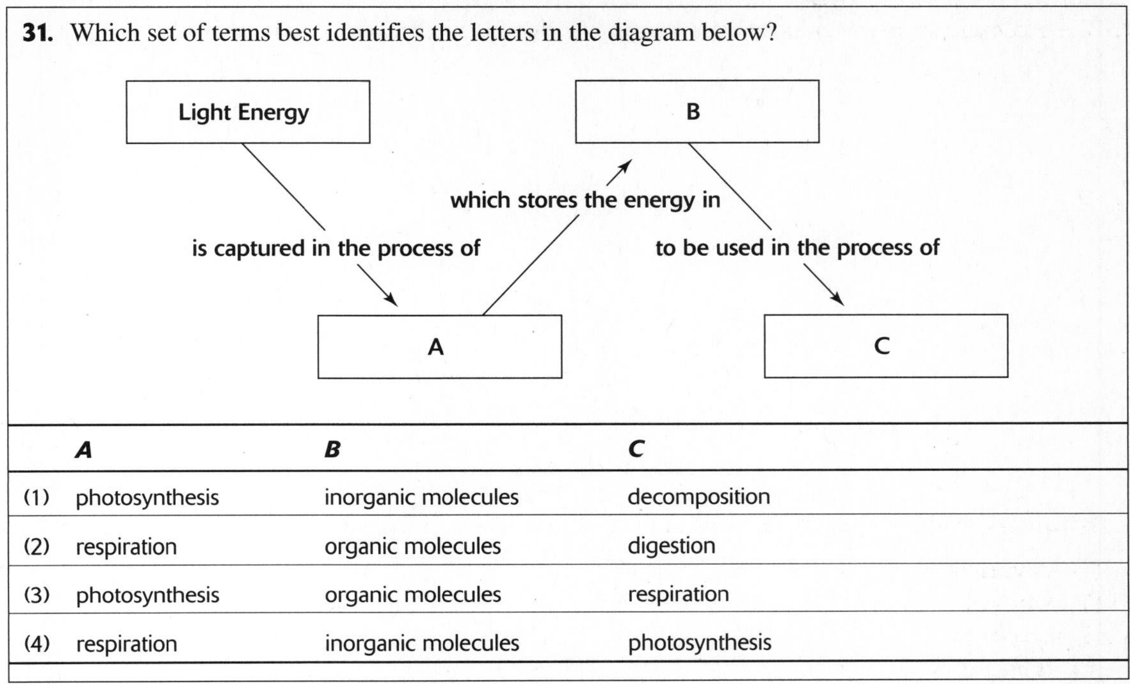


| | *A* | *B* | *C* |
|---|---|---|---|
| (1) | photosynthesis | inorganic molecules | decomposition |
| (2) | respiration | organic molecules | digestion |
| (3) | photosynthesis | organic molecules | respiration |
| (4) | respiration | inorganic molecules | photosynthesis |

**Correct Answer: (3)** Light energy is captured by plants in the process of photosynthesis. Photosynthesis is the process by which plants use the energy from the sun to convert inorganic molecules, such as water and carbon dioxide, into organic molecules, such as sugars. Those sugars are then used by the plant for respiration to fuel activities such as growth and reproduction. *(Cell Structure)*

**32.** The diagram below shows the relative concentration of molecules inside and outside of a cell.

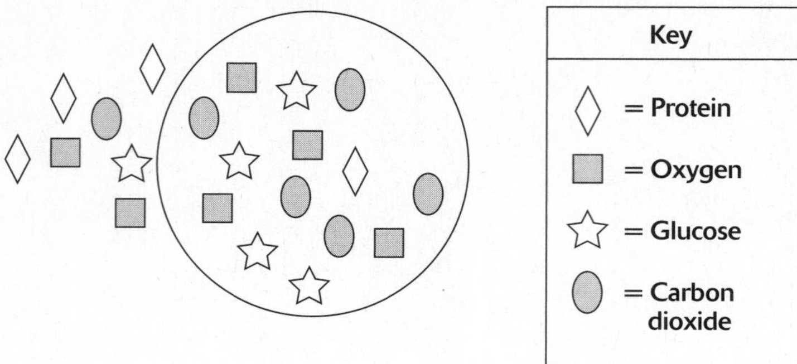


Which statement best describes the general direction of diffusion across the membrane of this cell?

**(1)** Glucose would diffuse into the cell.
**(2)** Protein would diffuse out of the cell.
**(3)** Carbon dioxide would diffuse out of the cell.
**(4)** Oxygen would diffuse into the cell.

**Correct Answer: (3)** Diffusion describes passive transport. Molecules will move from higher concentration to lower concentration. There are four carbon dioxide molecules inside the cell and only two carbon dioxide molecules outside of the cell. Movement will be from the inside (higher concentration) to the outside (lower concentration). *(Cells and Their Environment)*

**33.** In the diagram below, which structure performs a function similar to a function of the human lungs?

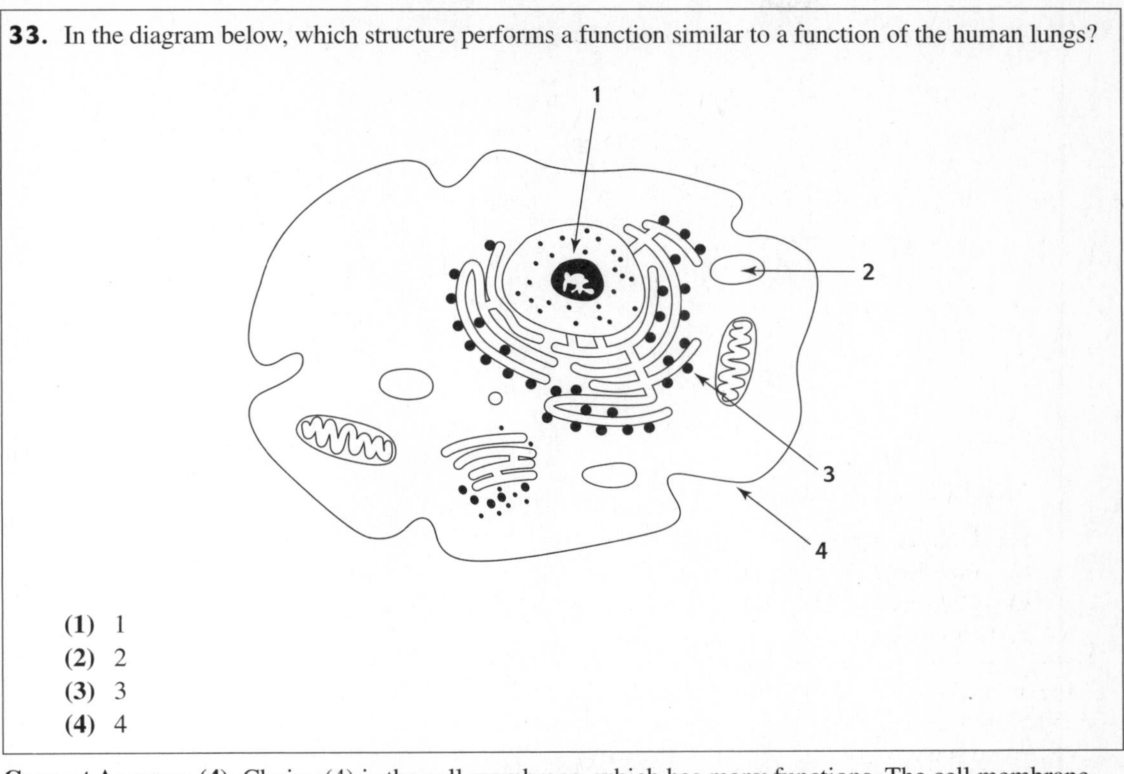


**(1)** 1
**(2)** 2
**(3)** 3
**(4)** 4

**Correct Answer: (4)** Choice (4) is the cell membrane, which has many functions. The cell membrane is most similar to the lungs because it allows for the diffusion of material into and out of the cell. The alveoli of the lungs carry out a similar function; this is where gases, carbon dioxide, and oxygen diffuse into and out of the capillaries surrounding the alveoli, into the alveoli. Choice (1) is the nucleus, which is where the cell is controlled. Choice (2) is a vacuole used for storage. Choice (3) is the endoplasmic reticulum, which is involved in transport. *(Cell Structure)*

**34.** Cellular communication is illustrated in the diagram below.

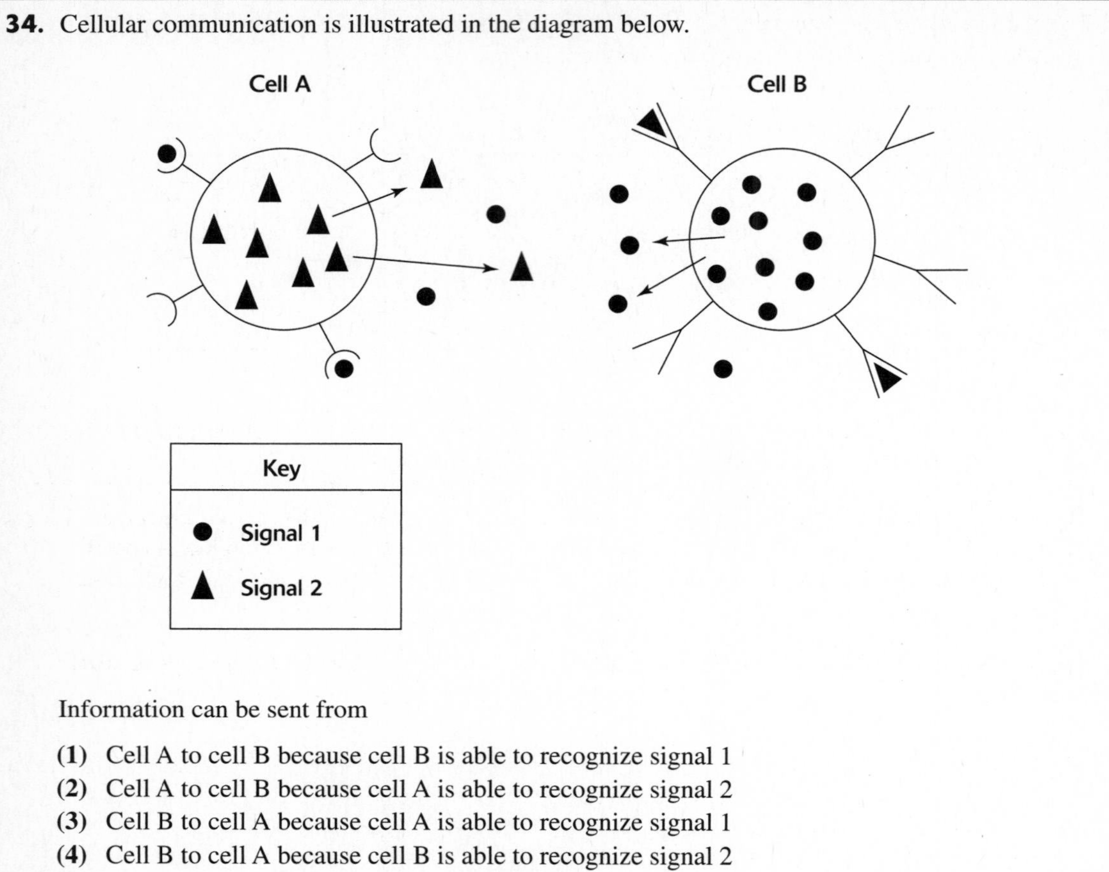


Information can be sent from

**(1)** Cell A to cell B because cell B is able to recognize signal 1
**(2)** Cell A to cell B because cell A is able to recognize signal 2
**(3)** Cell B to cell A because cell A is able to recognize signal 1
**(4)** Cell B to cell A because cell B is able to recognize signal 2

**Correct Answer: (3)** Cell A produces signal 2 (triangles), which can be seen inside the cell. Cell A, however, can recognize signal 1 (circles), and some of the receptors (which look like antennae) on the outside of cell A have received the message (circles) from cell B. Cell B produces signal 1 (circles), which can be seen inside the cell. Cell B, however, can recognize signal 2 (triangles), and some of the receptors on the outside of cell B have received the message (circles) from cell A. *(Cells and Their Environment)*

**35.** The chart below contains a number of characteristics for three different organisms. The characteristics can be used in classifying these organisms.

| *Characteristics* | *Organism A* | *Organism B* | *Organism C* |
|---|---|---|---|
| Number of cells | Unicellular | Multicellular | Unicellular |
| Type of nutrition | Autotrophic | Autotrophic | Heterotrophic |
| Nuclear membrane | Absent | Present | Absent |
| DNA | Present | Present | Present |

Which *two* organisms would be expected to have the most similar genetic material? Support your answer using information from the chart.

**Correct Answer: A and C** Organisms A and C would be expected to have the most similar genetic material because they have more characteristics in common than any other combination like A and B or B and C. Organisms A and C are both unicellular and the nuclear membrane is absent in both. *(The Characteristics of Life)*

Base your answers to questions 36 and 37 on the diagram below of a cell associated with coordination and on your knowledge of biology.

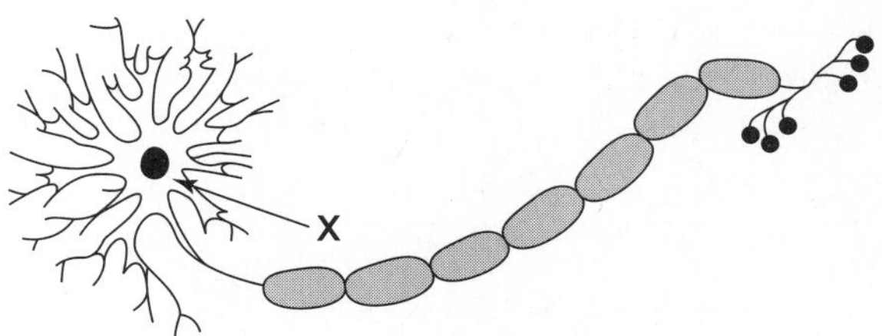


**36.** Structure X would be involved in the

**(1)** storage of digestive enzymes
**(2)** absorption of energy from the sun
**(3)** development of pathogens
**(4)** synthesis of proteins

**Correct Answer: (4)** This diagram represents a neuron or nerve cell, which communicates with other neurons to send and receive messages (also known as impulses). The choices offered really don't have anything to do with this function, so you need to pick the next best thing and that is choice (4): synthesis of proteins. *(Cell Structure)*

**37.** Which statement best describes a function of the entire structure shown in the diagram?

(1) It unites with an egg cell during fertilization.
(2) It synthesizes a hormone involved in the control of blood sugar level.
(3) It releases chemicals involved in cellular communication.
(4) It controls the replication of genetic material.

**Correct Answer: (3)** This diagram represents a neuron or nerve cell, which communicates with other neurons to send and receive messages (also known as impulses). Only sperm cells unite with egg cells for fertilization—choice (1). Neurons are for communication, not making hormones—choice (2). Choice (4) does not describe the function of the entire structure. *(Cell Structure)*

**38.** The types of human cells shown below are different from one another, even though they all originated from the same fertilized egg and contain the same genetic information.

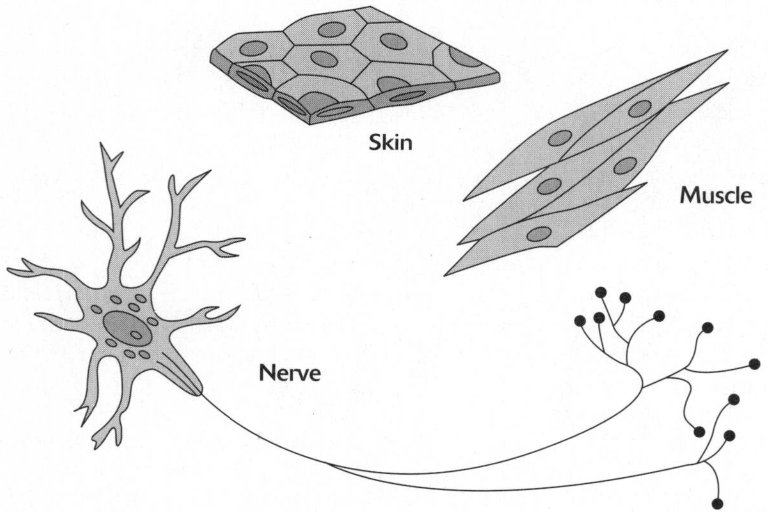


Explain why these genetically identical cells can differ in structure and function.

**Correct Answer:** Every cell of the human body is genetically identical, yet the cells do different jobs, as shown in the diagram. A skin cell will do the job of a skin cell for two reasons: First, a cell is judged by the company it keeps, its environment. If a cell is with other skin cells, it will act like a skin cell. If it is with muscle cells, it will act like a muscle cell. Second, different parts of the genetic information contained in all cells is used in different cells. It would not do a muscle cell any good to act like a nerve cell when it is surrounded by other muscle cells. The muscle cell will have the same information as the nerve cell, but it won't need it or use it.

So your answer should say something like: "Cells that are genetically alike can differ in structure and function because they are in different environments." (A skin cell is with other skin cells and so on.) Or, you could say: "Different parts of the genetic information is used by different cells." *(Cells and Their Environment)*

**39.** To determine which colors of light are best used by plants for photosynthesis, three types of underwater green plants of similar mass were subjected to the same intensity of light of different colors for the same amount of time. All other environmental conditions were kept the same. After 15 minutes, a video camera was used to record the number of bubbles of gas each plant gave off in a 30-second period of time. Each type of plant was tested six times. The average of the data for each plant type is shown in the table below.

| Average Number of Bubbles Given Off in 30 Seconds | | | | |
|---|---|---|---|---|
| **Plant Type** | **Red Light** | **Yellow Light** | **Green Light** | **Blue Light** |
| *Elodea* | 35 | 11 | 5 | 47 |
| *Potamogeton* | 48 | 8 | 2 | 63 |
| *Utricularia* | 28 | 9 | 6 | 39 |

Which statement is a valid inference based on the data?

**(1)** Each plant carried on photosynthesis best in a different color of light.
**(2)** Red light is better for photosynthesis than blue light.
**(3)** These types of plants make food at the fastest rates with red and blue light.
**(4)** Water must filter out red and green light.

**Correct Answer: (3)** The process of photosynthesis produces oxygen in the presence of light. The rate of photosynthesis and, therefore, oxygen production, is affected by the wavelengths (colors) of light absorbed by the plant. Green plants absorb red and blue light more than other wavelengths in the visible spectrum, causing the rate of photosynthesis to be much higher when exposed to these colors as opposed to green and yellow. *(The Characteristics of Life)*

Base your answers to questions 40 and 41 on the information below and on your knowledge of biology.

A biology student was given three unlabeled jars of pond water from the same source, each containing a different type of mobile unicellular organism: euglena, amoeba, and paramecium. The only information the student has is that the amoeba and paramecium are both heterotrophs and the euglena can be either heterotrophic or autotrophic, depending on its environment.

**40.** State *one* way the euglena's two methods of nutrition provide a survival advantage the other unicellular organisms do *not* have.

**Correct Answer:** The euglena has the advantage of being able to use either method, depending upon the materials that are available. If sunlight is available, the euglena can make its own food through the process of photosynthesis. If sunlight isn't available, the euglena can consume food. *(Single-Cell and Multicellular Organisms)*

**41.** Which procedure and resulting observation would help identify the jar that contains the euglena?

**(1)** Expose only one side of each jar to light. After 24 hours, only in the jar containing euglena will most of organisms be seen on the darker side of the jar.

**(2)** Expose all sides of each jar to light. After 48 hours, the jar with the highest dissolved carbon dioxide content will contain the euglena.

**(3)** Over a period of one week, determine the method of reproduction used by each type of organism. If mitotic cell division is observed, the jar will contain euglena.

**(4)** Prepare a wet-mount slide of specimens from each jar and observe each slide with a compound light microscope. Only the euglena will have chloroplasts.

**Correct Answer: (4)** Euglena have chloroplasts, the organelle where photosynthesis occurs. Amoeba and paramecia don't have chloroplasts, which is why they are considered heterotrophic—they must eat to stay alive. *(Single-Cell and Multicellular Organisms)*

Base your answers to questions 42 through 44 on the diagrams below of two cells, X and Y, and on your knowledge of biology.

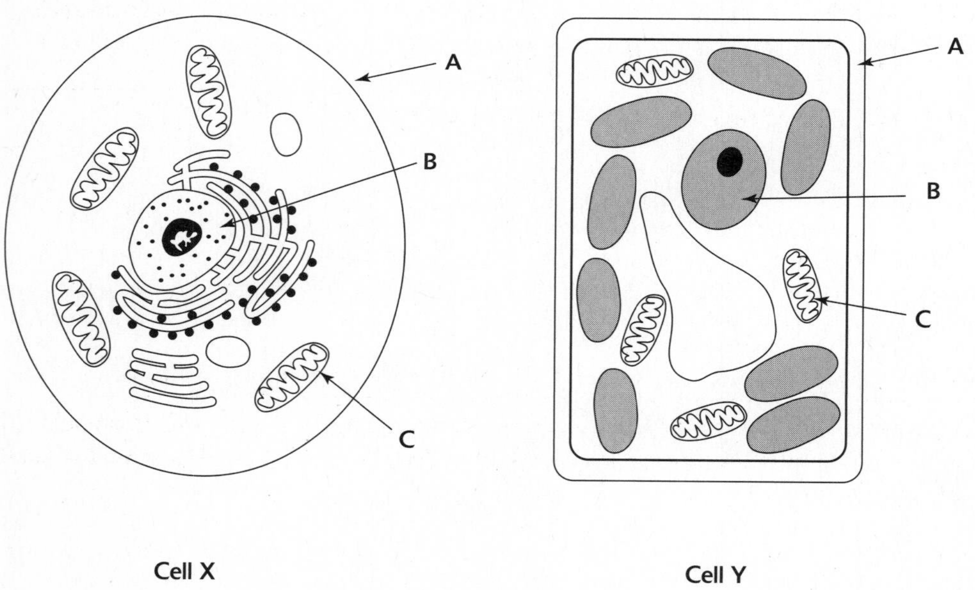


**42.** Select one lettered organelle and write the letter of that organelle in the space below.

__________

Identify the organelle you selected.

**Correct Answer:** All the letters in both cells X and Y are pointing to the same structures. A is pointing to the cell membrane; B is pointing to the nucleus; C is pointing to a mitochondrion. You will rarely be asked to identify other organelles like the endoplasmic reticulum, golgi bodies, or lysosomes. Your best bet is to play it safe and identify the nucleus—it's always recognizable in every cell (except in bacteria and mature red blood cells). *(Cell Structure)*

**43.** State one function of the organelle that you identified in question 43.

**Correct Answer:** Again, keep things simple, and go with the nucleus. The nucleus controls all cell activities. If you're feeling brave, you can state that the function of the cell membrane is to allow some things to pass into and out of the cell. Or, you could say that the function of the mitochondrion is to produce energy by carrying out cellular respiration. *(Cell Structure)*

**44.** Identify one process that is carried out in Cell Y that is *not* carried out in Cell X.

**Correct Answer:** In order to answer this question, you have to know the difference between Cell X and Cell Y. The animal cell is round and the plant cell is rectangular. Now that you've identified which cell is which, just remember that plant cells carry out photosynthesis and animal cells do not. *(The Characteristics of Life)*

**45.** Arrange the following structures from largest to smallest.

a chromosome

a nucleus

a gene

Largest ____________________

____________________

Smallest ____________________

**Correct Answer:** The nucleus is the largest structure. It contains chromosomes (which should be in the second blank), and chromosomes are made up of sections of DNA called *genes,* which are the smallest structure. *(Cell Structure)*

Base your answers to question 46 on the diagram of a cell below.

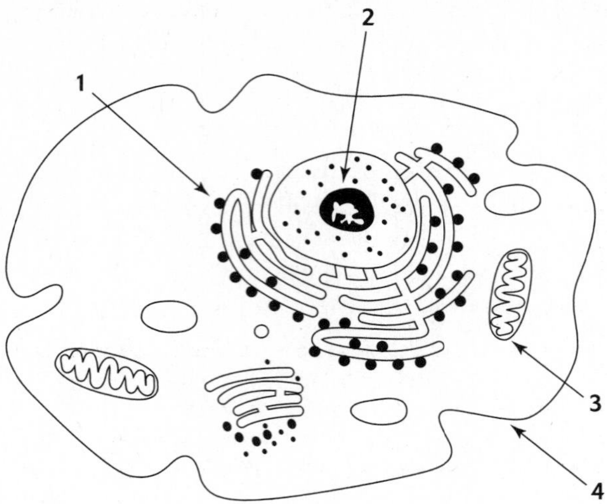


**46.** Choose either structure 3 or structure 4, write the number of the structure on the line below, and describe how it aids the process of protein synthesis.

__________

**Correct Answer:** Structure 3 is a mitochondria, and structure 4 is the cell membrane. Mitochondria is the organelle that provides energy for cellular processes—in this case, protein manufacture. The cell membrane allows the components of proteins to enter the cell, and some of the proteins to leave the cell for use elsewhere. *(Cell Structure)*

Base your answers to questions 47 and 48 on the information below and on your knowledge of biology.

Carbon exists in a simple organic molecule in a leaf and in an inorganic molecule in the air humans exhale.

**47.** Identify the simple organic molecule formed in the leaf and the process that produces it.

**Correct Answer:** An organic molecule formed in a leaf is glucose, produced through the process of photosynthesis. A simple sugar, monosaccharide or $C_6H_{12}O_6$, may be used in place of glucose. *(The Characteristics of Life)*

**48.** Identify the carbon-containing molecule that humans exhale and the process that produces it.

**Correct Answer:** Humans exhale carbon dioxide, a byproduct of aerobic cellular respiration. *(The Characteristics of Life)*

**49.** Describe how *two* of the cell structures listed below interact to help maintain a balanced internal environment in a cell:

mitochondrion
ribosome
cell membrane
nucleus
vacuole

In your answer be sure to:

- select *two* of these structures, write their names, and state *one* function of each
- describe how each structure you selected contributes to the functioning of the other

**Correct Answer:** Be sure to answer all the parts of the question:

- Mitochondrion: Breaks down organic molecules, such as glucose, to release energy (ATP) for cell reactions
- Ribosome: Site where proteins are made from amino acids
- Cell membrane: Regulates which particles enter and leave the cell
- Nucleus: Contains the genetic material and thus regulates all the functions of the cell
- Vacuole: storage
- The cell membrane regulates what particles come into the cell and allows glucose to enter the cell. This glucose is used by the mitochondrion to produce ATP. The ATP provides the energy to allow active transport of some particles.

or

- The nucleus contains the genetic code that is used by the ribosome to produce proteins. The proteins produced by the ribosome are used to keep the cell alive.

*(Cell Structure)*

Base your answers to questions 50 and 51 on the diagram below, which illustrates a role of hormones.

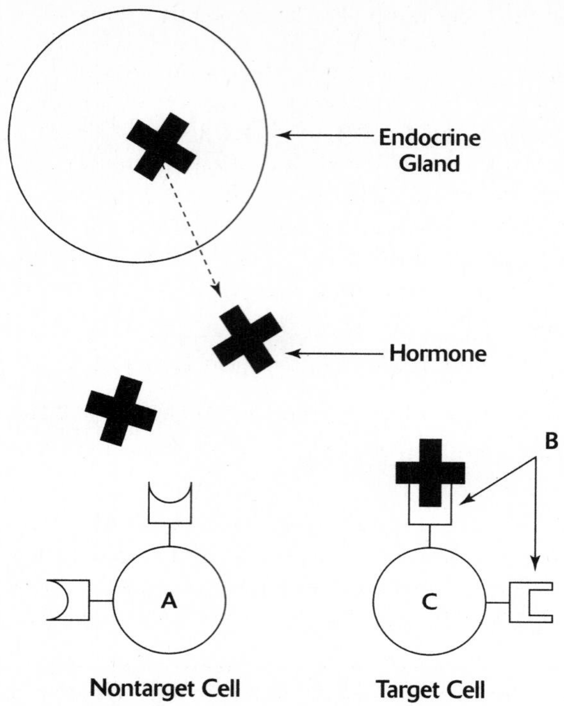


**50.** Letter B indicates

(1) ribosomes
(2) receptor molecules
(3) tissues
(4) inorganic substances

**Correct Answer: (2)** Receptor molecules on the surface of a cell recognize and bind to only those molecules that fit the receptor's specific three-dimensional shape. *(Cell Structure)*

**51.** Explain why cell A is a nontarget cell for the hormone illustrated in the diagram.

**Correct Answer:** Cell A, the nontarget cell, does not possess the receptor molecule with the specific shape needed to bind to the indicated hormone. *(Cell Structure)*

Base your answer to question 52 on the information below and on your knowledge of biology.

It has been discovered that plants utilize chemical signals for communication. Some of these chemicals are released from leaves, fruits, and flowers and play various roles in plant development, survival, and gene expression. For example, bean plant leaves infested with spider mites release chemicals that result in an increase in the resistance to spider mites in uninfested leaves on the same plant and the expression of self-defense genes in uninfested bean plants nearby. Plants can also communicate with insects. For example, corn, cotton, and tobacco under attack by caterpillars release chemical signals that simultaneously attract parasitic wasps to destroy the caterpillars and discourage moths from laying their eggs on the plants.

**52.** Identify the specialized structures in the cell membrane that are involved in communication.

**Correct Answer: Receptors** Cells have membranes that are made up of a phospholipid bilayer and various protein molecules. Certain types of protein molecules known as receptors are involved in the communication between cells. *(Cell Structure)*

**53.** Organelles carry out specific processes involving chemical reactions. In the chart below, identify *two* organelles and, for each, identify a process involving chemical reactions that occurs there. Describe *one* specific way each process identified is important to the functioning of the organism.

| *Organelle* | *Process Involving Chemical Reactions That Occur in the Organelle* | *How the Process Is Important to the Functioning of the Organism* |
|---|---|---|
| (1) | | |
| (2) | | |

**Correct Answer:** The best organelles to choose for this question would be the mitochondrion, the chloroplast, or the ribosome, because you've probably learned about the chemical reactions that take place there and can state why those processes are important for the functioning of the organism.

| *Organelle* | *Process Involving Chemical Reactions That Occur in the Organelle* | *How the Process Is Important to the Functioning of the Organism* |
|---|---|---|
| Mitochondrion | Cell respiration | Provides energy for life functions |
| Chloroplast | Photosynthesis | Provides food for plants |
| Ribosome | Protein synthesis | Proteins can be enzymes that control chemical reactions |

*(Cell Structure)*

# Genetics

**Directions:** For each statement or question, choose the *number* of the word or expression that best completes the statement or answers the question. Then check your answer against the one that immediately follows the question. Try not to look at the answer before making your selection.

**1.** Cloning an individual usually produces organisms that

**(1)** contain dangerous mutations
**(2)** contain identical genes
**(3)** are identical in appearance and behavior
**(4)** produce enzymes different from the parent

**Correct Answer: (2)** Cloning uses the techniques of genetic engineering to produce individuals that are genetically identical to the parent. In the process of cloning, a nucleus (including an entire set of chromosomes and genes) is removed from a somatic (body) cell using microdissection tools and inserted into a haploid egg cell that has had its nucleus removed. *(Genetic Engineering)*

**2.** Which statement best describes the relationship between cells, DNA, and proteins?

**(1)** Cells contain DNA that controls the production of proteins.
**(2)** DNA is composed of proteins that carry coded information for how cells function.
**(3)** Proteins are used to produce cells that link amino acids together into DNA.
**(4)** Cells are linked together by proteins to make different kinds of DNA molecules.

**Correct Answer: (1)** DNA controls everything. Don't make the common mistake of confusing DNA with proteins, choice (2); they are two different things. Also, don't be fooled by seeing proteins, amino acids, and DNA in the same sentence—choice (3). Amino acids are the building blocks of proteins, not the other way around. *(The Structure of DNA/RNA)*

**3.** A single gene mutation results from

**(1)** a change in a base sequence in DNA
**(2)** recombination of traits
**(3)** the failure of chromosomes to separate
**(4)** blocked nerve messages

**Correct Answer: (1)** A mutation is an error in the DNA sequence of a chromosome. The error can be a change in one or more DNA bases that make up the genes of a particular chromosome. Most mutations are not beneficial. *(The Structure of DNA/RNA)*

4. In a cell, information that controls the production of proteins must pass from the nucleus to the

(1) cell membrane
(2) chloroplasts
(3) mitochondria
(4) ribosomes

**Correct Answer: (4)** Protein production occurs at the ribosomes, which are found in the cytosol, outside the nucleus. mRNA that has been transcribed from DNA leaves the nucleus and travels to the ribosomes to be translated into a polypeptide. *(How a Gene Becomes a Protein)*

5. Some mammals have genes for fur color that produce pigment only when the outside temperature is above a certain level. This pigment production is an example of how the environment of an organism can

(1) destroy certain genes
(2) cause new mutations to occur
(3) stop the process of evolution
(4) influence the expression of certain genes

**Correct Answer: (4)** Genes carry the basic information for all traits, but the physical appearance of an organism can sometimes be influenced by environmental factors that switch genes "on" and "off." *(Heredity)*

6. The largest amount of DNA in a plant cell is contained in

(1) a nucleus
(2) a chromosome
(3) a protein molecule
(4) an enzyme molecule

**Correct Answer: (1)** It doesn't matter what kind of cell it is, plant or animal; the nucleus contains all the DNA. You're probably thinking, "Don't chromosomes have genes and DNA?" Yes, they do, but they're in the nucleus. Choice (3), proteins, and choice (4), enzymes, are types of molecules. Proteins include enzymes, but they don't include DNA. *(The Structure of DNA/RNA)*

7. Which statement indicates that different parts of the genetic information are used in different kinds of cells, even in the same organism?

(1) The cells produced by a zygote usually have different genes.
(2) As an embryo develops, various tissues and organs are produced.
(3) Replicated chromosomes separate during gamete formation.
(4) Offspring have a combination of genes from both parents.

**Correct Answer: (2)** All cells within an organism contain the same genetic information; however, different kinds of cells use different parts of the DNA. As an embryo develops, different tissues and organs grow and develop as different parts of the DNA are used. Although choices (3) and (4) are true statements, they do not address the question. *(The Structure of DNA/RNA)*

**8.** The sequence of subunits in a protein is most directly dependent on the

(1) region in the cell where enzymes are produced
(2) DNA in the chromosomes in a cell
(3) type of cell in which starch is found
(4) kinds of materials in the cell membrane

**Correct Answer: (2)** Chromosomes are made up of deoxyribonucleic acid (DNA), the hereditary material in a cell. DNA contains the genetic information that controls which proteins are made and when to make them. Proteins are comprised of one or more polypeptides—long chains of amino acids linked together by peptide bonds. The order in which the amino acids are assembled is directed by the order of the four nitrogen-containing bases in a DNA strand—adenine (A), thymine (T), guanine (G), and cytosine (C). *(How a Gene Becomes a Protein)*

**9.** Which process is *least* likely to add to the variety of traits in a population?

(1) deletion of bases from DNA
(2) genetic engineering
(3) accurate replication of DNA
(4) exchange of segments between chromosomes

**Correct Answer: (3)** If DNA is accurately replicated or copied, it will not add to the variety of traits in a population. We want DNA to be accurately copied. All the other choices add variety to traits in a population. *(Heredity)*

**10.** A product of genetic engineering technology is represented below.

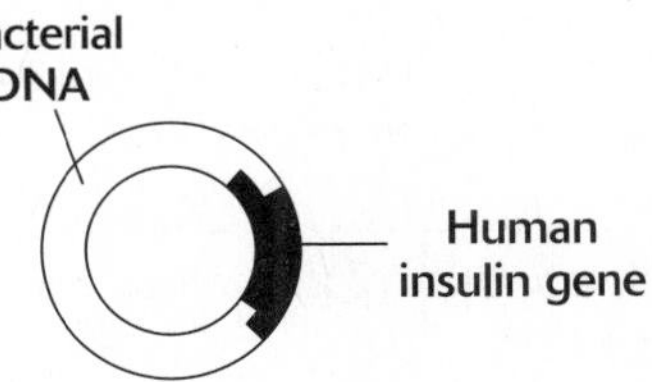


Which substance was needed to join the insulin gene to the bacterial DNA as shown?

(1) a specific carbohydrate
(2) a specific enzyme
(3) hormones
(4) antibodies

**Correct Answer: (2)** Enzymes are molecules that are responsible for doing two specific jobs: They either bring things together (as in protein synthesis) or take things apart (as in hydrolysis). Genetic engineering is accomplished by using restriction enzymes to cut the DNA and then using enzymes to join the bacterial plasmid and the human piece of DNA together. The most commonly used example of this process is for the production of insulin. *(Genetic Engineering)*

**11.** Which process can produce new inheritable characteristics within a multicellular species?

(1) cloning of the zygote
(2) mitosis in muscle cells
(3) gene alterations in gametes
(4) differentiation in nerve cells

**Correct Answer: (3)** For traits or characteristics to be inheritable, they must impact the gametes. Any changes to body cells may impact the organism but will not be transmitted to the next generation. *(Heredity)*

**12.** Three structures are represented in the diagram below.

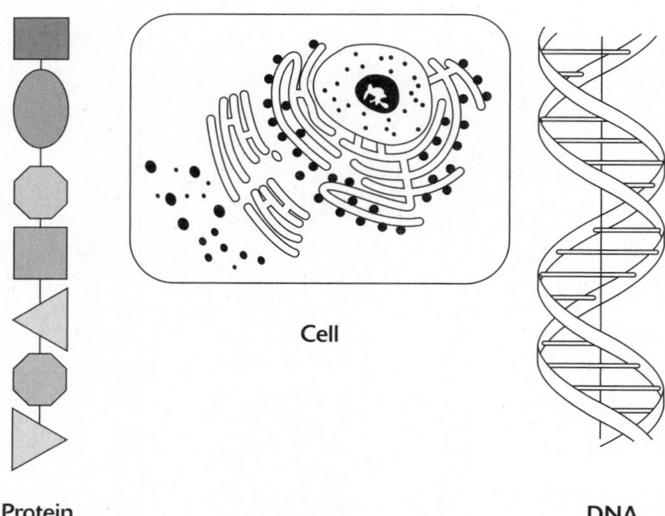


What is the relationship between these three structures?

(1) DNA is made up of proteins that are synthesized in the cell.
(2) Protein is composed of DNA that is stored in the cell.
(3) DNA controls the production of protein in the cell.
(4) The cell is composed only of DNA and protein.

**Correct Answer: (3)** DNA is composed of nucleotides and controls the production of proteins within all cells. *(How a Gene Becomes a Protein)*

**13.** Variation in the offspring of sexually reproducing organisms is the direct result of

(1) sorting and recombining of genes
(2) replication and cloning
(3) the need to adapt and maintain homeostasis
(4) overproduction of offspring and competition

**Correct Answer: (1)** Sexual reproduction requires two parents. The process of meiosis uses sorting and recombination to make sure that each gamete is genetically unique. This is how diversity is maintained in a population. *(Heredity)*

**14.** Fruit flies with the curly-wing trait will develop straight wings if kept at a temperature of 16°C during development and curly wings if kept at 25°C. The best explanation for this change in the shape of wings is that the

(1) genes for curly wings and genes for straight wings are found on different chromosomes
(2) type of genes present in the fruit fly is dependent on environmental temperature
(3) environment affects the expression of the genes for this trait
(4) higher temperature produces a gene mutation

**Correct Answer: (3)** Genes carry the basic information for all traits, but the physical appearance of an organism can sometimes be influenced by environmental factors that switch genes "on" and "off." *(Heredity)*

**15.** The chart below shows relationships between genes, the environment, and coloration of tomato plants. Which statement best explains the final appearance of these tomato plants?

| *Inherited Gene* | *Environmental Condition* | *Final Appearance* |
|---|---|---|
| A | Light | Green |
| B | Light | White |
| A | Dark | White |
| B | Dark | White |

(1) The expression of gene A is not affected by light.
(2) The expression of gene B varies with the presence of light.
(3) The expression of gene A varies with the environment.
(4) Gene B is expressed only in darkness.

**Correct Answer: (3)** Gene expression can be influenced by the environment. In green plants, some genes are switched "on" and "off" by light. In this case, the tomato plant with gene B has a final appearance of white whether exposed to light or dark. The tomato plant with gene A has a final appearance of green when exposed to light, and white when not exposed to light. Therefore, light is the variable that influences the expression of gene A. *(Heredity)*

**16.** An error in genetic information present in a body cell of a mammal would most likely produce

**(1)** rapid evolution of the organism in which the cell is found
**(2)** a mutation that will affect the synthesis of a certain protein in the cell
**(3)** an adaptation that will be passed on to other types of cells
**(4)** increased variation in the type of organelles present in the cell

**Correct Answer: (2)** Genetic information codes for the production of proteins. An error in genetic information may affect the production of the protein for which the information codes. *(How a Gene Becomes a Protein)*

**17.** The genetic code of a DNA molecule is determined by a specific sequence of

**(1)** ATP molecules
**(2)** sugar molecules
**(3)** chemical bonds
**(4)** molecular bases

**Correct Answer: (4)** DNA is made up of repeating nucleotides. A nucleotide is composed of the five-carbon sugar deoxyribose, a phosphate group, and one of four nitrogen-containing bases: adenine, thymine, guanine, or cytosine. The order of bases in a DNA molecule is what determines which proteins will be made. *(The Structure of DNA/RNA)*

**18.** The diagram below represents a section of a molecule that carries genetic information.

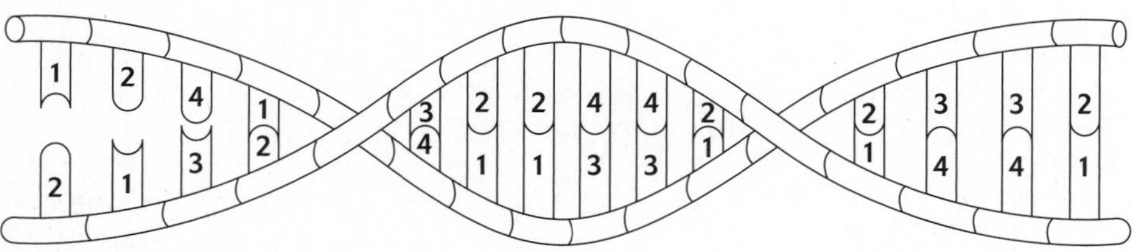


The pattern of numbers represents

**(1)** a sequence of paired bases
**(2)** the order of proteins in a gene
**(3)** folds of an amino acid
**(4)** positions of gene mutations

**Correct Answer: (1)** The diagram shows a section of DNA, the numbers representing a sequence of base pairs that make up the "rungs" of the double helix. The bases must pair with each other in specific ways because of their structure. There are two types of bases—purines and pyrimidines. Purines have two rings of carbon and nitrogen atoms and pyrimidines have one ring of carbon and nitrogen atoms. A purine always pairs with a pyrimidine. Adenine and guanine (both purines) always pair with thymine and cytosine (both pyrimidines). More specifically, adenine pairs with thymine and cytosine pairs with guanine. The base pairs are of uniform length, allowing the DNA helix to have a uniform shape—most commonly a right-hand twist with ten base pairs in each turn. *(The Structure of DNA/RNA)*

**19.** Genes involved in the production of abnormal red blood cells have an abnormal sequence of

(1) ATP molecules
(2) amino acids
(3) sugars
(4) bases

**Correct Answer: (4)** The question is making reference to sickle cell anemia, in which the amino acid valine is substituted for the amino acid glutamic acid. You aren't expected to know these amino acids or which replaces which. But you are expected to know that the amino acids are switched because of a change in the RNA bases that code for these amino acids. It is the change in the sequence of bases that causes the change in the amino acids. *(How a Gene Becomes a Protein)*

**20.** A mutation occurs in the liver cells of a certain field mouse. Which statement concerning the spread of this mutation through the mouse population is correct?

(1) It will spread because it is beneficial.
(2) It will spread because it is a dominant gene.
(3) It will not spread because it is not in a gamete.
(4) It will not spread because it is a recessive gene.

**Correct Answer: (3)** A cell in the liver will stay in that one mouse; it will not spread to any other mice. The only way for a mutation to spread is if it occurs in a gamete—an egg or a sperm. Only if the mutation is in either one of these cells when that cell is involved in fertilization will the mutation be passed to another organism. *(Heredity)*

**21.** Which process is illustrated in the diagram below?

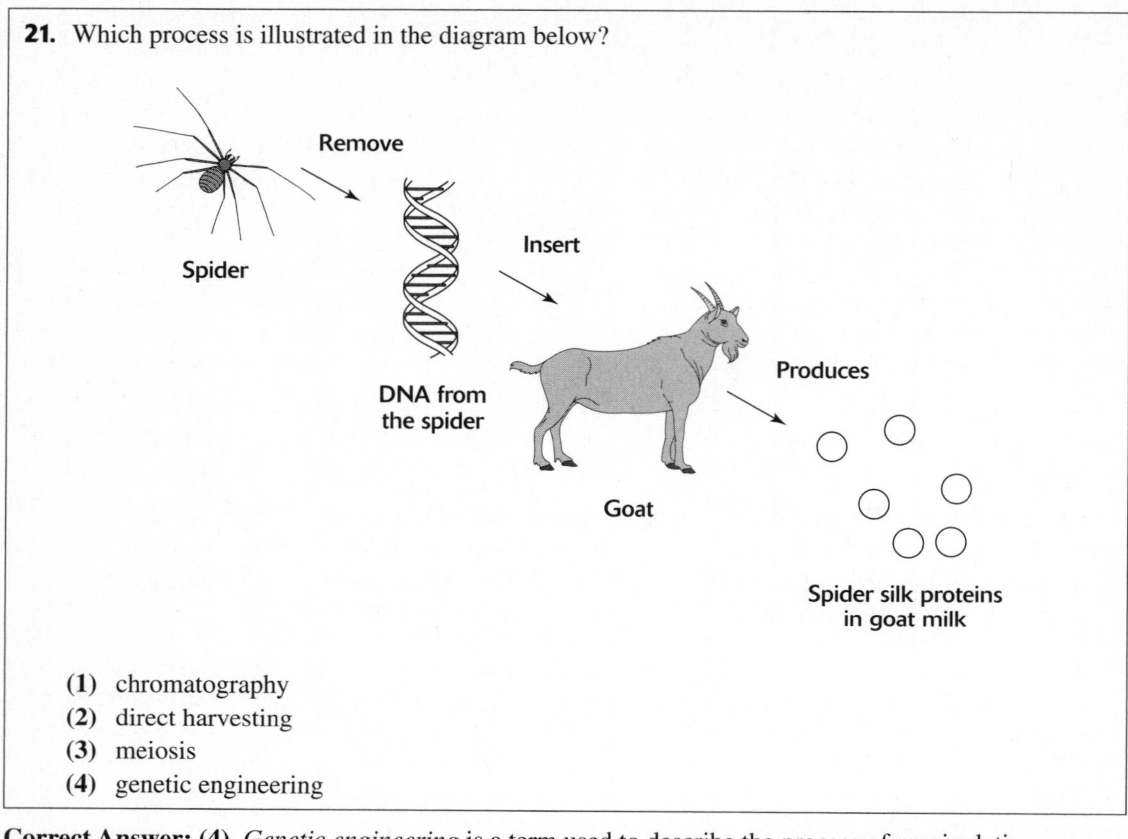


(1) chromatography
(2) direct harvesting
(3) meiosis
(4) genetic engineering

**Correct Answer: (4)** *Genetic engineering* is a term used to describe the process of manipulating genes. The image shows a sample of DNA from a spider being manipulated and incorporated into the DNA of a goat. This way, the goat can produce the proteins that the spider's DNA codes for. *(Genetic Engineering)*

**22.** The production of certain human hormones by genetically engineered bacteria results from

(1) inserting a specific group of amino acids into the bacteria
(2) combining a portion of human DNA with bacterial DNA and inserting this into bacteria
(3) crossing two different species of bacteria
(4) deleting a specific amino acid from human DNA and inserting it into bacterial DNA

**Correct Answer: (2)** Genetic engineering, or gene splicing, is a technique used by scientists to produce substances such as hormones in large amounts. The first step is to isolate the gene of interest using restriction enzymes to cut the DNA at specific sites. The second step is to insert the gene of interest into a bacterial plasmid. After the gene is inserted, the bacteria will produce the protein specified by the donor gene. *(Genetic Engineering)*

**23.** A gene that codes for resistance to glyphosate, a biodegradable weedkiller, has been inserted into certain plants. As a result, these plants will be more likely to

(1) produce chemicals that kill weeds growing near them
(2) die when exposed to glyphosate
(3) convert glyphosate into fertilizer
(4) survive when glyphosate is applied to them

**Correct Answer: (4)** Through the process of gene splicing, the DNA of two different organisms may be combined to form recombinant DNA. This new DNA is able to produce the proteins coded for in the original organisms. When the gene for resistance to glyphosate is inserted into a plant that is normally not resistant, the plant will be able to produce the protein that provides the resistance. *(Genetic Engineering)*

**24.** A biotechnology firm has produced tobacco plants that synthesize human antibodies that prevent bacterial diseases. One of the first steps in the production of these plants required

(1) using natural selection to increase the survival of antibody-producing tobacco plants
(2) inserting human DNA segments into the cells of tobacco plants
(3) using selective breeding to increase the number of antibody genes in tobacco plants
(4) growing tobacco plants in soil containing a specific fertilizer

**Correct Answer: (2)** The process of genetic engineering requires isolating a gene of interest using restriction enzymes—in this case, the gene that codes for the production of specific human antibodies. This gene of interest is inserted into the DNA of another organism, which is then able to synthesize the antibodies. *(Genetic Engineering)*

**25.** Researchers Cohn and Boyer transferred a gene from an African clawed frog into a bacterium. To accomplish this, these scientists had to use

(1) enzymes to cut out and insert the gene
(2) hereditary information located in amino acids
(3) radiation to increase the gene mutation rate of the bacterial cells
(4) cancer cells to promote rapid cell division

**Correct Answer: (1)** Whenever you read that a gene is transferred from one organism to another, *especially* a bacteria, it's always genetic engineering. This is what it's all about: genetic manipulation—taking the genes of one organism and inserting them into another organism, thereby changing the second organism's genes. *(Genetic Engineering)*

Base your answer to question 26 on the diagram below, which represents the human female reproductive system.

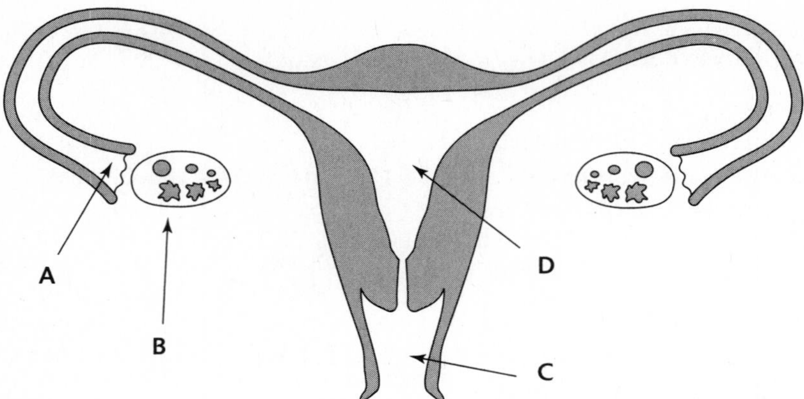


**26.** New inherited characteristics may appear in offspring as a result of new combinations of existing genes or may result from mutations in genes contained in cells produced by structure

(1) A
(2) B
(3) C
(4) D

**Correct Answer: (2)** The structure indicated by B is the ovary. The ovary contains haploid eggs, or sex cells of a female. Only changes in sex cells can be passed on to offspring. *(Heredity)*

**27.** A tree produces only seedless oranges. A small branch cut from this tree produces roots after it is planted in soil. When mature, this new tree will most likely produce

(1) oranges with seeds only
(2) oranges without seeds only
(3) a majority of oranges with seeds and only a few oranges without seeds
(4) oranges and other kinds of fruit

**Correct Answer: (2)** If the tree doesn't have the genetic information to produce seeds, then the new tree, which came from cells from the old tree, will not have the genetic information either. *(Heredity)*

**28.** A basketball player develops speed and power as a result of practice. This athletic ability will *not* be passed on to her offspring because

(1) muscle cells do not carry genetic information
(2) mutations that occur in body cells are not inherited
(3) gametes do not carry complete sets of genetic information
(4) base sequences in DNA are not affected by this activity

**Correct Answer: (4)** Information contained in one's DNA will be passed on to future generations. Learned or acquired skills are the result of hard work and are not present in one's DNA at birth. Learned or acquired skills are not passed on to future generations. *(Heredity)*

**29.** The characteristics of a developing fetus are most influenced by

(1) gene combinations and their expression in the embryo
(2) hormone production by the father
(3) circulating levels of white blood cells in the placenta
(4) milk production in the mother

**Correct Answer: (1)** The characteristics of a developing fetus are most influenced by the genes that make up the embryo. Half the genes come from the egg cell of the mother, and the other half come from the sperm of the father. When a haploid egg cell is fertilized by a haploid sperm cell, the diploid number is restored in the zygote. The information contained in the genes inherited from the parents determines the traits of the embryo. *(Heredity)*

**30.** The Y-chromosome carries the SRY gene that codes for the production of testosterone in humans. Occasionally, a mutation occurs resulting in the SRY gene being lost from the Y-chromosome and added to the X-chromosome, as shown in the diagram below.

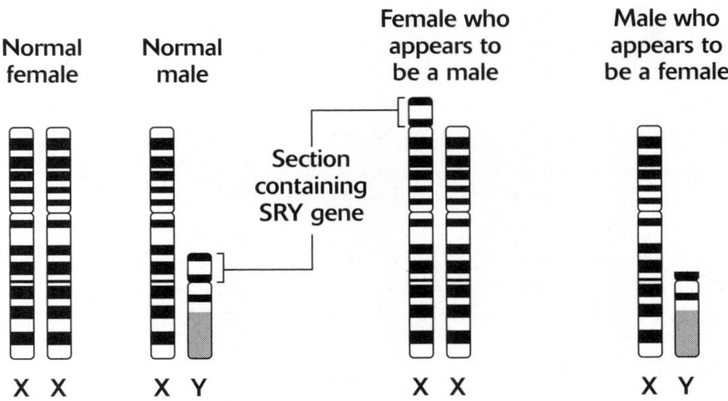


Based on the diagram, which statement is correct?

(1) The production of testosterone influences the development of male characteristics.
(2) Reproductive technology has had an important influence on human development.
(3) Normal female characteristics develop from a single X-chromosome.
(4) Male characteristics only develop in the absence of X-chromosomes.

**Correct Answer: (1)** Testosterone affects the development of male characteristics. *(How a Gene Becomes a Protein)*

**31.** A mutation occurs in a cell. Which sequence best represents the correct order of the events involved for this mutation to affect the traits expressed by this cell?

(1) a change in the sequence of DNA bases → joining amino acids in sequence → appearance of characteristic
(2) joining amino acids in sequence → a change in the sequence of DNA bases → appearance of characteristic
(3) appearance of characteristic → joining amino acids in sequence → a change in the sequence of DNA bases
(4) a change in the sequence of DNA bases → appearance of characteristic → joining amino acids in sequence

**Correct Answer: (1)** Mutations occur in a cell's DNA. The sequence of bases in DNA determines the order of amino acids in the proteins that are made. The function of the protein helps to determine traits expressed by a cell. *(How a Gene Becomes a Protein)*

**32.** Enzymes are used in moving sections of DNA that code for insulin from the pancreas cells of humans into a certain type of bacterial cell. This bacterial cell will reproduce, giving rise to offspring that are able to form

(1) human insulin
(2) antibodies against insulin
(3) enzymes that digest insulin
(4) a new type of insulin

**Correct Answer: (1)** The technique described is referring to genetic engineering. Restriction enzymes are used to cut DNA into small pieces that contain a particular gene, or gene of interest. In this case, the gene of interest codes for the production of human insulin. The desired gene is inserted into another species, such as a bacterial cell. The bacterial cell will then be able to make the protein specified by the gene of interest. *(Genetic Engineering)*

Base your answers to questions 33 through 36 on the passage below and on your knowledge of biology.

## Better Rice

The production of new types of food crops will help raise the quantity of food grown by farmers. Research papers released by the National Academy of Sciences announced the development of two new superior varieties of rice—one produced by selective breeding and the other by biotechnology.

One variety of rice, called *Nerica* (New Rice for Africa), is already helping farmers in Africa. *Nerica* combines the hardiness and weed resistance of rare African rice varieties with the productivity and faster maturity of common Asian varieties.

Another variety, called Stress-Tolerant Rice, was produced by inserting a pair of bacterial genes into rice plants for the production of trehalose (a sugar). Trehalose helps plants maintain healthy cell membranes, proteins, and enzymes during environmental stress. The resulting plants survive drought, low temperatures, salty soils, and other stresses better than standard rice varieties.

**33.** Which substance from bacteria was most likely inserted into rice plants in the development of the trehalose-producing rice?

**(1)** sugar
**(2)** enzymes
**(3)** DNA
**(4)** trehalose

**Correct Answer: (3)** The passage states that Stress-Tolerant Rice "was produced by inserting a pair of bacterial genes into rice plants." Genes are found on the chromosomes that are made of DNA. *(Genetic Engineering)*

**34.** *Nerica* was most likely produced by

**(1)** crossing a variety of African rice with a variety of Asian rice
**(2)** cloning genes for hardiness and weed resistance from Asian rice
**(3)** using Asian rice to compete with rare African varieties
**(4)** inserting genes for productivity and faster maturity into Asian rice

**Correct Answer: (1)** The passage states that "*Nerica* combines the hardiness and weed resistance of rare African rice varieties with the productivity and faster maturity of common Asian varieties." This statement reveals that *Nerica* has a combination of desirable traits from African and Asian varieties of rice. The introductory paragraph states that one variety of rice was produced by selective breeding and the other was produced by biotechnology. Because the last paragraph of the passage discusses the biotechnology by which the Stress-Tolerant Rice variety was produced, *Nerica* would have to have been produced by selective breeding, or crossing a variety of African rice with a variety of Asian rice. *(Heredity)*

**35.** Which strain of rice was produced as a result of genetic engineering? Support your answer.

**Correct Answer:** Stress-Tolerant Rice was produced by genetic engineering because it was made by inserting genes from a bacteria that produces trehalose, which allows it to be more tolerant of environmental stresses. *(Genetic Engineering)*

**36.** State *one* reason that further testing must be done before rice plants that produce trehalose are approved for human consumption.

**Correct Answer:** One reason that further testing must be done on these genetically engineered rice plants is to determine whether the plants are safe for human consumption. Another possibility is to test whether the plant has nutritional value. *(Genetic Engineering)*

Base your answer to question 37 on the passage below and on your knowledge of biology.

## In Search of a Low-Allergy Peanut

Many people are allergic to substances in the environment. Of the many foods that contain allergens (allergy-inducing substances), peanuts cause some of the most severe reactions. Mildly allergic people may only get hives. Highly allergic people can go into a form of shock. Some people die each year from reactions to peanuts.

A group of scientists is attempting to produce peanuts that lack the allergy-inducing proteins by using traditional selective breeding methods. They are searching for varieties of peanuts that are free of the allergens. By crossing those varieties with popular commercial types, they hope to produce peanuts that will be less likely to cause allergic reactions and still taste good. So far, they have found one variety that has 80 percent less of one of three complex proteins linked to allergic reactions. Removing all three of these allergens may be impossible, but even removing one could help.

Other researchers are attempting to alter the genes that code for the three major allergens in peanuts. All of this research is seen as a possible long-term solution to peanut allergies.

**37.** How does altering the DNA of a peanut affect the proteins in peanuts that cause allergic reactions?

**(1)** The altered DNA is used to synthesize changed forms of these proteins.
**(2)** The altered DNA leaves the nucleus and becomes part of the allergy-producing protein.
**(3)** The altered DNA is the code for the antibodies against the allergens.
**(4)** The altered DNA is used as an enzyme to break down the allergens in peanuts.

**Correct Answer: (1)** Altering the DNA of a peanut would affect the proteins that cause allergic reaction because DNA holds the code for all proteins that are synthesized by the organism. If the DNA is altered, new proteins will be synthesized by the cells that may not cause allergies. *(How a Gene Becomes a Protein)*

Base your answers to questions 38 and 39 on the information and chart below and on your knowledge of biology.

In DNA, a sequence of three bases is a code for the placement of a certain amino acid in a protein chain. The table below shows some amino acids with their abbreviations and DNA codes.

| *Amino Acid* | *Abbreviation* | *DNA Code* |
|---|---|---|
| Phenylalanine | Phe | AAA, AAG |
| Tryptophan | Try | ACC |
| Serine | Ser | AGA, AGG, AGT, AGC, TCA, TCG |
| Valine | Val | CAA, CAG, CAT, CAC |
| Proline | Pro | GGA, GGG, GGT, GGC |
| Glutamine | Glu | GTT, GTC |
| Threonine | Thr | TGA, TGG, TGT, TGC |
| Asparagine | Asp | TTA, TTG |

**38.** Which amino acid chain would be produced by the DNA base sequence below?

**C-A-A-G-T-T-A-A-A-T-T-A-T-T-G-T-G-A**

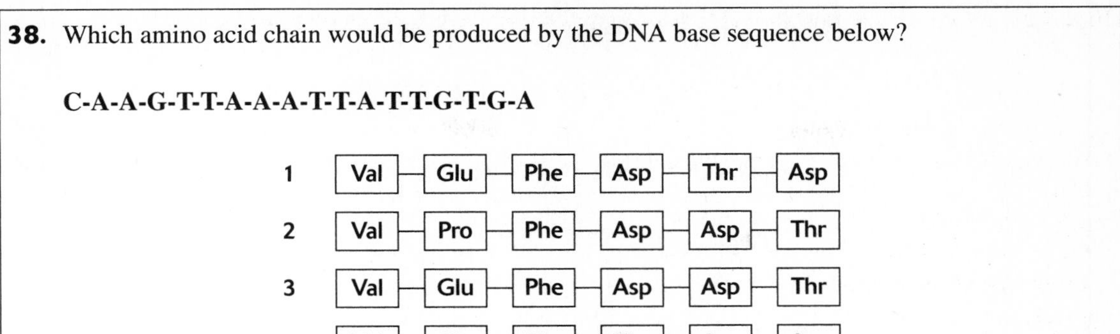


**Correct Answer: (3)** According to the table, the DNA code CAA is valine, GTT is glutamine, AAA is phenylalanine, TTA is asparagine, TTG is also asparagine, and TGA is threonine. *(How a Gene Becomes a Protein)*

**39.** Describe how a protein would be changed if a base sequence mutates from GGA to TGA.

**Correct Answer:** If a base sequence mutates from GGA to TGA, the amino acid proline would be replaced with threonine. The shape of the protein would be changed. The protein would not be able to fit as well with the proper substrate or function as effectively as it could if the original amino acid were present. The protein may not be able to function at all. *(How a Gene Becomes a Protein)*

Base your answer to question 40 on the information below and on your knowledge of biology.

**Variations in Lake Water Level**

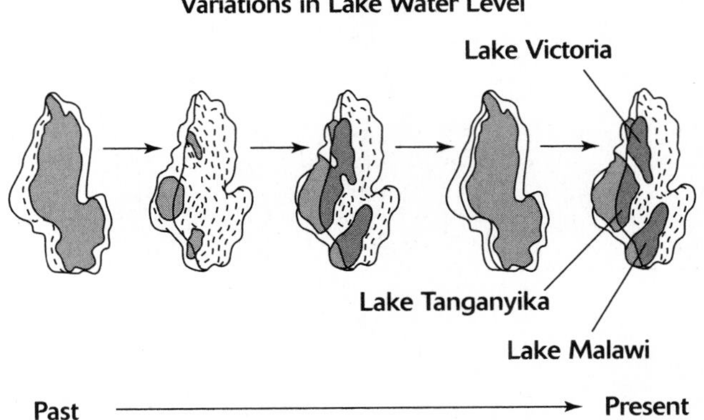


The three great lakes in Africa (Victoria, Tanganyika, and Malawi) contain a greater number of fish species than any other lake in the world. Lake Malawi alone has 200 species of cichlid fish. The diversity of cichlid species in these African lakes could have been caused by changes in water level over thousands of years.

According to one hypothesis, at one time the three lakes were connected as one large lake and all the cichlids could interbreed. When the water level fell, groups of cichlids were isolated in smaller lakes as shown in the diagram. Over time, the groups of cichlids developed genetic differences. When the water levels rose again, the isolated populations were brought back into contact. Due to significant genetic differences, these populations were unable to interbreed. Variations in water level over thousands of years resulted in today's diversity of cichlid species.

**40.** Each cichlid population is genetically different from the other cichlid populations. State *one* reason for these genetic differences.

**Correct Answer:** There are numerous potential answers to this question, and each answer could be a reason for the genetic differences in each fish population. Think about how the populations become different. Evolution could cause them to be different. Natural selection or sexual reproduction also cause them to be different. *Remember:* You don't have to give an explanation, only a reason. An answer that covers all the bases would be, "Each cichlid population is genetically different from the other cichlid populations because mutations occurred in their DNA making them genetically different." *(Heredity)*

Base your answer to question 41 on the diagram of a cell below.

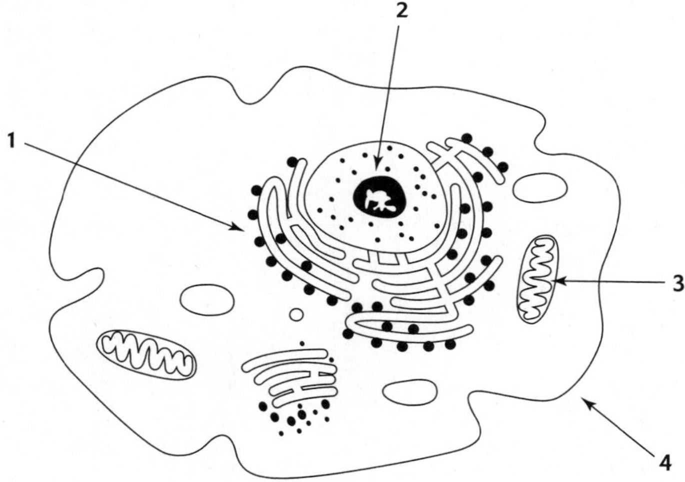


**41.** Describe how structures 1 and 2 interact in the process of protein synthesis.

**Correct Answer:** Structure 1 is a ribosome (or Rough ER) and structure 2 is the nucleus. Structure 2 contains the DNA that provides the directions for the proteins that are assembled in the cytosol at the ribosomes, Structure 1. *(How a Gene Becomes a Protein)*

**42.** One variety of wheat is resistant to disease. Another variety contains more nutrients of benefit to humans. Explain how a new variety of wheat with disease resistance and high nutrient value could be developed. In your answer, be sure to:

- identify *one* technique that could be used to combine disease resistance and high nutrient value in a new variety of wheat
- describe how this technique would be carried out to produce a wheat plant with the desired characteristics
- describe *one* specific difficulty (other than stating that it does not always work) in developing a new variety using this technique

**Correct Answer:** There are two ways this could be done: selective breeding and genetic engineering.

In selective breeding, two wheat plants are chosen with the desired qualities: disease resistance and high nutrient value. Next the plants are crosspollinated (the pollen of one plant is placed in the pistil of the other plant). The plants are allowed to germinate and, hopefully, the new plant offspring will have both traits.

- Selective breeding
- Take the pollen of one plant and crosspollinate it with the other plant.
- Offspring may not have both traits (because one trait might be recessive).

If you choose genetic engineering, do the same thing—short and simple answers:

- Genetic engineering
- Remove the gene for one trait from one plant and insert it into the DNA of the other plant.
- The trait may not be expressed (because it may be recessive and it needs two copies to be expressed).

There are other explanations, but they become too complicated. *(Genetic Engineering)*

**43.** Animal cells utilize many different proteins. Discuss the synthesis of proteins in an animal cell. Your answer must include at least:

- the identity of the building blocks required to synthesize these proteins
- the identity of the sites in the cell where the proteins are assembled
- an explanation of the role of DNA in the process of making proteins in the cell

**Correct Answer:** In animals, the building blocks required to synthesize proteins are amino acids. In an animal cell, protein assembly occurs at the ribosomes in the cytoplasm. DNA acts as the template or directions that tell the cell which proteins to make. DNA is transcribed into mRNA in the nucleus. mRNA leaves the nucleus and travels to a ribosome in the cytoplasm where the mRNA is translated. At the ribosome, tRNA molecules attach amino acids in a particular order according to the mRNA being translated. *(How a Gene Becomes a Protein)*

Base your answer to question 44 on the passage below and on your knowledge of biology.

## In Search of a Low-Allergy Peanut

Many people are allergic to substances in the environment. Of the many foods that contain allergens (allergy-inducing substances), peanuts cause some of the most severe reactions. Mildly allergic people may only get hives. Highly allergic people can go into a form of shock. Some people die each year from reactions to peanuts.

A group of scientists is attempting to produce peanuts that lack the allergy-inducing proteins by using traditional selective breeding methods. They are searching for varieties of peanuts that are free of the allergens. By crossing those varieties with popular commercial types, they hope to produce peanuts that will be less likely to cause allergic reactions and still taste good. So far, they have found one variety that has 80 percent less of one of three complex proteins linked to allergic reactions. Removing all three of these allergens may be impossible, but even removing one could help.

Other researchers are attempting to alter the genes that code for the three major allergens in peanuts. All of this research is seen as a possible long-term solution to peanut allergies.

**44.** Explain how selective breeding is being used to try to produce commercial peanuts that will *not* cause allergic reactions in people.

**Correct Answer:** To create new varieties of peanuts that can be produced commercially, scientists would choose to breed varieties of peanuts that are low in or free of allergens and cross these with commercial varieties. The offspring would be tested for good taste (commercial quality) as well as allergy-causing proteins. *(Genetic Engineering)*

# Evolution: Change over Time

**Directions:** For each statement or question, choose the *number* of the word or expression that best completes the statement or answers the question. Then check your answer against the one that immediately follows the question. Try not to look at the answer before making your selection.

**1.** The evolutionary pathways of ten different species are represented in the diagram below.

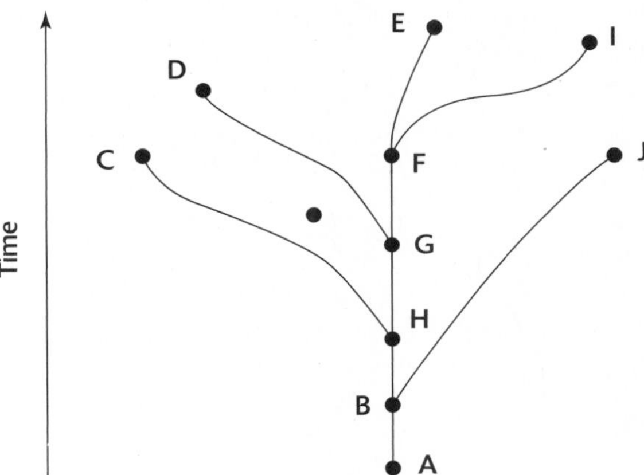


Which two species are the most closely related?

(1) C and D
(2) E and I
(3) G and J
(4) A and F

**Correct Answer: (2)** Evolutionary relationships can be shown in a diagram or "tree." The organisms at the base of the tree are the ancestors to those at the top of the tree. The most closely related species are those that can be traced from the same branch. In this diagram, for example, Species F was a common ancestor for species E and I. Species G is a common ancestor for species D, F, E, and I. Species A is the common ancestor for all the species in the diagram. *(Patterns of Evolution)*

**2.** Which factor could be the cause of the other three in an animal species?

(1) the inability of the species to adapt to changes
(2) a lack of genetic variability in the species
(3) extinction of the species
(4) a decrease in the survival rate of the species

**Correct Answer: (2)** The best way to approach this question is to read each statement separately and ask yourself, "Does choice (1) cause choice (2)?" The answer is no. Do the same with choice (2): "Does choice (2) cause choice (3)?" The answer is yes. Repeat with choice (3): "Does choice (3) cause choice (4)?" The answer is no. Repeat with choice (4): "Does choice (4) cause choice (1)?" The answer is no. The correct answer is choice (2), the lack of genetic variability. Genetic variability, or the possessing of traits (or not possessing them), is the principal cause of evolution. *(Mechanisms of Evolution)*

**3.** Which two processes result in variations that commonly influence the evolution of sexually reproducing species?

**(1)** mutation and genetic recombination
**(2)** mitosis and natural selection
**(3)** extinction and gene replacement
**(4)** environmental selection and selective breeding

**Correct Answer: (1)** Evolution is the change in a species over time. In order for that change (such as a change in the fur color) to impact the species, it must be heritable and, therefore, affect the DNA. Changes to DNA are brought about by mutation (a genetic "mistake") or recombination (a "reshuffling" of the DNA attained by crossing over). Although natural selection is considered the mechanism of evolution, it relies on some change to the DNA. *(Mechanisms of Evolution)*

**4.** In a group of mushrooms exposed to a poisonous chemical, only a few of the mushrooms survived. The best explanation for the resistance of the surviving mushrooms is that the resistance

**(1)** was transmitted to the mushrooms from the poisonous chemical
**(2)** resulted from the presence of mutations in the mushrooms
**(3)** was transferred through the food web to the mushrooms
**(4)** developed in response to the poisonous chemical

**Correct Answer: (2)** Each individual organism within a population is genetically different. Mutations can occur within some of these individuals. These mutations, whether harmful or helpful, are transferred from one generation to the next and can ultimately lead to changes within in the species. Resistance of some mushrooms to a lethal chemical can only be explained by variation in DNA. Beneficial mutations cannot develop in response to something in the environment, such as a chemical. *(Mechanisms of Evolution)*

**5.** The presence of some similar structures in all vertebrates suggests that these vertebrates

**(1)** all develop at the same rate
**(2)** evolved from different animals that appeared on Earth at the same time
**(3)** all develop internally and rely on nutrients supplied by the mother
**(4)** may have an evolutionary relationship

**Correct Answer: (4)** One of the theories about evolution is that, if organisms share similarities, they share a common ancestor. The similarities they could share and the sciences that study them include: structures (studied in comparative anatomy), proteins and DNA (studied in comparative biochemistry), embryos (studied in comparative embryology), and cells (studied in comparative cytology). *(Patterns of Evolution)*

**6.** Natural selection and its evolutionary consequences provide a scientific explanation for each of the following *except*

**(1)** the fossil record
**(2)** protein and DNA similarities between different organisms
**(3)** similar structures among different organisms
**(4)** stable physical environment

**Correct Answer: (4)** Natural selection is used to explain what happens to organisms, which are living things. It cannot explain changes in the physical environment. All the other choices are a result of natural selection. *(Mechanisms of Evolution)*

**7.** The illustration below shows an insect resting on some green leaves.

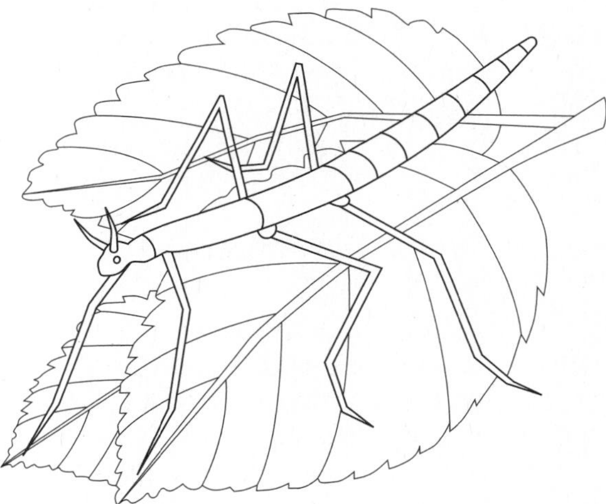

The size, shape, and green color of this insect are adaptations that would most likely help the insect to

**(1)** compete successfully with all birds
**(2)** make its own food
**(3)** hide from predators
**(4)** avoid toxic waste materials

**Correct Answer: (3)** Some insects take on the shape and color of the leaves upon which they live. This allows them to blend in with their background so that they are difficult to see. This camouflage helps them to avoid predators. *(The Theory of Evolution)*

**8.** If mitotic cell division is the only way a particular species of a single-celled organism can reproduce, it is most likely that

(1) mutations *cannot* occur in this species
(2) the rate of evolution in this species is slower than in one that reproduces sexually
(3) the number of organisms of this species in an area will remain constant
(4) this species belongs to the animal kingdom

**Correct Answer: (2)** Mitosis is a form of asexual reproduction in which the offspring is genetically identical to the parent. In sexually reproducing species, the offspring possess genes and phenotypic traits of both parents. Sexual reproduction, in addition to random genetic mutation, creates variation within a species. For evolution to proceed, there must be a source of genetic variation that will produce characteristics the environment may act upon. The only source of genetic variation in asexually reproducing species is mutation. Because most mutations are harmful, the chance of a beneficial mutation occurring in a species is low, causing the rate of evolution to be significantly slower than in sexually reproducing organisms that have more sources of genetic variation that are not generally harmful. *(Mechanisms of Evolution)*

**9.** Which factor contributed most to the extinction of many species?

(1) changes in the environment
(2) lethal mutation
(3) inability to evolve into simple organisms
(4) changes in migration patterns

**Correct Answer: (1)** If organisms did not possess the adaptations that matched their environment, then they were naturally selected to not survive. So, when the environment changed, and the organisms lacked the genetic variation to survive, they most likely became extinct. *(The Theory of Evolution)*

**10.** In order for new species to develop, there *must* be a change in the

(1) temperature of the environment
(2) migration patterns within a population
(3) genetic makeup of a population
(4) rate of succession in the environment

**Correct Answer: (3)** Speciation is the formation of new species. New species may be formed when the number of beneficial or favorable adaptations increase in a species and unfavorable adaptations decrease over time. Eventually, the species becomes so different from what it used to be that it can no longer be considered the same species. Speciation is thought to occur in two stages. Populations of a species first become geographically isolated by some kind of natural barrier that does not allow gene mixing between the different populations. The populations become adapted to their own environments, which may eventually result in reproductive isolation. The populations may become so different physically or behaviorally, for example, that even if they could bridge the barrier, they would not be able to reproduce. Species are considered to be separate when they lose the ability to mate and produce viable offspring that can also reproduce. *(Mechanisms of Evolution)*

**11.** Which statement describing a cause of extinction includes the other three?

(1) Members of the extinct species were unable to compete for food.
(2) Members of the extinct species were unable to conceal their presence by camouflage.
(3) Members of the extinct species lacked adaptations essential for survival.
(4) Members of the extinct species were too slow to escape from predators.

**Correct Answer: (3)** This is a difficult question because, if taken separately, all four answers are true statements. In this question, the key word is *adaptations.* It takes precedence over all the other significant terms like *survival, compete, camouflage,* or *predators.* The extinct species was unable to compete for food, was unable to conceal its presence, and was too slow to escape—all because of lacking adaptations. *(Mechanisms of Evolution)*

**12.** Mutations that occur in skin or lung cells have little effect on the evolution of a species because mutations in these cells

(1) usually lead to the death of the organism
(2) cannot be passed on to offspring
(3) are usually beneficial to the organism
(4) lead to more serious mutations in offspring

**Correct Answer: (2)** Mutations must be passed on to offspring in order for them to have an impact on evolution. The only way that genetic information is passed on to offspring is through the gametes. So, in order for a mutation to be passed on to offspring, it must affect the gametes. Mutations of skin or lung cells have little impact on evolution because they do not affect the formation of gametes and cannot be passed on to offspring. *(Mechanisms of Evolution)*

**13.** Which factor is *least* likely to contribute to an increase in the rate of evolution?

(1) presence of genetic variations in a population
(2) environmental selection of organisms best adapted to survive
(3) chromosomal recombinations
(4) a long period of environmental stability

**Correct Answer: (4)** A good strategy to use when reading questions with superlatives (like *least, most, greatest,* and so on) is to take each answer choice separately, put it at the *beginning* of the statement, and see whether it's true. For example, with choice (4): A long period of environmental stability is *least* likely to contribute to an increase in the rate of evolution. This is a true statement. Repeating this same process with choices (1), (2), and (3) shows that those statements are not true. *(Mechanisms of Evolution)*

**14.** The teeth of carnivores are pointed and are good for puncturing and ripping flesh. The teeth of herbivores are flat and are good for grinding and chewing. Which statement best explains these observations?

**(1)** Herbivores have evolved from carnivores.
**(2)** Carnivores have evolved from herbivores.
**(3)** The two types of teeth most likely evolved as a result of natural selection.
**(4)** The two types of teeth most likely evolved as a result of the needs of an organism.

**Correct Answer: (3)** Evolution occurs as a result of natural selection, not need. Those organisms that had teeth that allowed them to survive better also reproduced more and left behind offspring that had similar teeth. Over time, the result of natural selection was organisms with teeth that best fit the types of food they consumed. *(Mechanisms of Evolution)*

**15.** Scientists compared fossil remains of a species that lived 5,000 years ago with members of the same species living today. Scientists concluded that this species had changed very little over the entire time period. Which statement best accounts for this lack of change?

**(1)** The environment changed significantly, and those offspring without favorable characteristics died.
**(2)** The environment changed significantly, but the species had no natural enemies for a long period of time.
**(3)** The environment did not change significantly, and those offspring expressing new characteristics survived their natural enemies.
**(4)** The environment did not change significantly, and those offspring expressing new characteristics did not survive.

**Correct Answer: (4)** If offspring were born with new traits and they did not survive, then that would explain how the species had changed very little in the past 5,000 years. If they had survived, then those with new traits would not look like the ones 5,000 years before—they would appear different. But that is not what the scientists found. All the other choices would have organisms that do not resemble those of 5,000 years earlier. *(Patterns of Evolution)*

**16.** Which statement is *not* part of the concept of natural selection?

**(1)** Individuals that possess the most favorable variations will have the best chance of reproducing.
**(2)** Variation occurs among individuals in a population.
**(3)** More individuals are produced than will survive.
**(4)** Genes of an individual adapt to a changing environment.

**Correct Answer: (4)** The concept of natural selection is part of Charles Darwin's Theory of Evolution, explained in his book *On the Origin of Species by Means of Natural Selection,* published in 1859. Natural selection includes the idea that individuals with traits or adaptations that make them better suited to their environment will most likely live to reproduce and pass their genes on to the next generation. Genes don't adapt. If a gene is responsible for some trait that allows an organism to better survive a changing condition better than another organism, the chance that the gene will be passed on to a future generation increases. *(The Theory of Evolution)*

**17.** Woolly mammoths became extinct thousands of years ago, while other species of mammals that existed at that time still exist today. These other species of mammals most likely exist today because, unlike the mammoths, they

**(1)** produced offspring that all had identical inheritable characteristics
**(2)** did not face a struggle for survival
**(3)** learned to migrate to new environments
**(4)** had certain inheritable traits that enabled them to survive

**Correct Answer: (4)** In a changing environment, organisms better equipped to handle the changes will live, reproduce, and have offspring with the same traits that helped their parents survive. Organisms not well equipped will be more likely to die and be less likely to produce offspring. The wooly mammoth had traits that were not well suited for the environment, and they died. *(The Theory of Evolution)*

**18.** The evolutionary pathways of seven living species are shown in the diagram below.

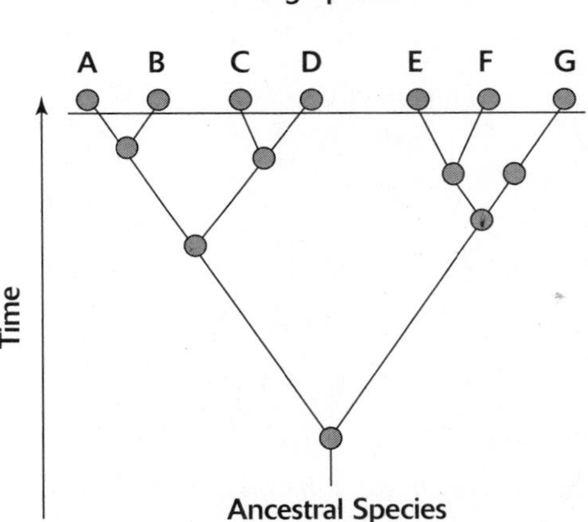


Which two species are likely to have the most similar DNA base sequence?

**(1)** B and G
**(2)** E and G
**(3)** B and C
**(4)** C and D

**Correct Answer: (4)** Species C and D are the most closely related, because they are closer to each other on the diagram. The more closely related two organisms are, the more similar their DNA base sequences will be. All the other choices show two organisms that are split farther apart than C and D. *(Mechanisms of Evolution)*

**19.** The bones in the forelimbs of three mammals are shown below.

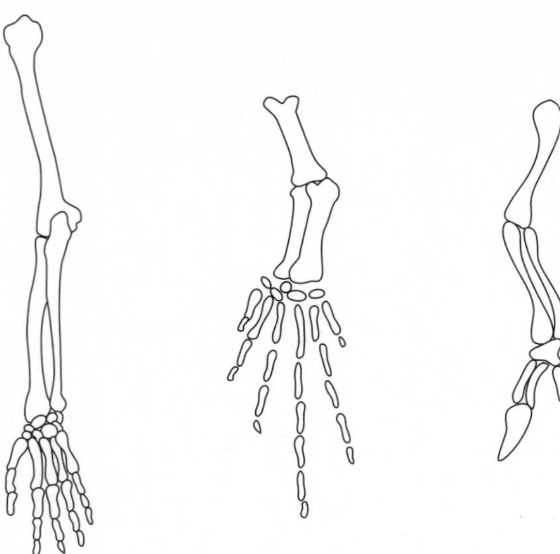

For these mammals, the number, position, and shape of the bones most likely indicate that they may have

**(1)** developed in a common environment
**(2)** developed from the same earlier species
**(3)** identical genetic makeup
**(4)** identical methods of obtaining food

**Correct Answer: (2)** The bones in the forelimbs of the three mammals are homologous—they are structurally similar but have different functions. Homologous structures result from modifications of a specific trait or attribute. The presence of homologous features indicates that the different species shared a common ancestor. A common environment—choice (1)—may lead to similar advantageous features that are not structurally identical. If these mammals had identical genetic makeup—choice (3)—they would look the same. Methods of obtaining food—choice (4)—are not indicated by the bone structure. *(The Theory of Evolution)*

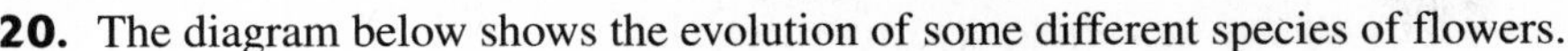

**20.** The diagram below shows the evolution of some different species of flowers.

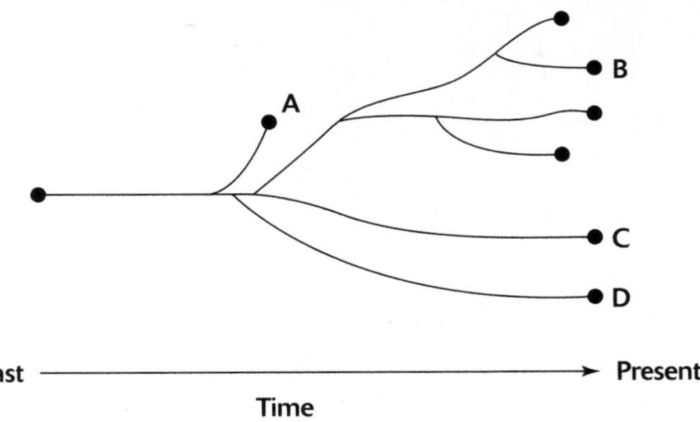


Which statement about the species is correct?

(1) Species A, B, C, and D came from different ancestors.
(2) Species C evolved from species B.
(3) Species A, B, and C can interbreed successfully.
(4) Species A became extinct.

**Correct Answer: (4)** The diagram is a phylogenetic tree, which shows the evolutionary history of a group of related organisms. Because the line showing the history of species A stops at some distance before the present, where species B, C, and D are shown to exist, it is assumed species A became extinct. Another possibility is that evidence of species A after the time of its presumed extinction has not yet been found. *(Patterns of Evolution)*

**21.** The theory of biological evolution includes the concept that

(1) species of organisms found on Earth today have adaptations not always found in earlier species
(2) fossils are the remains of present-day species and were all formed at the same time
(3) individuals may acquire physical characteristics after birth and pass these acquired characteristics on to their offspring
(4) the smallest organisms are always eliminated by the larger organisms within the ecosystem

**Correct Answer: (1)** Biological evolution is the idea that species change over a long period of time. The change is made possible through genetic variation in response to pressures from the environment. As a particular trait becomes more favorable, the population of those *without* the trait decreases and the population that exhibits the trait increases. Over time, the species will have adaptations not present in earlier forms. *(The Theory of Evolution)*

**22.** Which species is most likely to survive changing environmental conditions?

(1) a species that has few variations
(2) a species that reproduces sexually
(3) a species that competes with similar species
(4) a species that has a limited life span

**Correct Answer: (2)** Genetic variation is brought about by mutation, recombination by independent assortment or crossing over during meiosis, and sexual reproduction (or the random fusion of gametes). Darwin's theory of natural selection states that organisms with beneficial variations, or traits that make them better adapted to their environment, are more likely to survive and reproduce than organisms with unfavorable variations. Genetic variation allows a species to adapt to a changing environment. *(The Theory of Evolution)*

Base your answer to question 23 on the information below and on your knowledge of biology.

The dodo bird inhabited the island of Mauritius in the Indian Ocean, where it lived undisturbed for years. It lost its ability to fly and it lived and nested on the ground where it ate fruits that had fallen from trees. There were not mammals living on the island.

In 1505, the first humans set foot on Mauritius. The island quickly became a stopover for ships engaged in the spice trade. The dodo was a welcome source of fresh meat for the sailors and large numbers of dodos were killed for food. In time, pigs, monkeys, and rats brought to the island ate the dodo eggs in the ground nests.

**23.** Which statement describes what most likely happened to the dodo bird within 100 years of the arrival of humans on Mauritius?

(1) Dodo birds developed the ability to fly in order to escape predation and their population increased.
(2) The dodo bird population increased after the birds learned to build their nests in trees.
(3) Human exploitation and introduced species significantly reduced dodo bird populations.
(4) The dodo bird population became smaller because they preyed upon the introduced species.

**Correct Answer: (3)** The things humans did on the island (using the birds for food, the animals they brought with them eating the bird eggs) had a negative impact on the dodo birds. *(Mechanisms of Evolution)*

Base your answers to questions 24 through 26 on the diagram below, which shows some evolutionary pathways. Each letter represents a different species.

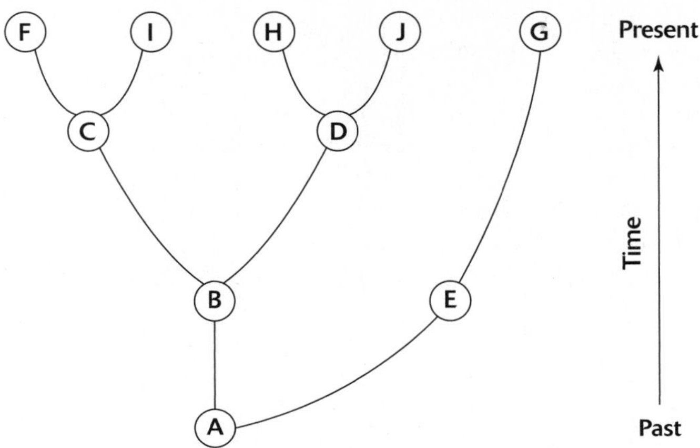


**24.** Which two organisms are most closely related?

(1) F and I
(2) F and H
(3) A and G
(4) G and J

**Correct Answer: (1)** Evolutionary history is often represented in a "tree" diagram. Each branch of the tree represents a point at which offspring of a common ancestor gave rise to a different group. In this diagram, species A is the common ancestor for all the other species. Species B, however descended from species A, and gave rise to species C, F, I, D, H, and J. Within each of those two branches are distinctly different groups—bears and raccoons, for example. Any organisms that arose from a common ancestor are related. The closer they are to the point of divergence, the more closely related they are. *(Patterns of Evolution)*

**25.** The most recent ancestor of organisms D and F is

(1) A
(2) B
(3) C
(4) I

**Correct Answer: (2)** The species at the top of the tree diagram are those that are currently alive (species F, I, H, J, and G). They arose from ancestor species that can be traced as you move down the branches. To find the common ancestor of species on different branches (D and F), look for the point at which their branches meet—in this case, species B. *(Patterns of Evolution)*

**26.** If A represents a simple multicellular heterotrophic organism, B would most likely represent

**(1)** a single-celled photosynthetic organism
**(2)** an autotrophic mammal
**(3)** a complex multicellular virus
**(4)** another type of simple multicellular heterotroph

**Correct Answer: (4)** Because species A and B are directly connected on a branch of the evolutionary tree, they're likely to be very similar to each other. Photosynthetic organisms, mammals, and viruses are all very different from simple multicellular heterotrophic organisms, such as species A. *(Patterns of Evolution)*

**27.** According to the diagram below, which three species lived on Earth during the same time period?

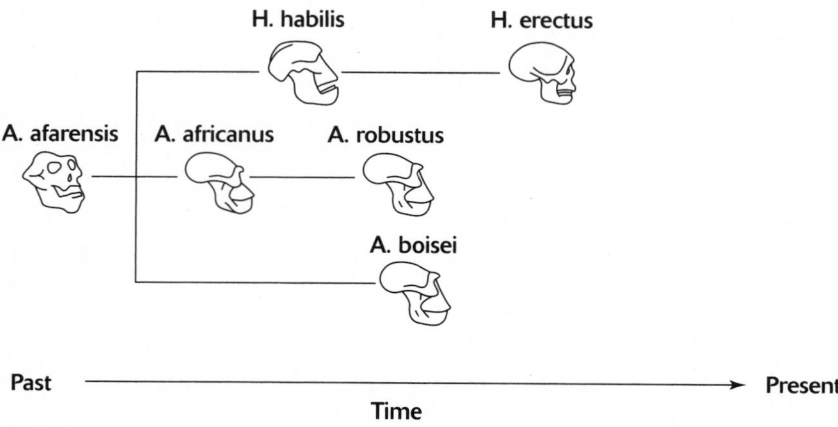


**(1)** *robustus, africanus, afarensis*
**(2)** *habilis, erectus, afarensis*
**(3)** *habilis, robustus, boisei*
**(4)** *africanus, boisei, erectus*

**Correct Answer: (3)** In order to answer this question, you don't need to know anything about these human ancestors. What you *do* need to know is how to interpret the diagram. First, the common ancestor to all these species is *A. afarnesis;* this is because this species is at the beginning of the diagram and all the other species branch off from it. Second, any one particular species, represented by the skull, is present until the line it is on makes it to the next skull. For example, look at the top line. It shows *H. habilis* connected to the common ancestor, *A. afarnesis* on the left, and the line leads from the *H. habilis* skull until it reaches the skull for *H. erectus.* This means that *H. habilis* lived up until the time *H. erectus* evolved. If you look at the second and third lines, they too have the common ancestor of *A. afarensis.* Based on the diagram, *A. robustus* and *A. boisei* existed at the same time. And, *H. habilis* also existed at the same time because it is present until the line it is on meets the next ancestor. Choice (3) is the only choice that has the three ancestors that existed at the same time. *(Patterns of Evolution)*

Base your answer to question 28 on the diagram below and on your knowledge of biology.

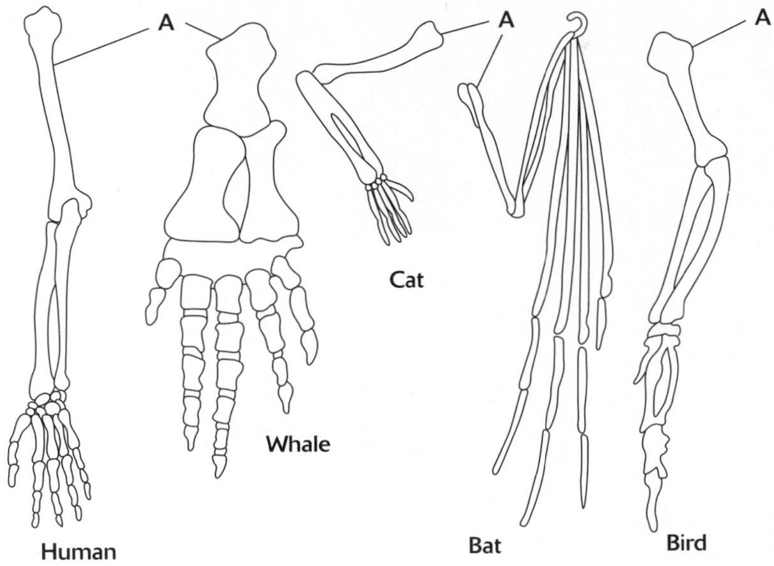


**28.** The similarities of the bones labeled A provide evidence that

(1) the organisms may have evolved from a common ancestor
(2) all species have one kind of bone structure
(3) the cells of the bones contain the same type of mutations
(4) all structural characteristics are the same in animals

**Correct Answer: (1)** The structures are homologous, which means that the bones are arranged in a very similar manner, even though they are used for different purposes. The structures are so similar that they provide evidence that these organisms all evolved from a common ancestor. *(The Theory of Evolution)*

Base your answers to questions 29 through 31 on the information below and on your knowledge of biology.

Color in peppered moths is controlled by genes. A light-colored variety and a dark-colored variety of a peppered moth species exist in nature. The moths often rest on tree trunks, and several different species of birds are predators of this moth.

Before industrialization in England, the light-colored variety was much more abundant than the dark-colored variety and evidence indicates that many tree trunks at that time were covered with light-colored lichens. Later, industrialization developed and brought pollution which killed the lichens leaving the tree trunks covered with dark-colored soot. The results of a study made in England are shown below.

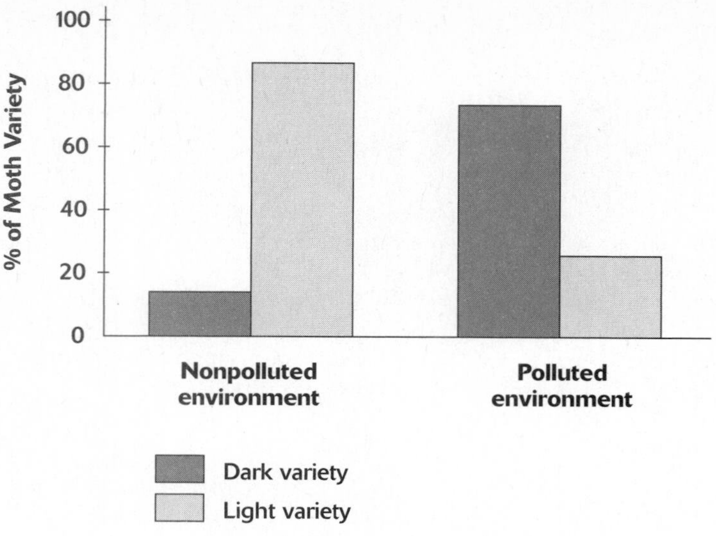


**29.** State one possible reason that a larger number of the dark-colored variety was present in the polluted environment.

**Correct Answer:** The dark-colored moths were able to avoid predators by blending into their environment, which included the trees that were covered in dark soot. They were better adapted to their environment than the light-colored moths. *(Mechanisms of Evolution)*

**30.** State one possible reason that the light-colored variety was not completely eliminated from the polluted environment.

**Correct Answer:** Reasons that the light-colored moth was not completely eliminated from the polluted environment include the following:

- The genes for light color may be dominant.
- Light-colored moths may be resting in areas in which they were better adapted, or better able to blend in.
- Light-colored moths from neighboring communities may be immigrating.
- Light-colored moths may have an adaptation that allows them to survive in the environment.

*(The Theory of Evolution)*

**31.** Which conclusion can best be drawn from the information given?

**(1)** The trait for dark coloration better suits the peppered moth for survival in nonpolluted environments.
**(2)** The trait for light coloration better suits the peppered moth for survival in polluted environments.
**(3)** The variation of color in the peppered moth has no influence on survival of the moth.
**(4)** A given trait may be a favorable adaptation in one environment, but not in another environment.

**Correct Answer: (4)** The environment selects which traits of an organism are beneficial and which traits are not. A trait may be beneficial to a population in one environment and detrimental to the population in a different environment. *(The Theory of Evolution)*

Base your answers to questions 32 and 33 on the information below and on your knowledge of biology.

**Variations in Lake Water Level**

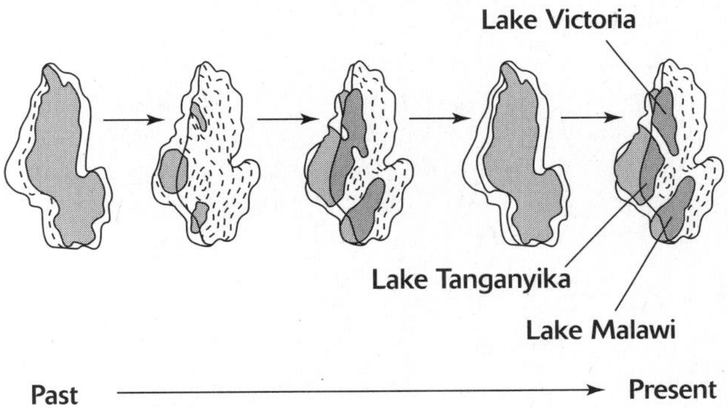

Lake Victoria

Lake Tanganyika

Lake Malawi

Past ⟶ Present

The three great lakes in Africa (Victoria, Tanganyika, and Malawi) contain a greater number of fish species than any other lake in the world. Lake Malawi alone has 200 species of cichlid fish. The diversity of cichlid species in these African lakes could have been caused by changes in water level over thousands of years.

According to one hypothesis, at one time the three lakes were connected as one large lake and all the cichlids could interbreed. When the water level fell, groups of cichlids were isolated in smaller lakes as shown in the diagram. Over time, the groups of cichlids developed genetic differences. When the water levels rose again, the isolated populations were brought back into contact. Due to significant genetic differences, these populations were unable to interbreed. Variations in water level over thousands of years resulted in today's diversity of cichlid species.

**32.** Which discovery would support this explanation of cichlid diversity?

(1) The water level changed little over time.
(2) The local conditions in each of the small lakes were very different.
(3) Differences between cichlid species are small and interbreeding is possible.
(4) Once formed, the lakes remained isolated from each other.

**Correct Answer: (2)** Because the conditions in each of the small lakes were different, the fish that possessed the adaptations that matched the environmental conditions of each lake were able to survive and reproduce. The differences in the lakes led to diversity of the fish. *(Patterns of Evolution)*

**33.** As the water level of the lakes changed, many species of cichlid survived while others became extinct. State why some species survived while others became extinct.

**Correct Answer:** When some species survive while others die out, it is always due to one thing: the possession of adaptations (or absence thereof) that allows them to survive (or die). Your answer should be: Those species survived because they possessed adaptations that matched their environment. *(Patterns of Evolution)*

**34.** Growers of fruit trees have always had problems with insects. Insects can cause visible damage to fruits, making them less appealing to consumers. As a result of this damage, much of the fruit cannot be sold. Insecticides have been useful for controlling these insects, but, in recent years, some insecticides have been much less effective. In some cases, insecticides do nothing to stop the insect attacks.

Provide a biological explanation for this loss of effectiveness of the insecticides. In your answer, be sure to:

- identify the original event that resulted in the evolution of insecticide resistance in some insects
- explain why the percentage of resistant insects in the population has increased
- describe *one* alternative form of insect control, other than using a different insecticide, that fruit growers could use to protect their crops from insect attack

**Correct Answer:** Be sure to answer all parts of the question:

- A genetic mutation (or genetic change) that is heritable would have likely caused the resistance to the insecticide.
- The percentage of resistant insects in the population increases each generation because those that are not resistant to the insecticide are killed by it. These survivors then reproduce and their offspring, which are also resistant to the insecticide, also survive and reproduce, while the nonresistant insects are killed.
- An alternative form of insect control would be to release natural predators of the insects, such as ladybugs or praying mantis, into the fruit tree orchards. These predators would eat the insects that damage the fruit. Another possibility would be to genetically engineer insect-resistant plants that the insects would not eat.

*(Mechanisms of Evolution)*

**35.** A hawk has a genetic trait that gives it much better eyesight than other hawks of the same species in the same area. Explain how this could lead to evolutionary change within this species of hawk over a long period of time. In your answer, be sure to include an explanation of

- competition within the hawk population
- survival of various individuals in the population
- how the frequency of the better-eyesight trait would be expected to change over time within the population
- what would most likely happen to the hawks having the better eyesight trait if they also had unusually weak wing muscles

**Correct Answer:** Be sure to answer all parts of the question:

- In terms of competition, the better-eyesight hawks would be better able to find food than hawks with poorer eyesight.
- In terms of survival, those hawks with better eyesight would be more likely to survive than those that did not have better eyesight.
- In terms of the frequency of better-eyesight hawks, the frequency would increase because they would be more likely to survive and, therefore, reproduce.
- In terms of better-eyesight hawks having weak wing muscles, they would decrease because they would possess an adaptation that would make it less likely for them to survive.

*(Patterns of Evolution)*

# Reproduction and Development

**Directions:** For each statement or question, choose the *number* of the word or expression that best completes the statement or answers the question. Then check your answer against the one that immediately follows the question. Try not to look at the answer before making your selection.

**1.** Most of the hereditary information that determines the traits of an organism is located in

**(1)** only those cells of an individual produced by meiosis
**(2)** the nuclei of body cells of an individual
**(3)** certain genes in the vacuoles of body cells
**(4)** the numerous ribosomes in certain cells

**Correct Answer: (2)** DNA is the hereditary information that determines the traits of an organism. Body (somatic) cells contain 46 chromosomes that hold the total amount of genetic information for the individual. Sex cells (egg and sperm) are haploid (1n) and contain only half the amount (23 chromosomes) of the genetic information that make up an organism. *(Types of Reproduction)*

**2.** The arrows in the diagram below illustrate processes in the life of a species that reproduces sexually.

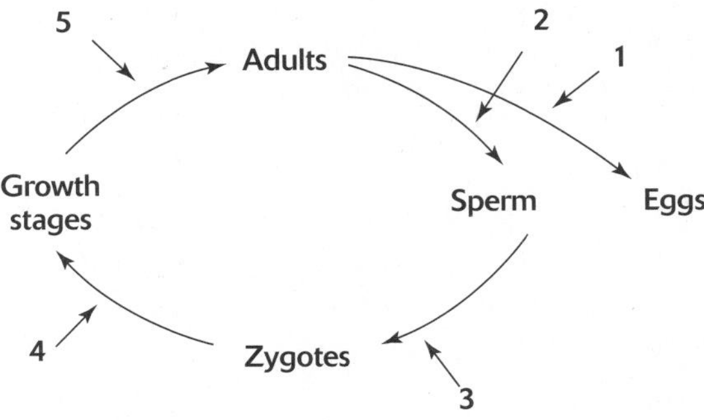


Which processes result directly in the formation of cells with half the amount of genetic material that is characteristic of the species?

**(1)** 1 and 2
**(2)** 2 and 3
**(3)** 3 and 4
**(4)** 4 and 5

**Correct Answer: (1)** Adult sex cells go through the processes of meiosis, or gametogenesis—oogenesis and spermatogenesis, specifically—to create haploid (1n) egg and sperm cells. These cells contain half the genetic information of an organism. An egg cell will be fertilized by a sperm cell, which will restore the full number of chromosomes of the species. *(Types of Reproduction)*

**3.** Changes in the genetic code of a human can be transmitted to offspring if they occur in

(1) cancer cells
(2) gametes
(3) cell membranes
(4) antibodies

**Correct Answer: (2)** Changes in the genetic code of a human can only be transmitted to offspring if they occur in gametes. Gametes (egg and sperm cells) will form offspring after fertilization and formation of a zygote. *(Types of Reproduction)*

**4.** Which statement correctly describes the genetic makeup of the sperm cells produced by a human male?

(1) Each cell has pairs of chromosomes and the cells are usually genetically identical.
(2) Each cell has pairs of chromosomes and the cells are usually genetically different.
(3) Each cell has half the normal number of chromosomes and the cells are usually genetically identical.
(4) Each cell has half the normal number of chromosomes and the cells are usually genetically different.

**Correct Answer: (4)** Gametes, such as sperm and eggs, are formed during meiosis. Meiosis involves two cell divisions and a reduction of the normal number of chromosomes by half. Chromosomes are rearranged during meiosis so that individual gametes are usually genetically different from each other. *(Cell Division)*

**5.** To produce large tomatoes that are resistant to cracking and splitting, some seed companies use the pollen from one variety of tomato plant to fertilize a different variety of tomato plant. This process is an example of

(1) selective breeding
(2) DNA sequencing
(3) direct harvesting
(4) cloning

**Correct Answer: (1)** Selective breeding is a technique used to produce an organism with desirable traits. In this case, artificial pollination, a technique by which pollen is intentionally transferred from one plant to another by humans, was used to produce a tomato plant with certain characteristics. *(Technology of Reproduction)*

**6.** Which cell process occurs only in organisms that reproduce sexually?

**(1)** mutation
**(2)** replication
**(3)** meiosis
**(4)** mitosis

**Correct Answer: (3)** Meiosis is the process in which gametes (the eggs and sperm), which are necessary in order for sexual reproduction to occur, are produced. All the other choices occur in sexually and asexually reproducing organisms. *(Types of Reproduction)*

**7.** In an environment that undergoes frequent change, species that reproduce sexually may have an advantage over species that reproduce asexually because the sexually reproducing species produce

**(1)** more offspring in each generation
**(2)** identical offspring
**(3)** offspring with more variety
**(4)** new species of offspring in each generation

**Correct Answer: (3)** Asexual reproduction produces offspring that are genetically identical, while sexual reproduction produces offspring that are genetically different from each other. If an environmental change occurs (such as an increase in temperature), only those organisms that have a genetic makeup that allows them to survive under those new conditions will survive. Asexual organisms are genetically identical, so if they encounter an environmental change, and they do not have the genetic makeup that allows them to survive under those new conditions, they will all die because they are all equally unfit for that environment. If sexual organisms encounter an environmental change, some may have the genetic makeup that allows them to survive under those new conditions because all individuals in the population are genetically different. If the environment is frequently changing, any one of those changes could wipe out the entire population of asexual organisms. However, because sexual organisms are genetically varied, some may survive the constantly changing environmental conditions. *(Types of Reproduction)*

**8.** Research has shown that certain body cells, known as stem cells, can develop into a variety of specialized cells. Various factors can cause stem cells to develop into different types of mature cells. These different types of mature cells result from

**(1)** different antibodies and mitotic cell division
**(2)** identical genetic codes and meiotic cell division
**(3)** different environments of the cells and the functioning of different parts of the genetic code
**(4)** similar steps in the development of the cells and a reduction in the number of chromosomes in each cell

**Correct Answer: (3)** Cells are known by the company they keep. If a stem cell is placed in the pancreas, it will behave like a pancreas cell. Likewise, if a stem cell is placed in a lung, it will behave like a lung cell. How can this be? How can the same kind of cell (a stem cell) function in two different ways? The answer lies in the genes. All body cells of an organism contain the same genetic information. So the cell in the pancreas has the same information as the cell in the lung. Because they are in their respective places—the pancreas and the lung—the part of the genetic code that functions for that type of cell will take over and the stem cell will divide and start functioning like the cells around it. *(Technology of Reproduction)*

**9.** The development of specialized tissues and organs in a multicellular organism directly results from

**(1)** cloning
**(2)** differentiation
**(3)** meiosis
**(4)** evolution

**Correct Answer: (2)** After fertilization, a zygote begins a series of mitotic divisions called *cleavage.* As the cells continue to divide and grow, they begin to differentiate into specialized cells that will make up the tissues and organs of the embryo. *(Cell Division)*

**10.** The *least* genetic variation will probably be found in the offspring of organisms that reproduce using

**(1)** mitosis to produce a larger population
**(2)** meiosis to produce gametes
**(3)** fusion of eggs and sperm to produce zygotes
**(4)** internal fertilization to produce an embryo

**Correct Answer: (1)** The process of mitosis is asexual. It occurs when a cell clones itself resulting in two identical cells. The question asks for the "least" genetic variation, and clones have the least variation because they are all identical. The other three choices are sexual processes that provide variation. *(Types of Reproduction)*

**11.** Reproduction in humans usually requires

**(1)** the process of cloning
**(2)** mitotic cell division of gametes
**(3)** gametes with chromosomes that are not paired
**(4)** the external fertilization of sex cells

**Correct Answer: (3)** In order to answer this question, you must know that gametes are the sex cells—eggs and sperm—and that the gametes have half as many chromosomes (23) as other cells. This is because when they combine with each other during fertilization, the resulting zygote will have the proper number of chromosomes, 46. Cloning—choice (1)—is the making of an exact copy of an organism; this is not how humans reproduce. Mitosis—choice (2)—is similar to cloning in that the offspring cells that are made are just like the parent cell they came from. External fertilization—choice (4)—means that eggs and sperm are placed outside the body and fertilization takes place outside the body; humans do not reproduce this way. *(Technology of Reproduction)*

**12.** The human reproductive system is regulated by

(1) restriction enzymes
(2) antigens
(3) complex carbohydrates
(4) hormones

**Correct Answer: (4)** Several hormones are involved in human reproduction: estrogen, follicle stimulating hormone (FSH), leutinizing hormone (LH), and human chorionic gonadatropin (HCG). Each hormone has a specific function, but all you need to be concerned about is making a connection between these hormones and the fact that they're involved in reproduction. *(Human Reproduction)*

**13.** Which statement is true of both mitosis and meiosis?

(1) Both are involved in asexual reproduction.
(2) Both occur only in reproductive cells.
(3) The number of chromosomes is reduced by half.
(4) DNA replication occurs before the division of the nucleus.

**Correct Answer: (4)** The first stage of meiosis is the same as mitosis: DNA, in the form of chromosomes, replicates or doubles. Only mitosis is involved in asexual reproduction—choice (1). Mitosis occurs in body cells (also called somatic cells), while meiosis occurs in the formation of sex cells (also called gametes). Only in meiosis is the chromosome number reduced to half the original number. In meiosis, the chromosome number is reduced to one-fourth the original number. *(Cell Division)*

**14.** In sexually reproducing species, the number of chromosomes in each body cell remains the same from one generation to the next as a direct result of

(1) meiosis and fertilization
(2) mitosis and mutation
(3) differentiation and aging
(4) homeostasis and dynamic equilibrium

**Correct Answer: (1)** Meiosis is a type of cell division that results in the formation of haploid (1n) gametes (egg and sperm) from a diploid (2n) parent cell in sexually reproducing species. Each gamete contains half the total number of chromosomes, so that upon fertilization, when the sperm nuclei joins with the egg nuclei forming a zygote, the diploid number is restored. *(Types of Reproduction)*

**15.** A cell resulting from the fertilization of an egg begins to divide. Two cells are formed that normally remain attached and could develop into a new individual. If the two cells become separated, which statement describes what would most likely occur?

(1) The cells would each have all of the needed genetic information, and both could survive.
(2) The cells would each have only one-half of the needed genetic information, so both would die.
(3) One cell would have all of the needed genetic information and would survive, but the other would have none of the needed genetic information and would die.
(4) Each cell would have some of the needed genetic information, but would be unable to share it, so both would die.

**Correct Answer: (1)** This question is referring to the process in which identical twins are formed. The fertilized egg splits into two separate cells instead of staying together. Because the cells are the result of mitosis of the fertilized egg, each cell possesses identical genetic information necessary for life. If all goes well, identical twins will be born. *(Human Reproduction)*

**16.** The human brain, kidney, and liver all develop from the same zygote. This fact indicates that cells formed by divisions of the zygote are able to

(1) differentiate
(2) mutate
(3) undergo cloning
(4) be fertilized

**Correct Answer: (1)** It is pretty amazing that, from one fertilized egg and then one zygote, an entire human being can arise. A human has many different tissues, organs, and structures, and they are all different. That's what *differentiate* means: to develop into different tissues and organs. *(Human Reproduction)*

**17.** Which diagram best illustrates an event in sexual reproduction that would most directly lead to the formation of a human embryo?

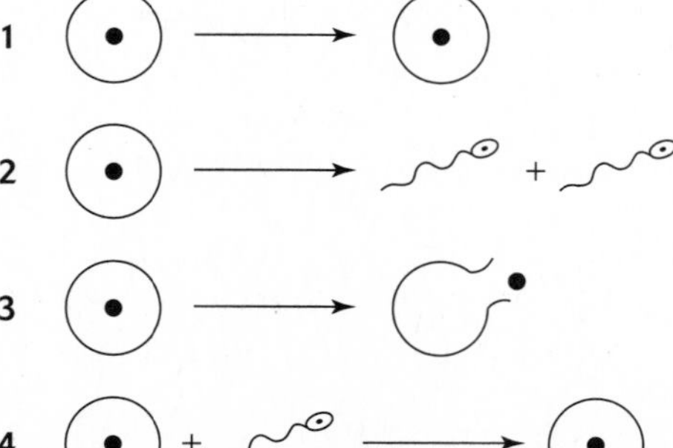

**Correct Answer: (4)** Sexual reproduction involves the union of a sperm cell and an egg cell. These two cells come together in during fertilization and ultimately lead to the formation of a human embryo. *(Human Reproduction)*

Base your answer to question 18 on the diagram below, which represents the human female reproductive system.

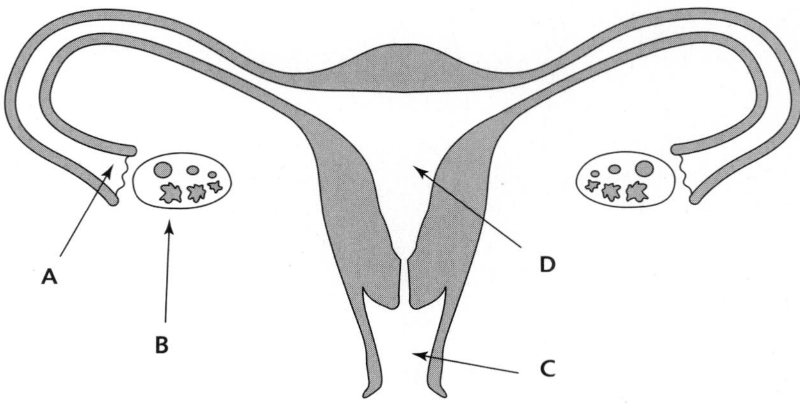


**18.** In which part of this system does a fetus usually develop?

**(1)** A
**(2)** B
**(3)** C
**(4)** D

**Correct Answer: (4)** The uterus is where the fertilized egg, or zygote, implants and begins its development. The structure indicated by D is the uterus. *(Human Reproduction)*

**19.** Marine sponges contain a biological catalyst that blocks a certain step in the separation of chromosomes. Which cellular process would be directly affected by this catalyst?

**(1)** mitosis
**(2)** diffusion
**(3)** respiration
**(4)** photosynthesis

**Correct Answer: (1)** Mitosis is asexual cellular division. The chromosomes double and then separate so that each new cell has a copy. If the chromosomes were not able to separate, mitosis would be interrupted. *(Cell Division)*

**20.** A certain bacterial colony originated from the division of a single bacterial cell. Each cell in this colony will most likely

(1) express adaptations unlike those of the other cells
(2) replicate different numbers of genes
(3) have a resistance to different antibiotics
(4) synthesize the same proteins and enzymes

**Correct Answer: (4)** Bacteria that have reproduced asexually will be genetically identical. Unless mutations occur, everything about all the cells in the colony will be identical, including the synthesis of proteins and enzymes. *(Types of Reproduction)*

**21.** One function of the placenta in a human is to

(1) surround the embryo and protect it from shock
(2) allow for mixing of maternal blood with fetal blood
(3) act as the heart of the fetus, pumping blood until the fetus is born
(4) permit passage of nutrients and oxygen from the mother to the fetus

**Correct Answer: (4)** The placenta is a temporary organ formed between the mother and an embryo when a woman becomes pregnant. The placenta allows nutrients, gases, waste, drugs, and other substances to pass between the mother and the fetus through the umbilical cord. Blood of the mother and fetus do not mix. Blood from the fetus passes through the umbilical cord to the placenta where waste materials diffuse out across membranes to the mother's circulatory system and nutrients diffuse in from the mother. Blood that has been rid of wastes and enriched by nutrients travels back to the developing fetus through the umbilical cord. The placenta also secretes a hormone that stops the menstrual cycle during pregnancy. Amniotic fluid is what surrounds the fetus and protects it from shock. *(Human Reproduction)*

**22.** Down syndrome is a genetic disorder caused by the presence of an extra chromosome in the body cells of humans. This extra chromosome occurs in a gamete as a result of

(1) an error in the process of cloning
(2) an error in meiotic cell division
(3) a gene mutation
(4) replication of a single chromosome during mitosis

**Correct Answer: (2)** During meiosis, the chromosomes replicate or double before any splitting of the cytoplasm occurs. During this process, when the chromosomes are lined up at the equator of the cell, there are two pairs of chromosomes called a tetrad that are attached together for a total of four chromosomes. Normally, the tetrad divides evenly in a process called disjunction, in which one pair of chromosomes goes toward one side of the cell and the other pair heads toward the other side, or pole, of the cell.

When the tetrad fails to separate evenly in a process called nondisjunction, one of the pairs of chromosomes ends up with an extra chromosome, making it three instead of two. The remaining cell will only contain one chromosome instead of a pair. *(Cell Division)*

**23.** The reproductive cycle of a human is usually regulated by

(1) gametes
(2) hormones
(3) natural selection
(4) immune responses

**Correct Answer: (2)** The human reproductive cycle is highly regulated by hormones such as estrogen, follicle stimulating hormone (FSH), leutinizing hormone (LH), and human chorionic gonadatropin (HCG). The rule for any hormones is that they are released from one organ of the body and travel through the blood to another organ, called the target organ, where they cause some response from that organ. *(Human Reproduction)*

**24.** Removal of one ovary from a human female would most likely

(1) affect the production of eggs
(2) make fertilization impossible
(3) make carrying a fetus impossible
(4) decrease her ability to provide essential nutrients to an embryo

**Correct Answer: (1)** The ovaries are the organs in which eggs are produced. Removal of one ovary (normal females have two ovaries) will reduce the number of eggs that the female will produce, but will not impact her ability to carry a fetus or provide nutrients for an embryo. Also, the removal of only one ovary will not make the female infertile. *(Human Reproduction)*

**25.** Each of the offspring that result from meiosis and fertilization has

(1) twice as many chromosomes as its parents
(2) one-half as many chromosomes as its parents
(3) gene combinations different from those of either parent
(4) gene combinations identical to those of each parent

**Correct Answer: (3)** Meiosis is a type of cell division that is involved in producing the gametes. During meiosis, the number of chromosomes is reduced by half and this insures that the number of chromosomes remains constant from one generation to the next. Meiosis also allows for each gamete to be genetically unique. As a result, each offspring (after fertilization) has the same number of chromosomes as their parents, but also a gene combination that is unique to itself. *(Cell Division)*

**26.** Which statement describes asexual reproduction?

(1) Adaptive traits are usually passed from parent to offspring without genetic modification.
(2) Mutations are not passed from generation to generation.
(3) It always enables organisms to survive in changing environmental conditions.
(4) It is responsible for many new variations in offspring.

**Correct Answer: (1)** Don't let the beginning words "Adaptive traits" scare you. It is the end of the statement that is key: "from parent to offspring without genetic modification." This basically sums up what asexual reproduction is. If the parents have a mutation—choice (2)—the mutation *will* be passed on to any offspring. Asexual reproduction will not allow organisms to survive in changing environmental conditions—choice (3). Only sexual reproduction, with its crossing over and variations, helps organism survive in changing environmental conditions. *(Types of Reproduction)*

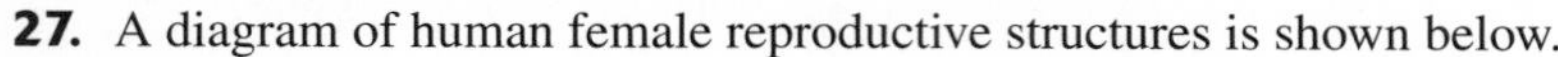

**27.** A diagram of human female reproductive structures is shown below.

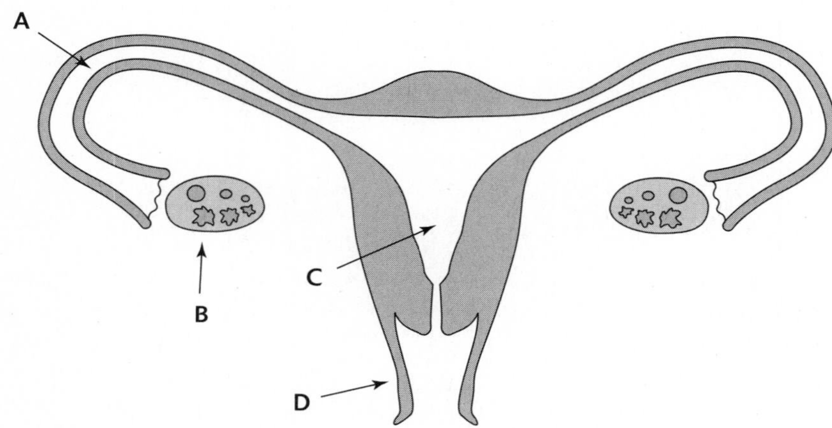


Which structure is correctly paired with its function?

(1) A—releases estrogen and progesterone
(2) B—produces and releases the egg
(3) C—provides the usual site for fertilization
(4) D—nourishes a developing embryo

**Correct Answer: (2)** B is an ovary. The ovary is the site of egg production. *(Human Reproduction)*

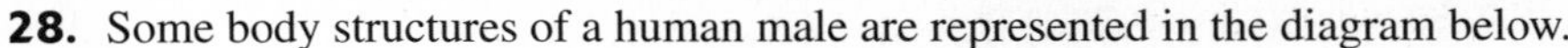

**28.** Some body structures of a human male are represented in the diagram below.

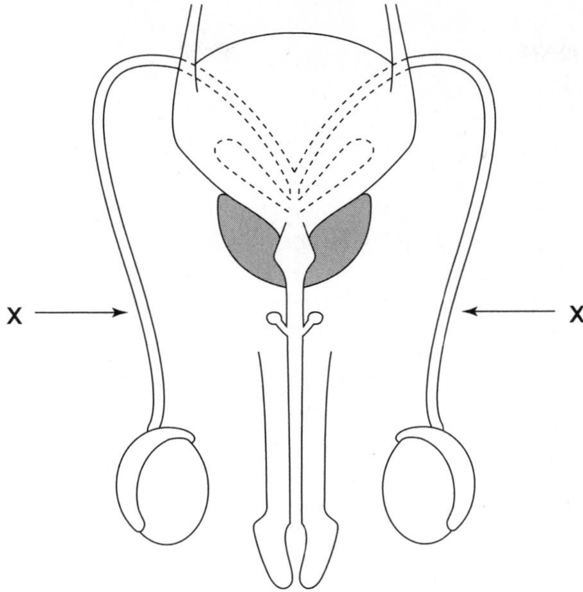


An obstruction in the structures labeled X would directly interfere with the

(1) transfer of sperm to a female
(2) production of sperm
(3) production of urine
(4) transfer of urine to the external environment

**Correct Answer: (1)** Structure X indicates the vas deferens, a pair of ducts that originate at the epididymis (where sperm mature) and assist passage of sperm and other secretions out through the penis. *(Human Reproduction)*

**29.** Which phrase best describes a process represented in the diagram below?

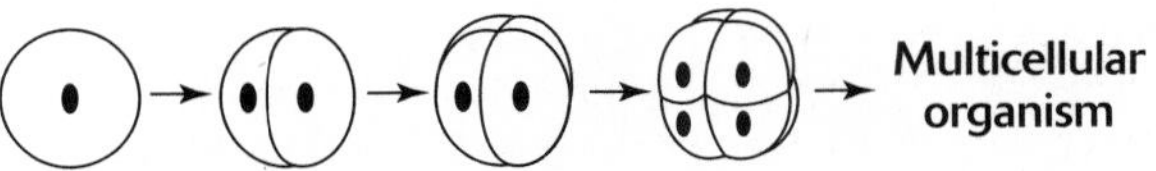


(1) a zygote dividing by mitosis
(2) a zygote dividing by meiosis
(3) a gamete dividing by mitosis
(4) a gamete dividing by meiosis

**Correct Answer: (1)** After an egg is fertilized, the zygote begins a series of cell divisions called cleavage. During cleavage, the zygote divides by mitosis, resulting in two smaller identical cells. Mitosis is a form of cell division whereby one cell divides into two identical cells. Those two cells will also divide by mitosis, producing a total of four cells. This process continues, eventually forming a solid ball of cells called a *morula. (Types of Reproduction)*

**30.** Which reproductive structure is correctly paired with its function?

**(1)** uterus—usual site of fertilization
**(2)** testis—usual location for egg development
**(3)** ovary—delivers nutrients to the embryo
**(4)** sperm—transports genetic material

**Correct Answer: (4)** This is a different way to think of the function of sperm, but it is accurate. The sperm holds the DNA of the father, just as the egg holds the DNA of the mother. The sperm is the vehicle, so to speak, that the male uses to get his genetic information to the egg of the female. The uterus—choice (1)—is the place in the female where the fertilized egg becomes attached and grows. The testis—choice (2)—is the place where sperm are made. The ovary—choice (3)—is where the eggs are stored in the female. *(Human Reproduction)*

**31.** Which developmental process is represented by the diagram below?

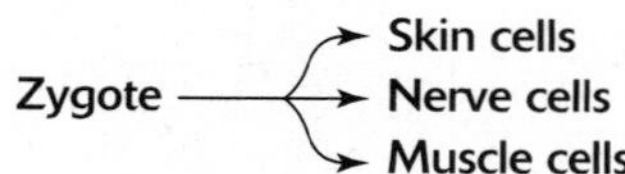


**(1)** fertilization
**(2)** differentiation
**(3)** evolution
**(4)** mutation

**Correct Answer: (2)** During development, the zygote grows and develops into an embryo and ultimately a fetus. Development involves cell differentiation; the change from a generalized cell to a specialize cell such as a skin cell, nerve cell, or muscle cell. *(Cell Division)*

**32.** Which substance usually passes in the greatest amount through the placenta from the blood of the fetus to the blood of the mother?

(1) oxygen
(2) carbon dioxide
(3) amino acids
(4) glucose

**Correct Answer: (2)** The placenta is the tissue in which substances (gases, nutrients, and wastes) are transferred between the blood of mother and fetus. This transfer occurs by diffusion; always from high concentration to low concentration. The fetus produces carbon dioxide as a waste product of cellular respiration and at the placenta, the concentration of carbon dioxide is higher in the blood of the fetus than in the blood of the mother. Because of the differences in concentration, carbon dioxide is transferred from fetus to mother. *(Human Reproduction)*

**33.** The diagram below represents a human reproductive system.

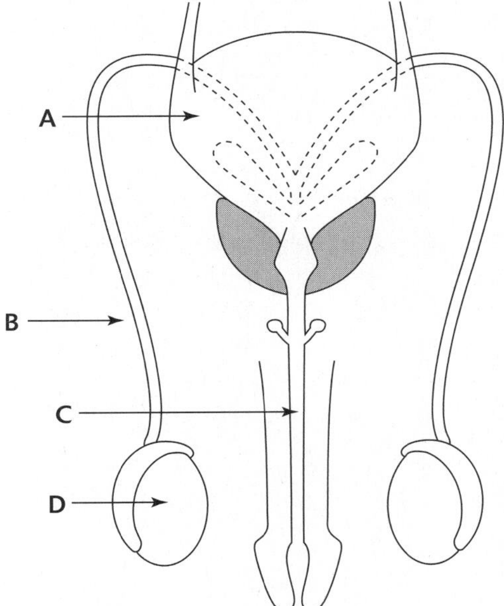


Meiosis occurs within Structure

(1) A
(2) B
(3) C
(4) D

**Correct Answer: (4)** Structure D represents one of the testes. The testes in the male and the ovaries in the female produce the gametes sperm and egg, respectively. *(Human Reproduction)*

**34.** Most mammals have adaptations for

(1) internal fertilization and internal development of the fetus
(2) internal fertilization and external development of the fetus
(3) external fertilization and external development of the fetus
(4) external fertilization and internal development of the fetus

**Correct Answer: (1)** This is basically the definition of fertilization and development in most mammals. *(Types of Reproduction)*

**35.** Toxins can harm a developing fetus. They usually enter the fetus by the process of

(1) blood flow from the mother to the fetus
(2) active transport from the ovary
(3) diffusion across the placental membranes
(4) recombination of genes from the fetus to the mother

**Correct Answer: (3)** Nutrients, gases, and toxins must diffuse through the placenta into the circulatory system of the fetus. *(Human Reproduction)*

**36.** Which statement about embryonic organ development in humans is accurate?

(1) It is affected primarily by the eating habits and general health of the father.
(2) It may be affected by the diet and general health of the mother.
(3) It will not be affected by any medication taken by the mother in the second month of pregnancy.
(4) It is not affected by conditions outside the embryo.

**Correct Answer: (2)** Fertilization and development occur in the female. During this time, the female is responsible for supplying the developing embryo and fetus with nutrients. Poor nutrition will adversely affect the developing embryo. *(Human Reproduction)*

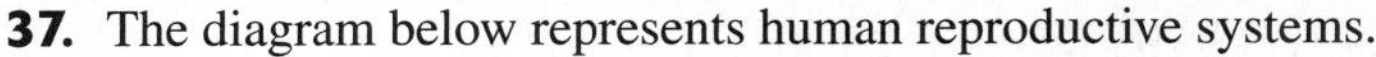

**37.** The diagram below represents human reproductive systems.

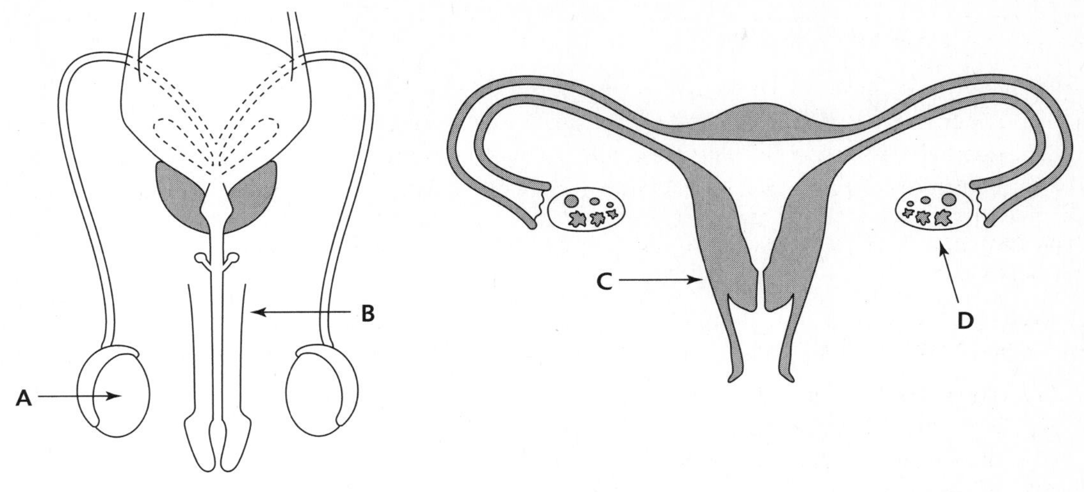


Which statement best describes part of the human reproductive process?

(1) Testosterone produced in A is transferred to D, where it influences embryonic development.
(2) Testosterone produced in D influences formation of sperm within B.
(3) Estrogen and progesterone influence the activity of C.
(4) Progesterone stimulates the division of the egg within C.

**Correct Answer: (3)** The male reproductive system is shown in the figure with labels A and B, while the female reproductive system is shown in the figure with labels C and D. Estrogen, progesterone, and testosterone are sex hormones that are produced by members of both sexes. Males, however, produce high levels of testosterone in the testes (Structure A), while the female ovaries (Structure D) produce high levels of estrogen and progesterone. Estrogen and progesterone levels rise and fall throughout the menstrual cycle and impact the state of the uterus (Structure C). *(Human Reproduction)*

**38.** Which phrase does not describe cells cloned from a carrot?

(1) They are genetically identical.
(2) They are produced sexually.
(3) They have the same DNA codes.
(4) They have identical chromosomes.

**Correct Answer: (2)** Cloning is a form of asexual reproduction in which the offspring are genetically identical to the parent. Sexual reproduction involves the union of gametes producing offspring that are not genetically identical to either parent. *(Types of Reproduction)*

**39.** Human egg cells are most similar to human sperm cells in their

(1) degree of motility
(2) amount of stored food
(3) chromosome number
(4) shape and size

**Correct Answer: (3)** Human egg and sperm cells, or gametes, are both haploid. They contain only one set of chromosomes. Gametes are formed by meiosis—cell division—which results in gametes with half the number of chromosomes as the parent cell. Fertilization of the egg by the sperm restores the original number of chromosomes to the zygote. *(Human Reproduction)*

**40.** The diagram below represents the reproductive system of a mammal.

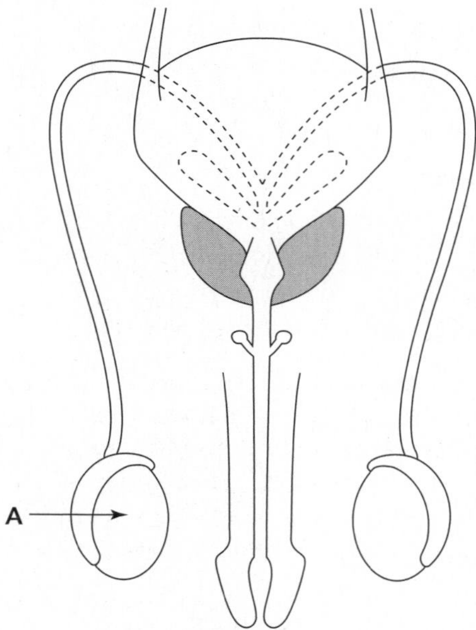


The hormone produced in structure A most directly brings about a change in

(1) blood sugar concentration
(2) physical characteristics
(3) the rate of digestion
(4) the ability to carry out respiration

**Correct Answer: (2)** Structure A is a male gonad, or sex gland, called a testis. The two testes produce the hormone testosterone, which is responsible for the development of secondary sex characteristics in the male. Physical traits that appear in an adolescent male include body hair, a deeper voice, and muscle development. *(Human Reproduction)*

**41.** The diagram below represents a series of events in the development of a bird.

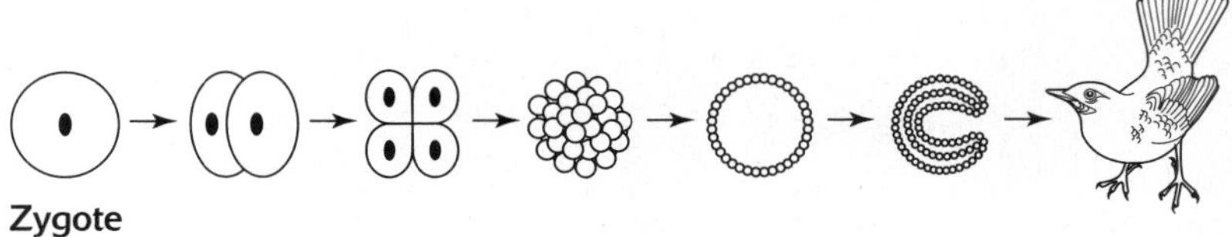


Which series of terms best represents the sequence of processes shown?

**(1)** meiosis → growth → differentiation
**(2)** meiosis → differentiation → growth
**(3)** mitosis → meiosis → differentiation
**(4)** mitosis → differentiation → growth

**Correct Answer: (4)** Gametes (sperm and eggs) are produced by meiosis. A zygote is produced from the fusion of gametes. The zygote grows when cells undergo mitosis. The zygote develops into a bird as it grows and differentiates. Differentiation is the process by which cells become specialized and develop into different types of tissues and organs. *(Cell Division)*

**42.** A variation causes the production of an improved variety of apple. What is the best method to use to obtain additional apple trees of this variety in the shortest period of time?

**(1)** selective breeding
**(2)** natural selection
**(3)** asexual reproduction
**(4)** hormone therapy

**Correct Answer: (3)** The best method to obtain apples of the same variety in the shortest amount of time would be asexual reproduction—specifically, grafting. Grafting is the process by which the bud or branch of one plant is attached to the root or stem of a second plant. The second plant must have the vascular tissue that can match up with the vascular tissue of the attached section so that the apples may get the nutrients and water they need. *(Types of Reproduction)*

**43.** Part of embryonic development in a species is illustrated in the diagram below.

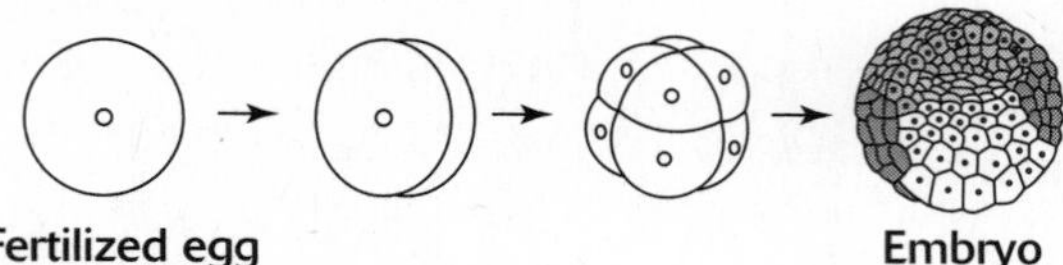


Which set of factors plays the most direct role in controlling the events shown in the diagram?

**(1)** genes, hormones, and cell location
**(2)** antibodies, insulin, and starch
**(3)** ATP, amino acids, and inorganic compounds
**(4)** abiotic resources, homeostasis, and selective breeding

**Correct Answer: (1)** The best way to answer this question is to identify the key word in the question: *controlling*. You should always associate *control* or *controlling* with DNA, genes, and chromosomes. *(Cell Division)*

**44.** Which phrase belongs in box X of the flowchart below?

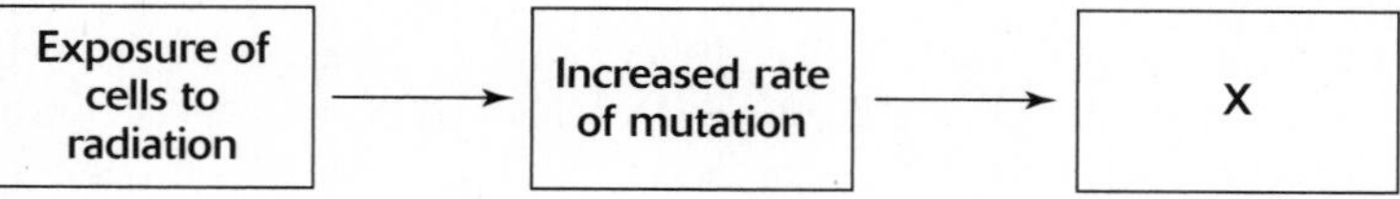


**(1)** Increased chance of cancer
**(2)** Increase in the production of functional gametes
**(3)** Decrease in genetic variability of offspring
**(4)** Decreased number of altered genes

**Correct Answer: (1)** Cancer occurs when a cell loses the ability to control the cell cycle. Cells divide uncontrollably, producing a tumor. Radiation and certain chemicals have been linked to causing an increased rate of mutation, which may result in cancer. *(Cell Division)*

**45.** The chromosome content of a skin cell that is about to form two new skin cells is represented in the diagram below.

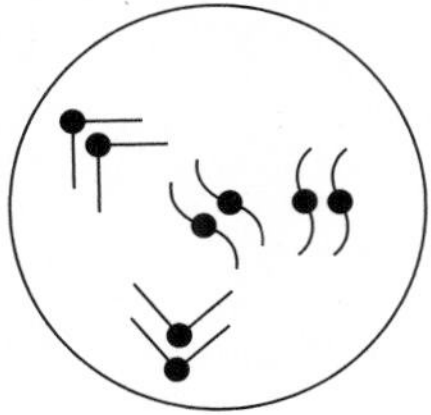

Which diagram best represents the chromosomes that would be found in the two new skin cells produced as a result of this process?

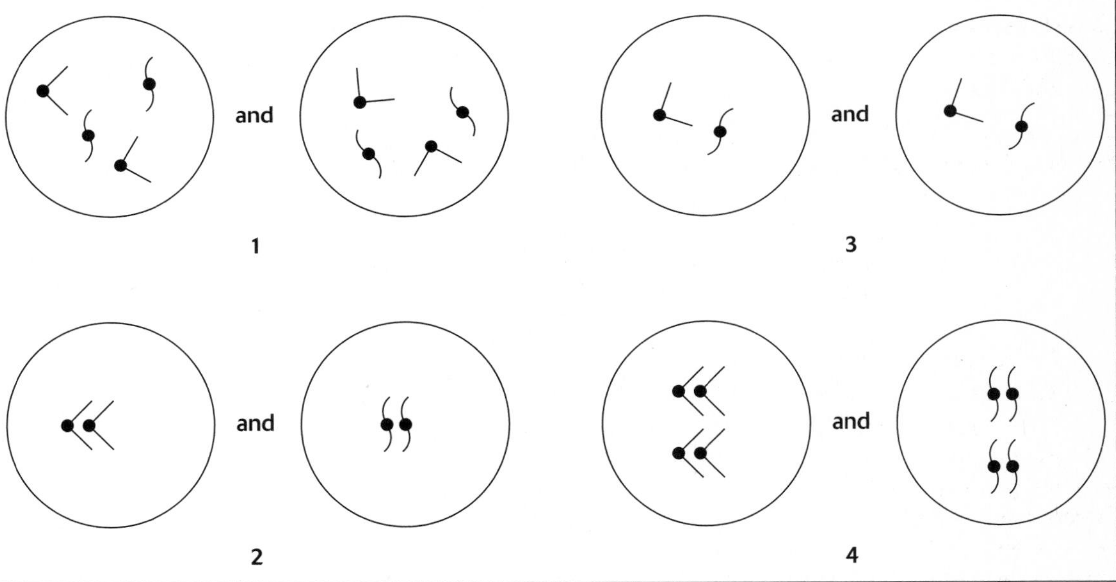


**Correct Answer: (1)** Skin cells multiply by the process of mitosis, which creates cells that are identical to the parent cell. *(Types of Reproduction)*

**46.** The diagram below represents processes involved in human reproduction.

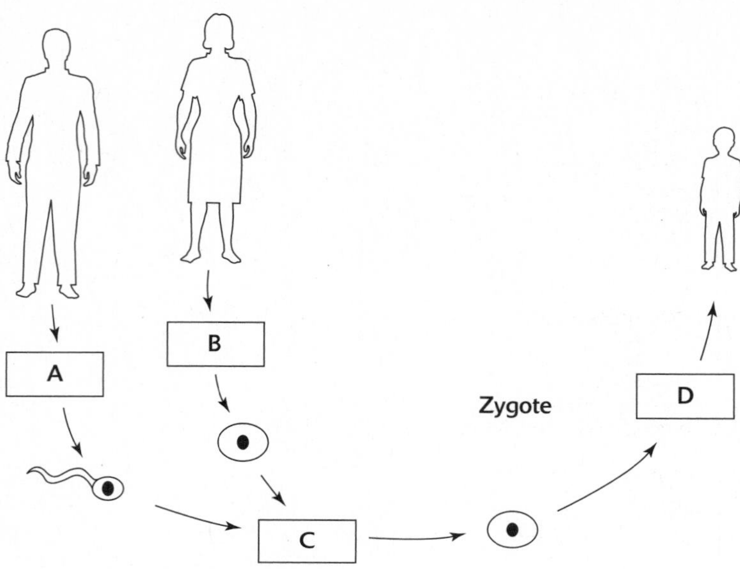


Which row in the chart below correctly identifies the processes represented by the letters in the diagram?

| | *A* | *B* | *C* | *D* |
|---|---|---|---|---|
| (1) | mitosis | meiosis | fertilization | differentiation |
| (2) | meiosis | meiosis | fertilization | differentiation |
| (3) | meiosis | mitosis | differentiation | fertilization |
| (4) | mitosis | mitosis | differentiation | fertilization |

**Correct Answer: (2)** The diagram presents a human male and female. Beneath each figure are the gametes or sex cells that come from each person—sperm from the male, egg from the female. These sex cells are both produced by the process of meiosis, which is letters A and B in the diagram. Letter C represents the coming together of these cells, which is also known as *fertilization.* The result of fertilization is the zygote, which will develop into the child represented at D. The cells of the zygote will develop into the specialized cells that will form the various tissues and organs of the developing fetus. This process is referred to as *differentiation.* No other choices are appropriate. *(Human Reproduction)*

Base your answers to questions 47 through 50 on the diagram below and on your knowledge of biology. The diagram represents a single-celled organism, such as an amoeba, undergoing the changes shown.

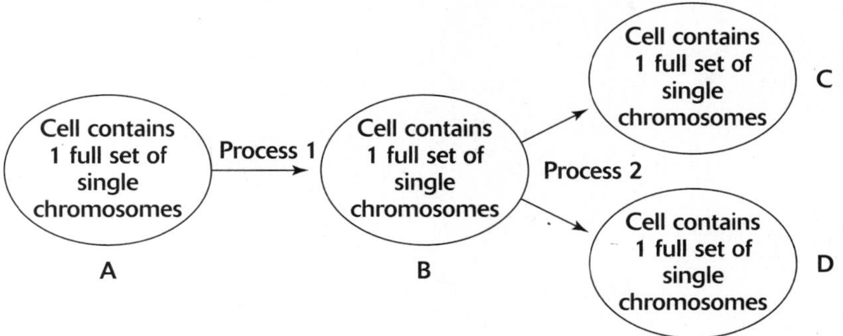


**47.** As a result of these processes, the single-celled organism accomplishes

(1) gamete production
(2) energy production
(3) sexual reproduction
(4) asexual reproduction

**Correct Answer: (4)** Processes 1 and 2 are both stages of mitosis. Cells A and B are the same cell, except that Cell B has a full set of double chromosomes, while Cell A has only single chromosomes. To accomplish this, Process 1 is chromosome replication. Process 2 involves cell division and the resulting daughter cells (cells C and D), have one full set of single chromosomes and these cells are identical to the mother cell (Cell A). Mitosis can be utilized for growth and asexual reproduction, since both involve the production of cells that are genetically identical to the original cell. *(Types of Reproduction)*

**48.** Process 1 is known as

(1) replication
(2) meiosis
(3) differentiation
(4) digestion

**Correct Answer: (1)** The main difference between cells A and B is that Cell B has a set of double chromosomes. This was accomplished during interphase of mitosis when chromosome replication occurred. *(Cell Division)*

**49.** Process 1 and Process 2 are directly involved in

(1) meiotic cell division
(2) mitotic cell division
(3) fertilization
(4) recombination

**Correct Answer: (2)** Processes A and B both occur during mitosis. If meiosis were involved, there would be a halving of the number of chromosomes. If fertilization were involved, there would be a joining of cells and the original cells (gametes) would have had half the number of chromosomes. Recombination involves the insertion of new DNA and is not shown in the diagram. *(Cell Division)*

**50.** The genetic content of C is usually identical to the genetic content of

**(1)** B but not D
**(2)** both B and D
**(3)** D but not A
**(4)** both A and D

**Correct Answer: (4)** Cells C and D are genetically identical to Cell A because they were produced through mitosis. The only difference between these cells and Cell B is that Cell B has double the number of chromosomes. *(Cell Division)*

**51.** A sperm cell from an organism is represented in the diagram below.

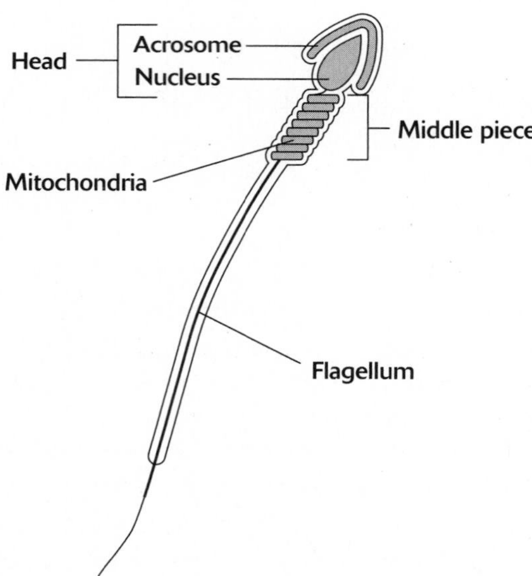


Which statement regarding this sperm cell is *not* correct?

**(1)** The acrosome contains half the normal number of chromosomes.
**(2)** Energy to move the flagellum originates in the middle piece.
**(3)** The head may contain a mutation.
**(4)** This cell can unite with another cell resulting in the production of a new organism.

**Correct Answer: (1)** Choice (2) is correct: If you look closely and carefully at the middle section, there is a label to mitochondria. *Remember:* Mitochondria produce energy through the process of cellular respiration. Choice (3) is correct: The head of the sperm contains the nucleus where the chromosomes are, where mutations occur. Choice (4) is correct: The sperm can unite with another cell, an egg (called fertilization), and create a new organism. This leaves you with Choice (1), which is *not* correct. Look carefully at the diagram. The chromosomes (which are half the normal number) are contained in the nucleus, not in the acrosome. *(Human Reproduction)*

**52.** The diagram below illustrates the process of cell division.

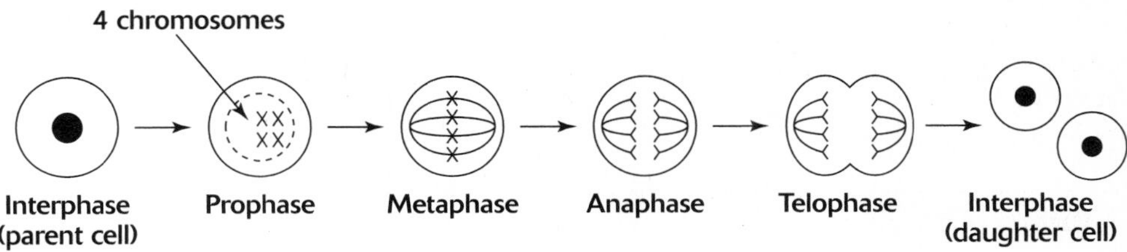


What is the significance of anaphase in this process?

**(1)** Anaphase usually ensures that each daughter cell has the same number of chromosomes as the parent cell.
**(2)** Anaphase usually ensures that each daughter cell has twice as many chromosomes as the parent cell.
**(3)** In anaphase, the cell splits in half.
**(4)** In anaphase, the DNA is being replicated.

**Correct Answer: (1)** Cell division is about making new cells (daughter cells) from one original cell. It is also about splitting up the nuclear material or chromosomes between the new daughter cells. In cell division (also known as mitosis), the number of chromosomes in the daughter cells is the same number of chromosomes as in the parent cell. It is during the step known as anaphase that the chromosome pairs are split up and half of each pair is pulled to the opposite sides or poles of the cell. When this happens, each daughter cell receives the same number of chromosomes as the parent cell. *(Cell Division)*

**53.** Sexually produced offspring often resemble, but are not identical to, either of their parents. Explain why they resemble their parents but are *not* identical to either parent.

**Correct Answer:** The only way to get an exact copy of an organism is to clone it. But the problem with that is that the offspring would look like only one of the parents, not both. Sexual reproduction involves the blending of the traits from both parents. The egg and sperm contain half the number of chromosomes of other cells of an organism. Each egg and sperm carry random combinations of traits from the respective parent. So when the egg and sperm combine during fertilization, the future offspring now has some of both parents' characteristics—the offspring might have the father's nose and hair color, but the mother's attached ear lobes and eye color. *(Types of Reproduction)*

Base your answer to question 54 on the information and the data table below and on your knowledge of biology.

Biologists investigated the effect of the presence of aluminum ions on root tips of a variety of wheat. They removed 2mm sections of the tips of roots. Half of the root tips were placed in a nutrient solution with aluminum ions, while the other half were placed in an identical nutrient solution without aluminum ions. The length of the root tips, in millimeters, was measured every hour for seven hours. The results are shown in the data table below.

**Data Table**

| *Time (hr)* | *Length of Root Tips in Solution with Aluminum Ions (mm)* | *Length of Root Tips in Solution without Aluminum Ions (mm)* |
|---|---|---|
| 0 | 2.0 | 2.0 |
| 1 | 2.1 | 2.2 |
| 2 | 2.2 | 2.4 |
| 3 | 2.4 | 2.8 |
| 4 | 2.6 | 2.9 |
| 5 | 2.7 | 3.2 |
| 6 | 2.8 | 3.7 |
| 7 | 2.8 | 3.9 |

**54.** The aluminum ions most likely affected

**(1)** photosynthetic rate
**(2)** the union of gametes
**(3)** mitotic cell division
**(4)** starch absorption from the soil

**Correct Answer: (3)** According to the graph, the root tip in the nutrient solution with aluminum ions didn't grow as much as the one in the nutrient solution without aluminum ions. Growth and development in an organism is the result of mitotic cell division. *(Cell Division)*

**55.** The diagram below illustrates asexual reproduction in bread mold. Reproductive structures known as spores were released from bread mold A. One of these spores developed into bread mold B.

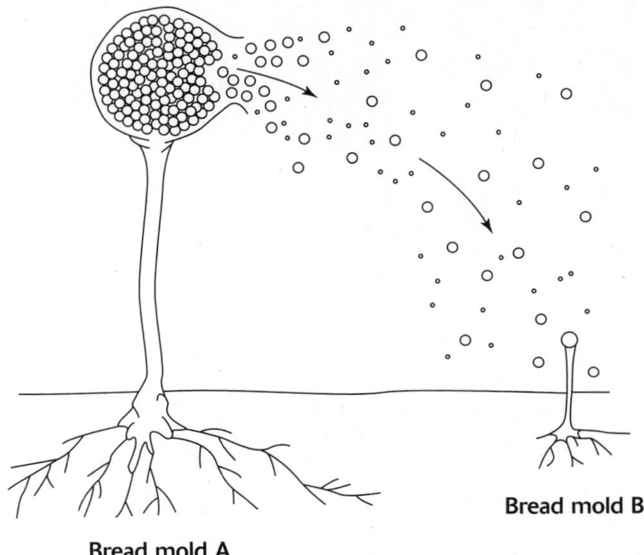


State how the genetic information in the nuclei of cells in bread mold B compares to the genetic information in the nuclei of cells in bread mold A.

**Correct Answer:** Bread mold produces spores through the process of asexual reproduction. The type of cell division involved in asexual reproduction is mitosis. Mitosis is a type of cell division in which a parent cell makes an exact copy of itself. In organisms that reproduce this way, the parent and offspring are genetically identical. *(Types of Reproduction)*

Base your answers to questions 56 and 57 on the statement below and on your knowledge of biology.

Selective breeding has been used to improve the racing ability of horses.

**56.** Define selective breeding and state how it would be used to improve the racing ability of horses.

**Correct Answer:** Selective breeding is when you choose parents based upon desired traits. If two fast horses were mated, the offspring may inherit the characteristics that lead to the ability to run fast. *(Types of Reproduction)*

**57.** State *one* disadvantage of selective breeding.

**Correct Answer:** The following answers apply:

- Undesirable traits of parents may be expressed in the offspring.
- Unexpected combinations of genes may result.
- Unpredictable results may result.
- Decreased variation in racehorses may result.

*(Types of Reproduction)*

Base your answers to questions 58 and 59 on the statement and diagram below and on your knowledge of biology.

Women are advised to avoid consuming alcoholic beverages during pregnancy.

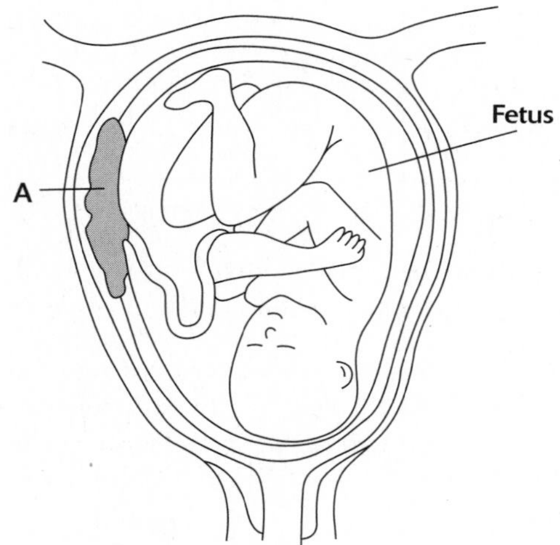


**58.** Identify the structure labeled A and explain how the functioning of Structure A is essential for the normal development of the fetus.

**Correct Answer:** Structure A is the placenta and is responsible for the exchange of nutrients, wastes, and gases (carbon dioxide and oxygen) between mother and fetus. *(Human Reproduction)*

**59.** Explain why consumption of alcoholic beverages by a pregnant woman is likely to be more harmful to her fetus than to herself.

**Correct Answer:** The consumption of alcohol by the pregnant woman is more harmful to the fetus than to the mother because the fetus is still developing and the alcohol could cause abnormalities. *(Human Reproduction)*

**60.** Define fertilization and describe the resulting development of a human embryo. In your answer, be sure to include a definition of fertilization and the functions of the ovary, uterus, and placenta. Circle the terms *fertilization, ovary, uterus,* and *placenta* in your description.

**Correct Answer:** Fertilization is defined as the union of the sperm and the egg. The function of the ovary is to produce the egg cell. After fertilization occurs, the fertilized egg, called a zygote, becomes attached to the wall of the uterus where it develops. The placenta is an organ that develops in the uterus whose function is to supply the developing embryo with nutrients and oxygen and to remove waste products.

Base your answers to questions 61 and 62 on the information below and on your knowledge of biology.

- The reproductive cycle in a human female is not functioning properly.
- An imbalance of hormones is diagnosed as the cause.

**61.** Identify one hormone directly involved in the human female reproductive system that could cause this problem.

**Correct Answer:** There are several hormones involved in the functioning of the human female reproductive system. You can name estrogen, progesterone, follicle stimulating hormone (FSH), or leutinizing hormone (LH). *(Human Reproduction)*

**62.** Explain why some cells in a female's body respond to reproductive hormones while other cells do not.

**Correct Answer:** To answer this question, you have to know what hormones are and how they work. Hormones are proteins that are produced in one place in the body and carried through the bloodstream to another part of the body called a *target organ.* Like all proteins, hormones are specific: They only act on certain organs. This would be your best answer: Specific reproductive hormones act on specific cells. *(Human Reproduction)*

**63.** Compare asexual reproduction to sexual reproduction. In your comparison, be sure to include:

- which type of reproduction results in offspring that are usually genetically identical to the previous generation and explain why this occurs
- one other way these methods of reproduction differ

**Correct Answer:**

| | ***Asexual Reproduction*** | ***Sexual Reproduction*** |
|---|---|---|
| Number of parents | One | Two |
| Union of gametes | No | Yes |
| Offspring genetically identical to parents | Yes | No |
| Method of cell division | Mitosis | Meiosis |

Asexual reproduction occurs through the process of mitosis—a form of cell division in which the daughter cells are genetically identical to the parent cell. *(Types of Reproduction)*

# Homeostasis

**Directions:** For each statement or question, choose the *number* of the word or expression that best completes the statement or answers the question. Then check your answer against the one that immediately follows the question. Try not to look at the answer before making your selection.

**1.** Which row in the chart below best describes the active transport of molecule X through a cell membrane?

| *Row* | *Movement of Molecule X* | *ATP* |
|---|---|---|
| (1) | high concentration → low concentration | used |
| (2) | high concentration → low concentration | not used |
| (3) | low concentration → high concentration | used |
| (4) | low concentration → high concentration | not used |

**Correct Answer: (3)** Active transport is the movement of molecules from an area of low concentration to an area of high concentration. This movement occurs only with the use of ATP (a source of energy for cells). Molecules can move from an area of high concentration to an area of low concentration without the use of ATP, but this process is diffusion, not active transport. *(Biochemistry)*

**2.** Hormones and secretions of the nervous system are chemical messengers that

**(1)** store genetic information
**(2)** carry out the circulation of materials
**(3)** extract energy from nutrients
**(4)** coordinate system interactions

**Correct Answer: (4)** The body constantly maintains homeostasis through the coordinated activities of the nervous and endocrine systems. The central nervous system (CNS), consisting of the brain and spinal cord, controls most body activities using sense receptors to gather information about conditions around and inside the body. This information is received by the CNS, which responds by sending messages to muscles and glands. Chemical messengers released into the bloodstream in one part of the body are recognized by specific tissues elsewhere in the body. *(Feedback)*

**3.** Which statement concerning simple sugars and amino acids is correct?

(1) They are both wastes resulting from protein synthesis.
(2) They are both building blocks of starch.
(3) They are both needed for the synthesis of larger molecules.
(4) They are both stored as fat molecules in the liver.

**Correct Answer: (3)** Simple sugars such as glucose and amino acids are the building blocks of carbohydrates and proteins, respectively. *(Biochemistry)*

**4.** Molecule X moves across a cell membrane by diffusion. Which row in the chart below best indicates the relationship between the relative concentrations of molecule X and the use of ATP for diffusion?

| *Row* | *Movement of Molecule X* | *Use of ATP* |
|---|---|---|
| (1) | high concentration → low concentration | used |
| (2) | high concentration → low concentration | not used |
| (3) | low concentration → high concentration | used |
| (4) | low concentration → high concentration | not used |

**Correct Answer: (2)** Diffusion is the movement of molecules from an area of high concentration to an area of low concentration. This movement occurs without the use of ATP (a source of energy for cells). Molecules can move from an area of low concentration to an area of high concentration with the use of ATP, but this process is active transport, not diffusion. *(Biochemistry)*

**5.** Muscle cells in athletes often have more mitochondria than muscle cells in nonathletes. Based on this observation, it can be inferred that the muscle cells in athletes

(1) have a smaller demand for cell proteins than the muscle cells of nonathletes
(2) reproduce less frequently than the muscle cells of nonathletes
(3) have nuclei containing more DNA than nuclei in the muscle cells of nonathletes
(4) have a greater demand for energy than the muscle cells of nonathletes

**Correct Answer: (4)** Mitochondria are the sites of aerobic cellular respiration, a process that creates energy for cells. An athlete would have a higher demand for energy (more energy at a faster rate) than a nonathlete and would, therefore, require more mitochondria to produce that energy. *(Human Body Systems)*

**6.** Most of the starch stored in the cells of a potato is composed of molecules that originally entered these cells as

**(1)** enzymes
**(2)** simple sugars
**(3)** amino acids
**(4)** minerals

**Correct Answer: (2)** Starch is a complex carbohydrate that is made up of simple sugars. Enzymes are proteins, and proteins are made up of amino acids. *(Biochemistry)*

**7.** In the body of a human, the types of chemical activities occurring within cells are most dependent on the

**(1)** biological catalysts present
**(2)** size of the cell
**(3)** number of chromosomes in the cell
**(4)** kind of sugar found on each chromosome

**Correct Answer: (1)** Catalysts are protein molecules that increase the rate of chemical reactions in the body. Practically everything our bodies do is controlled by and made possible by chemical reactions. Catalysts speed up these reactions. If it were not for catalysts, these important chemical reactions would occur too slowly and the organism would not survive. *(Biochemistry)*

**8.** The enzyme pepsin is produced in the cells of the stomach but *not* in the cells of the small intestine. The small intestine produces a different enzyme, trypsin. The reason that the stomach and small intestine produce different enzymes is that the gene that codes for pepsin is

**(1)** in the cells of the stomach, but not in the cells of the small intestine
**(2)** expressed in the stomach, but not in the cells of the small intestine
**(3)** mutated in the small intestine
**(4)** digested by the trypsin in the small intestine

**Correct Answer: (2)** The expression of genes is what the trait that the gene codes for looks like or does. All the cells in our bodies (with the exception of mature red blood cells) have the same exact DNA as all the other cells. *(Biochemistry)*

**9.** Which statement concerning proteins is *not* correct?

**(1)** Proteins are long, usually folded, chains.
**(2)** The shape of a protein molecule determines its function.
**(3)** Proteins can be broken down and used for energy.
**(4)** Proteins are bonded together, resulting in simple sugars.

**Correct Answer: (4)** Proteins are chains of amino acids that can be long and often folded into specific shapes that determine their function. Proteins, from the food we eat, can be broken down and used for energy. *(Biochemistry)*

**10.** All chemical breakdown processes in cells directly involve

**(1)** reactions that are controlled by catalysts
**(2)** enzymes that are stored in mitochondria
**(3)** the production of catalysts in vacuoles
**(4)** enzymes that have the same genetic base sequence

**Correct Answer: (1)** Enzymes are proteins that serve catalysts in chemical breakdown. A catalyst is a substance that increases the rate of a chemical reaction but remains unchanged by that reaction. Enzymes are made and used in the cytoplasm, and each enzyme is made from a unique genetic code. *(Biochemistry)*

**11.** The use of a vaccine to stimulate the immune system to act against a specific pathogen is valuable in maintaining homeostasis because

**(1)** once the body produces chemicals to combat one type of virus, it can more easily make antibiotics
**(2)** the body can digest the weakened microbes and use them as food
**(3)** the body will be able to fight invasions by the same type of microbe in the future
**(4)** the more the immune system is challenged, the better it performs

**Correct Answer: (3)** A vaccine is a dead or weakened form of a pathogen that stimulates the body's immune system and provides active immunity. Active immunity is when the organism makes its own antibodies in response to antigens—usually proteins—on the surface of the foreign cells. The body has special cells that "remember" the pathogen so that any future exposure to the same pathogen will cause the body to make antibodies right away and maintain homeostasis. *(Human Body Systems)*

**12.** Which statement does *not* describe an example of a feedback mechanism that maintains homeostasis?

**(1)** The guard cells close the openings in leaves, preventing excess water loss from a plant.
**(2)** White blood cells increase the production of antigens during an allergic reaction.
**(3)** Increased physical activity increases the heart rate in humans.
**(4)** The pancreas releases insulin, helping humans to keep blood sugar levels stable.

**Correct Answer: (2)** White blood cells make antibodies during an allergic reaction. They do not make antigens. Antigens are the substances that cause the immune response. *(Feedback)*

**13.** Which order of metabolic processes converts nutrients consumed by an organism into cell parts?

(1) digestion → absorption → circulation → diffusion → synthesis
(2) absorption → circulation → digestion → diffusion → synthesis
(3) digestion → synthesis → diffusion → circulation → absorption
(4) synthesis → absorption → digestion → diffusion → circulation

**Correct Answer: (1)** Digestion is the breakdown of food into tiny particles that can be absorbed by the small intestine and moved to the circulatory system, where they are transported throughout the body. These tiny particles then diffuse from the blood (where they are found in relatively high concentrations) to body cells (where they are found in relatively low concentrations). Lastly, the cells can manufacture or synthesize new compounds that are needed to maintain cell function. *(Human Body Systems)*

**14.** Experiments revealed the following information about a certain molecule:

- It can be broken down into amino acids.
- It can break down proteins into amino acids.
- It is found in high concentrations in the small intestine of humans.

This molecule is most likely

(1) an enzyme
(2) an inorganic compound
(3) a hormone
(4) an antigen

**Correct Answer: (1)** An enzyme is a protein catalyst, which allows chemical reactions to occur at a faster rate. Because enzymes are proteins, they can be broken down into amino acids. Because they are catalysts, they are involved in chemical reactions that break down other molecules. They are found in high concentrations in the small intestine, where digestion occurs. *(Biochemistry)*

**15.** Which activity is *not* a function of white blood cells in response to an invasion of the body by bacteria?

(1) engulfing these bacteria
(2) producing antibodies to act against this type of bacteria
(3) preparing for future invasions of this type of bacteria
(4) speeding transmissions of nerve impulses to detect this bacteria

**Correct Answer: (4)** Choices (1), (2), and (3) are all true statements. That leaves choice (4). The detection of bacteria invading the body is not a function of the nervous system and neurons. It is a function of the immune system and is carried out chemically, not electrically by the nervous system. *(Human Body Systems)*

**16.** The diagram below represents a structure involved in cellular respiration

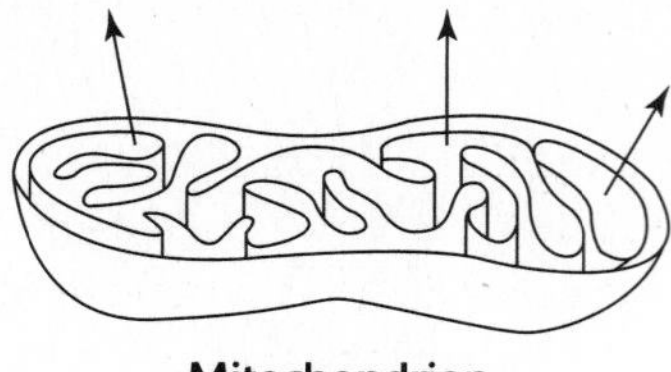

Mitochondrion

The release of which substance is represented by the arrows?

(1) glucose
(2) oxygen
(3) carbon dioxide
(4) DNA

**Correct Answer: (3)** The structure in the diagram is a mitochondrion. Mitochondria are organelles that are responsible for aerobic cellular respiration. In order to produce ATP, cells take in glucose and oxygen. As waste products, the cells release carbon dioxide ($CO_2$) and water ($H_2O$). The arrow in the diagram is moving away from the structure indicating that it is a waste product. Carbon dioxide is the only waste product of the four choices. *(Biochemistry)*

**17.** The diagram below represents a series of reactions that can occur in an organism.

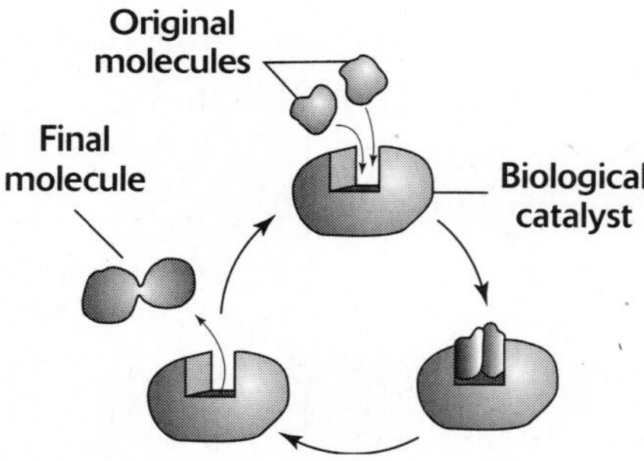


This diagram best illustrates the relationship between

(1) enzymes and synthesis
(2) amino acids and glucose
(3) antigens and immunity
(4) ribosomes and sugars

**Correct Answer: (1)** By definition, enzymes are protein molecules that are involved in chemical reactions. They can, as in this diagram, synthesize (or put together) two simple molecules to make a more complex one, or they can take molecules apart. Either way, they are also, by definition, catalysts, as indicated in the diagram. *(Biochemistry)*

**18.** The diagram below represents what can happen when homeostasis in an organism is threatened. Which statement provides a possible explanation for these events?

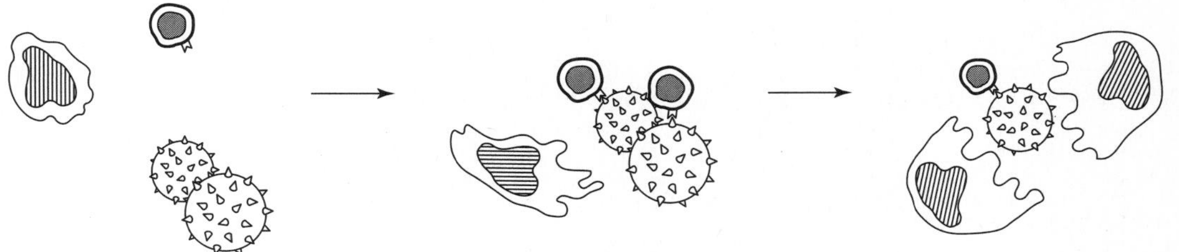

(1) Antibiotics break down harmful substances by the process of digestion.
(2) Some specialized cells mark and other cells engulf microbes during immune reactions.
(3) Embryonic development of essential organs occurs during pregnancy.
(4) Cloning removes abnormal cells produced during differentiation.

**Correct Answer: (2)** The diagram is showing the body's immune response. When the body recognizes a foreign cell or molecule, the body makes antibodies. Antibodies are proteins that bind to foreign substances, helping the body destroy them. White blood cells function in the immune response by engulfing the unwanted cells or substances. *(Human Body Systems)*

**19.** Arrows A, B, and C in the diagram below represent the processes necessary to make the energy stored in food available for muscle activity.

Food $\xrightarrow{A}$ Simpler molecules $\xrightarrow{B}$ Mitochondria $\xrightarrow{C}$ ATP in muscle cells

The correct sequence of processes represented by A, B, and C is

(1) diffusion → synthesis → active transport
(2) digestion → diffusion → cellular respiration
(3) digestion → excretion → cellular respiration
(4) synthesis → active transport → excretion

**Correct Answer: (2)** Digestion is the process by which food is broken down into simple molecules. In order for the energy from food to be used by the body, or muscle cells in this case, the materials needed for cellular respiration must be present in the organelle that carries out this process—the mitochondria. Oxygen and organic molecules diffuse into the mitochondria so they may be converted into a form of energy the body can use—ATP—by the process of cellular respiration. *(Biochemistry)*

**20.** The graph below shows the effect of temperature on the relative rate of action of enzyme X on a protein.

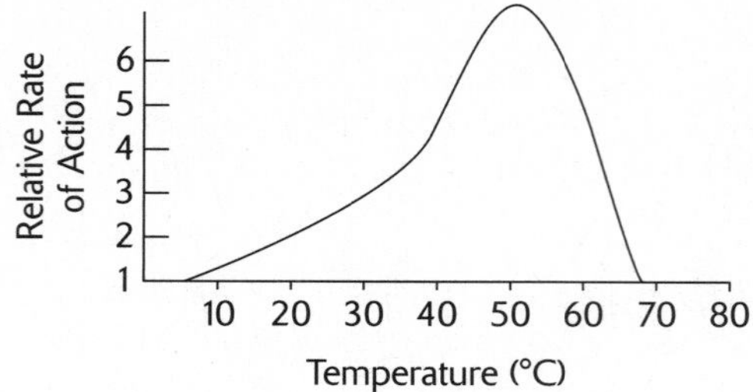


Which change would *not* affect the relative rate of action of enzyme X?

(1) the addition of cold water when the reaction is at 50°C
(2) an increase in temperature from 70°C to 80°C
(3) the removal of the protein when the reaction is at 30°C
(4) a decrease in temperature from 40°C to 10°C

**Correct Answer: (2)** According to the graph, the rate of enzyme action starts to decrease once the temperature reaches about 55°C and returns to its lowest rate of 1 by the time 70°C is reached. So, raising the temperature from 70°C to 80°C will have no effect because the enzyme has already basically stopped working. If cold water is added when the reaction is at 50°C—choice (2)—the reaction rate will decrease. If the protein is removed—choice (3)—the reaction will stop altogether because there will be nothing for the enzyme to act upon. A decrease in temperature from 40°C to 10°C—choice (4)—will also affect the enzyme rate by causing it to decrease. *(Biochemistry)*

**21.** The interaction between guard cells and a leaf opening would *not* be involved in

(1) diffusion of carbon dioxide
(2) maintaining homeostasis
(3) heterotrophic nutrition
(4) feedback mechanisms

**Correct Answer: (3)** The question gives information about plants: guard cells and a leaf opening. Plants carry out autotrophic nutrition by the process of photosynthesis, so the parts mentioned in the question would *not* be involved in heterotrophic nutrition. Choices (1), (2), and (4) are all functions of these parts of a plant leaf. *(Feedback)*

**22.** Scientists have genetically altered a common virus so that it can destroy the most lethal type of brain tumor without harming the healthy tissue nearby. This technology is used for all of the following *except*

(1) treating the disease
(2) curing the disease
(3) controlling the disease
(4) diagnosing the disease

**Correct Answer: (4)** The genetically altered virus will take care of the tumor after it has already been found. The question doesn't mention anything about discovering or locating a tumor. A separate procedure must be used to diagnose (discover) the tumor. *(Human Body Systems)*

**23.** Some human white blood cells help destroy pathogenic bacteria by

(1) causing mutations in the bacteria
(2) engulfing and digesting the bacteria
(3) producing toxins that compete with bacterial toxins
(4) inserting part of their DNA into the bacterial cells

**Correct Answer: (2)** White blood cells called macrophages engulf and digest antigens such as bacteria. T-cells, which are also part of a body's immune response, produce toxins that kill body cells infected with a virus, but they are not part of an immune response to bacteria, nor is there any competition among toxins. Human cells are not able to insert their DNA into bacteria. *(Disease)*

**24.** Which process illustrates a feedback mechanism in plants?

(1) Chloroplasts take in more nitrogen, which increases the rate of photosynthesis.
(2) Chloroplasts release more oxygen in response to a decreased rate of photosynthesis.
(3) Guard cells change the size of leaf openings, regulating the exchange of gases.
(4) Guard cells release oxygen from the leaf at night.

**Correct Answer: (3)** A feedback mechanism involves a cycle in which the state of one part of the system changes or reinforces an action by another part of the system. For example, the guard cells of a leaf cell open pores in the leaf in response to ample water within the leaf. As long as water remains sufficient in the leaf, the guard cells maintain the open pores, and gas exchange takes place. However, if water becomes depleted in the leaf, the guard cells respond by closing the pores, and gas exchange slows or ceases. *(Feedback)*

**25.** Which statement best describes what will most likely happen when an individual receives a vaccination containing a weakened pathogen?

(1) The ability to fight disease will increase due to antibodies received from the pathogen.
(2) The ability to fight disease caused by the pathogen will increase due to antibody production.
(3) The ability to produce antibodies will decrease after the vaccination.
(4) The ability to resist most types of diseases will increase.

**Correct Answer: (2)** A vaccine is made of a dead or weakened form of a bacteria or virus that, when injected into the body, is not capable of causing disease, but can still activate the body's immune response. The immune system produces antibodies and other special cells that not only inactivate the foreign substance but are specific to each one as well. When a specific type of antigen found on a pathogen (disease-causing microorganism) initially enters the body, measurable amounts of antibodies or specialized immune cells aren't present until after the first five days. Over the next one to two weeks the level of antibodies and special cells increases. If the same antigen enters the body a second time, high levels of antibodies and special cells are present in the blood within two days of infection. *(Human Body Systems)*

**26.** When organisms break the bonds of organic compounds, the organisms can

(1) use the smaller molecules to plug the gaps in the cell membrane to slow diffusion
(2) use the energy obtained to digest molecules produced by respiration that uses oxygen
(3) obtain energy or reassemble the resulting materials to form different compounds
(4) excrete smaller amounts of solid waste materials during vigorous exercise

**Correct Answer: (3)** Don't be frightened by the phrase *organic compounds.* Although you should know that the question is referring to carbohydrates, lipids, and proteins, the question is really determining whether you know that breaking bonds releases energy. The problem is, do you know what that energy is going to be used for? The best answer is choice (3). This is exactly why breaking bonds occurs—to provide energy and to use that energy for the synthesis of other compounds. *(Biochemistry)*

**27.** Feedback interactions in the human body are important because they

(1) determine the diversity necessary for evolution to occur
(2) direct the synthesis of altered genes that are passed on to every cell in the body
(3) regulate the shape of molecules involved in cellular communication
(4) keep the internal body environment within its normal range

**Correct Answer: (4)** Feedback and homeostasis are about maintaining a stable internal environment. Choice (3) is a reasonable answer, but feedback is not regulating the shapes of molecules. Instead, it regulates the metabolic processes that are needed to maintain the body in a stable state. *(Feedback)*

**28.** The production of energy-rich ATP molecules is the direct result of

(1) recycling of light energy to be used in the process of photosynthesis
(2) releasing the stored energy of organic compounds by the process of respiration
(3) breaking down starch by the process of digestion
(4) copying coded information during the process of protein synthesis

**Correct Answer: (2)** This a standard definition for respiration: the release of energy that is stored in organic compounds. Energy that is stored in glucose (the organic compound) is converted to ATP, the energy molecule. The respiration referred to in this question is cellular respiration, not the "breathing" respiration. *(Biochemistry)*

**29.** When a certain plant is without water for an extended period of time, guard cells close openings in the leaves of the plant. This activity conserves water and illustrates

(1) cellular communication involving the action of nerve cells and receptor sites
(2) an increase in rate of growth due to a low concentration of water
(3) maintenance of a dynamic equilibrium through detection and response to stimuli
(4) a response to one biotic factor in the environment

**Correct Answer: (3)** Water is absorbed through the roots of a plant and is drawn up the stem to the leaves where it finally evaporates through openings in leaves called stomates. This process is called *transpiration*. The rate of transpiration is dependent upon the availability of water and is controlled by guard cells surrounding the openings. A stomate opens when the guard cells take in water through the process of osmosis and swell, becoming turgid. This pressure causes the walls of the cells to bow outward, creating a space between the cells. When the guard cells lose water, becoming less turgid, the space between the guard cells closes as the cell walls relax. Stomates are generally open during the day, when there is sufficient water available. Stomates close usually at night, when it is cold, and when there is a lack of available water. *(Feedback)*

**30.** The purpose of introducing weakened microbes into the body of an organism is to stimulate the

(1) production of living microbes that will protect the organism from future attacks
(2) production of antigens that will prevent infections from occurring
(3) immune system to react and prepare the organism to fight future invasions by these microbes
(4) replication of genes that direct the synthesis of hormones that regulate the number of microbes

**Correct Answer: (3)** This question is the description of a vaccine. Vaccines contain dead or weakened bacteria or virus particles that are injected into the body. These bacteria and virus particles are not enough to cause the disease, but they are enough to stimulate the immune system to make antibodies against the disease, as well as to prepare white blood cells for future attacks of these bacteria and viruses. *(Disease)*

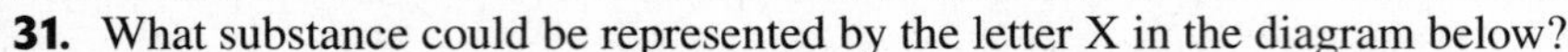

**31.** What substance could be represented by the letter X in the diagram below?

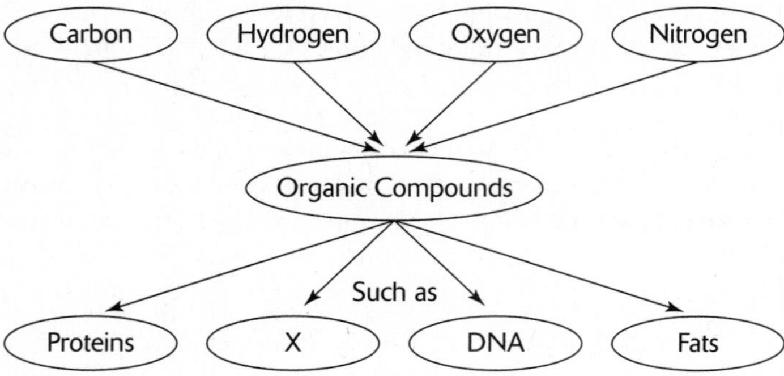


(1) carbohydrates
(2) ozone
(3) carbon dioxide
(4) water

**Correct Answer: (1)** Organic compounds contain both carbon (C) and hydrogen (H). Carbohydrates have a molecular formula of $C_6H_{12}O_6$. Ozone ($O_3$), carbon dioxide ($CO_2$) and water ($H_2O$) do not contain both C and H. *(Biochemistry)*

**32.** Information concerning a metabolic activity is shown below.

$$X \xrightarrow{\text{enzyme}} \text{products + energy metabolism}$$

Substance X is most likely

(1) DNA
(2) oxygen
(3) ATP
(4) chlorophyll

**Correct Answer: (3)** ATP (adenosine triphosphate) is a source of stored energy for a cell that may be used to perform chemical reactions. *(Biochemistry)*

**33.** A part of the Hepatitis B virus is synthesized in the laboratory. This viral particle can be identified by the immune system as a foreign material, but the viral particle is not capable of causing disease. Immediately after this viral particle is injected into a human, it

**(1)** stimulates the production of enzymes that are able to digest the Hepatitis B virus
**(2)** triggers the formation of antibodies that protect against the Hepatitis B virus
**(3)** synthesizes specific hormones that provide immunity against the Hepatitis B virus
**(4)** breaks down key receptor molecules so that the Hepatitis B virus can enter body cells

**Correct Answer: (2)** A virus is a type of pathogen that causes disease. A vaccine consists of a dead or weakened form of a bacteria or virus that can no longer cause disease but can still act as an antigen and trigger the immune response. Antigens, usually proteins on the outer surface of the bacteria or virus, are substances that cause an immune response. The immune system produces antibodies and other types of cells that bind to and inactivate the pathogen. *(Disease)*

**34.** Which condition is necessary for enzymes and hormones to function properly in the human body?

**(1)** These chemicals must have a specific shape.
**(2)** These chemicals must be able to replicate.
**(3)** Body temperature must be above 40°C.
**(4)** Body pH must be above 10.

**Correct Answer: (1)** Enzymes and hormones are specific and only work on molecules that fit their shape. Both are sensitive to temperature and pH, but within the human body they work best at normal body temperature (37°C) and a pH close to that of the part of the body in which they occur (a human body with a pH above 10 would be dead). Chemicals are not alive and cannot replicate. *(Biochemistry)*

**35.** The data in the table below indicate the presence of specific reproductive hormones in blood samples taken from three individuals. An X in the hormone column indicates a positive lab test for the appropriate levels necessary for normal reproductive functioning in that individual.

**Data Table**

| *Individuals* | *Hormones Present* | | |
|---|---|---|---|
| | *Testosterone* | *Progesterone* | *Estrogen* |
| 1 | | X | X |
| 2 | | | X |
| 3 | X | | |

Which processes could occur in individual 3?

(1) production of sperm only
(2) production of sperm and production of eggs
(3) production of eggs and embryonic development
(4) production of eggs only

**Correct Answer: (1)** Individual 3 is producing testosterone. Testosterone is the principal male sex hormone. The largest amount of testosterone is produced in the testes along with the production of sperm. *(Human Body Systems)*

**36.** A process that occurs in the human body is represented in the diagram below.

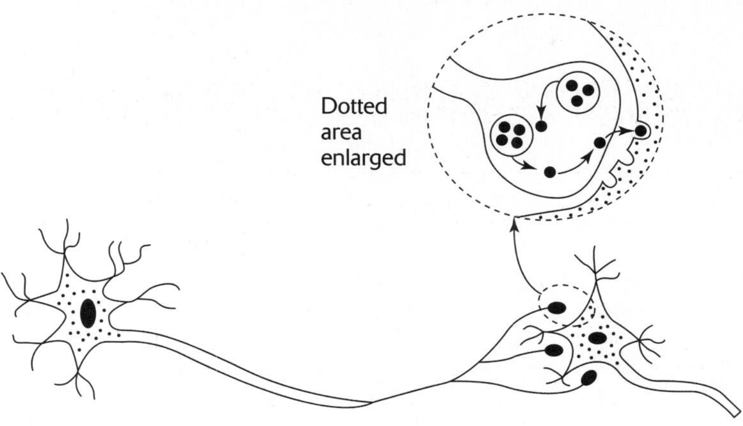


Which statement is most closely associated with the diagram?

**(1)** Small molecules are obtained from large molecules during digestion.
**(2)** Certain molecules are replicated by means of a template.
**(3)** Receptor molecules play an important role in communication between cells.
**(4)** Energy from nutrients is utilized for waste disposal.

**Correct Answer: (3)** The diagram shows the end of a nerve cell (neuron) next to the beginning of another neuron. The circle area shows a close-up of the section where they meet and shows small molecules going from the end of one neuron into the space between the two and into a pocket on the next neuron. This is how nerve cells communicate; this is how a message or impulse is sent from one neuron to the next neuron. What is needed for this to happen is those small black dots that represent molecules called *neurotransmitters.* These neurotransmitters go from one cell to the next, attaching to those pockets or receptors and allowing the message to continue from one nerve cell to the next. In order to be able to answer this question, you have to be able to recognize that the diagram shows two nerve cells. When this is shown, nine times out of ten it will be related to cell communication and receptors. *(Human Body Systems)*

Base your answers to questions 37 through 39 on the diagram below and on your knowledge of biology.

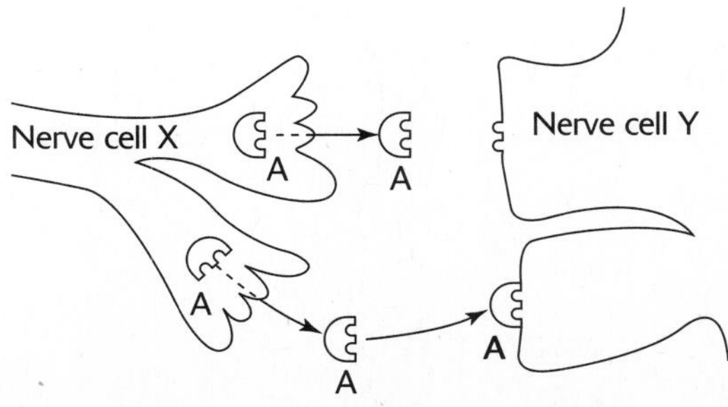

**37.** The process represented in the diagram best illustrates

(1) cellular communication
(2) muscle contraction
(3) extraction of energy from nutrients
(4) waste disposal

**Correct Answer: (1)** The diagram is showing the transmission of an impulse between two nerve cells, X and Y. Nerve cells, or neurons, carry chemical and electrical messages, or impulses, throughout the body between sensory organs and glands or muscles. *(Human Body Systems)*

**38.** Which statement best describes the diagram?

(1) Nerve Cell X is releasing receptor molecules.
(2) Nerve Cell Y is signaling nerve Cell X.
(3) Nerve Cell X is attaching to nerve Cell Y.
(4) Nerve Cell Y contains receptor molecules for Substance A.

**Correct Answer: (4)** The diagram is showing the transmission of an impulse between two nerve cells, X and Y. Nerve cells, or neurons, carry chemical and electrical messages, or impulses, throughout the body between sensory organs and glands or muscles. Impulses are carried from one nerve cell to another across a space called a synapse by special chemicals called neurotransmitters. In the diagram, Substance A is being released from Cell X across the synaptic gap, to be received by special receptor proteins in the membrane of Cell Y. *(Human Body Systems)*

**39.** A drug is developed that, due to its molecular shape, blocks the action of Substance A. Which shape would the drug molecule most likely resemble?

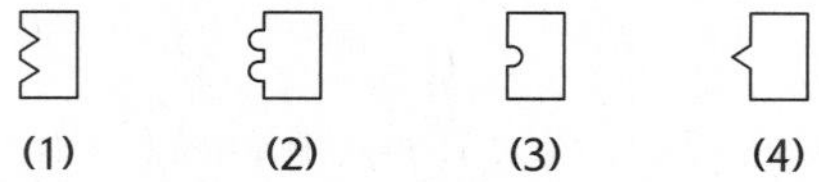

(1) (2) (3) (4)

**Correct Answer: (2)** The shape of Molecule 2 fits exactly with the shape of Substance A. If Molecule 2 were to bind to Substance A before it could travel across the synaptic gap to Cell Y, Substance A would not have the correct shape to bind to the receptors on Cell Y's membrane. In that way, Molecule 2 would block the action of Substance A. *(Human Body Systems)*

**40.** Enzymes have an optimum temperature at which they work best. Temperatures above and below this optimum will decrease enzyme activity. Which graph best illustrates the effect of temperature on enzyme activity?

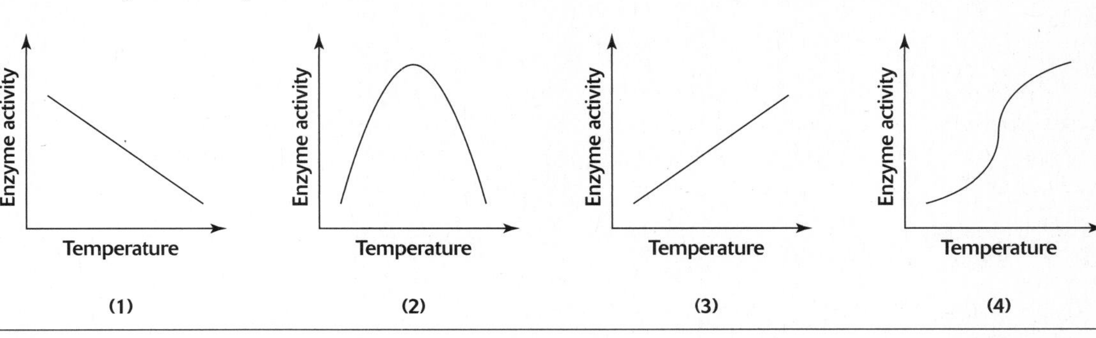


**Correct Answer:** (2)

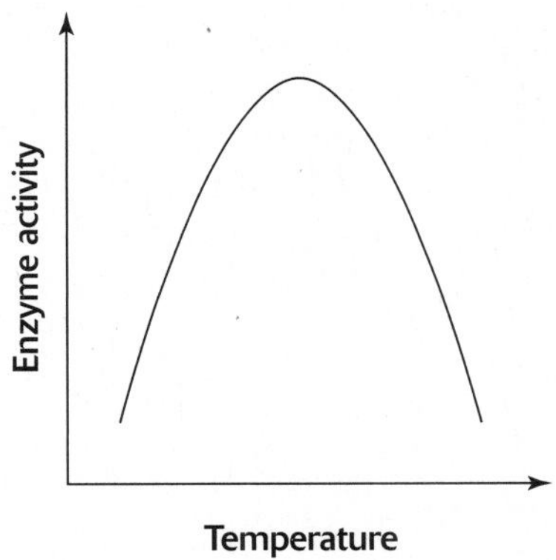


As temperature increases, the rate of enzyme activity increases until a certain point. At temperatures beyond this point, the enzyme starts to denature and its effectiveness decreases. *(Biochemistry)*

**41.** A word equation is shown below.

$$\text{Starch molecules} \xrightarrow{\text{(biological catalyst)}} \text{Simple sugars}$$

This reaction is most directly involved in the process of

**(1)** reproduction
**(2)** protein synthesis
**(3)** replication
**(4)** heterotrophic nutrition

**Correct Answer: (4)** The reaction shows large, complex starch molecules being broken by enzymes into their building blocks, simple sugars. This process takes place during digestion in heterotrophs so that the materials can be absorbed into the body and used for energy or the synthesis of other compounds. *(Biochemistry)*

Base your answers to questions 42 and 43 on the information in the diagram below and on your knowledge of biology.

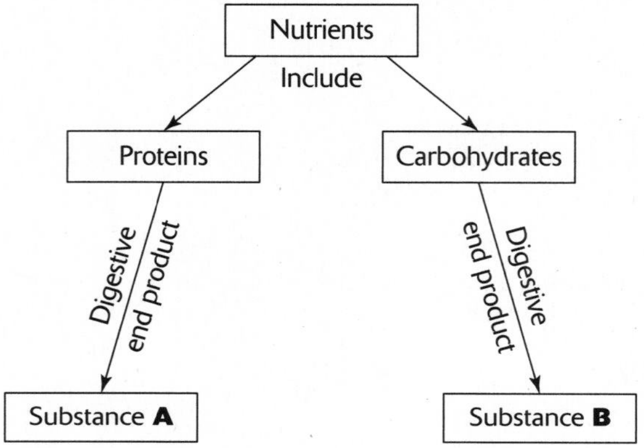


**42.** In an autotrophic organism, Substance B functions as a

**(1)** source of energy
**(2)** hormone
**(3)** vitamin
**(4)** biotic resource

**Correct Answer: (1)** Complex carbohydrates are broken down during digestion into simple sugars, such as glucose. These simple sugars are then used during respiration in the production of ATP (an energy molecule that the cell can utilize for growth, development, and division). *(Biochemistry)*

**43.** In a heterotrophic organism, Substance A could be used directly for

**(1)** photosynthesis
**(2)** synthesis of enzymes
**(3)** a building block of starch
**(4)** a genetic code

**Correct Answer: (2)** Proteins are broken down during digestion into amino acids. The cell can utilize these amino acids to synthesize enzymes, a special type of protein. *(Biochemistry)*

Base your answers to questions 44 and 45 on the diagram below and on your knowledge of biology. The diagram illustrates a process by which energy is released in organisms.

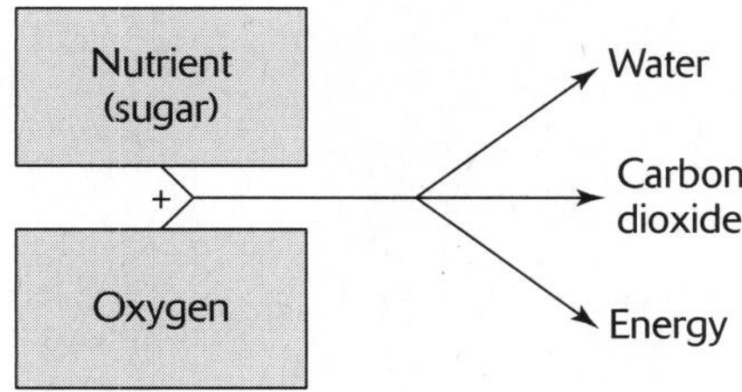


**44.** Cells usually transfer the energy that is released directly to

**(1)** glucose
**(2)** ATP
**(3)** oxygen
**(4)** enzymes

**Correct Answer: (2)** The image describes the process of aerobic cellular respiration. The purpose of cellular respiration is to take the energy that is stored in organic molecules and transfer it to the ATP molecule for easier use. *(Biochemistry)*

**45.** The energy released in this process was originally present in

**(1)** sunlight and then transferred to sugar
**(2)** sunlight and then transferred to oxygen
**(3)** the oxygen and then transferred to sugar
**(4)** the sugar and then transferred to oxygen

**Correct Answer: (1)** The process described is photosynthesis. In photosynthesis, the energy from sunlight is used to make organic molecules (sugar). *(Biochemistry)*

**46.** An experimental setup is shown in the diagram below.

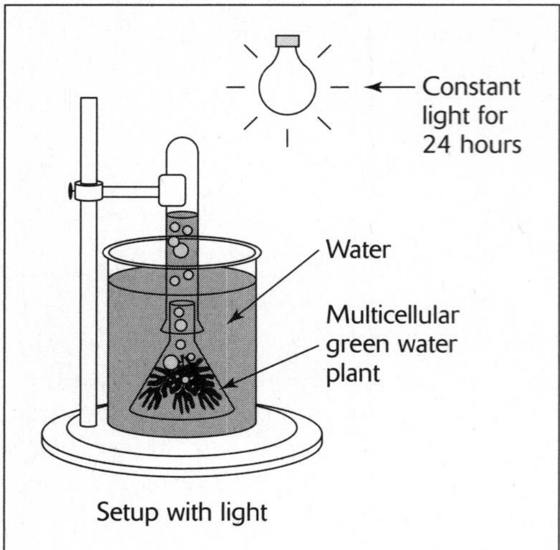


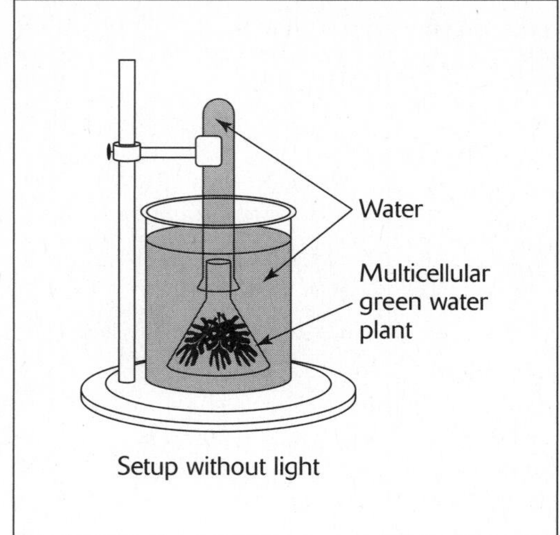


Which hypothesis would most likely be tested using this setup?

**(1)** Green water plants release a gas in the presence of light.
**(2)** Roots of water plants absorb minerals in the absence of light.
**(3)** Green plants need light for cell division.
**(4)** Plants grow best in the absence of light.

**Correct Answer: (1)** Plants photosynthesize in the presence of light. One of the waste products of photosynthesis is the gas oxygen. In the experiment shown, the plant in the first setup is exposed to light. Bubbles are produced and funneled into the test tube. Those bubbles are the gaseous waste product of photosynthesis (oxygen). In a similar setup without light, no oxygen bubbles are evident. In the 24-hour period in which this experiment was conducted, roots were not present and growth was not evident. *(Biochemistry)*

**47.** Using appropriate information, fill in spaces A and B in the chart below. In space A, identify an organ in the human body where molecules diffuse into the blood. In space B, identify a specific molecule that diffuses into the blood at this organ.

| ***An organ in the human body where molecules diffuse into the blood*** | ***A specific molecule that diffuses into the blood at this organ*** |
|---|---|
| A | B |
| | |

**Correct Answer:** Examples of acceptable responses include the following:

| ***An organ in the human body where molecules diffuse into the blood*** | ***A specific molecule that diffuses into the blood at this organ*** |
|---|---|
| Lungs | Oxygen |
| Small intestine | Glucose |
| Large intestine | Water |
| Pancreas | Insulin |

Oxygen molecules diffuse across the cell membrane of the alveoli in the lungs to the capillaries surrounding them. The products of carbohydrate digestion (simple sugars such as glucose) diffuse across the membrane of villi in the small intestine into the bloodstream. The products of protein digestion (amino acids) are also absorbed into the bloodstream through the villi. (***Note:*** The products of fat digestion [fatty acids and glycerol] are absorbed into lacteals and the lymph system—not directly into the bloodstream.) Water is absorbed from indigestible food found in the large intestine into the bloodstream. Insulin is absorbed into the bloodstream in the pancreas. *(Human Body Systems)*

Base your answer to question 48 on the diagram below and on your knowledge of biology.

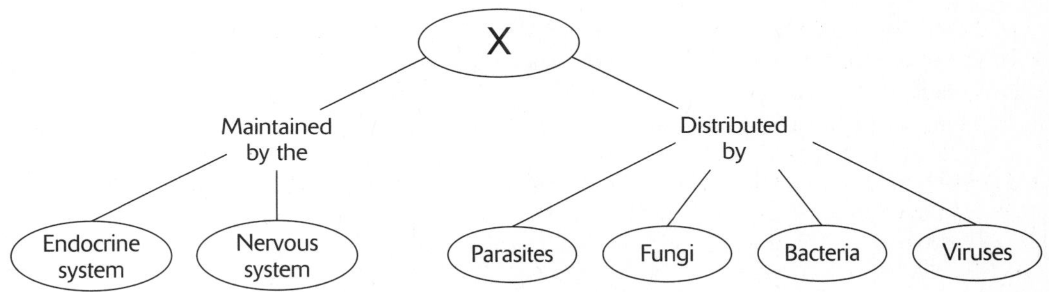


**48.** What term or phrase does letter X most likely represent?

**Correct Answer:** Homeostasis. X has to be something that is maintained by the endocrine and nervous systems—both part of the regulatory system, and able to be disrupted by microorganisms. The endocrine and nervous systems both work to regulate body functions to maintain homeostasis. *(Human Body Systems)*

**49.** The diagrams below represent some of the systems that make up the human body.

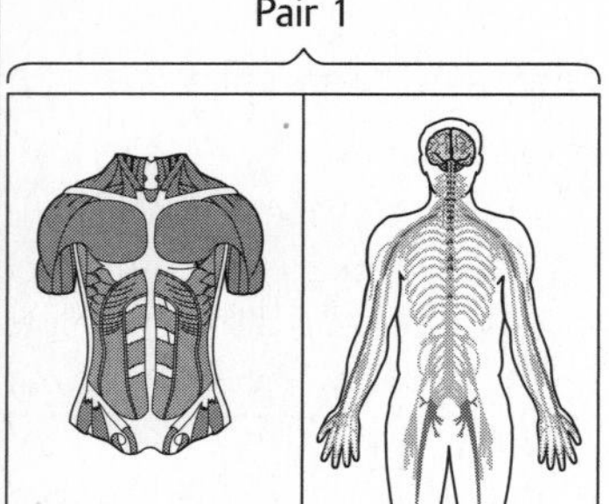


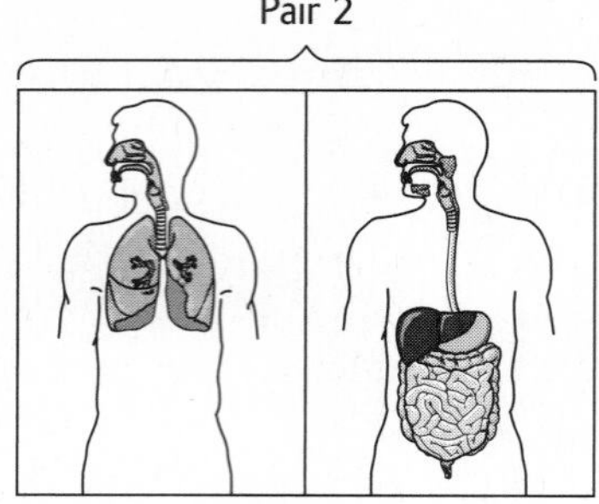


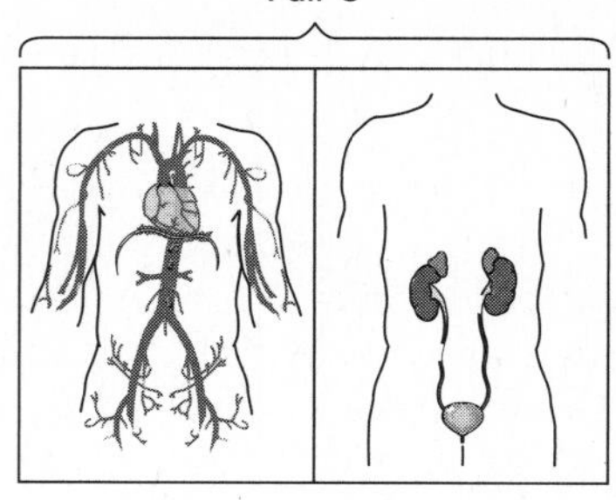


Select one of the pairs of systems and write its number below. For the pair selected, identify each system and state one function of that system. Explain how the two systems work together to help maintain homeostasis in an individual.

Pair _____

**Correct Answer:** Pair 1 represents the muscular system and the nervous system. The nervous system receives stimuli and sends messages to the muscles so they may react to the stimuli.
Pair 2 represents the respiratory system and the digestive system. The digestive system breaks down large food molecules into a form the body can use. The respiratory system takes in oxygen. Both products are required in the process of cellular respiration to provide energy for the body.
Pair 3 represents the circulatory system and the excretory (urinary) system. The circulatory system delivers nutrients and oxygen to body cells and picks up waste products. The waste products are filtered out in the kidneys and the final waste product, urine, is delivered to the urinary bladder until its elimination through the urethra. *(Human Body Systems)*

**50.** State *one* specific way white blood cells help to protect the human body from pathogens.

**Correct Answer:** Don't just say, "White blood cells help fight infection." The question says that you must state a *specific* way that white blood cells protect the human body. White blood cells do two things: They produce antibodies against pathogens, and other white blood cells engulf them. Either of those answers would work. *(Disease)*

**51.** Identify *two* body systems that help maintain glucose levels in the blood and describe how each system is involved.

**Correct Answer:** **(1)** The first system that comes to mind is one you may not be that familiar with: the endocrine system. The endocrine system makes hormones, chemicals that travel through the blood from where they are made to a target organ, which performs some function. In this case, the endocrine system secretes insulin from the pancreas, which goes into the blood to help get glucose into the cells. The other system is the digestive system, which is responsible for breaking down food into the usable form of glucose. You could also choose the circulatory system for its role in carrying the insulin from the pancreas through the blood to the entire body. *(Disease)*

Base your answer to question 52 on the passage below and on your knowledge of biology.

## In Search of a Low-Allergy Peanut

Many people are allergic to substances in the environment. Of the many foods that contain allergens (allergy-inducing substances), peanuts cause some of the most severe reactions. Mildly allergic people may only get hives. Highly allergic people can go into a form of shock. Some people die each year from reactions to peanuts.

A group of scientists is attempting to produce peanuts that lack the allergy-inducing proteins by using traditional selective breeding methods. They are searching for varieties of peanuts that are free of the allergens. By crossing those varieties with popular commercial types, they hope to produce peanuts that will be less likely to cause allergic reactions and still taste good. So far, they have found one variety that has 80 percent less of one of three complex proteins linked to allergic reactions. Removing all three of these allergens may be impossible, but even removing one could help.

Other researchers are attempting to alter the genes that code for the three major allergens in peanuts. All of this research is seen as a possible long-term solution to peanut allergies.

**52.** Allergic reactions usually occur when the immune system produces

(1) antibiotics against usually harmless antigens
(2) antigens against usually harmless antibodies
(3) antibodies against usually harmless antigens
(4) enzymes against usually harmless antibodies

**Correct Answer: (3)** Allergic reactions are caused when the body reacts to antigens (foreign substance) that have invaded the body. In response to this invasion, the body produces antibodies (a protein produced by the immune system to kill the antigen). Typical allergy symptoms accompany this production of antibodies as the body attempts to kill and rid itself of the invading antigens. *(Disease)*

**53.** Humans require multiple systems for various life functions. Two vital systems are the circulatory system and the respiratory system. Select one of these systems, write its name in the chart below, and then identify two structures that are part of that system, and state how each structure you identified functions as part of the system.

| ***System:*** | |
|---|---|
| ***Structure*** | ***Function*** |
| (1) | |
| (2) | |

**Correct Answer:**

| ***System: Circulatory*** | |
|---|---|
| ***Structure*** | ***Function*** |
| (1) Heart | Pumps blood throughout the body |
| (2) Artery | Carries blood from the heart to the body |
| (3) Vein | Returns blood from the body to the heart |
| (4) Blood cells | Carries oxygen to the body |
| (5) Capillaries | Allows for exchange of materials between body cells and the bloodstream |

| ***System: Respiratory*** | |
|---|---|
| ***Structure*** | ***Function*** |
| (1) Lungs | Takes in oxygen and releases carbon dioxide |
| (2) Alveoli | Air sacs where gases are exchanged between the environment and the bloodstream |
| (3) Cilia in nose and throat | Filters particulates from the air before it enters the lungs |
| (4) Diaphragm | When contracted, draws air into the lungs; when relaxed, forces air out of the lungs |

*(Human Body Systems)*

Base your answer to question 54 on the information and chart below and on your knowledge of biology.

In DNA, a sequence of three bases is a code for the placement of a certain amino acid in a protein chain. The table below shows some amino acids with their abbreviations and DNA codes.

| ***Amino Acid*** | ***Abbreviation*** | ***DNA Code*** |
|---|---|---|
| Phenylalanine | Phe | AAA, AAG |
| Tryptophan | Try | ACC |
| Serine | Ser | AGA, AGG, AGT, AGC, TCA, TCG |
| Valine | Val | CAA, CAG, CAT, CAC |
| Proline | Pro | GGA, GGG, GGT, GGC |
| Glutamine | Glu | GTT, GTC |
| Threonine | Thr | TGA, TGG, TGT, TGC |
| Asparagine | Asp | TTA, TTG |

**54.** Identify one environmental factor that could cause a base sequence in DNA to be changed to a different base sequence.

**Correct Answer:** An environmental factor that could cause a base sequence in DNA to be changed would be some kind of mutagenic agent such as UV rays, X-rays and other types of radiation, chemicals, viruses, or pollutants. *(Disease)*

**55.** An incomplete graph is shown below.

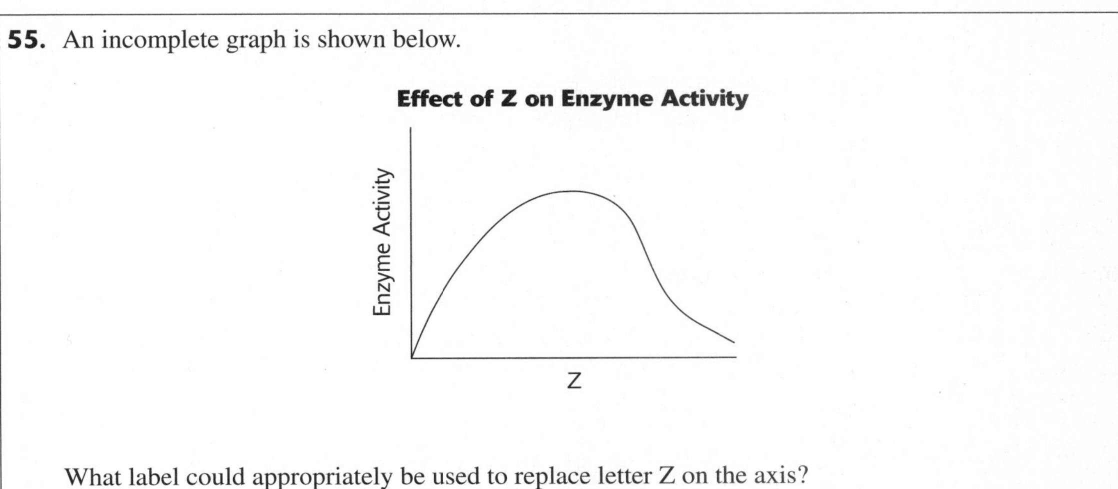


What label could appropriately be used to replace letter Z on the axis?

**Correct Answer:** Letter *Z* must be something that can have an effect on the activity of an enzyme, such as temperature, concentration of substrate, concentration of the enzyme, or pH. *(Biochemistry)*

Base your answers to questions 56 through 59 on the diagram below and on your knowledge of biology. The arrows in the diagram represent biological processes.

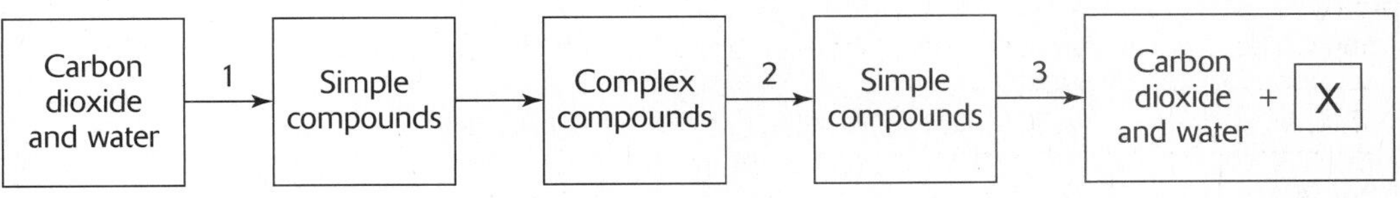


**56.** Identify *one* type of organism that carries out Process 1.

**Correct Answer:** Process 1 is photosynthesis, which is the conversion of carbon dioxide and water into simple compounds. Photosynthesis is carried out by plants, also called producers or autotrophs. *(Biochemistry)*

**57.** Explain why Process 2 is essential in humans.

**Correct Answer:** Process 2 is the breakdown of complex compounds into simple ones. This digestion of food is necessary to make the molecules small enough to be transported throughout the body and diffused into cells. This process is necessary so that energy can be released from the food that we eat. *(Biochemistry)*

**58.** Identify Process 3.

**Correct Answer:** Process 3 is respiration, which releases energy (ATP molecules) from simple compounds. Carbon dioxide and water are waste products in this reaction. *(Biochemistry)*

**59.** Identify what letter X represents.

**Correct Answer:** Letter X represents the energy (ATP molecules) released during respiration. *(Biochemistry)*

Base your answer to question 60 on the data table below and on your knowledge of biology. The table contains information about glucose production in a species of plant that lives in the water of a salt marsh.

| *Temperature (°C)* | *Glucose Production (mg/hr)* |
|---|---|
| 10 | 5 |
| 20 | 10 |
| 30 | 15 |
| 40 | 5 |

**60.** State *one* possible reason for the change in glucose production when the temperature was increased from 30°C to 40°C.

**Correct Answer:** Photosynthesis is responsible for producing glucose in plants. The process of photosynthesis is accomplished through a series of complex chemical reactions. Chemical reactions are affected by temperature. The data in this table support this conclusion. Enzymes are involved in most chemical reactions (including photosynthesis). Enzymes are sensitive to heat and can be destroyed at high temperatures. The data in this table also support this conclusion. *(Biochemistry)*

**61.** Organ systems of the human body interact to maintain a balanced internal environment. As blood flows through certain organs of the body, the composition of the blood changes because of interactions with those organs. State one change in the composition of the blood as it flows through the digestive system.

**Correct Answer:** This is a two-part question: Its purpose is to determine whether you know the function of the blood and circulatory system and the function of the digestive system. First, the blood and vessels of the circulatory system are responsible for carrying gases (oxygen and carbon dioxide), wastes, and nutrients throughout the body. The digestive system is involved with breaking down food into simpler molecules that the body can use. So the answer is: As the blood flows through the digestive system, it changes from being low in nutrients to being high in nutrients. *(Human Body Systems)*

**62.** Describe *one* example of diffusion in the human body. In your description be sure to:

- Identify the place where the diffusion takes place.
- Identify a substance that diffuses there.
- Identify where that substance diffuses from and where it diffuses to, at that place.

**Correct Answer:** Diffusion is the movement of particles from an area of high concentration to an area of low concentration. Where in the human body does this occur? Everywhere—but you need to be more specific than that. Some examples are in the lungs, where oxygen and carbon dioxide diffuse into and out of the capillaries and alveoli; in the small intestine, where nutrients diffuse out of the villi of the small intestine into the capillaries that surround the villi; or in the kidneys, where wastes diffuse out of the capillaries into the nephron or water that diffuses out of the nephron and into the capillaries. In general, diffusion occurs at every cell in the body, allowing nutrients, water, and oxygen in, and carbon dioxide and wastes out. If you choose to use lungs as your answer, your answer could be:

- Diffusion occurs in the lungs.
- Oxygen diffuses in the lungs.
- The oxygen will diffuse out of the alveoli and into the capillaries that surround it.

*(Human Body Systems)*

**63.** AIDS is an infectious disease that has reached epidemic proportions. Describe the nature of this disease and identify *two* ways to prevent or control the spread of infectious diseases such as AIDS. In your response be sure to include

- the type of pathogen that causes AIDS
- the system of the body that is attacked by that pathogen
- the effect on the body when this system is weakened by AIDS
- *two* ways to prevent or control the spread of infectious diseases such as AIDS

**Correct Answer:** The pathogen that causes acquired immune deficiency syndrome (AIDS) is the human immunodeficiency virus (HIV). HIV attacks the helper T cells of the immune system, the body's defense against disease. As the number of helper T cells drops, the immune system's responses to pathogens becomes less effective. The person is unable to fight infections and develops AIDS. The spread of infectious diseases such as AIDS can be prevented by avoiding sexual contact/exchange of body fluids, especially saliva, mucus, semen, and vaginal secretions. Blood-to-blood contact also spreads the disease, as when IV drug users share needles. *(Disease)*

Base your answers to questions 64 and 65 on the information below and on your knowledge of biology.

Cell communication involves a cell detecting and responding to signals from other cells. Receptor molecules play an important role in these reactions. Human cells have insulin receptors that are needed for the movement of glucose out of the blood.

**64.** State one way that the shape of the insulin receptor is related to its role in cell communication.

**Correct Answer:** The insulin receptor on a cell has a particular shape that is specific to (allows it to only match up with) the insulin molecule. If insulin is released and attaches to its specific receptor, then glucose may be stored as glycogen in the liver. If the receptor does not match up with insulin, glucose will not be stored. Insulin has no other receptor that will match its shape and allow the uptake of glucose. *(Feedback)*

**65.** A typical human liver cell can have over 90,000 insulin receptors. If a genetic error occurred, resulting in each liver cell in a person having only 1,000 insulin receptors, what specific effect would this have on the liver cells?

**Correct Answer:** If a person had only 1,000 insulin receptors in each liver cell instead of the usual 90,000 or more, the person would not be able to take in or absorb the normal amount of insulin, store glucose as efficiently, or regulate blood sugar levels as efficiently. *(Feedback)*

Base your answer to question 66 on the information below and on your knowledge of biology.

It has been discovered that plants utilize chemical signals for communication. Some of these chemicals are released from leaves, fruits, and flowers and play various roles in plant development, survival, and gene expression. For example, bean plant leaves infested with spider mites release chemicals that result in an increase in the resistance to spider mites in uninfested leaves on the same plant and the expression of self-defense genes in uninfested bean plants nearby. Plants can also communicate with insects. For example, corn, cotton, and tobacco under attack by caterpillars release chemical signals that simultaneously attract parasitic wasps to destroy the caterpillars and discourage moths from laying their eggs on the plants.

**66.** Explain why chemicals released from one plant species may not cause a response in a different plant species.

**Correct Answer:** The chemicals released and the receptors they bind to are very specific. Only certain chemicals will bind with certain receptors. *(Biochemistry)*

Base your answers to questions 67 and 68 on the statement below and on your knowledge of biology.

Some internal environmental factors may interfere with the ability of an enzyme to function efficiently.

**67.** Identify *two* internal environmental factors that directly influence the rate of enzyme action.

**Correct Answer:** Environmental factors that cause changes in enzyme action include: temperature, pH, enzyme concentration, and substrate concentration. *(Biochemistry)*

**68.** Explain why changing the shape of an enzyme could affect the ability of the enzyme to function.

**Correct Answer:** Enzyme shape is specific to the substrate upon which it acts, much like the shape of a key is specific to the lock that it opens. If the shape of the enzyme changes, it will no longer fit the same substrate. *(Biochemistry)*

Base your answers to questions 69 through 71 on the diagram below of activities in the human body.

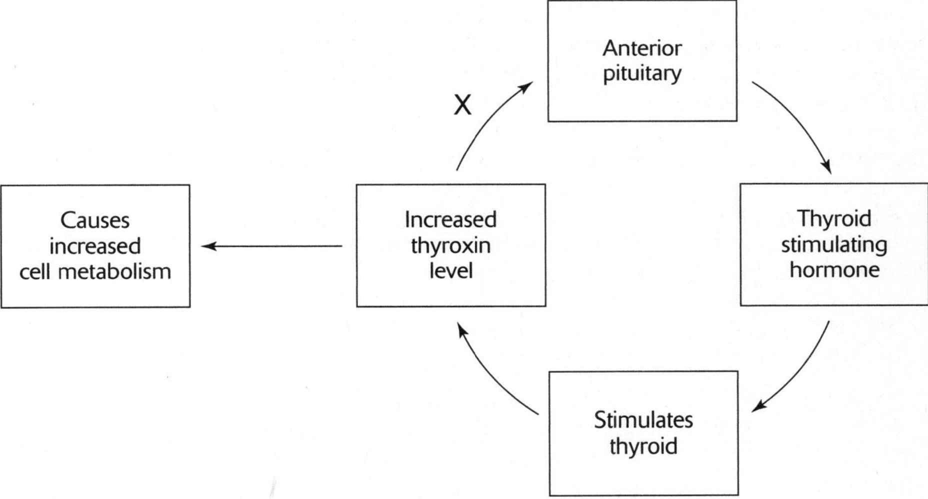


**69.** This diagram illustrates part of

(1) a feedback mechanism
(2) an enzyme pathway
(3) a digestive mechanism
(4) a pattern of learned behavior

**Correct Answer: (1)** The diagram shows a continuous cycle in which change in, say, A causes a change in B, which subsequently affects A. Positive feedback reinforces the first change. In this case, an increase in A causes an increase in B, which causes another increase in A, and so on. Negative feedback opposes the first change. In this case, an increase in A would cause an increase in B, which would then cause a decrease in A, further decreasing B. *(Feedback)*

**70.** Describe the action represented by the arrow labeled X in the diagram and state one reason that this action is important.

**Correct Answer:** Thyroxin is a hormone secreted by the thyroid gland that regulates the rate of metabolism. A low thyroxin level triggers the hypothalamus to stimulate the anterior pituitary gland to secrete thyroid stimulating hormone (TSH). TSH stimulates the production and release of thyroxin by the thyroid gland. When the concentration of thyroxin reaches a particular level, the hypothalamus stops stimulating the pituitary, inhibiting the secretion of TSH. This form of negative feedback is important because it maintains the proper level of thyroxin in the body. *(Feedback)*

**71.** Identify one hormone involved in another biological relationship and an organ that is directly affected by the hormone you identified.

**Correct Answer:** Insulin, glucagon, and secretin affect the pancreas. Estrogen and progesterone affect the ovaries or uterus. Follicle stimulating hormone (FSH) affects the ovaries and testes. Oxytocin affects the uterus. Vasopressin affects the kidneys. Epinephrine affects the heart, liver, and lungs. Steroids affect the liver and kidneys. *(Feedback)*

Base your answers to questions 72 through 74 on the information below and on your knowledge of biology.

> Cells of the immune system and the endocrine system of the human body contribute to the maintenance of homeostasis. The methods and materials these two systems use as they carry out this critical function are different.

**72.** State *two* ways cells of the immune system fight disease.

**Correct Answer:** The immune system is made up of various types of white blood cells. Some of the white cells produce antibodies and some engulf and destroy those labeled with antibodies. *(Human Body Systems)*

**73.** Identify the substance produced by the cells of all the endocrine glands that helps maintain homeostasis.

**Correct Answer:** Hormones. Hormones are chemicals produced by the cells of the endocrine glands in order to regulate homeostasis. *(Human Body Systems)*

**74.** Identify *one* specific product of one of the endocrine glands and state how it aids in the maintenance of homeostasis.

**Correct Answer:** Name any hormone that the body produces and explain what that hormone does. For example, insulin and glucagon help to regulate blood sugar levels. *(Human Body Systems)*

# Ecology

**Directions:** For each statement or question, choose the *number* of the word or expression that best completes the statement or answers the question. Then check your answer against the one that immediately follows the question. Try not to look at the answer before making your selection.

**1.** When brown tree snakes were accidentally introduced onto the island of Guam, they had no natural predators. These snakes sought out and ate many of the eggs of insect-eating birds. What probably occurred following the introduction of the brown tree snakes?

(1) The bird population increased.
(2) The insect population increased.
(3) The bird population began to seek a new food source.
(4) The insect population began to seek a new food source.

**Correct Answer: (2)** The insect population increased because the bird population decreased. If the snakes ate bird eggs, the bird population declined. There were fewer birds to eat the insects so the insect population increased. *(Organisms in Their Environment)*

**2.** The size of a mouse population in a natural ecosystem tends to remain relatively constant due to

(1) the carrying capacity of the environment
(2) the lack of natural predators
(3) cycling of energy
(4) increased numbers of decomposers

**Correct Answer: (1)** Population sizes depend on the ability of the environment to support them. If the environment remains relatively stable, the populations within them tend to do the same. *(Organisms in Their Environment)*

**3.** In most habitats, the removal of predators will have the most immediate impact on a population of

(1) producers
(2) decomposers
(3) herbivores
(4) microbes

**Correct Answer: (3)** Animals that feed on other animals are carnivores. Some carnivores are scavengers, which feed on dead animals that they have not killed themselves, and some are predators, which attack their prey and eat it. Herbivores are animals that feed only on plants (producers). *(Energy Flow in Ecosystems)*

**4.** Organisms from a particular ecosystem are shown below.

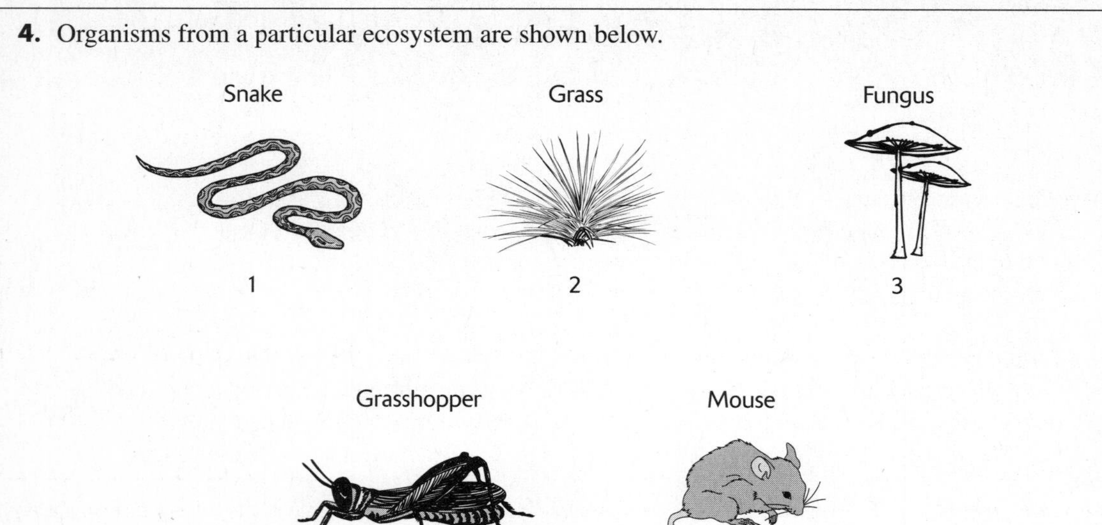


Which statement concerning an organism in this ecosystem is correct?

**(1)** Organism 2 is heterotrophic.
**(2)** Organism 3 helps recycle materials.
**(3)** Organism 4 obtains all its nutrients from an abiotic source.
**(4)** Organism 5 must obtain its energy from Organism 1.

**Correct Answer: (2)** Organism 3 is a mushroom, a type of fungi. Mushrooms are saprobes, organisms that get their nutrients by breaking down the remains of dead plants and animals and absorbing the nutrients. Nutrients are also added back into the soil to be recycled. *(The Structure of Ecosystems)*

**5.** Which statement best explains the change shown in the diagram below?

**(1)** Gene expression in an organism can be modified by interactions with the environment.
**(2)** Certain rabbits produce mutations that affect genes in specific areas of the body.
**(3)** Sorting and recombination of genes can be influenced by very cold temperatures.
**(4)** Molecular arrangement in existing proteins can be altered by environmental factors.

**Correct Answer: (1)** The expression of certain genes may be altered by environmental cues. The ability to alter gene expression helps organisms to be more fit in their environments. *(Organisms in Their Environment)*

**6.** After a rabbit population reaches the carrying capacity of its habitat, the population of rabbits will most likely

**(1)** decrease only
**(2)** increase only
**(3)** alternately increase and decrease
**(4)** remain unchanged

**Correct Answer: (3)** The carrying capacity refers to the limited number of rabbits that the environment is capable of supporting. The rabbit population can't live above the carrying capacity for very long because the resources in the environment are limited. As the rabbit population reaches the carrying capacity, resources will become scarce and the population will begin to decrease. As the population begins to decrease, resources will replenish and the population will rise again. *(Energy Flow in Ecosystems)*

**7.** A food web is represented below.

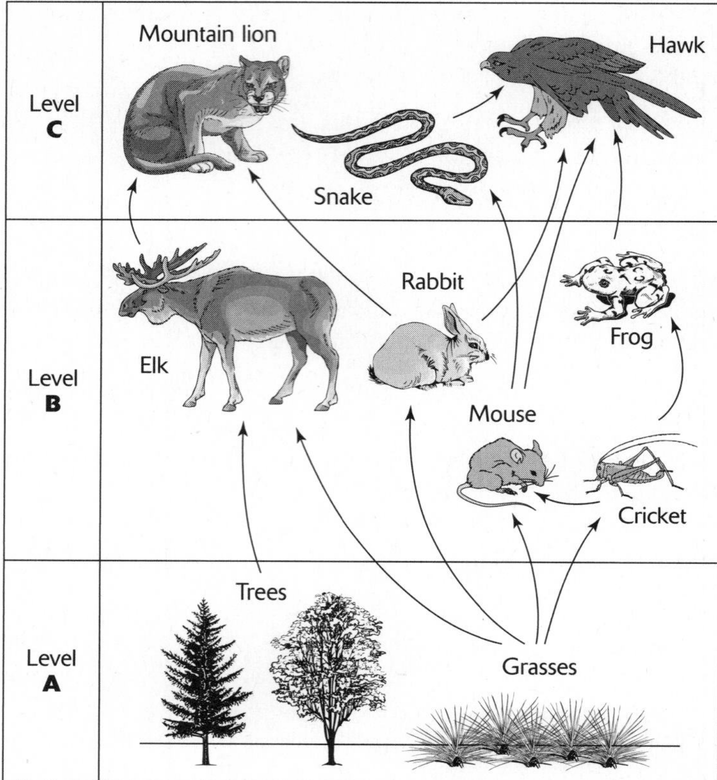


Which statement best describes energy in this food web?

**(1)** The energy content of Level B depends on the energy content of Level C.
**(2)** The energy content of Level A depends on energy provided from an abiotic source.
**(3)** The energy content of Level C is greater than the energy content of Level A.
**(4)** The energy content of Level B is transferred to Level A.

**Correct Answer: (2)** Energy within a food web moves from the level of the producer (Level A) to the primary consumers (Level B) and then ultimately the secondary consumers (Level C). Energy is used within each level to build the bodies of the organisms. Some energy is lost as heat from each level. As a result of this energy use and loss, each level of the food web has less energy than the level below it. The energy that drives the whole food web comes from the sun, an abiotic (nonliving) source. *(Energy Flow in Ecosystems)*

**8.** In 1993, there were only 30 panthers in Florida. They were all closely related and many had reproductive problems. To avoid extinction and restore health to the population, biologists introduced eight female panthers from Texas. Today, there are more than 80 panthers in Florida and most individuals have healthy reproductive systems. The success of this program was most likely due to the fact that the introduced females

**(1)** produced more reproductive cells than the male panthers in Texas
**(2)** solved the reproductive problems of the species by asexual methods
**(3)** increased the genetic variability of the panther population in Florida
**(4)** mated only with panthers from Texas

**Correct Answer: (3)** The original Florida parents were all closely related. That means that their DNA were all similar. The Texas panthers came from an entirely different gene pool. This brought variation into the population. Variation is important for the survival of a species. *(Biodiversity)*

**9.** What would most likely happen if most of the bacteria and fungi were removed from an ecosystem?

**(1)** Nutrients resulting from decomposition would be reduced.
**(2)** Energy provided for autotrophic nutrition would be reduced.
**(3)** The rate of mutations in plants would increase.
**(4)** Soil fertility would increase.

**Correct Answer: (1)** Bacteria and fungi in the soil of an ecosystem cause decomposition of dead organisms. This decomposition releases nutrients into the soil and causes soil fertility to increase. If the bacteria and fungi were removed from an ecosystem, decomposition would be greatly reduced, causing a decrease in soil fertility. Autotrophs (plants) would suffer from reduced nutrients in the soil, but their energy comes from the sun and would not be reduced. *(Energy Flow in Ecosystems)*

**10.** Organisms that have the ability to use an atmospheric gas to produce an organic nutrient are known as

**(1)** herbivores
**(2)** decomposers
**(3)** carnivores
**(4)** autotrophs

**Correct Answer: (4)** Autotrophs are organisms that are able to make their own organic nutrients. Photoautotrophs use solar energy, carbon dioxide, and water for the process of photosynthesis. *(Energy Flow in Ecosystems)*

**11.** Cattail plants in freshwater swamps in New York State are being replaced by purple loosestrife plants. The two species have very similar environmental requirements. This observation best illustrates

(1) variations within a species
(2) dynamic equilibrium
(3) random recombination
(4) competition between species

**Correct Answer: (4)** Two species that have similar environmental requirements may result in competition between species. If the two species share a niche, the one that has some advantage over the other can force the disadvantaged species to leave the habitat or possibly die out. *(Organisms in Their Environment)*

**12.** One biotic factor that limits the carrying capacity of any habitat is the

(1) availability of water
(2) level of atmospheric oxygen
(3) activity of decomposers
(4) amount of soil erosion

**Correct Answer: (3)** The only answer that indicates a biotic (living) factor is choice (3). Decomposers are organisms that break down dead and decaying organisms and return the organic matter to the environment to be recycled. *(Organisms in Their Environment)*

**13.** One arctic food chain consists of polar bears, fish, seaweed, and seals. Which sequence demonstrates the correct flow of energy between these organisms?

(1) seals → seaweed → fish → polar bears
(2) fish → seaweed → polar bears → seals
(3) seaweed → fish → seals → polar bears
(4) polar bears → fish → seals → seaweed

**Correct Answer: (3)** Food chains represent the flow of energy through a series of organisms. The path of energy flow always begins with producers, or autotrophs that are able to make their own organic nutrients. *(Energy Flow in Ecosystems)*

**14.** A greater stability of the biosphere would most likely result from

(1) decreased finite resources
(2) increased deforestation
(3) increased biodiversity
(4) decreased consumer populations

**Correct Answer: (3)** Biodiversity refers to the different organisms in an area and may be measured by species richness, species evenness, and genetic diversity. A stable biosphere would have a variety of organisms that could adapt to a changing environment. Any disruption in a species-rich ecosystem would not be as devastating as having only a few organisms in the ecosystem. *(Biodiversity)*

**15.** Many species of plants interact with harmless underground fungi. The fungi enable the plants to absorb certain essential minerals, and the plants provide the fungi with carbohydrates and other nutrients. This describes an interaction between a

**(1)** parasite and its host
**(2)** predator and its prey
**(3)** scavenger and a decomposer
**(4)** producer and a consumer

**Correct Answer: (4)** Plants are referred to as producers because they are able to use the sun's energy to convert carbon dioxide into glucose. Glucose is the carbohydrate that the question refers to. If the fungi take in the carbohydrates and the nutrients the plants provide, they are considered to be consumers. *(Energy Flow in Ecosystems)*

**16.** Four students each drew an illustration to show the flow of energy in a field ecosystem. Which illustration is *most* accurate?

(1) Sun → Oats → Mouse
Oats → Decomposers; Mouse → Decomposers

(2) Sun → Wheat → Woodchuck
Woodchuck → Decomposers; Decomposers → Wheat; Decomposers → Sun

(3) Sun → Grasses → Cow
Grasses → Decomposers; Cow → Decomposers; Decomposers → Sun

(4)
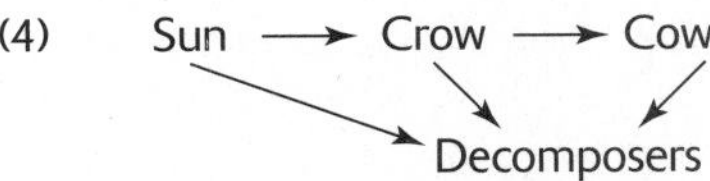


**Correct Answer: (1)** The most accurate diagram shows the energy flow from the sun to the producers (oats). Energy never flows back to the sun and decomposers do not utilize energy directly from the sun. *(Energy Flow in Ecosystems)*

**17.** The diagram below represents an energy pyramid.

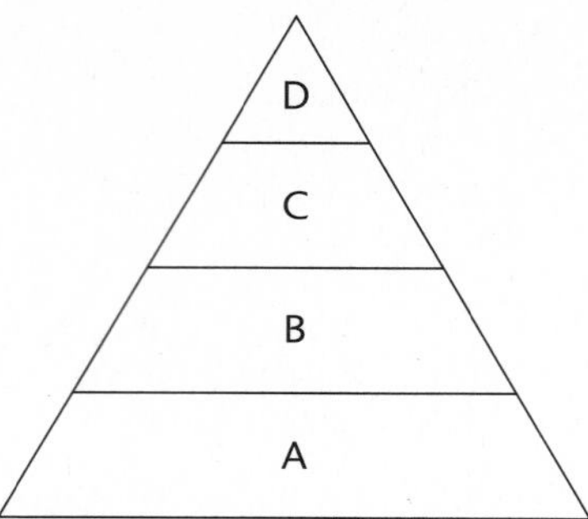


At each successive level from A to D, the amount of available energy

**(1)** increases only
**(2)** decreases only
**(3)** increases, then decreases
**(4)** remains the same

**Correct Answer: (2)** Energy flow in an ecosystem as represented in this energy pyramid decreases as you move from the bottom to the top. The bottom is always occupied by plants (also known as autotrophs or producers). Plants supply the energy for all the organisms located in the levels above it. The amount of energy decreases going up because the organisms found in each level need some of that energy for themselves to keep themselves alive. They need some of that energy for their own metabolic processes. *(Energy Flow in Ecosystems)*

**18.** As succession proceeds from a shrub community to a forest community, the shrub community modifies its environment, eventually making it

**(1)** more favorable for itself and less favorable for the forest community
**(2)** more favorable for itself and more favorable for the forest community
**(3)** less favorable for itself and more favorable for the forest community
**(4)** less favorable for itself and less favorable for the forest community

**Correct Answer: (3)** During ecological succession, communities change the environment making it make less favorable for itself and more favorable for the next community. This is accomplished by growing plants producing shade and leaf litter that inhibit the growth of similar types of plants. The progression goes from an open field with herbs and grasses, to an overgrown field with lots of shrubs, to a forest. In the case of this type of succession, the forest is the climax, or the final community, to occur on that site. *(The Structure of Ecosystems)*

**19.** In an ocean, the growth and survival of seaweed, small fish, and sharks depends on abiotic factors such as

(1) sunlight, temperature, and minerals
(2) sunlight, pH, and type of seaweed
(3) number of decomposers, carbon dioxide, and nitrogen
(4) number of herbivores, carbon, and food

**Correct Answer: (1)** Abiotic factors are nonliving. Sunlight, temperature, and minerals are all nonliving factors that are needed by living things to survive. *(The Structure of Ecosystems)*

**20.** What impact do the amounts of available energy, water, and oxygen have on an ecosystem?

(1) They act as limiting factors.
(2) They are used as nutrients.
(3) They recycle the residue of dead organisms.
(4) They control environmental temperature.

**Correct Answer: (1)** A limiting factor is any factor that limits the growth of organisms in the ecosystem. Energy, water, and oxygen can all be in limited supplies at one time or another and, therefore, act as limiting factors. *(The Structure of Ecosystems)*

**21.** Leaves of green plants contain openings known as stomates, which are opened and closed by specialized cells allowing for gas exchange between the leaf and the outside environment. Which phrase best represents the net flow of gases involved in photosynthesis into and out of the leaf through these openings on a sunny day?

(1) carbon dioxide moves in; oxygen moves out
(2) carbon dioxide and oxygen move in; ozone moves out
(3) oxygen moves in; nitrogen moves out
(4) water and ozone move in; carbon dioxide moves out

**Correct Answer: (1)** Green plants use the process of photosynthesis in the making of their own organic nutrients. Photosynthesis requires the presence of carbon dioxide, water, and sunlight to produce organic nutrients, oxygen gas, and water. Plants must take in carbon dioxide and release oxygen through the stomates. *(Organisms in Their Environment)*

**22.** Many years ago, a volcanic eruption killed many plants and animals on an island. Today the island looks much as it did before the eruption. Which statement is the best possible explanation for this?

(1) Altered ecosystems regain stability through the evolution of new plant species.
(2) Destroyed environments can recover as a result of the process of ecological succession.
(3) Geographic barriers prevent the migration of animals to island habitats.
(4) Destroyed ecosystems always return to their original state.

**Correct Answer: (2)** Because the island now looks much as it did before the volcanic eruption, evolution (a change in a species over time) is not involved. The process that explains the restoration of the island to its original state is ecological succession, the change in communities over time. *(Biodiversity)*

**23.** Some organizations are buying up sections of forest land. Once purchased, these sections of forest will never be cut down. The main reason for protecting these sections of forest is to

(1) cause the extinction of undesirable animal species
(2) prevent these trees from reproducing too fast
(3) maintain the diversity of the living environment
(4) provide more land for agricultural purposes

**Correct Answer: (3)** As the population of people throughout the world increases, more and more land is being used for homes, businesses, communities, and so forth. As a result, more and more forests are being cut down to make room for this spread of civilization and to supply wood for building. Organizations like the Nature Conservancy buy pieces of forest to preserve them and the diversity of life—both plant and animal—that is contained there. *(Biodiversity)*

**24.** When a particular white moth lands on a white birch tree, its color has a high adaptive value. If the birch trees become covered with black soot, the white color of this particular moth in this environment would most likely

(1) retain its adaptive value
(2) increase in adaptive value
(3) change to a more-adaptive black color
(4) decrease in adaptive value

**Correct Answer: (4)** A particular trait of an organism may be beneficial in some environments and less beneficial in others. In the case of the white moth, it has high adaptive value because it is able to blend into its environment to avoid predators. When the environment changes, the white color is no longer an advantage. The white moth is not able to blend as well, and the population decreases due to increased predation. *(Organisms in Their Environment)*

**25.** Which statement best describes the fruit fly population in the part of the curve labeled X in the graph shown below?

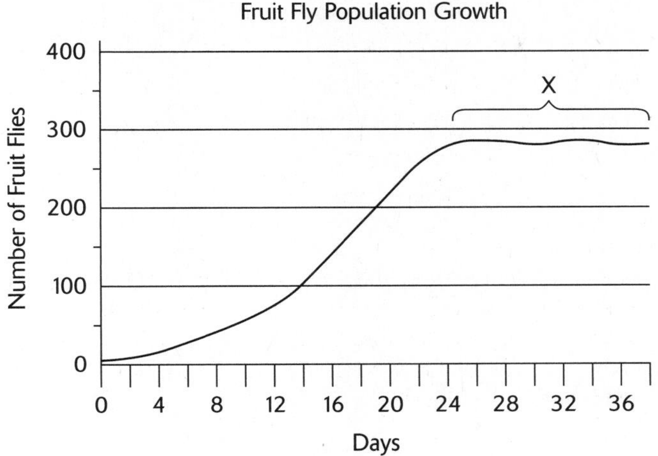


**(1)** The fruit fly population has reached the number of organisms the habitat can support.
**(2)** The fruit fly population can no longer mate and produce fertile offspring.
**(3)** The fruit fly population has an average life span of 36 days.
**(4)** The fruit fly population is no longer able to adapt to the changing environmental conditions.

**Correct Answer: (1)** As shown in the graph, the population of fruit flies remains relatively constant after day 24. Why doesn't the population keep increasing? The answer lies in something called *carrying capacity* (the number of organisms that an ecosystem is able to support). In any ecosystem, there are limits to the factors that organisms need to survive, and when that number of organisms is reached, there are no longer enough resources to support any more organisms.

If choice (2) were true, it could explain what the curve shows, but there is no way of knowing whether it is true or false, so you have to eliminate it as a choice. If fruit flies have a life span of 36 days, they would not all die at once, as in choice (3); if they did, then the curve would go back down to a population of 0. There is no evidence that the environment is changing, so you need to eliminate choice (4); if it were true, then the population would go back down to 0, just as it would in choice (3). *(Organisms in Their Environment)*

**26.** The growth of a population is shown in the graph below.

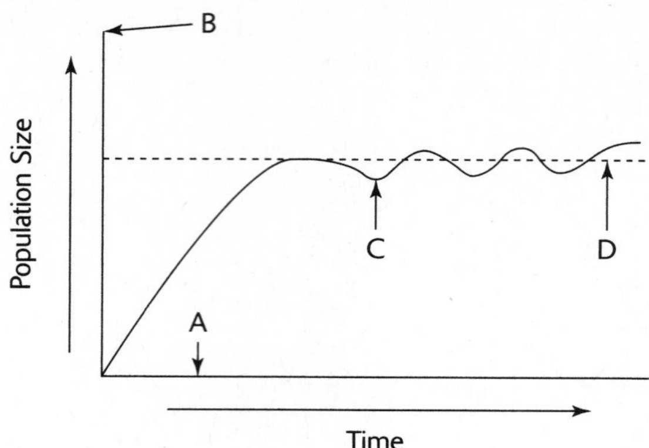


Which letter indicates the carrying capacity of the environment for this population?

(1) A
(2) B
(3) C
(4) D

**Correct Answer: (4)** The carrying capacity of a population is the maximum number of individuals that the environment can sustain. The population may fluctuate above and below the carrying capacity as individuals are born and die. *(Organisms in Their Environment)*

**27.** Carbon dioxide containing carbon-14 is introduced into a balanced aquarium ecosystem. After several weeks, carbon-14 will most likely be present in

(1) the plants only
(2) the animals only
(3) both the plants and animals
(4) neither the plants nor the animals

**Correct Answer: (3)** Over time, the plants will take in the carbon dioxide and convert it into glucose through the process of photosynthesis. The carbon-14 will be present in the glucose. The animals will eat the plants for the glucose. The carbon-14 will now be incorporated into the animals as well. *(Energy Flow in Ecosystems)*

**28.** The rapid destruction of tropical rain forests may be harmful because

(1) removing trees will prevent scientists from studying ecological succession
(2) genetic material that may be useful for future medical discoveries will be lost
(3) energy cycling in the environment will stop
(4) the removal of trees will limit the construction of factories that will pollute the environment

**Correct Answer: (2)** It is believed that the rain forest has the potential to reveal many substances found in the plants that exist there that would be useful in making medicines to fight disease. *(Biodiversity)*

**29.** A food web is represented in the diagram below.

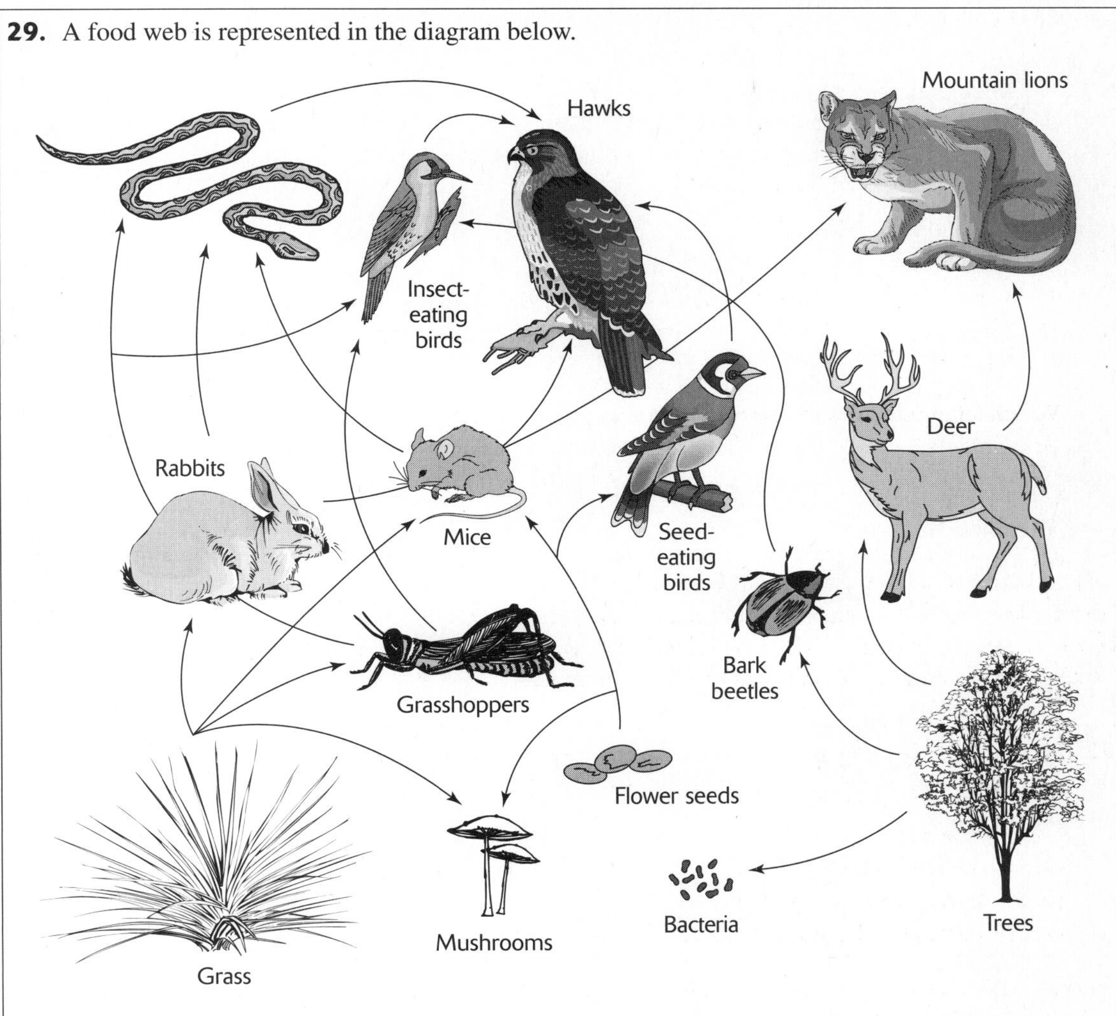


Which organisms are correctly paired with their roles in this food web?

(1) mountain lions, bark beetles — producers
hawks, mice — heterotrophs

(2) snakes, grasshoppers — consumers
mushrooms, rabbits — autotrophs

(3) all birds, deer — consumers
grasses, trees — producers

(4) seeds, bacteria — decomposers
mice, grasses — heterotrophs

**Correct Answer: (3)** Producers are autotrophs—organisms (usually plants) that can make their own food in the form of organic nutrients. Consumers are heterotrophs—organisms that are not able to make their own food and must get food from their environment. Consumers may eat producers as well as other consumers to obtain nutrients. *(Energy Flow in Ecosystems)*

**30.** A particular species of unicellular organism inhabits the intestines of termites, where the unicellular organisms are protected from predators. Wood that is ingested by the termites is digested by the unicellular organisms, forming food for the termites. The relationship between these two species can be described as

**(1)** harmful to both species
**(2)** parasite/host
**(3)** beneficial to both species
**(4)** predator/prey

**Correct Answer: (3)** The relationship between the species of unicellular organism and the termites they inhabit is one of mutualism, where both organisms benefit. The unicellular organism is protected from predators, while the termite is nourished by the products of digestion of the wood by the unicellular organism. *(Organisms in Their Environment)*

**31.** A population of chipmunks migrated to an environment where they had little competition. Their population quickly increased but eventually stabilized as shown in the graph. Which statement best explains why the population stabilized?

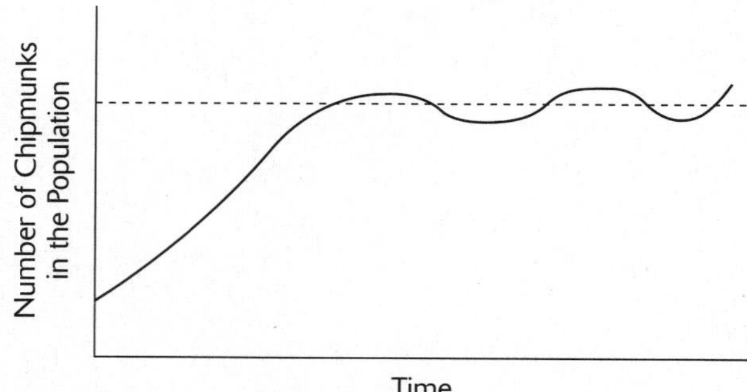


**(1)** Interbreeding between members of the population increased the mutation rate.
**(2)** The population size became limited due to factors such as availability of food.
**(3)** An increase in the chipmunk population caused an increase in the producer population.
**(4)** A predator species came to the area and occupied the same niche as the chipmunks.

**Correct Answer: (2)** The population of chipmunks increased because there was very little competition for resources in the environment, such as water, food, shelter, and space. Resources that control the size of a population are called *limiting factors*. The population of chipmunks continued to grow until the environment reached its carrying capacity and could not support more individuals in the population. *(Organisms in Their Environment)*

**32.** Cutting down a rain forest and planting agricultural crops, such as coffee plants, would most likely result in

(1) a decrease in biodiversity
(2) an increase in the amount of energy recycled
(3) a decrease in erosion
(4) an increase in the amount of photosynthesis

**Correct Answer: (1)** Within the rain forest are thousands of different species of plants and animals, perhaps some that have not even been discovered yet. Cutting down the rain forest and replacing it with one type of plant would definitely count as *decreasing* biodiversity. *(Biodiversity)*

**33.** An energy pyramid is represented below.

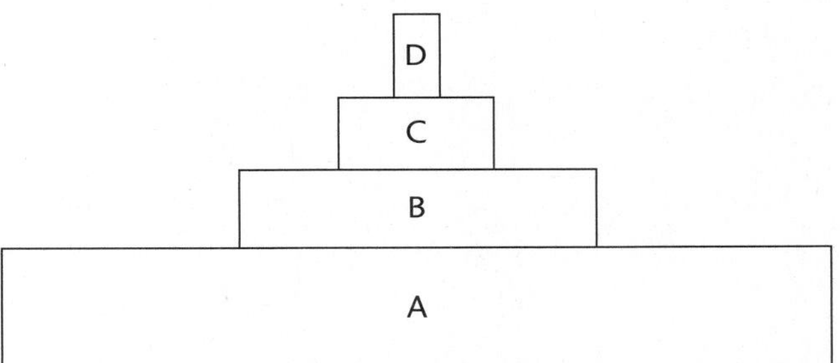


How much energy would be available to the organisms in Level C?

(1) all of the energy in Level A, plus the energy in Level B
(2) all of the energy in Level A, minus the energy in Level B
(3) a percentage of the energy contained in Level B
(4) a percentage of the energy synthesized in Level B and Level D

**Correct Answer: (3)** In an energy pyramid, 90 percent of the energy in a level is used for life processes or lost as heat during the lives of organisms. Organisms also die, and the energy that they have stored is then not available to the next level. Energy that drives the entire pyramid comes from the sun and cannot be synthesized at any level. *(Energy Flow in Ecosystems)*

**34.** Lichens and mosses are the first organisms to grow in an area. Over time, grasses and shrubs will grow where these organisms have been. The grasses and shrubs are able to grow in the area because the lichens and mosses

(1) synthesize food needed by producers in the area
(2) are at the beginning of every food chain in a community
(3) make the environment suitable for complex plants
(4) provide the enzymes needed for plant growth

**Correct Answer: (3)** The first organisms to grow in an ecosystem are called *pioneer organisms.* The lichens and mosses break down the rocks and soil in the area releasing minerals and enriching the soil so that other plants will grow in the area. *(The Structure of Ecosystems)*

**35.** The *negative* effect humans have on the stability of the environment is most directly linked to an increase in

(1) recycling activities by humans
(2) supply of finite resources
(3) predation and disease
(4) human population size

**Correct Answer: (4)** The key word in this question is *increase.* Human beings and all the things they do have the biggest negative impact on the stability of the environment. The more humans there are, the greater the impact.

It is great that humans recycle materials—choice (1)—but recycling is still not enough to counter the negative effects of our existence. If the supply of finite resources increased—choice (2)—then that would not be a negative impact, it would be a positive impact. *(The Structure of Ecosystems)*

**36.** The diagram below represents some energy transfers in an ecosystem.

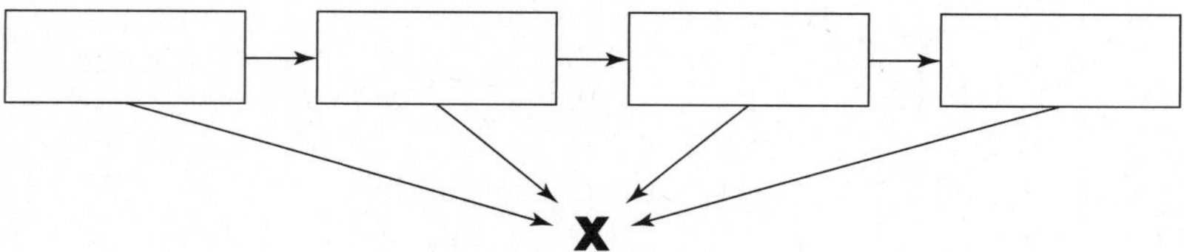


Which type of organism is most likely represented by letter X?

(1) decomposer
(2) autotroph
(3) producer
(4) herbivore

**Correct Answer: (1)** The organisms that acquire energy from all other organisms are decomposers because they are involved in the breakdown of dead organisms of all types. Autotrophs, also known as producers, utilize the sun and inorganic compounds to obtain energy. Herbivores consume plants (autotrophs) to obtain energy. *(Energy Flow in Ecosystems)*

**37.** Which statement describes all stable ecosystems?

(1) Herbivores provide energy for the autotrophs.
(2) The populations of predators are dependent on the populations of their prey.
(3) The number of autotrophs equals the number of heterotrophs.
(4) Consumers synthesize ATP from light energy.

**Correct Answer: (2)** The number of predators fluctuates with the number of prey: The fewer prey to feed on, the fewer predators that can survive.

Autotrophs provide energy for herbivores, not the other way around—choice (1). ***Remember:*** Autotrophs are producers and herbivores are consumers. The number of autotrophs must be greater than the number of heterotrophs—choice (3). If you recall an energy pyramid, the autotrophs are the largest layer on the bottom, and they must provide enough energy for the heterotrophs above it. It is true that consumers synthesize ATP, but they don't do it from light energy—choice (4). The only organisms that can synthesize ATP from light energy are plants and they accomplish this by photosynthesis. *(The Structure of Ecosystems)*

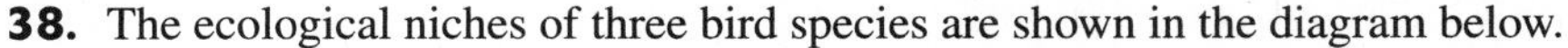

**38.** The ecological niches of three bird species are shown in the diagram below.

Cape May warblers feed in the upper area of the tree.
Bay-breasted warblers feed in the middle of the tree.
Yellow-rumped warblers feed in the lower part of the tree.

What is the advantage of each bird species having a different niche?

**(1)** As the birds feed higher in the tree, available energy increases.
**(2)** More abiotic resources are available for each bird.
**(3)** Predators are less likely to feed on birds in a variety of locations.
**(4)** There is less competition for food.

**Correct Answer: (4)** A *niche* is a role or a job that an organism does. In this case, the niche of each bird is to feed in a specific area of the tree. By doing so, the birds avoid competing with each other for food. The height of the tree where the birds feed—choice (1)—has nothing to do with the amount of available energy. The amount of abiotic resources—choice (2)—are the same for all species of birds. (Abiotic factors are light, air, water, and soil.) *(The Structure of Ecosystems)*

**39.** If humans remove carnivorous predators such as wolves and coyotes from an ecosystem, what will probably be the first observable result?

**(1)** The natural prey will die off.
**(2)** Certain plant populations will increase.
**(3)** Certain herbivores will exceed carrying capacity.
**(4)** The decomposers will fill the predator niche.

**Correct Answer: (3)** If carnivorous predators such as the wolf and coyote are removed from an ecosystem, the first observable result would be the increase in population of their prey—in this case, certain herbivores such as rabbits and deer. Carnivorous predators are animals that eat other animals they hunt and kill, while herbivores are animals that only eat plants. The population of herbivores would initially increase beyond the capacity of the environment to sustain them because other limiting factors (such as a decrease in the amount of food available, the introduction of another type of predator, or an increase in the number of other existing predators) would not have immediate effects. *(Organisms in Their Environment)*

**40.** Which diagram best illustrates the relationship between humans (H) and ecosystems (E)?

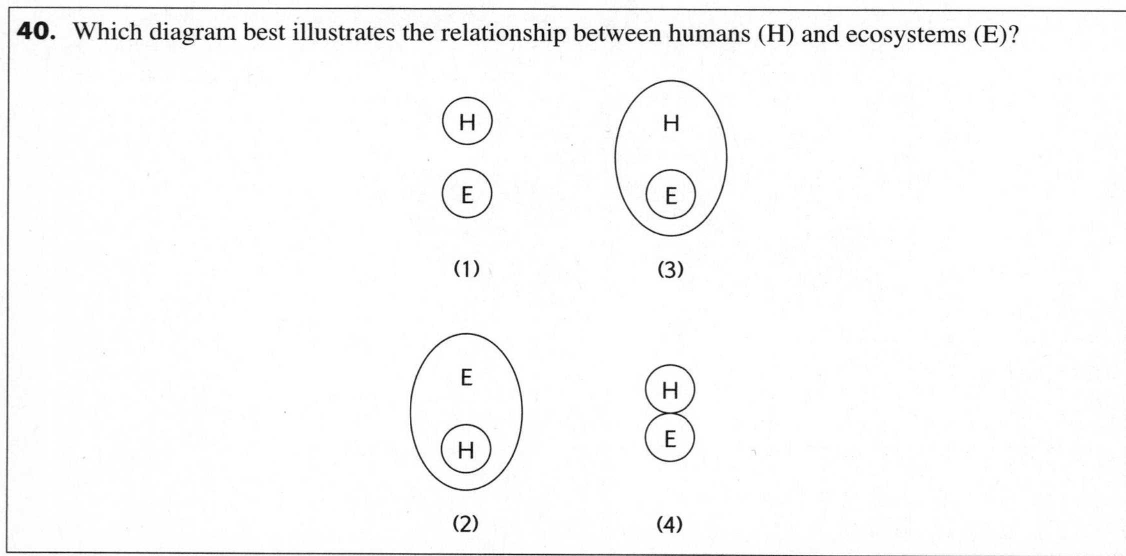


**Correct Answer: (2)** By definition, an ecosystem is the interaction between the biotic (living) and abiotic (nonliving) factors in the environment. Choice (2) best represents this relationship. It shows human beings in the ecosystem. The other choices do not represent this. *(The Structure of Ecosystems)*

**41.** The graph below shows the number of birds in a population.

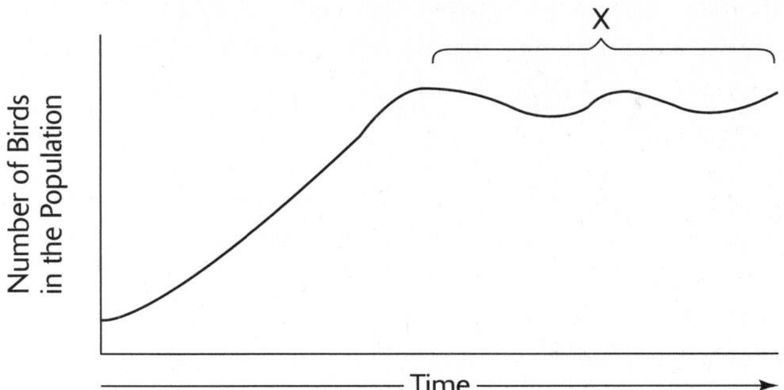


Which statement best explains section X of the graph?

(1) Interbreeding between members of this population increased the mutation rate.
(2) An increase in the bird population caused an increase in the producer population.
(3) The population reached a state of dynamic equilibrium due to limiting factors.
(4) Another species came to the area and provided food for the birds.

**Correct Answer: (3)** The key to getting this question right is knowing the vocabulary. Dynamic equilibrium means that even though things are changing (dynamic), they are staying the same (maintaining equilibrium). That's why the X region is a wavy line: It's changing but basically staying the same. The other term, *limiting factors,* refers to those things in the environment that limit the population from expanding more than the environment can support it. These factors would be food, water, mates, and shelter. *(The Structure of Ecosystems)*

**42.** Four environmental factors are listed below.

A. energy
B. water
C. oxygen
D. minerals

Which factors limit environmental carrying capacity in a land ecosystem?

(1) A only
(2) B, C, and D only
(3) A, C, and D only
(4) A, B, C, and D

**Correct Answer: (4)** Carrying capacity is the greatest number of individuals of a population that a specific environment can support. All organisms need energy, water, oxygen, and minerals to survive and their carrying capacity would depend on these factors. *(Organisms in Their Environment)*

**43.** The removal of nearly all the predators from an ecosystem would most likely result in

(1) an increase in the number of carnivore species
(2) a decrease in new predators migrating into the ecosystem
(3) a decrease in the size of decomposers
(4) an increase in the number of herbivores

**Correct Answer: (4)** If all predators (mountain lions and wolves, for example) are removed from an ecosystem, the herbivore (deer) population would increase drastically because they are not being killed by the predators. This increase, however, is temporary because the herbivore population would eventually increase to the point at which they have exceeded their carrying capacity and they would begin to die from starvation. *(Organisms in Their Environment)*

**44.** Stage D in the diagram below is located on land that was once a bare field.

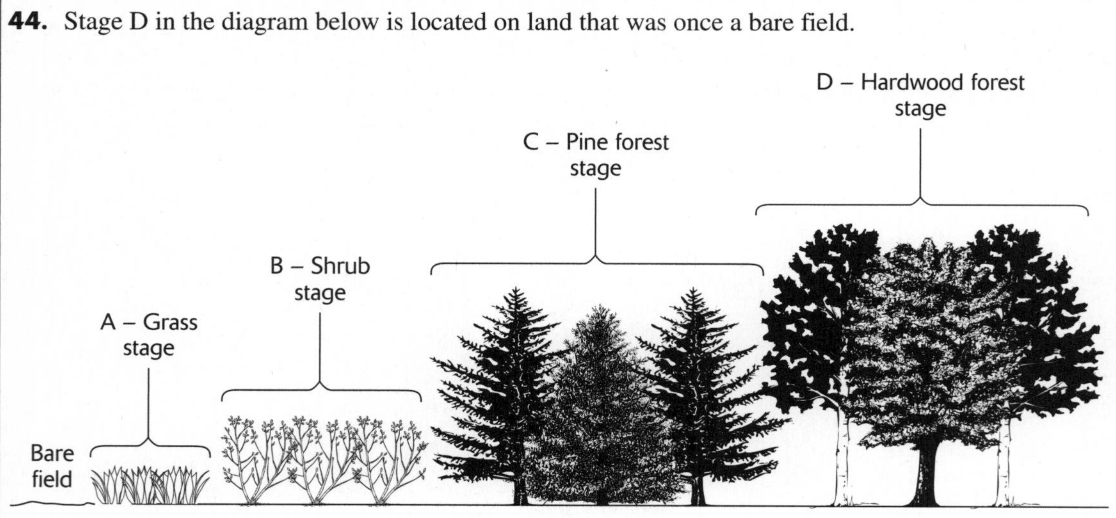


The sequence of stages leading from bare field to Stage D best illustrates the process known as

(1) replication
(2) recycling
(3) feedback
(4) succession

**Correct Answer: (4)** Ecological succession is the process by which a community is gradually replaced by another community until a stable, or climax, community is reached. In land environments, plants determine the type of community because they are the producers. In the above example, a bare field was the initial community. Left undisturbed by humans, organisms in that community would have caused the environment to change, which would make the environment less suitable for those organisms and more suitable for other organisms. The original organisms are slowly replaced by other organisms, and, over time, a new community would replace the previous one until the hardwood forest stage was reached. *(The Structure of Ecosystems)*

**45.** Which statement best describes what happens to energy and molecules in a stable ecosystem?

(1) Both energy and molecules are recycled in an ecosystem.
(2) Neither energy nor molecules is recycled in an ecosystem.
(3) Energy is recycled and molecules are continuously added to the ecosystem.
(4) Energy is continuously added to the ecosystem and molecules are recycled.

**Correct Answer: (4)** Energy from the sun is used by autotrophs in the process of photosynthesis to make organic nutrients. Autotrophs are consumed by animals, which use the chemical energy stored in the organic nutrients for their own metabolic processes. When autotrophs and their consumers die, decomposers cause decay by breaking down complex molecules of those organisms into simple ones, returning those molecules to the environment or absorbing them. In this way, molecules are returned to the environment to be used again by autotrophs. *(Energy Flow in Ecosystems)*

**46.** The graph below shows the populations of two species of ants. Ants of Species 2 have a thicker outer covering than the ants of Species 1. The outer covering of an insect helps prevent excessive evaporation of water.

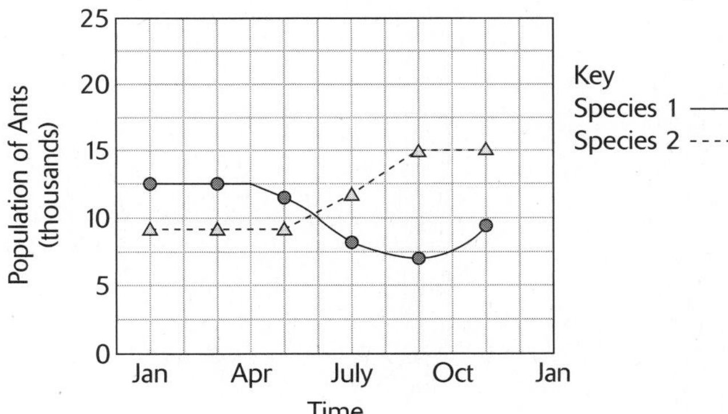


Which statement would best explain the population changes shown in the graph?

(1) The food sources for Species 1 increased while the food sources for Species 2 decreased from January through November.
(2) Disease killed off Species 1 beginning in May.
(3) The weather was hotter and dryer than normal from April through September.
(4) Mutations occurred from April through September in both species, resulting in both species becoming better adapted to the environment.

**Correct Answer: (3)** According to the graph, from April through September, the population of Species 2 increased and the population of Species 1 decreased. A logical explanation is that the thicker outer covering of Species 2 would be advantageous if the area experienced higher temperatures and drier conditions than normal. Species 2 would be able to retain more moisture and have an advantage over Species 1. *(Organisms in Their Environment)*

**47.** Which information concerning a desert is provided by the quotation below?

"The desert is arid, with less than 25 cm of rain per year. The plants are spaced far apart, or are grouped around water sources. Most of the animals are active at night."

**(1)** daily temperature range and types of autotrophs
**(2)** time of rainy season and type of food used by heterotrophs
**(3)** identity of a limiting factor and behavior of heterotrophs
**(4)** type of nutrition in animals and distribution

**Correct Answer: (3)** A limiting factor is something that, in this case, will limit the number of organisms that can survive in an ecosystem. The limiting factor here is the amount of rainfall: "less than 25 cm of rain per year." Choice (3) also states that the animals are active at night; this is their behavior and they are heterotrophs.

Even though the quote is about the desert and you know that deserts are hot, there is nothing in the quote about the temperature range so you can exclude choice (1). The quote states neither when the rainy season occurs nor what the heterotrophs eat—choice (2). Choice (4) is a possibility because it talks about where the plants are located, their distribution, but it does not really say anything about what the animals eat, their type of nutrition. *(The Structure of Ecosystems)*

**48.** Which statement concerning ecosystems is correct?

**(1)** Stable ecosystems that are changed by natural disaster will slowly recover and may again become stable if left alone for a long period of time.
**(2)** Competition does not influence the number of organisms that live in ecosystems.
**(3)** Climatic change is the principal cause of habitat destruction in ecosystems in the last 50 years.
**(4)** Stable ecosystems, once changed by natural disaster, will never recover and become stable again, even if left alone for a long period of time.

**Correct Answer: (1)** After an ecosystem experiences some kind of disaster, ecological succession will take place. In ecological succession, one community is slowly replaced by another until a stable climax community is reached. That community will remain stable until the next catastrophic event. *(The Structure of Ecosystems)*

**49.** The diagram below represents a food web.

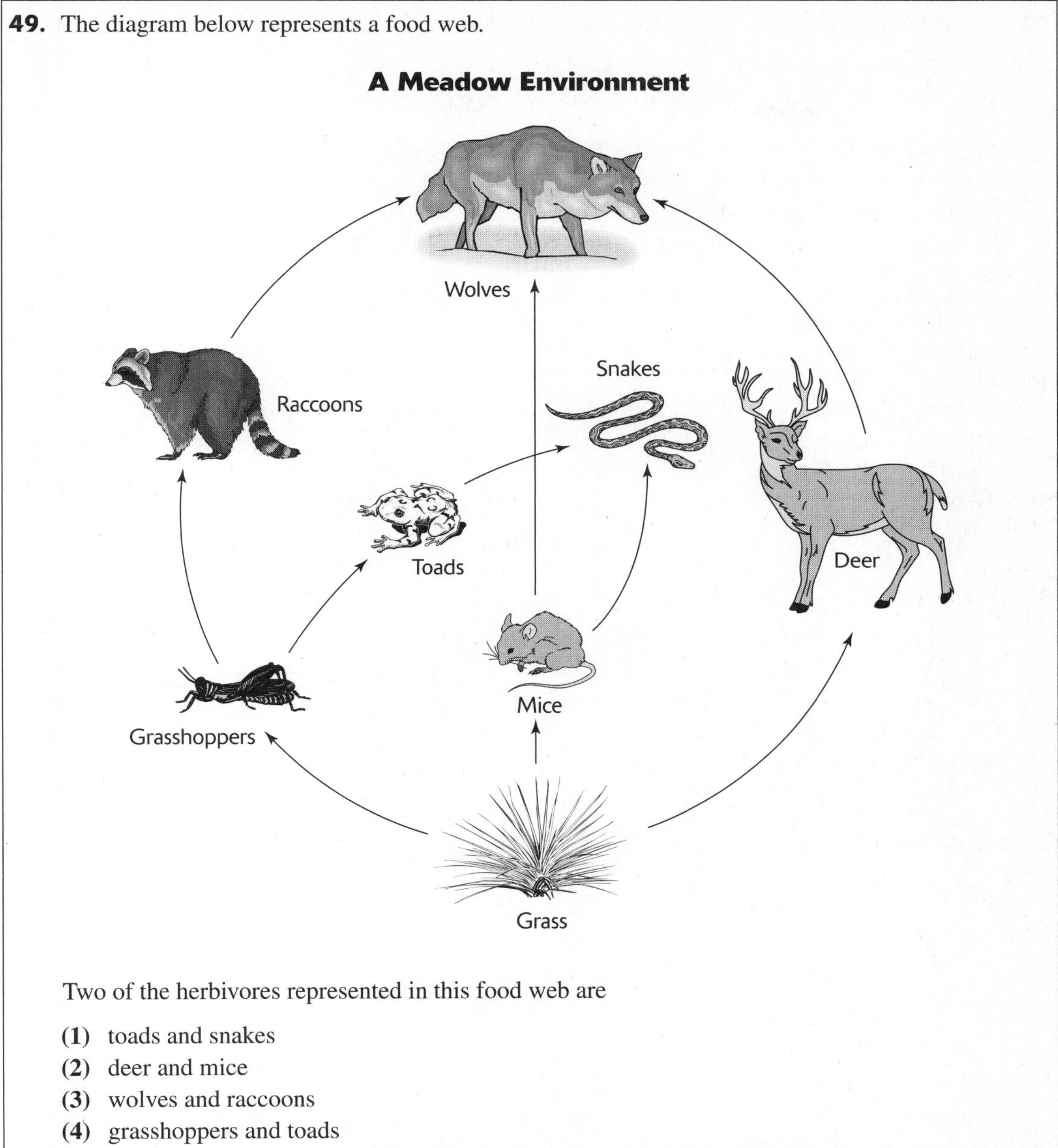


Two of the herbivores represented in this food web are

**(1)** toads and snakes
**(2)** deer and mice
**(3)** wolves and raccoons
**(4)** grasshoppers and toads

**Correct Answer: (2)** When interpreting a food web, it's important to remember that the arrow points to the organism that is *receiving* energy. Both the deer and the mice have arrows that point from the grass (the producer). Deer and mice eat grass and are, therefore, herbivores. *(Organisms in Their Environment)*

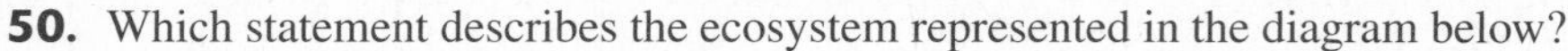

**50.** Which statement describes the ecosystem represented in the diagram below?

(1) This ecosystem would be the first stage in ecological succession.
(2) This ecosystem would most likely lack decomposers.
(3) All of the organisms in this ecosystem are producers.
(4) All of the organisms in this ecosystem depend on the activities of biological catalysts.

**Correct Answer: (4)** In this ecosystem, there are plants and animals, producers and consumers, autotrophs and heterotrophs. Even though they are not seen, there are also decomposers, bacteria, and fungi. All of them, as all living things, depend on the activities of biological catalysts. Catalysts are enzymes, protein molecules that speed up chemical reactions. Everything organisms do depends on chemical reactions, and catalysts make those reactions go as fast as they can, because if they didn't, life processes such as respiration, excretion, and digestion would take too long to occur and the organisms would not be able to stay alive.

This ecosystem is not in the first stage of ecological succession, as in choice (1); the first stage of ecological succession is small plants like lichens and moss that establish themselves in the area and prepare the soil for larger plants. All ecosystems need and have decomposers, bacteria, and fungi that recycle nutrients back into the ecosystem—choice (2). Both producers and consumers are in this ecosystem—choice (3). *(The Structure of Ecosystems)*

**51.** A scientist studied iguanas inhabiting a chain of small ocean islands. He discovered two species that live in different habitats and display different behaviors. His observations are listed in the table below.

**Observations of Two Species of Iguanas**

| *Species A* | *Species B* |
|---|---|
| spends most of its time in the ocean | spends most of its time on land |
| is rarely found more than 10 meters from shore | is found many meters inland from shore |
| eats algae | eats cactus and other land plants |

Which statement best describes these two species of iguanas?

**(1)** Both species evolved through the process of ecological succession.
**(2)** Each species occupies a different niche.
**(3)** The two species can interbreed.
**(4)** Species A is a scavenger and Species B is a carnivore.

**Correct Answer: (2)** These two species of iguanas live on different parts of the island: Species A is found mostly in or near the ocean, and Species B is found mostly on land and far from the shore. Each eats different types of food. This describes two species that occupy different niches, or unique roles, in the ecosystem. *(Organisms in Their Environment)*

Base your answers to questions 52 and 53 on the information and graph below and on your knowledge of biology.

A population of paramecia (single-celled aquatic organisms) was grown in a 200mL beaker of water containing some smaller single-celled organisms. Population growth of the organisms for 28 hours is shown in the graph below.

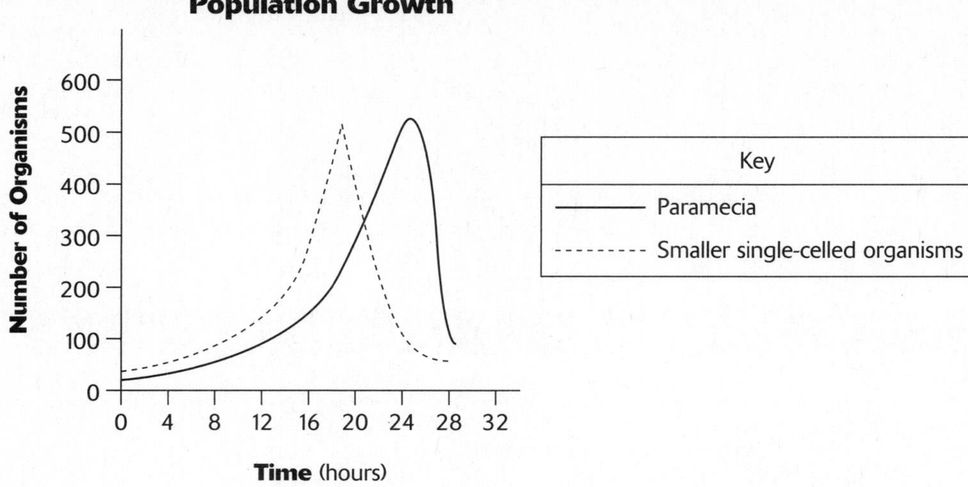


**52.** Which factor most likely accounts for the change in the paramecium population from 8 to 20 hours?

**(1)** an increase in the nitrogen content of water
**(2)** an increase in wastes produced
**(3)** an increase in available food
**(4)** an increase in water Ph

**Correct Answer: (3)** The paramecium population (solid line) increased during hours 8 to 20. Such an increase would be due to some factor in the environment that would have a positive impact on the population, such as availablity of food. A pH change, an increase in waste, and an increase in nitrogen (found in waste) would all cause a decrease in the size of the population. *(Organisms in Their Environment)*

**53.** One likely explanation for the change in the paramecium population from 26 hours to 28 hours is that the

**(1)** carrying capacity of the beaker was exceeded
**(2)** rate of reproduction increased
**(3)** time allowed for growth was not sufficient
**(4)** oxygen level was too high

**Correct Answer: (1)** The paramecium population (solid line) decreased during the hours 26 to 28. Such a decrease would be due to some factor in the environment that would have a negative impact on the population, such as lack of food. If the carrying capacity of the environment (beaker) was exceeded, meaning that the number of organisms was above what the environment could support, paramecia would begin to starve because of lack of food. This would cause the population to decrease as more and more organisms died due to lack of food. *(Organisms in Their Environment)*

**54.** A food web is shown below.

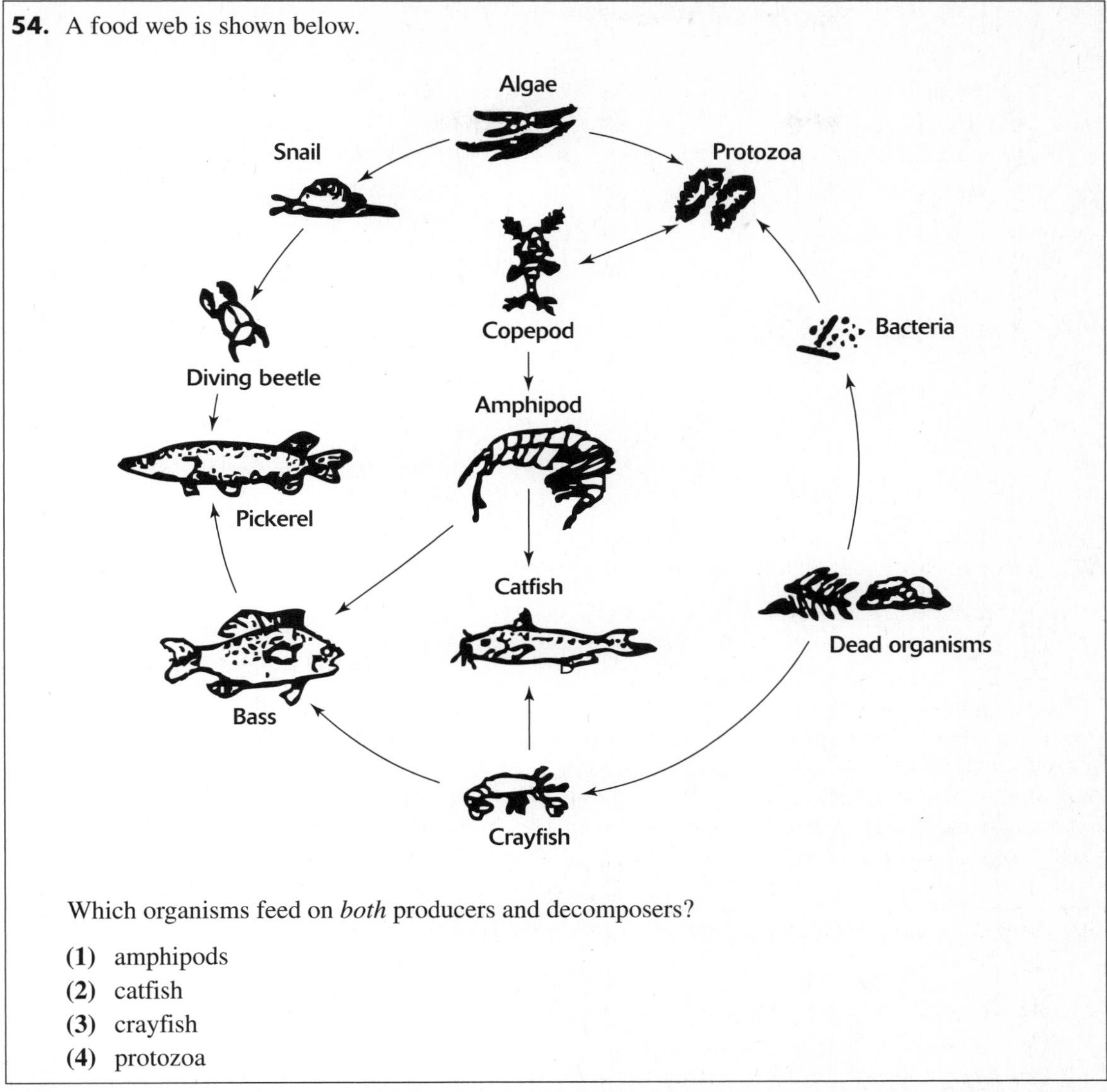


Which organisms feed on *both* producers and decomposers?

**(1)** amphipods
**(2)** catfish
**(3)** crayfish
**(4)** protozoa

**Correct Answer: (4)** This question becomes an easy one because the only decomposers shown are the bacteria. The direction of the arrows points away from what is eaten to what eats it: Bacteria are eaten by protozoa. The algae are the producers: They are autotrophs and carry out photosynthesis. Protozoa eat the algae. None of the other choices fulfills the same requirements. *(The Structure of Ecosystems)*

Base your answers to questions 55 through 57 on the passage below, which describes an ecosystem in New York State and on your knowledge of biology.

The Pine Bush ecosystem near Albany, New York, is one of the last known habitats of the nearly extinct Karner Blue butterfly. The butterfly's larvae feed on the wild green plant lupine. The larvae are, in turn, consumed by predatory wasps. The four groups below represent other organisms living in this ecosystem.

| Group A | Group B | Group C | Group D |
|---|---|---|---|
| algae<br>mosses<br>ferns<br>pine trees<br>oak trees | rabbits<br>tent caterpillars<br>moths | hawks<br>moles<br>hognosed snakes<br>toads | soil bacteria<br>molds<br>mushrooms |

**55.** The Karner Blue larvae belong in which group?

(1) A
(2) B
(3) C
(4) D

**Correct Answer: (2)** The groups of organisms are partitioned by their role in the ecosystem. Group A includes producers (organisms that make their own food); Group B includes primary consumers (organisms that eat producers); Group C includes secondary consumers (organisms that eat primary consumers); and Group D includes decomposers (organisms that break down all dead organisms). Because Karner Blue larvae eat the plant lupine, they are primary consumers. *(Energy Flow in Ecosystems)*

**56.** Which food chain best represents information in the passage?

(1) lupine → Karner Blue larvae → wasps
(2) wasps → Karner Blue larvae → lupine
(3) Karner Blue larvae → lupine → wasps
(4) lupine → wasps → Karner Blue larvae

**Correct Answer: (1)** Lupine is the food source for Karner Blue larvae. Karner Blue larvae are eaten by wasps. *(Energy Flow in Ecosystems)*

**57.** Which group contains decomposers?

(1) A
(2) B
(3) C
(4) D

**Correct Answer: (4)** Decomposers are organisms that break down all dead organisms. Soil bacteria, molds, and mushrooms are all decomposers and included in Group D. *(Energy Flow in Ecosystems)*

**58.** Oak trees in the northeastern United States have survived for hundreds of years, in spite of attacks by native insects. Recently, the gypsy moth, which has a caterpillar state that eats leaves, was imported from Europe. The gypsy moth now has become quite common in New England ecosystems. As a result, many oak trees are being damaged more seriously than ever before.

State *one* biological reason that this imported insect is a more serious problem for the trees than other insects that have been present in the area for hundreds of years.

**Correct Answer:** When nonnative organisms are brought into an ecosystem, such as the gypsy moth from Europe, usually there are no natural enemies that would prey on the organisms. With nothing to prey on the gypsy moths, their numbers will increase dramatically, which can cause significant damage. This is your best answer. *(Organisms in Their Environment)*

**59.** Certain insects are kept under control by sterilizing the males with X-rays so that sperm production stops. Explain how this technique reduces the survival of this insect species.

**Correct Answer:** Releasing sterile male insects into the wild is a form of biological control. It is not harmful to the environment, because it does not rely on chemical pesticides that have the potential to do more harm than good. Your answer should be: "When sterile male insects mate with female insects, no offspring are produced, because the males cannot produce sperm. Therefore, the insect population is reduced." *(Organisms in Their Environment)*

Base your answers to questions 60 through 62 on the graphs below, which show changes in the number of aspen trees and the beaver population in an area over a 50-year period.

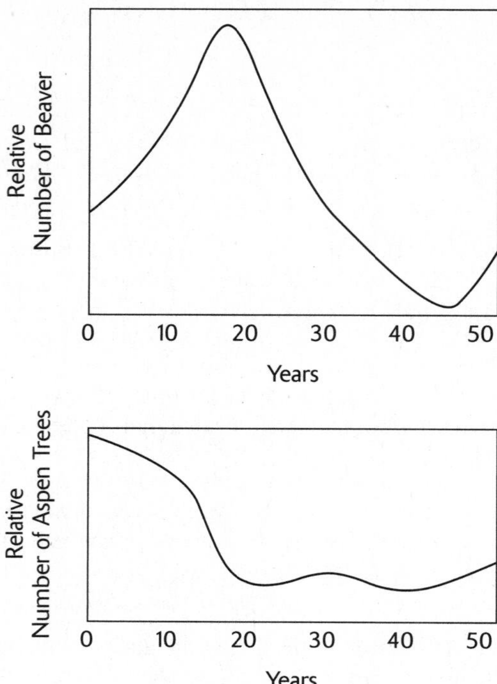


**60.** State the relationship that exists between the number of aspen trees and the beaver populations in this region during the first 15 years.

**Correct Answer:** Looking at the graphs you can see that, during the first 15 years, the number of beavers increased. During the same 15 years, the number of aspen trees decreased. Your answer should be: "As the number of beavers increased, the number of aspen trees decreased." Be careful that you don't phrase it the other way. *(Organisms in Their Environment)*

**61.** State *one* possible reason for the relationship between the aspen tree and the beaver populations.

**Correct Answer:** The most likely reason for this relationship is that the beavers used the trees for their survival. Your answer should be: "As more beavers were born, they needed more trees for food (or for shelter or to build dams)." *(Organisms in their Environment)*

**62.** Predict how the number of aspen trees would change if a parasite that targets the beaver population were introduced into the area during year 5. Explain your answer.

**Correct Answer:** If the beavers became infected with a parasite (parasites would harm the beavers, possibly making them sick and causing them to die), there would be fewer beavers to use the trees and the tree population would not decrease. Your answer should be: "I predict that the population of aspen trees would increase because the beaver parasite would decrease the beaver population and fewer trees would be destroyed." *(Organisms in Their Environment)*

Base your answer to question 63 on the passage below and on your knowledge of biology.

## Fighting Pollution with Bacteria

You may think that all bacteria are harmful. Think again! Some bacteria are working to clean up the damage humans have caused to the environment. In 1989, the oil tanker *Exxon Valdez* hit ground and a hole was ripped in its hull. Millions of gallons of crude oil spread along the coast of Alaska. In some places, the oil soaked 2 feet deep into the beaches. There seemed to be no way to clean up the spill. Then scientists decided to enlist the help of bacteria that are found naturally on Alaskan beaches. Some of these bacteria break down hydrocarbons (molecules found in oil) into simpler, less harmful substances such as carbon dioxide and water.

The problem was that there were not enough of these bacteria to handle the huge amount of oil. To make the bacteria multiply faster, the scientists sprayed a chemical that acted as a fertilizer along 70 miles of coastline. Within 15 days, the number of bacteria had tripled. The beaches that had been treated with the chemical were much cleaner than those that had not. Without this bacterial activity, Alaska's beaches might still be covered with oil.

This process of using organisms to eliminate toxic materials is called bioremediation. Bioremediation is being used to clean up gasoline that leaks into the soil under gas stations. At factories that process wood pulp, scientists are using microorganisms to break down phenols (a poisonous by-product of the process) into harmless salts. Bacteria also can break down acid drainage that seeps out of abandoned coal mines and explosives, such as TNT. Bacteria are used in sewage treatment plants to clean water. Bacteria also reduce acid rain by removing sulfur from coal before it is burned.

Because Americans produce more than 600 million tons of toxic waste a year, bioremediation may soon become a big business. If scientists can identify microorganisms that attack all the kinds of waste we produce, expensive treatment plants and dangerous toxic dumps might be put out of business.

**63.** The chemical was sprayed along the Alaskan coastline in order to

(1) introduce new bacteria to the beaches
(2) dissolve oil that was spilled on the shore
(3) increase the population of bacteria
(4) wash away oil that had been spilled

**Correct Answer: (3)** According to the passage, the chemical was sprayed to act as fertilizer and increase the population of the bacteria. *(Organisms in Their Environment)*

Base your answers to questions 64 and 65 on the information and table below and on your knowledge of biology.

The variety of organisms known as plankton contributes to the unique nutritional relationships in an ocean ecosystem. Phytoplankton include algae and other floating organisms that perform photosynthesis. Plankton that cannot produce food are known as zooplankton. Some nutritional relationships involving these organisms and several others are shown in the table below.

## Nutritional Relationships in a North Atlantic Ocean Community

| | ***Food Eaten by Animals in Community*** | | | | |
|---|---|---|---|---|---|
| ***Animals in Community*** | ***Codfish*** | ***Phytoplankton*** | ***Small Fish*** | ***Squid*** | ***Zooplankton*** |
| codfish | | | X | | |
| sharks | X | | | X | |
| small fish | | X | | | X |
| squid | X | | X | | |
| zooplankton | | X | | | |

**64.** According to the table, which organism can be classified as both an herbivore and a carnivore?

**Correct Answer:** In order to answer this question, you need to know what carnivores and herbivores are. A carnivore is an organism that eats other animals. An herbivore is an animal that eats plants. Based on the reading, phytoplankton include algae and other organisms that carry on photosynthesis. The reading also states that zooplankton are organisms that cannot produce their own food. In the chart, you can see that only small fish can be considered both carnivores (because they eat zooplankton) and herbivores (because they eat phytoplankton). *(Organisms in Their Environment)*

Base your answers to questions 65 through 67 on the food web and graph below and on your knowledge of biology. The graph represents the interaction of two different populations, A and B, in the food web.

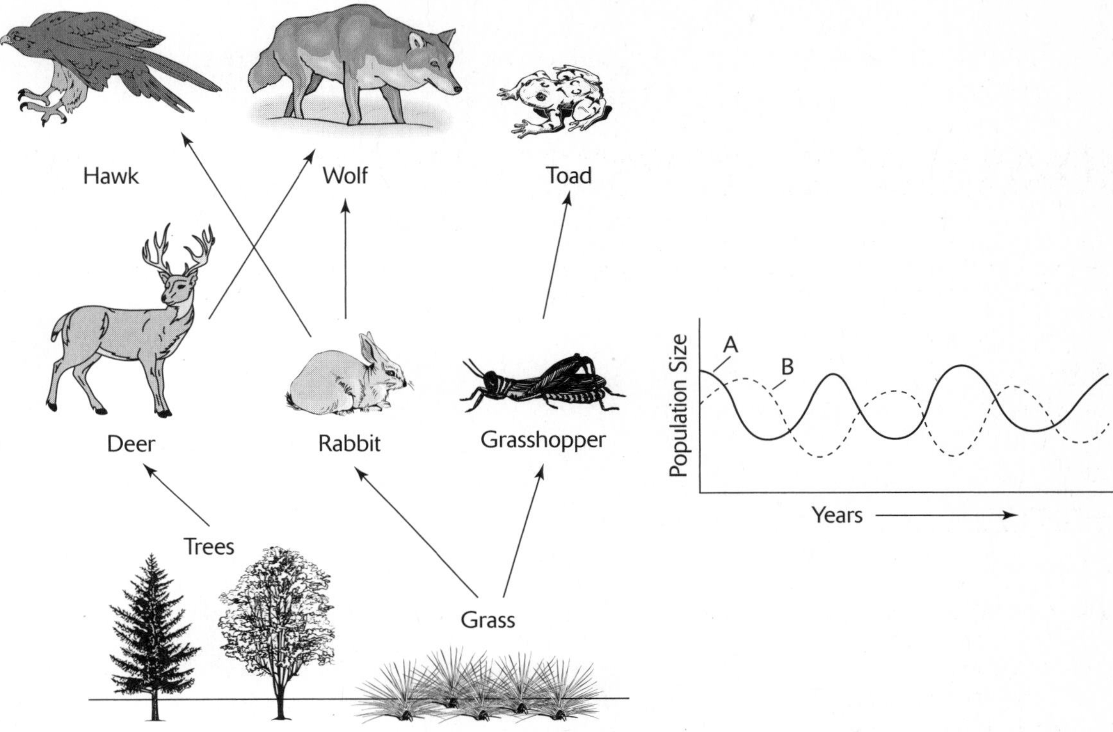


**65.** Population A is made up of living animals. The members of Population B feed on these living animals. The members of Population B are most likely

(1) scavengers
(2) autotrophs
(3) predators
(4) parasites

**Correct Answer: (3)** Predators are animals that hunt and kill other animals to consume them. Scavengers are animals that eat dead animals. *(Energy Flow in Ecosystems)*

**66.** Identify one heterotroph from the food web that could be a member of Population B.

**Correct Answer:** Heterotrophs that could be a member of Population B are the hawk, the wolf, and the toad. All three are predators. The hawk preys on the rabbit. The wolf preys on the rabbit. The frog preys on the cricket. *(Energy Flow in Ecosystems)*

**67.** An energy pyramid is shown below.

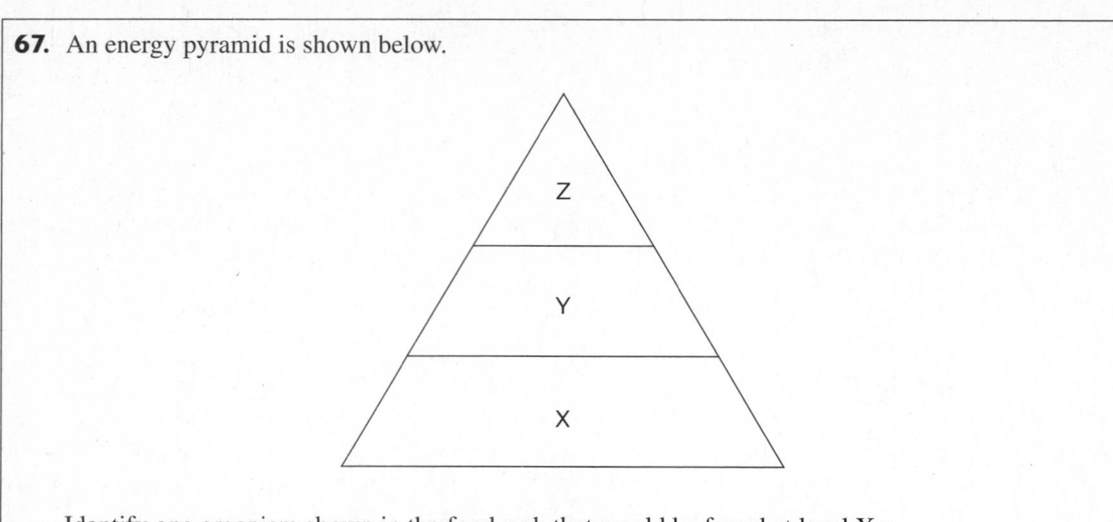


Identify one organism shown in the food web that would be found at level X.

**Correct Answer:** An organism from the food web that would be found at the bottom of the energy pyramid, which shows the amount of energy in an ecosystem would be trees or grass, both producers. The greatest amount of energy is found at the bottom of the pyramid, the least amount at the top. *(Energy Flow in Ecosystems)*

Base your answers to question 68 on the information below and on your knowledge of biology.

Color in peppered moths is controlled by genes. A light-colored variety and a dark-colored variety of a peppered moth species exist in nature. The moths often rest on tree trunks, and several different species of birds are predators of this moth.

Before industrialization in England, the light-colored variety was much more abundant than the dark-colored variety and evidence indicates that many tree trunks at that time were covered with light-colored lichens. Later, industrialization developed and brought pollution which killed the lichens leaving the tree trunks covered with dark-colored soot. The results of a study made in England are shown below.

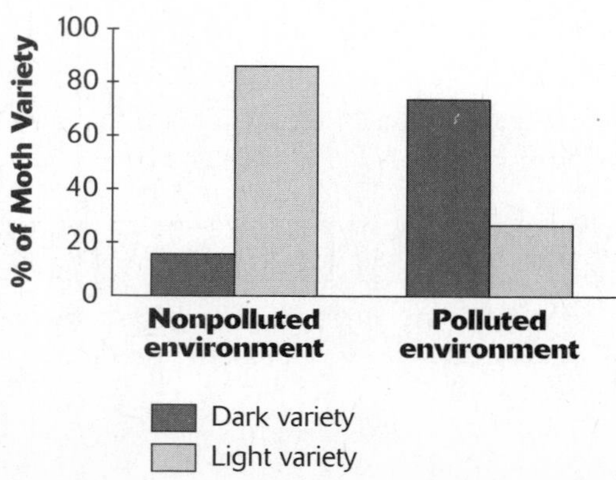

**68.** During the past few decades, air-pollution-control laws in many areas of England greatly limited the soot and other air pollutants coming from the burning of coal. State one way the decrease in soot and other air pollutants will most likely influence the survival of the light-colored variety of peppered moth.

**Correct Answer:** If the lichens are able to repopulate the polluted areas, the light-colored moth population may rise because they can better blend into their environment. The light-colored moth may be able to outcompete the dark colored moths and increase their population. *(Organisms in Their Environment)*

Base your answer to question 69 on the passage below and on your knowledge of biology.

## Great Effects on the Great Lakes due to Global Warming

Trees such as the jack pine, yellow birch, red pine, and white pine may no longer be able to grow in the Great Lakes region because summers are becoming warmer. However, other trees such as black walnut and black cherry may grow in the area, given enough time. The change in weather would favor these new tree species.

The Great Lakes region is the only place in the world where the endangered Kirtland's Warbler breeds. This bird species nests in young jack pine trees (5 to 23 years old). The vegetation must have specific characteristics or the birds will not nest. A specific area of Michigan is one of the few preferred areas. If the jack pines can no longer grow in this area, the consequences for the Kirtland's Warbler could be devastating.

Recent research findings also suggest that algae production in Lake Ontario and several other Great Lakes will be affected as warmer weather leads to warmer lake water. An increase in water temperature reduces the ability of water to hold dissolved oxygen. These changes have implications for the entire Great Lakes food web. Changes in deep-water oxygen levels and other habitat changes may prevent the more sensitive cold-water fish from occupying their preferred niches in a warmer climate.

All other factors being equal, climatic changes may not have a negative effect on every species in the Great Lakes region. This is because the length of the growing season would be increased. Some temperature-sensitive fish could move to cooler, deeper water when the surface water temperatures become too high. The total impact of global warming is difficult to predict.

**69.** Explain how the habitat of the Kirtland's Warbler may be changed as a result of global warming.

**Correct Answer:** The answer to this question lies in the first half of the passage. In the last sentence of the second paragraph, it says, "If the jack pines can no longer grow in this area, the consequences for the Kirkland's Warbler could be devastating." If the trees die, the birds' habitat will be gone. *(Biodiversity)*

**70.** What is the role of bacteria and fungi in an ecosystem?

**Correct Answer:** Bacteria and fungi are decomposers. Decomposers cause decay by breaking down complex molecules of those organisms into simple ones, returning those molecules to the environment or absorbing them. *(Energy Flow in Ecosystems)*

Base your answers to questions 71 through 73 on the passage below and on your knowledge of biology.

Research indicates that many plants prevent the growth of other plants in their habitat by releasing natural herbicides (chemicals that kill plants). These substances are known as allelochemcials and include substances such as quinine, caffeine, and digitalis. Experiments have confirmed that chemicals in the bark and roots of black walnut trees are toxic, and when released into the soil they limit the growth of crop plants such as tomatoes, potatoes, and apples. Allelochemicals can alter growth and enzyme action, injure the outer cover of a seed so the seed dies, or stimulate seed growth at inappropriate times of the year. Studies on allelochemical effects help explain the observation that almost nothing grows under a black walnut tree even though light and moisture levels are adequate for growth.

**71.** The release of allelochemicals into the soil under a black walnut tree will result in

(1) a decrease in biodiversity and a competitive advantage for the tree
(2) an increase in biodiversity and a competitive advantage for the tree
(3) a decrease in biodiversity and a competitive disadvantage for the tree
(4) an increase in biodiversity and a competitive disadvantage for the tree

**Correct Answer: (1)** If the black walnut tree gives off chemicals that stop other plants from growing nearby, then two things will happen: First, there will be fewer plants and, therefore, a decrease in biodiversity. Second, if there are fewer plants, then that becomes a competitive advantage for the black walnut tree. The advantage is that it will not have to compete with other plants for water and light, two factors essential for plant growth. None of the other choices correctly explains the interactions involved. *(Organisms in Their Environment)*

**72.** Explain why stimulation of seed growth by allelochemicals at inappropriate times of the year is considered a *disadvantage?*

**Correct Answer:** You don't need to know exactly what an allelochemical is to answer the question. The passage tells you what it does: It stimulates seeds to grow at the wrong time. Say, for example, the black walnut tree gives off this chemical in the fall and seeds start growing with winter coming. What's going to happen? The seeds won't survive because of the cold weather. Your answer should be: "It is a disadvantage because the seeds will start growing when they won't survive in the environment." *(Organisms in Their Environment)*

**73.** State *one* possible use of allelochemicals in agriculture.

**Correct Answer:** You know from the passage that these chemicals stop the growth of plants. Wouldn't it be great if farmers could use this chemical on plants that farmers don't want? They could spray or apply this chemical as a weedkiller. Because it is a natural chemical and not man-made, it is less likely to harm the environment like chemicals have in the past. Your answer should be: "This chemical could be used as a weedkiller to stop the growth of unwanted plants." *(Organisms in Their Environment)*

Base your answers to questions 74 and 75 on the information below and on your knowledge of biology.

A pond in the Adirondack Mountains of New York State was once a fishing spot visited by many people. It was several acres in size, and fishermen in boats were a common sight. Over time, the pond has become smaller in area and depth. Places where there was once open water are now covered by grasses and shrubs. Around the edges of the pond there are cattails and other wetland plants.

**74.** Identify the ecological process responsible for the changes to this pond.

**Correct Answer:** Ecological succession. Succession refers to changes in the ecosystem. Physical changes in the area lead to changes in the organisms that inhabit the ecosystem. *(The Structure of Ecosystems)*

**75.** Predict what will most likely happen to this pond area over the next hundred years if this process continues.

**Correct Answer:** The pond will grow smaller and may be completely filled in. As the vegetation increases, the size of the pond will decrease. *(The Structure of Ecosystems)*

Base your answers to questions 76 through 78 on the following diagram, which represents the changes in an ecosystem over a period of 100 years, and on your knowledge of biology.

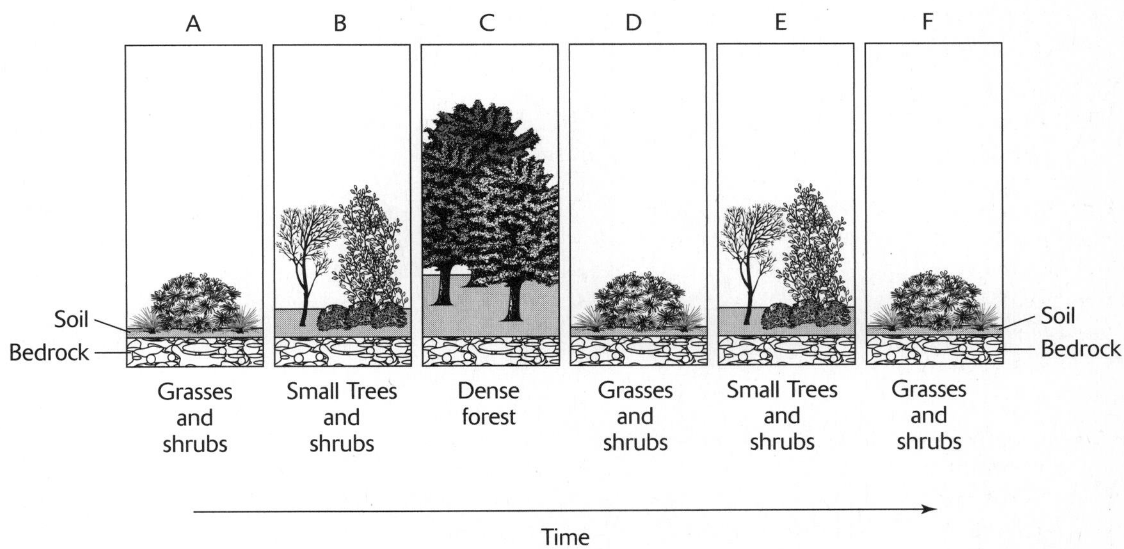


**76.** State one biological explanation for the changes in types of vegetation observed from A through C.

**Correct Answer:** A biological explanation for the changes in types of vegetation from A (grasses and shrubs) to C (dense forest) is ecological succession. Ecological succession is the gradual replacement of species over time as the environment changes. *(The Structure of Ecosystems)*

**77.** Identify one human activity that could be responsible for the change from C to D.

**Correct Answer:** Human activities that could be responsible for the change from C (dense forest) to D (grasses and shrubs) include clear cutting, fire (controlled burning or arson), and farming. *(The Structure of Ecosystems)*

**78.** Predict what would happen to the soil *and* vegetation of this ecosystem after stage F, assuming no natural disaster or human interference.

**Correct Answer:** Assuming no natural disaster or human interference, the soil and vegetation of the ecosystem after stage F (grasses and shrubs) would experience a similar progression as from A to C. The species may be different, but the gradual replacement of plant species that include grasses and shrubs to a mature forest climax community would remain the same. The soil may become nutrient rich as plant species die and their organic and inorganic material is returned to the soil by the action of decomposers. *(The Structure of Ecosystems)*

**79.** Identify one abiotic factor that would directly affect the survival of Organism A, shown in the diagram below.

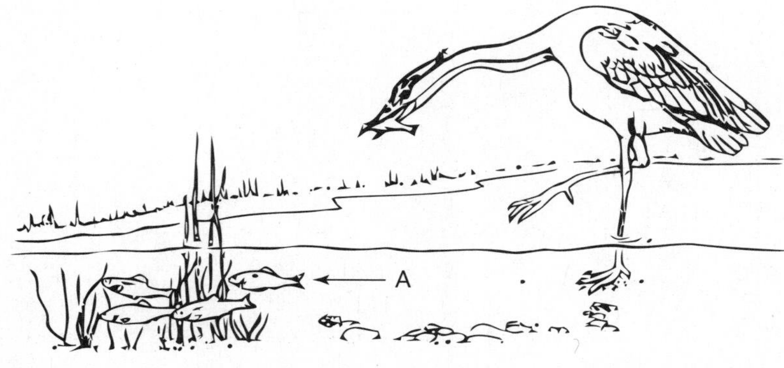


**Correct Answer:** Organism A is a fish. Abiotic factors are the parts of an ecosystem that are nonliving. Abiotic factors that would affect a fish include the following:

- the oxygen content of the water it lives in
- the pH of the water
- the temperature of the water
- the size of the water body it lives in

*(Organisms in Their Environment)*

**80.** Explain why most ecologists would agree with the statement, "A forest ecosystem is more stable than a cornfield."

**Correct Answer:** Ecosystems with greater biodiversity are more stable than those with lower biodiversity. Biodiversity is the number and kinds of species in an area. A forest ecosystem has many more species than a cornfield, which can have only one. *(Biodiversity)*

Base your answer to question 82 on the data table below and on your knowledge of biology. The table contains information about glucose production in a species of plant that lives in the water of a salt marsh.

| ***Temperature (°C)*** | ***Glucose Production (mg/hr)*** |
|---|---|
| 10 | 5 |
| 20 | 10 |
| 30 | 15 |
| 40 | 5 |

**81.** Which level of the energy pyramid below would contain the plant species of this salt marsh?

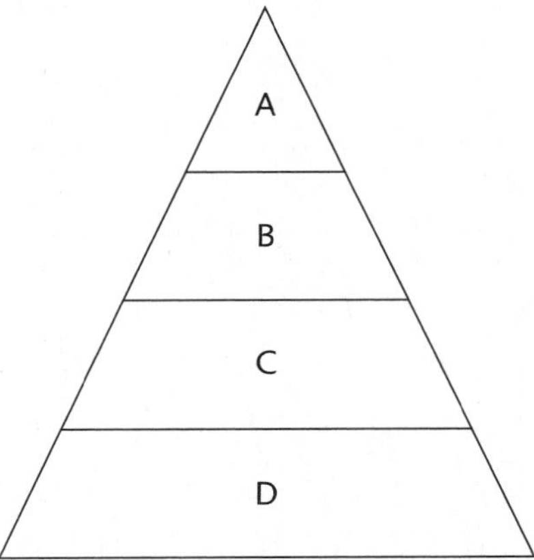


(1) A
(2) B
(3) C
(4) D

**Correct Answer: (4)** Plants always provide the energy for the rest of the organisms in the ecosystem because they're able to directly use energy from the sun to make their own food. All the plants in the ecosystem have more energy than any of the other organisms and always serve as the foundation of an energy pyramid. *(Energy Flow in Ecosystems)*

Base your answers to questions 83 through 86 on the information below and on your knowledge of biology.

A student uses a covered aquarium to study the interactions of biotic and abiotic factors in an ecosystem. The aquarium contains sand, various water plants, algae, small fish, snails, and decomposers. The water contains dissolved oxygen and carbon dioxide, as well as tiny amounts of minerals and salts.

**82.** Explain how oxygen is cycled between organisms in this ecosystem.

**Correct Answer:** Before you answer this question, be sure you know what *biotic* and *abiotic* mean. Biotic factors are those things in an ecosystem that are alive: In this ecosystem, the living things are the water plants, algae, small fish, snails, and decomposers. The *abiotic,* or nonliving, things are everything else: the water, sand, light, and any dissolved gases in the water. You need to remember what processes have oxygen in them. The animals in this ecosystem use oxygen to carry out the process of respiration. The plants or autotrophs in the ecosystem produce oxygen during the process of photosynthesis. Now that you have all the necessary background information, you can answer the question. Your answer should be: "The algae and various water plants take in carbon dioxide, which is given off by the snails and fish and use it to carry on photosynthesis, which produces oxygen. The fish and snails take in the oxygen during respiration and produce carbon dioxide, which is used by the plants." *(The Structure of Ecosystems)*

**83.** Describe *one* specific way the fish population changes the amount of *one* specific abiotic factor (other than oxygen) in this ecosystem.

**Correct Answer:** The question says that you cannot say anything about how oxygen changes in the ecosystem, but you can still mention carbon dioxide. As the fish and snails carry out respiration, what happens to the level of carbon dioxide? It increases. So, your answer could be: "The level of carbon dioxide increases." If you know anything else about the waste products produced by animals, you could say that nitrogen-containing wastes increase (urea, uric acid, and ammonia are such wastes). *(The Structure of Ecosystems)*

**84.** Identify *one* source of food for the decomposers in this ecosystem.

**Correct Answer:** Decomposers are bacteria and fungi. They are responsible for breaking down dead organisms into the molecules making them up—molecules like proteins, carbohydrates, and lipids. This question does not say anything about plants or animals dying, but if it is an ecosystem, those things are going to happen, so it becomes a legitimate answer. Your answer could be: "Dead plants and dead fish and snails." You could also mention the waste products: "Decomposers break down waste products." *(Organisms in Their Environment)*

**85.** Describe *one* specific way the use of this food by the decomposers benefits the other organisms in the aquarium.

**Correct Answer:** The decomposers recycle the nutrients of the ecosystem. *(The Structure of Ecosystems)*

Base your answer to question 87 on the information below.

Zebra mussels have caused several major changes in the ecosystem in the Hudson River. Native to Eurasia, zebra mussels were accidentally imported to the Great Lakes in ships during the late 1980s and first appeared in the Hudson in 1990.

In regions of the Hudson north of West Point, zebra mussels have depleted the levels of dissolved oxygen to the point where many native organisms either die or move to other waters. In addition, large amounts of phytoplankton (small photosynthetic organisms) are consumed by the zebra mussels.

Before the introduction of zebra mussels, one typical food chain in this part of the Hudson was:

phytoplankton → freshwater clams → other consumers

**86.** Describe some long-term changes in the Hudson River ecosystem that could be caused by zebra mussels. In your answer be sure to:

- state one likely change in the population of each of two different species (other than the zebra mussels) found in the Hudson
- identify one gas in this ecosystem and state how a change in its concentration due to the effects of zebra mussels would affect organisms other than the zebra mussels
- state how the death of many of the native organisms could affect the rate of decay and how this would affect the amount of material being recycled
- explain why the size of the zebra mussel population would decrease after an initial increase

**Correct Answer:** Zebra mussel consumption of phytoplankton may cause the phytoplankton population to decrease. The decrease in phytoplankton may cause the population of clams and other consumers that eat phytoplankton to decrease. The decrease in the populations of organisms that eat clams and other primary consumers may cause a decrease in higher-order consumers.

Zebra mussels may cause the death of fish in the Hudson due to low oxygen content.
The increased amount of decaying organisms may cause an increase in the population of decomposers and rate of decay, which would consume dissolved oxygen at an increased rate, rendering the bottom waters anoxic and killing fish and other aquatic species in the Hudson. The amount of material recycled would increase.

After experiencing a population explosion, the zebra mussel population would most likely crash due to lack of food and hostile environmental conditions such as low oxygen content. *(The Structure of Ecosystems)*

**87.** A tropical rain forest in the country of Belize contains over 100 kinds of trees as well as thousands of species of mammals, birds, and insects. Dozens of species living there have not yet been classified and studied. The rain forest could be a commercial source of food as well as a source of medicinal and household products. However, most of this forested area is not accessible because of a lack of roads and therefore, little commercial use has been made of this region. The building of paved highways into and through this rain forest has been proposed.

Discuss some aspects of carrying out this proposal to build paved highways. In your answer be sure to:

- state one possible impact on biodiversity and one reason for this impact
- state one possible reason for an increase in the number of some producers as a result of road building
- identify one type of consumer whose population would most likely increase as a direct result of an increase in a producer population
- state one possible action the road builders could take to minimize human impact on the ecology of this region

**Correct Answer:** Biodiversity, or the variety of species in a particular area, may decrease as a result of building paved highways into Belize. Habitats could be severely disrupted or destroyed. Species could lose their homes, food supplies, or breeding areas. Animals could be killed by vehicles. Animals could also be more easily poached because the roads are providing an easy access and escape route for poachers and others who would exploit the organisms there.

The creation of roads would open up the canopy and let light down to the forest floor, which may benefit producers living there.

A consumer whose population would likely increase as a direct result of an increase in a producer population would be humans, herbivores, or omnivores.

To minimize human impact on the ecology of the region, the road builders could:

- Limit the number of road-building vehicles.
- Limit the width of the road as well as the distance the road goes into the forest.
- Plant species alongside the road to prevent runoff and erosion.
- Create tunnels under the road for wildlife so they may cross the road safely.
- Use vehicles with pollution-control devices.
- Employ noise-control options.
- For every stretch of road built, the builders would have to plant trees in another area in need of them.
- A percentage of the profits could be used to fund the salaries of officers to protect the forest from poachers and exploiters.
- A percentage of the profits could be used to buy and donate other tracts of land for wildlife preservation.
- Use local manpower instead of hiring people who would have to fly or drive great distances to work the road.

*(Biodiversity)*

# Human Impact on the Environment

**Directions:** For each statement or question, choose the *number* of the word or expression that best completes the statement or answers the question. Then check your answer against the one that immediately follows the question. Try not to look at the answer before making your selection.

**1.** Some homeowners mow their lawns during the summer, collect the grass clippings, and dispose of them in a landfill. Instead of taking the clippings to a landfill, a more ecologically sound procedure would be to

(1) leave the clippings to decompose in the lawn to form materials that enrich the soil
(2) spray the clippings in the lawn with imported microbes that use them for food
(3) burn the clippings and add the ashes to the soil
(4) throw the clippings into a stream or river to provide extra food for organisms living there

**Correct Answer: (1)** The ecologically sound procedure would be to leave the clippings to decompose in the lawn. The materials in the grass would be returned to the soil where they could be reused by nearby autotrophs. This would reduce or eliminate the need to fertilize the soil. *(Positive Effects of Humans on the Environment)*

**2.** Which factor is primarily responsible for the destruction of the greatest number of habitats?

(1) human population growth
(2) decreased use of renewable resources
(3) spread of predatory insects
(4) epidemic diseases

**Correct Answer: (1)** The factor with the greatest negative impact on the environment is human population growth. An increase in population means a greater need for natural resources such as energy, food, and space to live. Energy consumption increases pollutants. Food production increases the use of pesticides and herbicides, and space requirements decrease the amount of land that can be preserved. *(Negative Effects of Humans on the Environment)*

**3.** When habitats are destroyed, there are usually fewer niches for animals and plants. This action would most likely *not* lead to a change in the amount of

(1) biodiversity
(2) competition
(3) interaction between species
(4) solar radiation reaching the area

**Correct Answer: (4)** When habitats are destroyed, the *biodiversity* (number of different types of organisms) decreases. Competition for remaining resources increases among the organisms that remain and this is a change in the interaction between species. However, the amount of sunlight (solar radiation) that reaches the habitat would not change. *(Negative Effects of Humans on the Environment)*

**4.** A new automobile manufacturing plant is opening in a certain town. It will have some negative environmental impacts. This is a trade-off that the town officials had to consider carefully before giving final approval. They most likely gave their approval because the negative impacts would be offset by the

(1) release of pollutants into the environment
(2) creation of new employment opportunities
(3) decrease of property values in the area around the plant
(4) increase of automobile traffic in the area around the plant

**Correct Answer: (2)** The negative impacts would have to be offset by something considered to be positive in the community, which would be the creation of new employment opportunities. The other choices are all examples of negative impacts. *(Negative Effects of Humans on the Environment)*

**5.** Which factor is a major cause of global warming?

(1) increased burning of fuels
(2) increased number of green plants
(3) decreased mineral availability
(4) decreased carbon dioxide in the atmosphere

**Correct Answer: (1)** Global warming is the rise in the Earth's temperature as a result of the increase in heat-trapping gases, such as carbon dioxide, in the atmosphere. The burning of fossil fuels such as natural gas and coal releases carbon dioxide into the atmosphere. Carbon dioxide levels in the atmosphere have increased steadily as the burning of fossil fuels has increased. *(Negative Effects of Humans on the Environment)*

**6.** In most states, automobiles must be inspected every year to make sure that the exhaust fumes they emit do not contain high levels of pollutants such as carbon monoxide. This process is a way humans attempt to

(1) control the water cycle
(2) recycle nutrients from one ecosystem to another
(3) control energy flow in natural ecosystems
(4) maintain the quality of the atmosphere

**Correct Answer: (4)** The effort to keep air pollution levels low is an attempt by humans to keep the quality of the atmosphere from declining. *(Positive Effects of Humans on the Environment)*

**7.** Which long-term change could directly cause the other three?

(1) pollution of air and water
(2) increasing human population
(3) scarcity of suitable animal habitats
(4) depletion of resources

**Correct Answer: (2)** Human activity affects every other facet of the environment. Humans pollute the land, air, and water; they use up resources; and they destroy the natural habitats of many organisms. *(Negative Effects of Humans on the Environment)*

**8.** Which human activity will most likely have a *negative* effect on global stability?

(1) decreasing water pollution levels
(2) increasing recycling programs
(3) decreasing habitat destruction
(4) increasing world population growth

**Correct Answer: (4)** The environment is capable of accommodating a limited number of people. If the world population increased infinitely, the Earth would run out of resources. The population level that an environment is able to support is referred to as the *carrying capacity*. As a population reaches its carrying capacity, members of the population must compete for limited resources. *(Negative Effects of Humans on the Environment)*

**9.** Which process helps reduce global warming?

(1) decay
(2) industrialization
(3) photosynthesis
(4) burning

**Correct Answer: (3)** Global warming is caused by greenhouse gases. One such greenhouse gas is carbon dioxide. Photosynthesis removes carbon dioxide from the atmosphere, thereby reducing global warming. *(Negative Effects of Humans on the Environment)*

**10.** The importation of organisms such as the Japanese beetle and gypsy moth to areas where they have no natural enemies best illustrates

(1) the use of abiotic factors to reduce pest species
(2) the selection of species to mate with each other to produce a new variety
(3) attempts by humans to protect extinct species
(4) a human activity that disrupts existing ecosystems

**Correct Answer: (4)** The importation (either on purpose or by accident) of organisms to an area with no natural enemies is an act that can cause a major disruption in native ecosystems. Predators, along with availability of food and space, are some of the limiting factors in an ecosystem. If the population of the imported species was not controlled by predators, the demands on the other limiting factors would increase with the increasing population. Food supply would decrease and space would be limited. *(Negative Effects of Humans on the Environment)*

**11.** Which situation has had the most *negative* effect on the ecosystems of Earth?

(1) use of air pollution controls
(2) use of natural predators to control insect pests
(3) recycling glass, plastic, and metals
(4) increasing human population

**Correct Answer: (4)** The other available choices (use of air pollution controls, use of natural predators to control insect pests, and recycling) are all positive effects on the ecosystems of the Earth. The increasing human population has resulted in an increase in the burning of fossil fuels to heat homes and businesses and to run vehicles; an increase in the destruction of forests to be used for farmland, living space, and building materials; an increase in air, water, and soil pollution from the waste products of factories, vehicle exhaust, farming practices, and landfills; and global warming. *(Negative Effects of Humans on the Environment)*

**12.** Humans have altered ecosystems in many ways. The most positive impact on an ecosystem would result from

(1) planting a single economically valuable crop in a 25-acre area
(2) seeding an area with valuable plants that are from another ecosystem
(3) planting many different plants that are native to the area in a vacant lot
(4) filling in a swamp and planting grass and trees for a community park

**Correct Answer: (3)** The best answer is choice (3), because you would be stopping erosion in the vacant lot and, more important, you would be planting a variety of plants (not just one kind) that are native to the area. This way, you're doing two things: providing biodiversity with the variety of plants and not risking introducing nonnative species that could take over the area and threaten native species. *(Positive Effects of Humans on the Environment)*

**13.** Which human activity would have the *least* negative impact on the quality of the environment?

(1) adding animal wastes to rivers
(2) cutting down tropical rain forests for plywood
(3) using species-specific sex attractants to trap and kill insect pests
(4) releasing chemicals into the groundwater

**Correct Answer: (3)** All these activities would have some impact on the environment. However, only using species-specific sex attractants to trap and kill insect pests has a positive impact. *(Negative Effects of Humans on the Environment)*

**14.** Methods used to reduce sulfur dioxide emissions from smokestacks are an attempt by humans to

(1) lessen the amount of insecticides in the environment
(2) eliminate diversity in wildlife
(3) lessen the environmental impact of acid rain
(4) use nonchemical controls on pest species

**Correct Answer: (3)** Sulfur dioxide is a gas produced when coal and oil that contain sulfur are burned. Sulfur dioxide reacts in the atmosphere to form sulfuric acid. Sulfuric acid is a major part of acid rain, which increases the acidity of ponds, lakes, and streams, causing the death of organisms or other negative health effects. Acid rain also causes erosion of limestone. *(Negative Effects of Humans on the Environment)*

**15.** Deforestation will most directly result in an immediate increase in

(1) atmospheric carbon dioxide
(2) atmospheric ozone
(3) wildlife populations
(4) renewable resources

**Correct Answer: (1)** Deforestation is the process of removing large expanses of trees. Trees take in carbon dioxide in the process of photosynthesis and release oxygen into the air. The removal of trees causes a buildup of carbon dioxide in the atmosphere. *(Negative Effects of Humans on the Environment)*

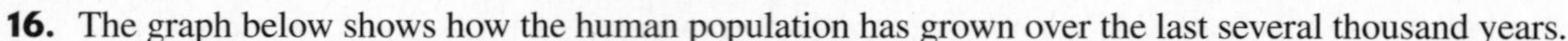

**16.** The graph below shows how the human population has grown over the last several thousand years.

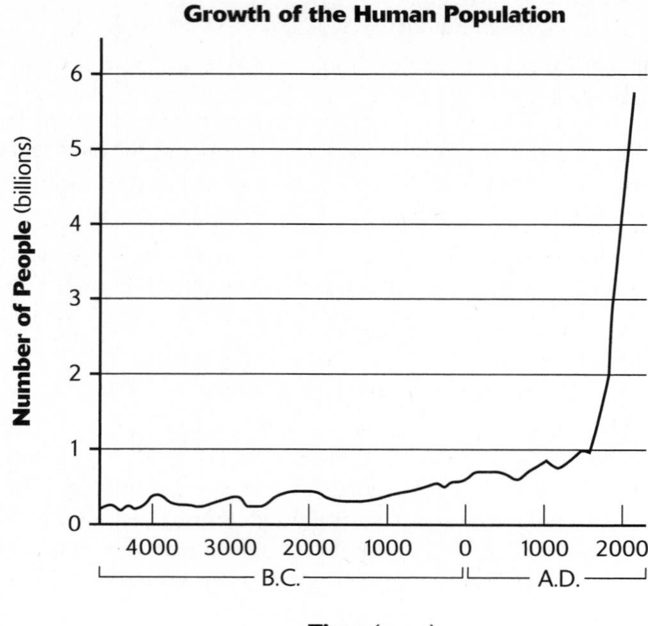


Which statement is a valid inference that can be made if the human population continues to grow at a rate similar to the rate shown between A.D. 1000 and A.D. 2000?

(1) Future ecosystems will be stressed and many animal habitats may be destroyed.
(2) Global warming will decrease as a result of a lower demand for fossil fuels.
(3) One hundred years after all resources are used up, the human population will level off.
(4) All environmental problems can be solved without a reduction in the growth rate of the human population.

**Correct Answer: (1)** If the human population continues to grow at a rate similar to that which we are experiencing now, more habitats will be destroyed to make way for cities and roads, global warming will increase, resources will be in short supply, and the human population will have to respond. This response will need to address cleaning up some environmental problems as well as reducing population growth. Without a reduction in population growth, environmental pollution and destruction of the habitat will continue. *(Negative Effects of Humans on the Environment)*

**17.** Which human activity would be *least* likely to disrupt the stability of an ecosystem?

(1) disposing of wastes in the ocean
(2) using fossil fuels
(3) increasing the human population
(4) recycling bottles and cans

**Correct Answer: (4)** Recycling of containers made from nonrenewable resources to be used again is a method of resource conservation. *(Positive Effects of Humans on the Environment)*

**18.** Compounds containing phosphorus that are dumped into the environment can upset ecosystems because phosphorus acts as a fertilizer. The graph below shows measurements of phosphorus concentrations taken during the month of June at two sites, from 1991 to 1997.

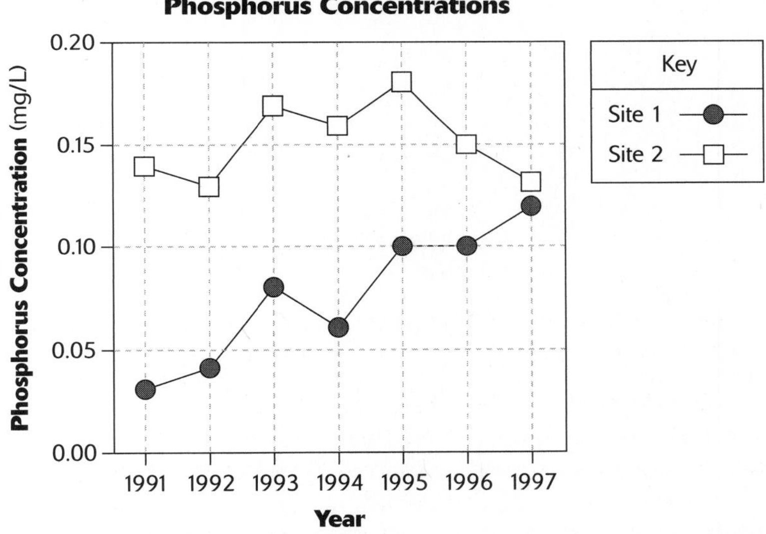


Which statement represents a valid inference based on information in the graph?

(1) There was no decrease in the amount of compounds containing phosphorus dumped at Site 2 during the period from 1991 to 1997.
(2) Pollution controls may have been put into operation at Site 1 in 1995.
(3) There was most likely no vegetation present near Site 2 from 1993 to 1994.
(4) There was a greater variation in phosphorous concentration at Site 1 than there was at Site 2.

**Correct Answer: (2)** The graph shows a steady decrease in phosphorous at Site 2 from 1995 on. Since Site 2 had higher phosphorous levels than Site 1, you may infer that pollution controls were put into operation to address the problem. *(Positive Effects of Humans on the Environment)*

Base your answer to question 19 on the passage below and on your knowledge of biology.

## Better Rice

The production of new types of food crops will help raise the quantity of food grown by farmers. Research papers released by the National Academy of Sciences announced the development of two new superior varieties of rice—one produced by selective breeding and the other by biotechnology.

One variety of rice, called *Nerica* (New Rice for Africa), is already helping farmers in Africa. *Nerica* combines the hardiness and weed resistance of rare African rice varieties with the productivity and faster maturity of common Asian varieties.

Another variety, called Stress-Tolerant Rice, was produced by inserting a pair of bacterial genes into rice plants for the production of trehalose (a sugar). Trehalose helps plants maintain healthy cell membranes, proteins, and enzymes during environmental stress. The resulting plants survive drought, low temperatures, salty soils, and other stresses better than standard rice varieties.

**19.** Why is the production of new varieties of food crops necessary?

**(1)** Essential food crops are rapidly becoming extinct.
**(2)** Technology for producing fresh water for agriculture has improved.
**(3)** Burning fossil fuels has decreased agricultural areas.
**(4)** World population continues to increase.

**Correct Answer: (4)** The first statement of the passage states that "The production of new types of food crops will help raise the quantity of food grown by farmers." More food is needed to feed the growing population of humans in the world. *(Negative Effects of Humans on the Environment)*

Base your answer to question 20 on the information and table below and on your knowledge of biology.

The variety of organisms known as plankton contributes to the unique nutritional relationships in an ocean ecosystem. Phytoplankton include algae and other floating organisms that perform photosynthesis. Plankton that cannot produce food are known as zooplankton. Some nutritional relationships involving these organisms and several others are shown in the table below.

**Nutritional Relationships in a North Atlantic Ocean Community**

| | *Food Eaten by Animals in Community* | | | | |
|---|---|---|---|---|---|
| ***Animals in Community*** | ***Codfish*** | ***Phytoplankton*** | ***Small Fish*** | ***Squid*** | ***Zooplankton*** |
| Codfish | | | X | | |
| Sharks | X | | | X | |
| Small fish | | X | | | X |
| Squid | X | | X | | |
| Zooplankton | | X | | | |

**20.** Humans are currently overfishing codfish in the North Atlantic. Explain why this could endanger *both* the shark population and the squid population in this community.

**Correct Answer:** By looking at the chart, you see that both sharks and squid feed on codfish. If the codfish are overfished, there will not be enough food for the sharks and squid. Your answer should be: "Overfishing of cod will endanger both sharks and squids because there will not be enough food for them to eat." *(Negative Effects of Humans on the Environment)*

Base your answers to questions 21 through 23 on the passage below and on your knowledge of biology.

## Fighting Pollution with Bacteria

You may think that all bacteria are harmful. Think again! Some bacteria are working to clean up the damage humans have caused to the environment. In 1989, the oil tanker *Exxon Valdez* hit ground and a hole was ripped in its hull. Millions of gallons of crude oil spread along the coast of Alaska. In some places, the oil soaked 2 feet deep into the beaches. There seemed to be no way to clean up the spill. Then scientists decided to enlist the help of bacteria that are found naturally on Alaskan beaches. Some of these bacteria break down hydrocarbons (molecules found in oil) into simpler, less harmful substances such as carbon dioxide and water.

The problem was that there were not enough of these bacteria to handle the huge amount of oil. To make the bacteria multiply faster, the scientists sprayed a chemical that acted as a fertilizer along 70 miles of coastline. Within 15 days, the number of bacteria had tripled. The beaches that had been treated with the chemical were much cleaner than those that had not. Without this bacterial activity, Alaska's beaches might still be covered with oil.

This process of using organisms to eliminate toxic materials is called bioremediation. Bioremediation is being used to clean up gasoline that leaks into the soil under gas stations. At factories that process wood pulp, scientists are using microorganisms to break down phenols (a poisonous by-product of the process) into harmless salts. Bacteria also can break down acid drainage that seeps out of abandoned coal mines and explosives, such as TNT. Bacteria are used in sewage treatment plants to clean water. Bacteria also reduce acid rain by removing sulfur from coal before it is burned.

Because Americans produce more than 600 million tons of toxic waste a year, bioremediation may soon become a big business. If scientists can identify microorganisms that attack all the kinds of waste we produce, expensive treatment plants and dangerous toxic dumps might be put out of business.

**21.** Which statement does *not* represent an example of bioremediation?

**(1)** Duckweed removes heavy metals from ponds and lakes.
**(2)** Ladybugs eliminate insect pests from plants.
**(3)** Bacteria break down hydrocarbons in oil.
**(4)** Ragweed plants remove lead from the ground around factory sites.

**Correct Answer: (2)** According to the passage, bioremediation is the process of using organisms to eliminate toxic materials. Insect pests are not toxic materials. Ladybugs eliminating insect pests from plants is an example of controlling pests biologically. *(Positive Effects of Humans on the Environment)*

**22.** State one economic advantage of bioremediation.

**Correct Answer:** Economic advantages of bioremediation include the following:

- Expensive treatment plants might be put out of business.
- The cost of manual or chemical cleanup could be reduced.
- Companies specializing in bioremediation could develop creating a new market and potentially many jobs.
- Costs associated with bioremediation are lower than the costs of manual or chemical cleanup.
- Society is becoming more environmentally conscious and people are willing to pay more for bioremediation versus chemical cleanup.
- Bioremediation can take place in areas that possess a potential health hazard for humans, which could save in health-care costs.
- Industries associated with water—such as fishing, cruises, tourism, and so on—will be able to thrive instead of being limited to "clean" areas.

*(Positive Effects of Humans on the Environment)*

**23.** Describe one biological problem that may possibly result from using microorganisms to fight pollution.

**Correct Answer:** Biological problems that may possibly result from using microorganisms to fight pollution include the following:

- The population of microorganisms increasing out of control if there are little or no environmental limiting factors such as predators and unlimited food supply.
- Due to the rapid increase in the population of bacteria as a result of the application of the fertilizer, the natural predators or consumers of the bacteria may increase in population, disrupting the food web.
- Some organisms may be harmful to humans or other animals, including those in the food industry (cattle and chickens, for example).
- The bacteria may have a negative impact on other species that share some of the same resources; other species may die off as a result.

*(Negative Effects of Humans on the Environment)*

Base your answers to questions 24 and 25 on the information below and on your knowledge of biology.

> The ice fields off Canada's Hudson Bay are melting an average of three weeks earlier than 25 years ago. The polar bears are, therefore, unable to feed on the seals on these ice fields during the last three weeks in spring. Polar bears have lost an average of 10% of their weight and have fewer cubs when compared to a similar population studied just 20 years ago. Scientists have associated the early melting of the ice fields with the fact that the average world temperature is about 0.6°C higher than it was a century ago and this trend is expected to continue.

**24.** What ecological problem most likely caused the earlier melting of the ice fields in the Hudson Bay area of Canada?

**Correct Answer:** This ecological problem could be caused by global warming. Other possible answers could include the greenhouse effect or too much carbon dioxide in the atmosphere. *(Negative Effects of Humans on the Environment)*

**25.** State *one* specific long-term action humans could take that might slow down or reduce the melting of the ice fields.

**Correct Answer:** If global warming is the cause of the melting of the ice fields, and if it is caused by too much carbon dioxide in the atmosphere, then the amount of carbon dioxide must be reduced. Your answer should be: "Humans should use alternative sources of energy that do not produce carbon dioxide." You could also say that humans should plant more trees (because trees take in carbon dioxide during photosynthesis) or they can cut down fewer trees. *(Positive Effects of Humans on the Environment)*

**26.** A farmer has been growing only corn in his fields for several years. Each year the corn stalks were cut off near the ground and processed to be used as food for cattle. The farmer observed that with each passing year, corn production in his fields decreased.

Explain why removing the dead corn stalks reduced corn production in these fields.

**Correct Answer:** In undisturbed ecosystems, plant litter falls to the ground and decomposes, forming a rich layer of soil called humus. On a farm, instead of plant litter being recycled back into soil so nutrients can be reused, the plants are harvested and the nutrients they contain do not get recycled back into the farm. With a lack of nutrients over time, crop yields decrease. *(Negative Effects of Humans on the Environment)*

Base your answers to questions 27 and 28 on the statement below and on your knowledge of biology.

The use of nuclear fuel can have positive and negative effects on an ecosystem.

**27.** State *one* positive effect on an ecosystem of using nuclear fuel to generate electricity.

**Correct Answer:** Any of the following apply:

- There is little air pollution from nuclear fuels.
- It doesn't contribute to acid rain.
- It doesn't use fossil fuels.
- It doesn't contribute to global warming by releasing carbon dioxide.

*(Positive Effects of Humans on the Environment)*

**28.** State *one* negative effect on an ecosystem of using nuclear fuel to generate electricity.

**Correct Answer:** Any of the following apply:

- results in nuclear waste
- dangers from radiation
- thermal pollution

*(Negative Effects of Humans on the Environment)*

Base your answers to questions 29 through 31 on the information and graph below.

Reducing toxic chemicals released into the environment often requires laws. When making decisions about whether or not to support the passing of such laws, individuals must weigh the benefits against the potential risks if the law is not passed.

The amounts of toxic chemicals released into the environment of New York State over a ten-year period are shown in the graph below.

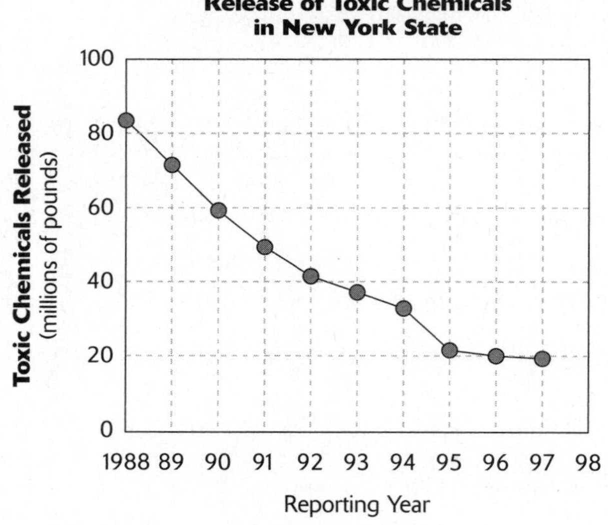


**29.** State one possible *negative* effect of passing a law to reduce the release of toxic chemicals.

**Correct Answer:** Possible negative effects of passing a law to reduce the release of toxic chemicals include: Costs associated with installing new technologies to make the reductions can be passed on to consumers, or can be too high to continue to stay in business, resulting in loss of jobs and tax revenue for the community; businesses may choose to pay fines (it may cost less) for exceeding limits of the release of chemicals rather than go out of business, or pass on the cost of installing new technologies to consumers in order to comply with the law. Because the law is at the state level and not a national level, a business may go to a state that does not have the law or move out of the country. *(Positive Effects of Humans on the Environment)*

**30.** State one possible explanation for why the amount of toxic chemicals released remained relatively constant between 1995 and 1997.

**Correct Answer:** Possible explanations for why the amount of toxic chemicals released remained relatively constant between 1995 and 1997 include:

- Businesses may have complied with the law keeping levels of chemicals at the required limit.
- Some businesses may have left the state or stopped producing the product resulting in the chemical waste.
- Fines associated with violating the law may have proven to be prohibitive to the company.
- Repeated violations may result in closing the business.
- State inspections of businesses may have increased in frequency.

*(Positive Effects of Humans on the Environment)*

**31.** State one other type of environmental problem that has been reduced by passing laws.

**Correct Answer:** Other types of environmental problems that have been reduced by passing laws include: air, water, and soil pollution; habitat loss; endangered species; use and disposal of certain chemicals (like DDT); landfills; and overhunting. *(Positive Effects of Humans on the Environment)*

**32.** The graph below shows the percentage of solid wastes recycled in New York State between 1987 and 1997.

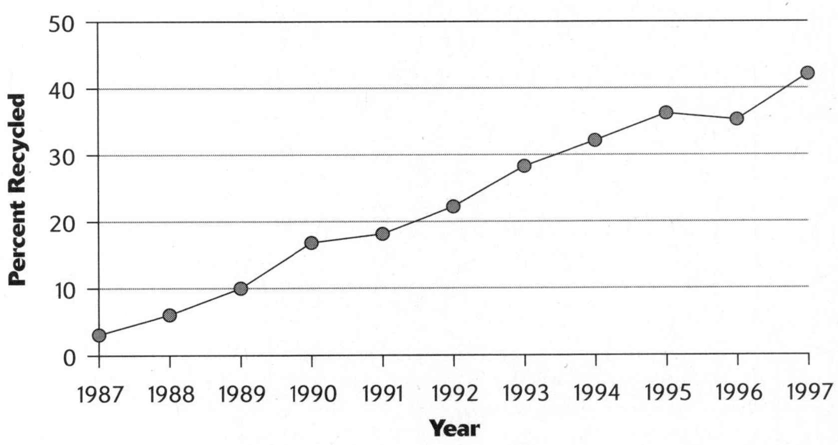


Discuss the impacts of recycling. In your answer be sure to

- explain what recycling is and provide one example of a material that is often recycled
- state one specific positive effect recycling has on the environment
- state one specific reason that the percentage of solid wastes recycled increased between 1987 and 1997

**Correct Answer:** Recycling is taking a product made of a particular material (such as glass, plastic, aluminum, or paper) and using it to make another product. Positive effects recycling has on the environment include

- not polluting the air with chemicals required to process the original product
- not using natural resources such as trees to make a product such as paper
- not adding to landfills
- reducing the amount of litter adding to the aesthetic quality of the environment

Reasons that the percentage of solid wastes recycled increased between 1987 and 1997 include

- increased public awareness and education about recycling
- more recycling centers
- more sanitation businesses that collect recyclables along with household garbage
- the economic benefit from recycling some materials
- the increased level of environmental awareness and concern for the environment
- more products being made from recycled materials
- tax or other economic incentives for businesses to use recycled materials
- tax or other economic incentives for businesses to recycle

*(Positive Effects of Humans on the Environment)*

Base your answers to questions 33 and 34 on the information below and on your knowledge of biology.

> Our national parks are areas of spectacular beauty. Current laws usually prohibit activities such as hunting, fishing, logging, mining, and drilling for oil and natural gas in these areas. Congress is being asked to change these laws to permit such activities.

**33.** Choose *one* of the activities listed above. State *one* way that activity could harm the ecosystem.

**Correct Answer:** The first two—hunting and fishing—disrupt food chains and food webs. Logging and mining destroy habitats. Drilling for oil and natural gas could lead to pollution in the ecosystem. Your answer could be:

> Activity: Hunting and fishing
>
> Harm: Overhunting and overfishing could disrupt food chains and food webs.

*(Negative Effects of Humans on the Environment)*

**34.** State *one* way allowing the activity you chose could benefit society.

**Correct Answer:** If you hunt deer, for example, there would be fewer deer that get into car accidents and fewer deer that eat and destroy crops. *(Positive Effects of Humans on the Environment)*

**35.** Currently, Americans rely heavily on the burning of fossil fuels as sources of energy. As a result of increased demand for energy sources, there is a continuing effort to find alternatives to burning fossil fuels.

Discuss fossil fuels and alternative energy sources. In your answer be sure to:

- state *one* disadvantage of burning fossil fuels for energy
- identify *one* energy source that is an alternative to using fossil fuels
- state *one* advantage of using this alternative energy source
- state *one* disadvantage of using this alternative energy source

**Correct Answer:** Be sure to address all the parts of the question.
Disadvantages of burning fossil fuel include the following:

- They pollute the air.
- They contribute to acid rain.
- They contribute to global warming.
- They are a limited or nonrenewable resource.

Alternative energy sources include:

- Solar energy
- Wind energy
- Water power
- Nuclear power
- Biofuels

Advantages of alternative energy sources include the following:

- They do not pollute the environment (all except nuclear power).
- They are renewable (all except nuclear power).
- Fossil fuels are not burned (all).

Disadvantages of alternative energy sources include the following:

- They are noisy (windmills).
- They destroy habitat (dams for water power).
- They produce dangerous waste (nuclear power).
- They are expensive.

*(Negative Effects of Humans on the Environment)*

**36.** Human activities continue to place strains on the environment. One of these strains on the environment is the loss of biodiversity. Explain what this problem is and describe some ways humans are involved in both the problem and the possible solutions. In your answer be sure to:

- state the meaning of the term *biodiversity*
- state one *negative* effect on humans if biodiversity continues to be lost
- suggest one practice that could be used to preserve biodiversity in New York State

**Correct Answer:** Biodiversity refers to the variety and relative numbers of species in an area. Loss of biodiversity is a decrease in the number of different species and individuals of a single species. If biodiversity continues to be lost, there will be far-reaching impacts on the remaining organisms and ecosystems involved. Fewer species would result in disruption of food chains; a reduction of genes in the gene pool (genetic variation) and possible sources of medical products. Methods of preserving biodiversity in New York State include setting limits on hunting and fishing, providing areas of wildlife preservation, habitat restoration, tax incentives for keeping land undeveloped; laws for pollution limits and clean-up responsibilities, requiring a certain percent of green space for new development; and education of the public. *(Positive Effects of Humans on the Environment)*

Base your answer to question 37 on the information below and on your knowledge of biology.

It has been discovered that plants utilize chemical signals for communication. Some of these chemicals are released from leaves, fruits, and flowers and play various roles in plant development, survival, and gene expression. For example, bean plant leaves infested with spider mites release chemicals that result in an increase in the resistance to spider mites in uninfested leaves on the same plant and the expression of self-defense genes in uninfested bean plants nearby. Plants can also communicate with insects. For example, corn, cotton, and tobacco under attack by caterpillars release chemical signals that simultaneously attract parasitic wasps to destroy the caterpillars and discourage moths from laying their eggs on the plants.

**37.** State *two* advantages of relying on chemicals released by plants rather than using manmade chemicals for insect control.

**Correct Answer:** The following answers apply:

- Chemicals released by plants are less harmful to the environment.
- Chemicals released by plants are cheaper.
- Chemicals released by plants do not cause pollution.

*(Positive Effects of Humans on the Environment)*

**38.** Deforestation is viewed as a problem in the world today. Describe a cause and an effect of deforestation and a way to lessen this effect. In your answer, be sure to:

- state *one* reason deforestation is occurring
- state *one* environmental problem that results from widespread deforestation
- state *one* way to lessen the effects of deforestation, other than planting trees

**Correct Answer:** Be sure to answer all parts of the question:

- Deforestation is occurring to produce lumber for building houses, furniture, and paper products. Forests are also cut down to create pastures for grazing animals such as cows.
- An environmental problem caused by widespread deforestation is habitat loss for native animals and plants. When forests are cut down, soil erosion increases. Lastly, the carbon dioxide that the forest plants would have used during photosynthesis remains in the atmosphere and may intensify global warming.
- A way to lessen the effects of deforestation would be to protect forested areas. Also, if demand for wood and paper products were decreased through recycling and reuse, then some forests could be spared from deforestation.

*(Negative Effects of Humans on the Environment)*

# Laboratory Skills: Scientific Inquiry and Technique

**Directions:** For each statement or question, choose the *number* of the word or expression that best completes the statement or answers the question. Then check your answer against the one that immediately follows the question. Try not to look at the answer before making your selection.

---

**1.** Researchers performing a well-designed experiment should base their conclusions on

**(1)** the hypothesis of the experiment
**(2)** data from repeated trials of the experiment
**(3)** a small sample size to insure a reliable outcome of the experiment
**(4)** results predicted before performing the experiment

**Correct Answer: (2)** If an experiment is well-designed, the proof of the researchers' conclusions is based on the data.

The hypothesis—choice (1)—is a reasonable explanation of what the experiment will show; you cannot base conclusions on something that has not happened yet. A small sample size—choice (3)—is the worst thing an experiment can have; a small sample size proves nothing. You cannot base conclusions on something that has not happened yet—choice (4). *(Scientific Method)*

**2.** In one variety of corn, the kernels turn red when exposed to sunlight. In the absence of sunlight, the kernels remain yellow. Based on this information, it can be concluded that the color of these corn kernels is due to the

**(1)** process of selective breeding
**(2)** rate of photosynthesis
**(3)** effect of environment on gene expression
**(4)** composition of the soil

**Correct Answer: (3)** This is a classic question asking you whether you recognize how the environment can affect how traits appear in an organism. In order to answer correctly, you need to know what gene expression means: what the trait looks like. In most cases, the trait can be seen, but in some cases a trait can't be seen with the eye—blood type would fall into this category. In the case of this question, the sun's presence or absence determines what color of corn is seen.

Choice (1) could be the answer if there were any information in the question about different varieties of corn being bred. You may be tempted to pick choice (2), because you're making a connection between light in the question and photosynthesis in the answer, but photosynthesis has nothing to do with changing the color of the kernels from red to yellow. Choice (4) is a possible answer if you assume that there could be chemicals in the soil that are affecting the plant, but you can't make that assumption. *(Scientific Method)*

**3.** The graph below shows the different concentrations of female reproductive hormones A, B, C, and D over a 28-day cycle.

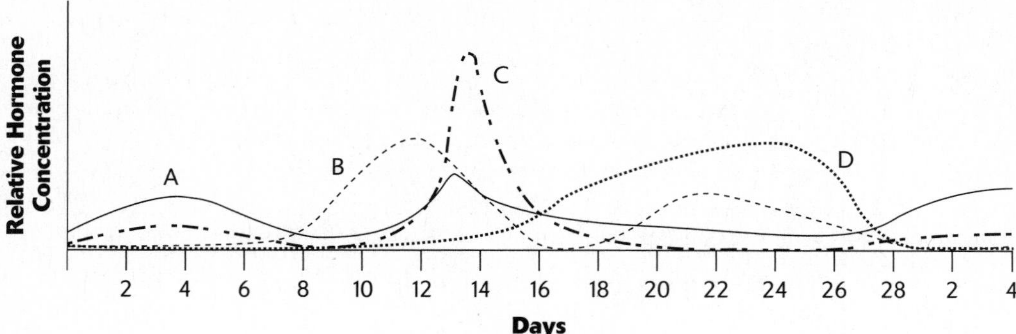


Although the data used to make this graph was originally entered in a data table, most scientists prefer to see the information in the form of a graph because

**(1)** the information in a graph is more accurate than the information in a data table
**(2)** it is easier to see relationships between variables in a graph than in a data table
**(3)** it is possible to put more information in a graph than in a data table
**(4)** only graphs can be used to predict future trends

**Correct Answer: (2)** Graphs of data are made because it is easier to see relationships between variables. The data used to make the graph should be the same data in the data table, so the accuracy is the same. *(Interpreting Graphs)*

**4.** Which graph illustrates changes that indicate a state of dynamic equilibrium in a mosquito population?

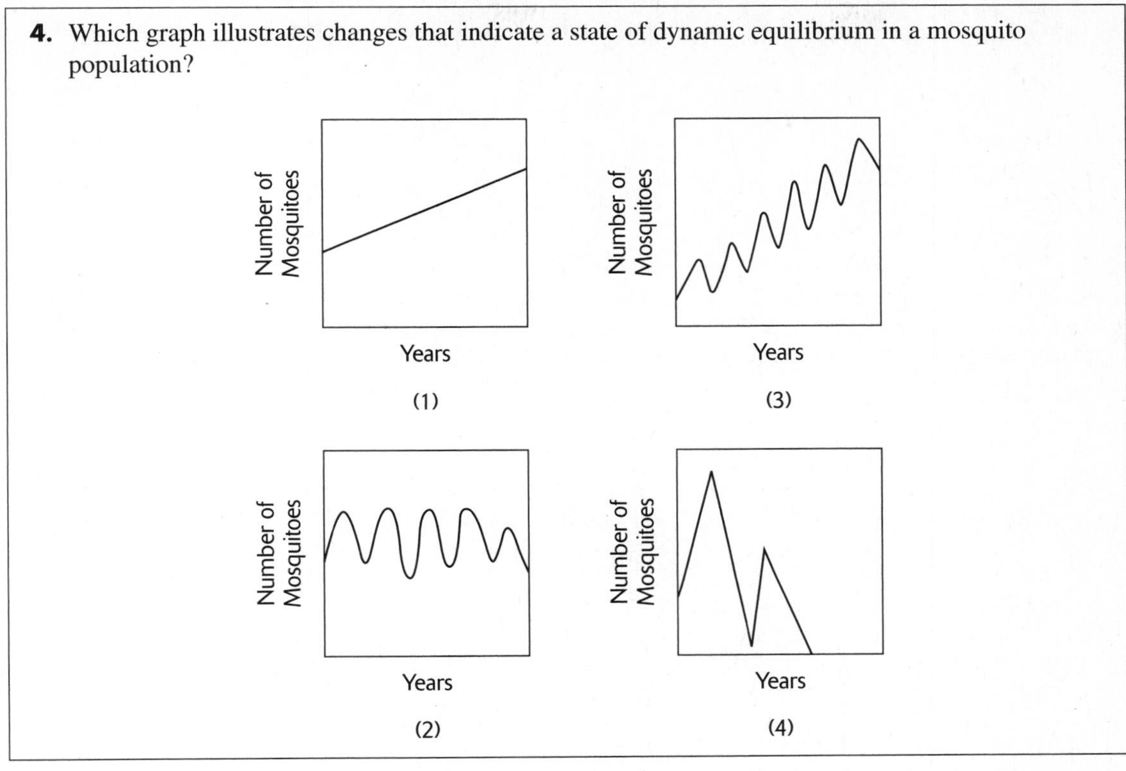


**Correct Answer: (2)** A dynamic equilibrium in this ecosystem is one in which there is a change in the number of mosquitoes, but overall (over many years) there is neither an increase nor a decrease in these numbers. *(Interpreting Graphs)*

**5.** Which situation is not an example of the maintenance of a dynamic equilibrium in an organism?

**(1)** Guard cells contribute to the regulation of water content in a geranium plant.
**(2)** Water passes into an animal cell causing it to swell.
**(3)** The release of insulin lowers the blood sugar level in a human after eating a big meal.
**(4)** A runner perspires while running a race on a hot summer day.

**Correct Answer: (2)** Homeostasis is the maintenance of a stable internal environment. The selectively permeable animal cell membrane allows some substances (and not others) to pass through it to maintain homeostasis. Water can pass freely through the cell membrane in either direction through a process called osmosis. Osmosis is the diffusion of water across a semipermeable membrane from a region of high concentration to a region of low concentration. Water can continue to pass through the cell membrane to the point at which the cell can burst. *(Diffusion/Osmosis)*

**6.** While viewing a specimen under the high power of a compound light microscope, a student noticed that the specimen was out of focus. Which part of the microscope should the student turn to obtain a clearer image under high power?

(1) eyepiece
(2) coarse adjustment
(3) fine adjustment
(4) nosepiece

**Correct Answer: (3)** The coarse and fine adjustment bring objects into focus. Under high power, only the fine adjustment should be used for two reasons. The coarse adjustment risks breaking the slide under high power and the adjustments are too great under that magnification. *(Microscopes)*

**7.** The graph below shows the effect of moisture on the number of trees per acre of five tree species.

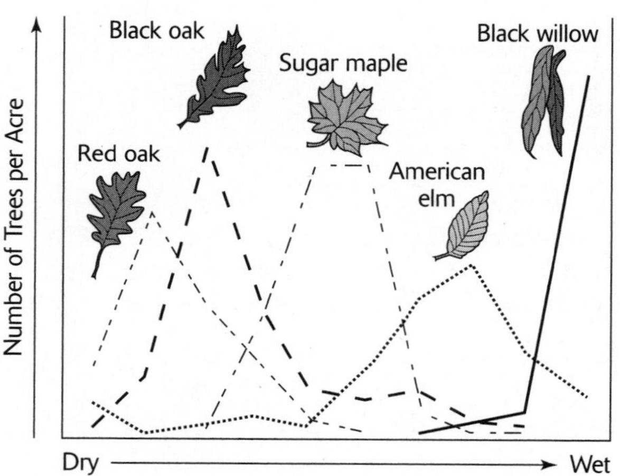


Which observation best represents information shown in the graph?

(1) All five species grow in the same habitat.
(2) The American elm grows in the widest range of moisture conditions.
(3) Red oaks can grow in wetter conditions than black willows.
(4) Sugar maples can grow anywhere black oaks can grow.

**Correct Answer: (2)** The graph shows the different relative moisture conditions in which five different tree species grow. The $x$-axis ranges from dry to wet, while the $y$-axis shows the abundance of trees of in a particular area along the gradient. Each different species is indicated by a different type of line (solid, dashed, dotted, and so on). The species that grow in the wettest conditions would have a higher abundance toward the rightmost side of the graph (such as black willow). Those that grow in the driest conditions would have a higher abundance on the leftmost side of the graph (such as red oak). Those that occur throughout the entire gradient of dry to wet would have some abundance at all different levels of moisture (such as American elm). *(Interpreting Graphs)*

**8.** An experimental setup is shown below.

Which hypothesis would most likely be tested using this setup?

**(1)** Light is needed for the process of reproduction.
**(2)** Glucose is not synthesized by plants in the dark.
**(3)** Protein synthesis takes place in leaves.
**(4)** Plants need fertilizers for proper growth.

**Correct Answer: (2)** The diagram shows a leaf of a plant and a light bulb. Part of the leaf is covered by black paper. What you should think of when you see the bulb and the leaf is that photosynthesis is taking place. But you need to go a little deeper—you need to realize that the process of photosynthesis produces glucose. The part of the leaf that is covered by the paper will not carry on photosynthesis and, therefore, will not synthesize or produce glucose.

Light is not needed for reproduction in plants—choice (1). Protein synthesis may take place in the leaves—choice (3)—but it does not require light. Plants do not need fertilizers for proper growth and nothing in the diagram has anything to do with fertilizers—choice (4). *(Scientific Method)*

Base your answer to question 9 on the information below and on your knowledge of biology.

In a class, each student made three models of the small intestine using three artificial membrane tubes. They filled each of the three tubes with equal amounts of water, starch, protein, and vitamin C. They added starch-digesting enzyme to tube 1. They added protein-digesting enzyme to tube 2. No enzyme was added to tube 3. The ends of the membrane tubes were sealed and the tubes were soaked for 24 hours in beakers of pure water. The beakers were numbered 1, 2, and 3, corresponding to the number of the tube they contained. At the end of the experiment, the students removed the tubes and tested the water in the beakers for the presence of nutrients.

**9.** Sugar would most likely be present in the water in

(1) beaker 1 only
(2) beaker 2 only
(3) beakers 1 and 3 only
(4) beakers 1, 2, and 3

**Correct Answer: (1)** The best thing to do here is to draw a picture of the experiment. Draw three beakers of water and the three membrane tubings, and label each with the stuff inside (water, starch, protein, and vitamin C). Label each beaker with what was added to it. When you have a picture, think about what enzymes do: They break stuff down. Lipids get broken down into fatty acids and glycerol, proteins get broken down into amino acids, and starches get broken down into sugars. So if each membrane tube contains starch, but only beaker 1 had starch-digesting enzyme added to it, then the only beaker that would test positive for the presence of sugars would be the first beaker. *(Diffusion/Osmosis)*

**10.** An investigation was carried out and the results are shown below. Substance X resulted from a metabolic process that produces ATP in yeast (a single-celled fungus).

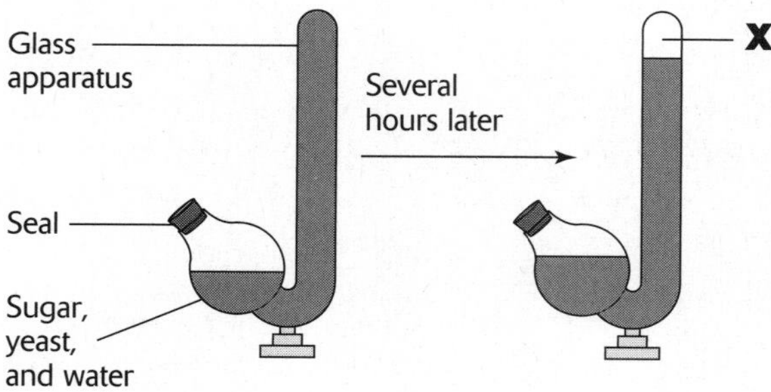


Which statement best describes substance X?

(1) It is oxygen released by protein synthesis.
(2) It is glucose that was produced in photosynthesis.
(3) It is starch that was produced during digestion.
(4) It is carbon dioxide released by respiration.

**Correct Answer: (4)** A metabolic process is something that organisms do to stay alive—digestion, excretion, regulation, and respiration are some examples. But yeast does something we can't do: It can ferment sugar. Yeast can turn sugar (glucose) into alcohol and carbon dioxide. In the diagram, the yeast will metabolize or use the sugar to produce energy in the form of ATP and in the same process make alcohol and carbon dioxide. The carbon dioxide will travel through the water in the J-tube and collect at the part labeled X. *(Scientific Method)*

**11.** A science researcher is reviewing another scientist's experiment and conclusion. The reviewer would most likely consider the experiment *invalid* if

(1) the sample size produced a great deal of data
(2) other individuals are able to duplicate the results
(3) it contains conclusions not explained by the evidence given
(4) the hypothesis was not supported by the data obtained

**Correct Answer: (3)** When one scientist reviews the research of another scientist, she is checking to make sure that the experiment was valid and had good experimental design. She would make sure that the sample size was sufficient and that there was a proper control. A good experiment could be repeated by other scientists and would have similar results. If the hypothesis were not supported by the data, the experiment would still be valid—only the hypothesis would be rejected, and another one would be proposed. The conclusions drawn from the experiment need support from the evidence (data) provided. Conclusions without evidential support would be invalid. *(Scientific Method)*

**12.** Which statement most accurately describes scientific inquiry?

(1) It ignores information from other sources.
(2) It does not allow scientists to judge the reliability of their sources.
(3) It should never involve ethical decisions about the application of scientific knowledge.
(4) It may lead to explanations that combine data with what people already know about their surroundings.

**Correct Answer: (4)** Scientific inquiry seeks to piece together patterns. Through observation and experimentation, scientists identify these patterns and share them with the scientific community so that others may benefit from and add to the information identified. *(Scientific Method)*

**13.** Which source would provide the most reliable information for use in a research project investigating the effects of antibiotics on disease-causing bacteria?

(1) the local news section of a newspaper from 1993
(2) a news program on national television about antigens produced by various plants
(3) a current professional science journal article on the control of pathogens
(4) an article in a weekly news magazine about reproduction in pathogens

**Correct Answer: (3)** This is really a vocabulary question: It's asking whether you know the definition of *pathogens.* The answer is in the question: "disease-causing bacteria." If you saw the connection here, then the next thing would be to recognize that a current scientific journal would be the best source of information for a research project.

Choices (1), (2), and (4), while all important for the purpose of keeping the average person informed, are not appropriate for use in a research project. *(Scientific Method)*

**14.** The diagrams below show four different one-celled organisms (shaded) in the field of view of the same microscope using different magnifications. Which illustration shows the largest one-celled organism?

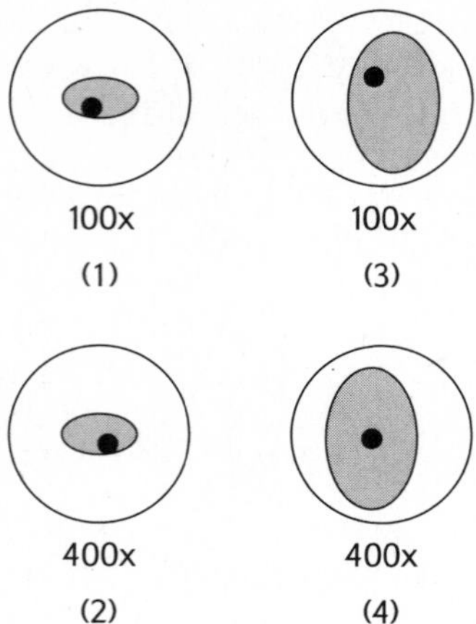


**Correct Answer: (3)** To answer this question, you have to remember some things about using the microscope. One thing is that an organism under low power will look bigger under high power. Another thing to consider is how much of the field of view the organism is taking up. In choice (1), the organism takes up about one-third of the field of view. In choice (2), the organism also takes up one-third of the field, but this is under high power (400X), so it is a pretty small organism. Choice (4) has the organism taking up almost the entire field of view under high power. But compare that to choice (3), which takes up about the same amount of the field, but under a lower power. If choice (3) were to be viewed under high power, the whole organism would not fit in the field of view. *(Microscopes)*

**15.** A student performed an experiment to determine if treating 500 tomato plants with an auxin (a plant growth hormone) will make them grow faster. The results are shown in the table below.

| *Days* | *Average Stem Height (cm)* |
|---|---|
| 1 | 10 |
| 5 | 13 |
| 10 | 19 |
| 15 | 26 |
| 20 | 32 |
| 25 | 40 |

Explain why the student *cannot* draw a valid conclusion from these results.

**Correct Answer:** To answer this question, you have to remember the first rule about experiments: You must have a control group. There isn't one in this experiment. Yes, the student is testing the auxin on a large number of plants, which is great. But the student doesn't have anything to compare it to. This would only be a valid experiment if the student also grew 500 tomato plants without auxin and then compared them. *(Scientific Method)*

**16.** After switching from the high-power to the low-power objective lens of a compound light microscope, the area of the low-power field will appear

**(1)** larger and brighter
**(2)** smaller and brighter
**(3)** larger and darker
**(4)** smaller and darker

**Correct Answer: (1)** The low-power field diameter is larger than the high-powered field diameter and allows more light to pass through it, causing the image to appear brighter. *(Microscopes)*

**17.** The diagram below shows a portion of a graduated cylinder.

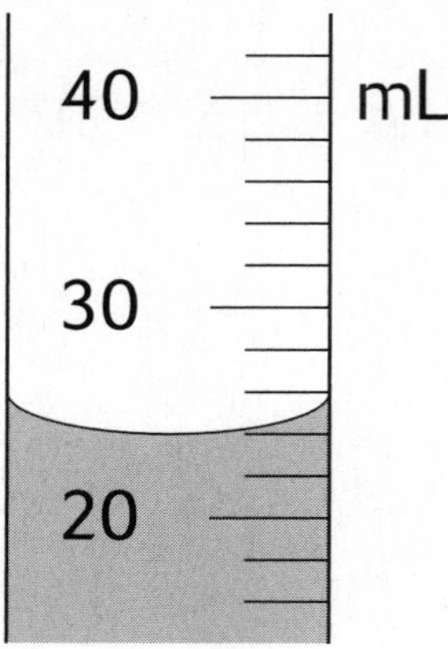


What is the volume of the liquid in this cylinder?

**(1)** 22 mL
**(2)** 24 mL
**(3)** 25 mL
**(4)** 26 mL

**Correct Answer: (2)** The volume of a liquid in a graduated cylinder is read at the bottom of the *meniscus,* the curved surface of the liquid in the cylinder. Each line on the cylinder is worth 2 mL. *(Lab Safety)*

**18.** The dichotomous key shown below can be used to identify birds W, X, Y, and Z.

| Dichotomous Key to Representative Birds | |
|---|---|
| 1. a. The beak is relatively long and slender | *Certhidea* |
| b. The beak is relatively stout and heavy | go to 2 |
| 2. a. The bottom surface of the lower beak is flat and straight | *Geospiza* |
| b. The bottom surface of the lower beak is curved | go to 3 |
| 3. a. The lower edge of the upper beak has a distinct bend | *Camarhynchus* |
| b. The lower edge of the upper beak is mostly flat | *Platyspiza* |

Bird X is most likely

(1) *Certhidea*
(2) *Geospiza*
(3) *Camarhynchus*
(4) *Platyspiza*

**Correct Answer: (4)** A dichotomous key is used to identify or classify organisms. A yes/no response to each statement takes the user through a series of steps that eliminates possibilities one by one. Each statement is followed by a direction that tells the user to go to another statement or provides the name of the organism. The user follows the statements until all the names are eliminated except one. In the dichotomous key given, Bird X has a "relatively stout and heavy" beak, with the "bottom surface on the lower beak curved" and "the lower edge of the upper beak mostly flat." *(Biodiversity)*

**19.** A peppered moth and part of a metric ruler are represented in the diagram below.

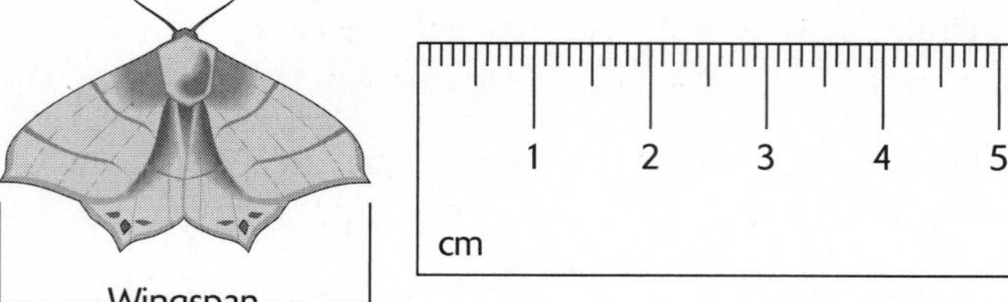


Which row in the chart below best represents the ratio of body length to wingspan of the peppered moth?

| *Row* | *Body Length:Wingspan* |
|---|---|
| (1) | 1:1 |
| (2) | 2:1 |
| (3) | 1:2 |
| (4) | 2:2 |

**Correct Answer: (3)** To determine the ratio of body length to wingspan of the peppered moth, measurements of each must first be taken. Body length = 13mm and wingspan = 30mm. In the proper format, the ratio of body length to wingspan is 13:30. Reducing this ratio to simplest terms, the ratio is approximately 1:2. One body length is approximately one-half the length of the wingspan of the peppered moth. In other words, the wingspan is twice as long as the body length. *(Scientific Method)*

**20.** Recently, scientists noted that stained chromosomes from rapidly dividing cells, such as human cancer cells, contain numerous dark, dot-like structures. Chromosomes from older human cells that have stopped dividing have very few, if any, dot-like structures. The best generalization regarding these dot-like structures is that they

**(1)** will always be present in cells that are dividing
**(2)** may increase the rate of mitosis in human cells
**(3)** definitely affect the rate of division in all cells
**(4)** can cure all genetic disorders

**Correct Answer: (2)** Without direct scientific evidence to support the actual function of the dot-like structures, the observation remains to be tested. Therefore, the idea that the dot-like structures *may* increase the rate of mitosis in human cells would be correct. *(Scientific Method)*

**21.** In an investigation to determine a factor that affects the growth of rats, a student exposed 100 rats of the same age and species to identical conditions, except for the amount of living space and the amount of food each rat received. Each day the student measured and recorded the weight of each rat. State one major error that the student made in performing this investigation.

**Correct Answer:** In an experiment, there may be only one variable. The student had two variables in the experiment—the amount of living space, and the amount of food received. *(Scientific Method)*

Base your answers to questions 22 and 23 on the information and diagram below and on your knowledge of biology.

Two test tubes, A and B, were set up as shown in the diagram below. Bromothymol blue, which turns blue to yellow in the presence of carbon dioxide, was added to the water at the bottom of each tube before the tubes were sealed. The tubes were maintained at the temperatures shown for six days. (Average room temperature is 20°C.)

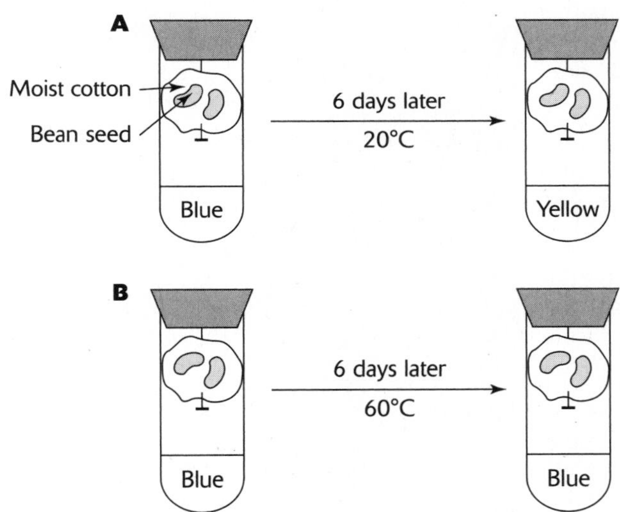


**22.** Identify the life process responsible for the change in Tube A.

**Correct Answer:** If you read the passage carefully, you note that the chemical, bromothymol blue, is in the water at the bottom of the tubes and that it changes color from blue to yellow when carbon dioxide is present. If Tube A changes from blue to yellow, that must mean that carbon dioxide is present. The only life process that produces carbon dioxide is cellular respiration. That is the answer. *(Scientific Method)*

**23.** Explain how the temperature difference could lead to the different results in tubes A and B after six days.

**Correct Answer:** The simplest answer would be to say that Tube B is too hot for the seeds to grow, so they won't carry out cellular respiration and won't produce carbon dioxide, which would change the water from blue to yellow. The secret lies in the temperature, which is 60°C. ***Remember:*** This is a Celsius temperature and 60°C is very, very hot—too hot for most plants to survive. The other thing to remember is that at high temperatures, enzymes will not work. Enzymes control virtually every life process in all living things. So, if the enzymes don't work due to high temperatures, then the organism will not carry out cell respiration (or any other process) and will die. *(Scientific Method)*

Base your answers to questions 24 through 28 on the information and data table below and on your knowledge of biology.

The effect of temperature on the action of pepsin, a protein-digesting enzyme present in stomach fluid, was tested. In this investigation, 20 milliliters of stomach fluid and 10 grams of protein were placed in each of 5 test tubes. The tubes were then kept at different temperatures. After 24 hours, the contents of each tube were tested to determine the amount of protein that had been digested. The results are shown in the table below.

**Protein Digestion at Different Temperatures**

| *Tube #* | *Temperature (°C)* | *Amount of Protein Digested (grams)* |
|---|---|---|
| 1 | 5 | 0.5 |
| 2 | 10 | 1.0 |
| 3 | 20 | 4.0 |
| 4 | 37 | 9.5 |
| 5 | 85 | 0.0 |

**24.** The dependent variable in this investigation is the

**(1)** size of the test tube
**(2)** time of digestion
**(3)** amount of stomach fluid
**(4)** amount of protein digested.

**Correct Answer: (4)** You can determine that the answer is choice (4) from the first sentence: "The effect of temperature on the action of pepsin . . . was tested." Ask yourself, "What depends on what?" Does the amount of proteins digested depend on the temperature or does the temperature depend on the amount of protein digested? You know that the two are related, so by asking yourself this question, it might be a little clearer.

It makes more sense that the amount of protein digested depends on the temperature than the other way around. Just look at the data: As the temperature increases, the amount of protein digested also increases up to 37°C and then decreases after that. The size of the test tube—choice (1)—really has no bearing on the experiment and nothing is said about their size. The time of digestion—choice (2)—sounds possible, but there is nothing in the experiment that says anything about time. The amount of stomach fluid—choice (3)—sounds like a possible answer, but keep in mind that you only need a small amount of enzymes to do the job, so this answer really doesn't matter. *(Scientific Method)*

*Directions* (25–26): Using the information in the data table, construct a line graph on the grid provided, following the directions below.

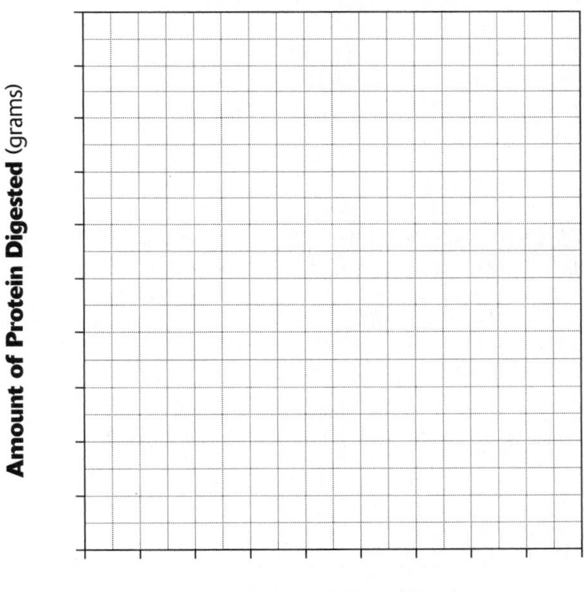


**25.** Mark an appropriate scale on each axis.

**Correct Answer:** Look at the grid. The axes are labeled "Temperature" and "Amount of Protein Digested (grams)." This helps you to know what numbers to plot and what the scale has to be.

The first thing you should do is to count the number of squares on each side of the grid. Along the bottom there are 18. Along the side there are 20. If you notice, on each axis the grid lines extend beyond the grid every other line. This is where you should write the numbers.

Next look at data in the table. First look at temperature. The temperature goes from 5°C to 85°C. The scale on this side must go beyond this highest number, 85, in order to make sure there is room for it on the graph. The "best" next highest number to use would be 90. Take 90 and divide it by the number of boxes on this side: 90 divided by 18 equals 5. Every box on this side is worth 5.

Because every other line of the grid extends beyond the grid, that's where you should write the numbers. You know that every line is worth 5, but every other line sticks out, so every other line is goes up by 10s. Start at the first line that extends beyond the grid and label it 10. Continue going up by 10s every other line: 20, 30, and so on until you reach 90.

Repeat the same process on the vertical axis. There are 20 boxes that have to cover from 0.0 to 9.5 grams of protein. Because the scale has to cover all the numbers, you need to go beyond the highest number, 9.5 to 10. Take the highest number, 10, and divide it by the number of boxes, 20—10 divided by 20 equals 0.5. Each box on the vertical scale is equal to 0.5. Again, because every other line extends beyond the grid, that is where we will place our numbers starting with 1.0 and continue up, labeling every other line increasing by 1.0. *(Interpreting Graphs)*

**26.** Plot the data on the grid. Surround each point with a small circle and connect the points.

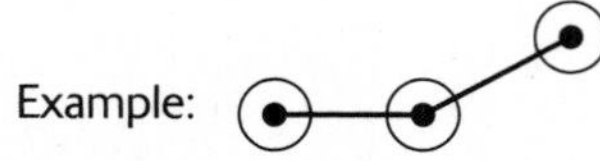


**Correct Answer:** Go to the data table, find the first set of points to plot: Temperature of 5 and amount of protein 0.5. Go to the first line, which would be 5°C. Move up this line to the first box of the "Amount of Protein," which would be 0.5, and make a point and circle it.

Go on to the next pair of points, temperature 10 and protein 1.0. Follow the same procedure. Find the 10°C line on the bottom, move up that line until it meets the 1.0 protein line, and make a point.

Continue to plot the rest of the data the same way. Your graph should be a line graph that increases as temperature increases until the temperature hits 37°C and then it drops down or decreases as the temperature continues up to 85°C. *(Interpreting Graphs)*

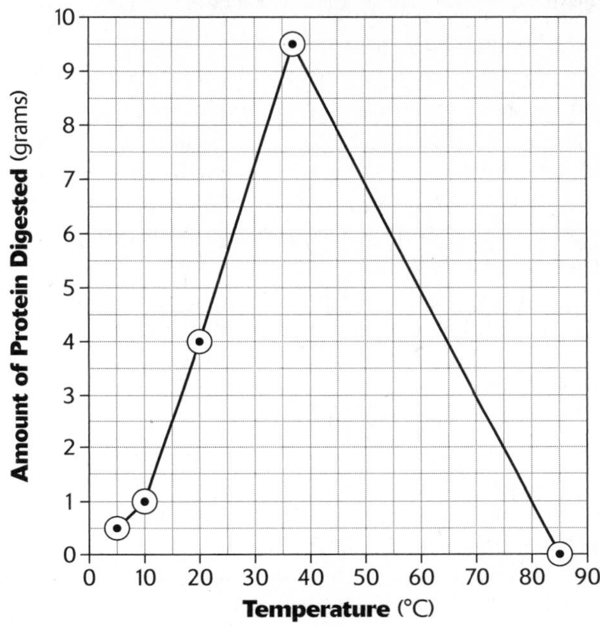


**27.** If a sixth test tube identical to the other tubes was kept at a temperature of 30°C for 24 hours, the amount of protein digested would most likely be

**(1)** less than 1.0 gram
**(2)** between 1.0 and 4.0 grams
**(3)** between 4.0 and 9.0 grams
**(4)** more than 9.0 grams

**Correct Answer: (3)** Based on the data table, 30°C is in between 20°C and 37°C. Therefore the amount of protein digested at 30°C would be between the amount of protein digested at the other two temperatures. This amount would be between 4.0 and 9.0 grams. The other choices—(1), (2), and (4)—do not fall within the proper range of temperatures. *(Interpreting Graphs)*

**28.** This investigation was repeated using 10 grams of starch instead of protein in each test tube. The contents of each tube were tested to determine the amount of starch that had been digested. The test results showed that no starch digestion occurred. Explain why no starch was digested.

**Correct Answer:** No starch was digested because enzymes are specific. They will only act on specific substances. The enzyme in the tubes will only digest protein, it will not digest starch. *(Interpreting Graphs)*

Base your answers to questions 29 through 32 on the information and data table below and on your knowledge of biology.

Biologists investigated the effect of the presence of aluminum ions on root tips of a variety of wheat. They removed 2mm sections of the tips of roots. Half of the root tips were placed in a nutrient solution with aluminum ions, while the other half were placed in an identical nutrient solution without aluminum ions. The length of the root tips, in millimeters, was measured every hour for seven hours. The results are shown in the following data table.

**Data Table**

| *Time (hr)* | *Length of Root Tips in Solution with Aluminum Ions (mm)* | *Length of Root Tips in Solution without Aluminum Ions (mm)* |
|---|---|---|
| 0 | 2.0 | 2.0 |
| 1 | 2.1 | 2.2 |
| 2 | 2.2 | 2.4 |
| 3 | 2.4 | 2.8 |
| 4 | 2.6 | 2.9 |
| 5 | 2.7 | 3.2 |
| 6 | 2.8 | 3.7 |
| 7 | 2.8 | 3.9 |

*Directions* (29–31): Using the information in the data table, construct a line graph on the grid provided, following the directions.

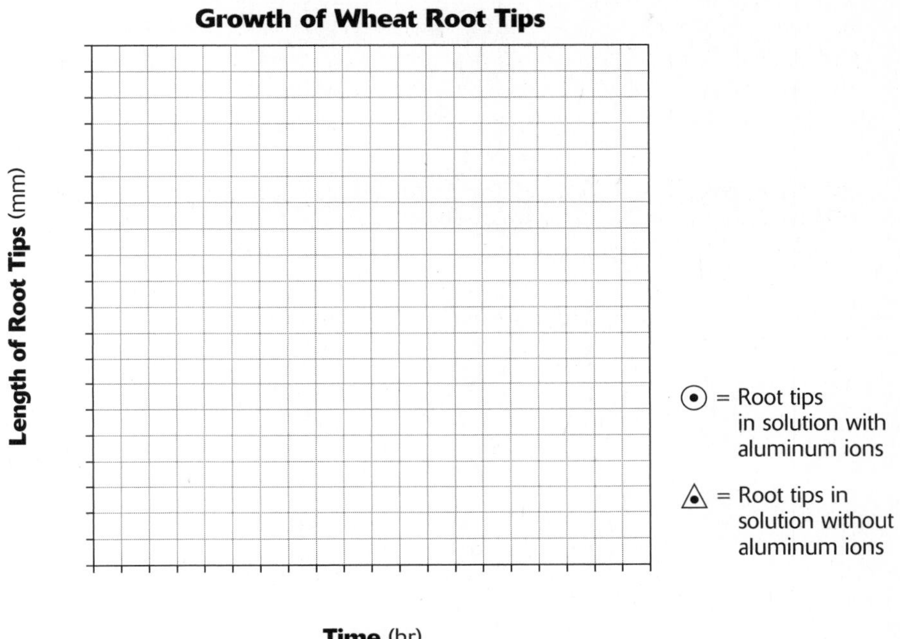


**29.** Mark an appropriate scale on each labeled axis.

**Correct Answer:** See graph after question 31. *(Interpreting Graphs)*

**30.** Plot the data for root tips in the solution with aluminum ions on the grid. Surround each point with a small circle and connect the points.

Example: 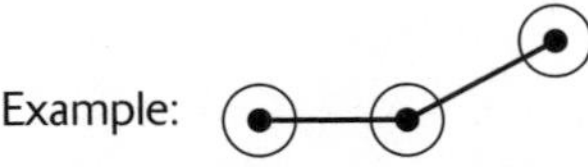

**Correct Answer:** See graph after question 31. *(Interpreting Graphs)*

**31.** Plot the data for root tips in the solution without aluminum ions on the grid. Surround each point with a small triangle and connect the points.

Example: 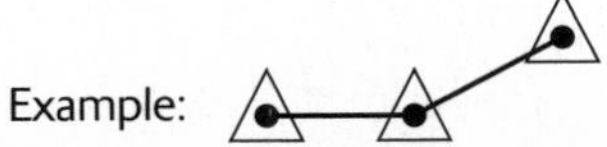

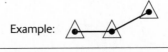

**Correct Answer:** *(Interpreting Graphs)*

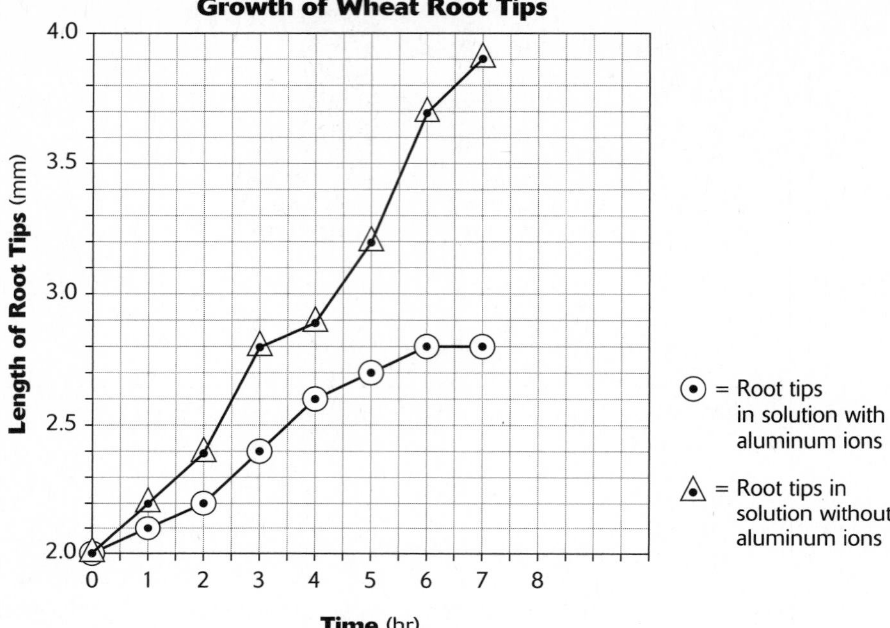


| **32.** Describe the effect of aluminum ions on the growth of the root tips of wheat. |
|---|

**Correct Answer:** The aluminum ions caused the root tip to grow at a slower rate, as indicated by the slope of the line on the graph. *(Interpreting Graphs)*

Base your answers to question 33 on the information below and on your knowledge of biology.

> Color in peppered moths is controlled by genes. A light-colored variety and a dark-colored variety of a peppered moth species exist in nature. The moths often rest on tree trunks, and several different species of birds are predators of this moth.
>
> Before industrialization in England, the light-colored variety was much more abundant than the dark-colored variety and evidence indicates that many tree trunks at that time were covered with light-colored lichens. Later, industrialization developed and brought pollution, which killed the lichens, leaving the tree trunks covered with dark-colored soot. The results of a study made in England are shown below.

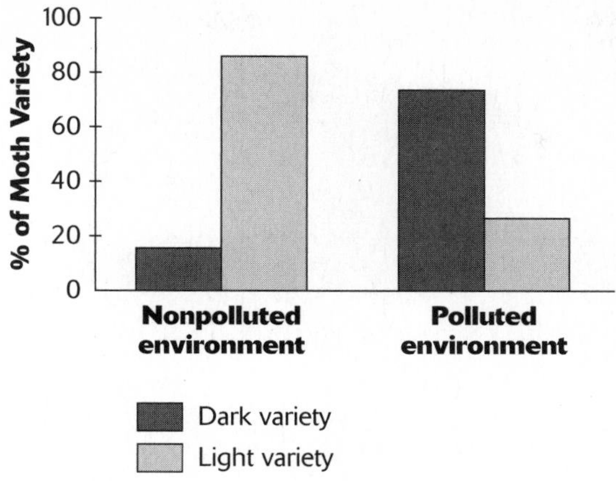


**33.** The percentage of light-colored moths in the polluted environment was closest to

**(1)** 16
**(2)** 24
**(3)** 42
**(4)** 76

**Correct Answer: (2)** According to the graph, the percentage of light-colored moths in the polluted environment was just above 20 percent. *(Interpreting Graphs)*

Base your answer to question 34 on the passage below and on your knowledge of biology.

## Great Effects on the Great Lakes due to Global Warming

Trees such as the jack pine, yellow birch, red pine, and white pine may no longer be able to grow in the Great Lakes region because summers are becoming warmer. However, other trees such as black walnut and black cherry may grow in the area, given enough time. The change in weather would favor these new tree species.

The Great Lakes region is the only place in the world where the endangered Kirtland's Warbler breeds. This bird species nests in young jack pine trees (5 to 23 years old). The vegetation must have specific characteristics or the birds will not nest. A specific area of Michigan is one of the few preferred areas. If the jack pines can no longer grow in this area, the consequences for the Kirtland's Warbler could be devastating.

Recent research findings also suggest that algae production in Lake Ontario and several other Great Lakes will be affected as warmer weather leads to warmer lake water. An increase in water temperature reduces the ability of water to hold dissolved oxygen. These changes have implications for the entire Great Lakes food web. Changes in deep-water oxygen levels and other habitat changes may prevent the more sensitive cold-water fish from occupying their preferred niches in a warmer climate.

All other factors being equal, climatic changes may not have a negative effect on every species in the Great Lakes region. This is because the length of the growing season would be increased. Some temperature sensitive fish could move to cooler, deeper water when the surface water temperatures become too high. The total impact of global warming is difficult to predict.

**34.** Which graph best shows the relationship between changes in temperature in the Great Lakes waters and the amount of dissolved oxygen those waters can hold?

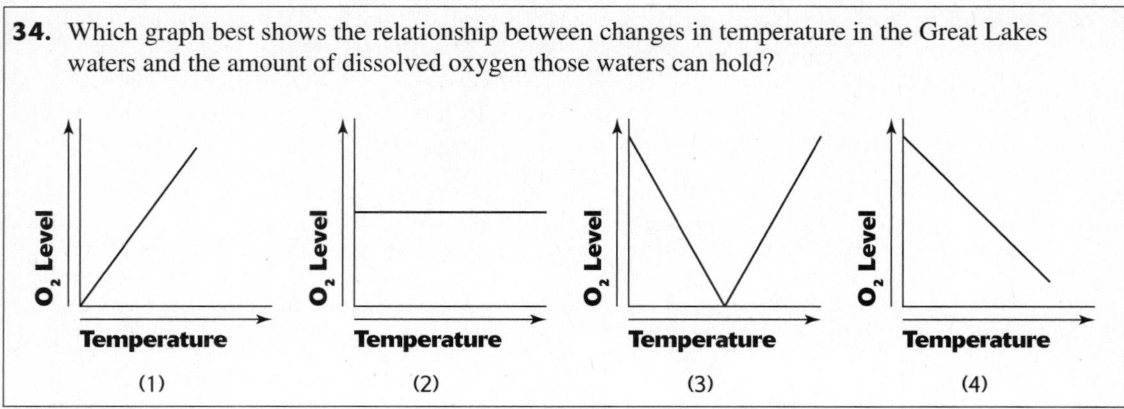


**Correct Answer: (4)** In this question, does the amount of dissolved oxygen affect the temperature of the water or does the temperature of the water affect the amount of dissolved oxygen? As stated in the third paragraph, "An increase in water temperature reduces the ability of water to hold dissolved oxygen." In other words, as the temperature increases, the amount of dissolved oxygen decreases. This is an inverse relationship. Look at each graph. You want to choose the graph that shows the temperature increasing and at the same time the amount of dissolved oxygen decreasing. The only graph that shows this is choice (4). Choice (1) shows a direct relationship: As the temperature increases, so does the amount of dissolved oxygen. Choice (2) shows a constant relationship: No matter how hot the water gets, the amount of dissolved oxygen remains the same. *(Interpreting Graphs)*

Base your answers to questions 35 through 38 on the data table below and on your knowledge of biology. The table contains information about glucose production in a species of plant that lives in the water of a salt marsh.

| *Temperature (°C)* | *Glucose Production (mg/hr)* |
|---|---|
| 10 | 5 |
| 20 | 10 |
| 30 | 15 |
| 40 | 5 |

**35.** Which terms describe temperature in this investigation?

**(1)** abiotic factor and independent variable
**(2)** abiotic factor and dependent variable
**(3)** biotic factor and independent variable
**(4)** biotic factor and dependent variable

**Correct Answer: (1)** Abiotic factors are those that are attributed to the environment, such as temperature, moisture, and light levels. Biotic factors are those that are attributed to living organisms, such as competition or predation. The independent variable is one that has an impact on the dependent variable. The dependent variable is the one that responds in some way to the impact of the independent variable. In this example, glucose production responds to an increase in temperature. Therefore, temperature is the independent variable and glucose is the dependent variable. *(Interpreting Graphs)*

**36.** What evidence from the data table shows that a salt-marsh plant is sensitive to its environment?

**Correct Answer:** The data in the table show that every time the temperature changes, the glucose production also changes. *(Interpreting Graphs)*

**37.** At which temperature would the plants most likely use the greatest amount of carbon dioxide?

(1) 10°C
(2) 20°C
(3) 30°C
(4) 40°C

**Correct Answer: (3)** Glucose is produced in plants as they photosynthesize. Carbon dioxide is used as glucose is produced. The higher the production of glucose, the more carbon dioxide is used. In the table given, the highest glucose production is observed at 30°C. This is the temperature at which carbon dioxide use would be the highest. *(Interpreting Graphs)*

**38.** How much oxygen will plants that live in water at 10°C most likely produce?

(1) twice the amount of oxygen produced at 20°C
(2) the same amount of oxygen produced at 40°C
(3) the most oxygen produced at any temperature
(4) more oxygen than is produced at 30°C

**Correct Answer: (2)** The amount of glucose produced at 10°C and 40°C is identical (5mg per hour). Therefore, the amount of oxygen that the plant would produce would also be identical. *(Interpreting Graphs)*

Base your answers to questions 39 and 40 on the passage below and on your knowledge of biology.

Research indicates that many plants prevent the growth of other plants in their habitat by releasing natural herbicides (chemicals that kill plants). These substances are known as allelochemcials and include substances such as quinine, caffeine, and digitalis. Experiments have confirmed that chemicals in the bark and roots of black walnut trees are toxic, and when released into the soil they limit the growth of crop plants such as tomatoes, potatoes, and apples. Allelochemicals can alter growth and enzyme action, injure the outer cover of a seed so the seed dies, or stimulate seed growth at inappropriate times of the year. Studies on allelochemical effects help explain the observation that almost nothing grows under a black walnut tree even though light and moisture levels are adequate for growth.

**39.** Which phrase best predicts the relative numbers of different plant species in regions A, B, and C in the diagram shown below?

**(1)** greater in C than B
**(2)** greater in A than C
**(3)** greater in A than B
**(4)** greater in B than C

**Correct Answer: (1)** The first sentence says that some plants give off chemicals that don't let other plants grow nearby. Look at the last part of the last sentence where it says, "almost nothing grows under a black walnut tree." Based on these two sentences, you can answer the question. It makes sense that the farther away from the tree you get, the more plants can grow. So, more plants grow at Area C than grow at Area B, and more plants grow at Area B than at area A. *(Scientific Method)*

**40.** A set of axes is shown below.

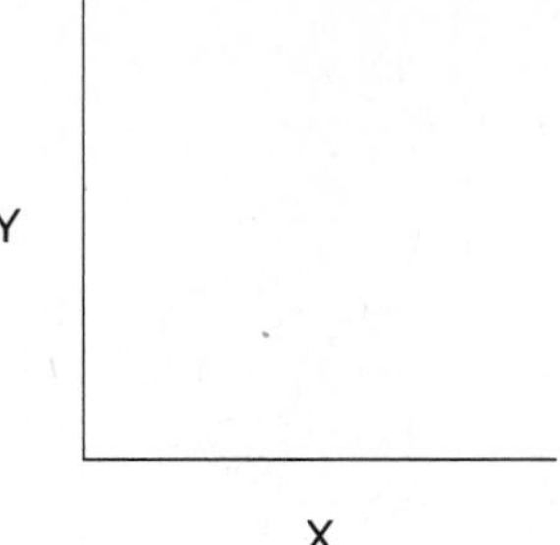


When using this set of axes to show the effect of black walnut allelochemicals on the number of plants, which labels would be appropriate for the *x*-axis and *y*-axis?

**(1)** *x*—Number of Plants, *y*—Distance from Walnut Tree Trunk (meters)
**(2)** *x*—Distance form Walnut Tree Trunk (meters), *y*—Number of Plants
**(3)** *x*—Number of Plants, *y*—Time (days)
**(4)** *x*—Time (days), *y*—Number of Plants

**Correct Answer:** You might say, "What difference does it make? Both choices have the same things." Well, it does matter because you have to know what belongs on the *x*-axis—the dependent variable belongs here. Again, you have to rely on common sense and ask yourself the question, "What depends on what?" Fill in the blanks. Does the number of plants depend on the distance from the tree or does the distance from the tree depend on the number of plants? Of course, it's the former. Choice (2) is the answer. *(Interpreting Graphs)*

**41.** The drugs usually used to treat high blood pressure do not affect blood vessels in the lungs. Bosentan is a new drug being studied as a treatment for high blood pressure in the lungs. In an experiment, patients treated with bosentan showed an improvement in the distance they could walk without fatigue within 12 weeks.

Design an experiment to test the effectiveness of bosentan as a drug to treat high blood pressure in the lungs. In your answer be sure to:

- state the hypothesis your experiment will test
- state how the control group will be treated differently from the experimental group
- state *two* factors that must be kept the same in both the experimental and control groups
- state the type of data that should be collected to determine if the hypothesis is supported

**Correct Answer:** To answer questions like this, take each bullet one at a time and keep your answers simple, but elegant.

The hypothesis is that bosentan will decrease the blood pressure in the lungs.

For the next bullet, remember, the control group gets nothing, the experimental group gets the treatment: The control group will not be given the drug, the experimental group will be given the drug.

Because the experiment is dealing with humans, you want to have as many similarities among both groups as possible. Both groups should be the same age, sex, height, weight, have the same level of high blood pressure, get the same food and hours of sleep, get the same dose of the drug at the same time, and have the same level of activity. You choose two factors.

The data to be collected would be blood pressure readings of the blood vessels in the lungs before treatment and after treatment. An alternative answer might be to measure the distance the people could walk before the drug and compare it with the distance they could walk after taking the drug. *(Scientific Method)*

**42.** A scientist wants to determine the best conditions for hatching brine shrimp eggs. In a laboratory, brine shrimp hatch at room temperature in glass containers of saltwater. The concentration of salt in the water is known to affect how many brine shrimp eggs will hatch.

Design an experiment to determine which of three saltwater concentrations—2 percent, 4 percent, or 6 percent—is best for hatching brine shrimp eggs. In your experimental design, be sure to:

- state how many containers to use in the experiment, and describe what would be added to each container in addition to the eggs
- state *two* factors that must be kept constant in all the containers
- state what data must be collected during this experiment
- state *one* way to organize the data so that they will be easy to analyze
- describe a result that would indicate the best salt solution for hatching brine shrimp eggs

**Correct Answer:** Be sure to address *all* the parts of the question:

- Three saltwater concentrations are indicated (2 percent, 4 percent, and 6 percent), so at least three containers would be needed for this experiment, each with a different salt concentration. Another acceptable experiment would utilize four containers—one for each of the salt concentrations listed above, and one with pure water.
- Many factors must be kept constant for this experiment to be a good one. These include: water temperature, the number of eggs in each container, the amount of water in each container, the size of the container, the amount of time the containers are observed, and the location in which the containers are placed.
- The data that should be collected during this experiment are how many eggs hatch in each container at each different salt concentration.
- Data are always most easily organized in a table (or spreadsheet). They can also be graphed to make them easy to analyze.
- A result that would indicate the best salt solution for hatching brine shrimp eggs would be the concentration in which the most eggs are observed to hatch. *(Scientific Method)*

**43.** The diagram below illustrates the result of growing a garlic bulb in a cup of distilled water over five days.

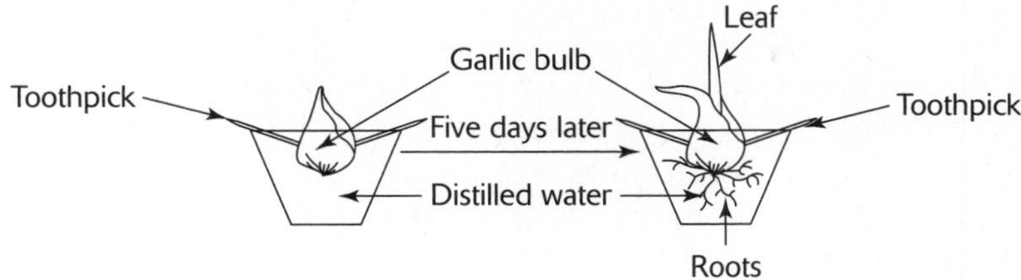


Design an experiment consisting of a control and three different experimental groups to test the prediction, "Garlic grows better as the salt concentration of the solution in which it is grown increases." In your answer, be sure to:

- describe the control to be used in the experiment
- describe the difference between the three experimental groups
- state *one* type of measurement that should be made to determine if the prediction is accurate
- describe *one* example of experimental results that would support the prediction

**Correct Answer:** Every experiment needs a control group to make it a valid experiment. The control group is treated to the same conditions as the experimental group, except that it is not given any treatment. Your answer should be: "The control group will be a garlic bulb in distilled water." (Keep your answers simple—the more you write, the more it will seem that you don't know what you're talking about.)

The three experimental groups need to be different. You can figure out what they should be by reading the hypothesis again: Garlic grows better as the salt concentration of the solution it is grown in increases. So, all you need to do is say something about the three experimental cups having different salt concentrations. Your answer should be: "The three experimental groups will have increasing salt concentrations."

State a type of measurement to be made: You probably want to say something like, "I will measure the size of the plant." Good answer, except for the fact that it doesn't say what specifically you're going to measure. Look at the diagram and think about the different things about the plant that you could measure. You could measure the height of the leaves, the number of leaves, the number of roots, the length of the roots. Whichever of these you choose, just be sure that your answer is specific.

An example of experimental results: Well, in the previous section you measured something; so, if your prediction is correct, what should you see in your measurements? You should see the measurements getting larger, increasing. You should say: "The length of the leaves is increasing." Or, you could say: "The number of roots is increasing." *(Scientific Method)*

**44.** For over 100 years, scientists have monitored the carbon dioxide concentrations in the atmosphere in relation to changes in the atmospheric temperature. The graphs below show the data collected for these two factors.

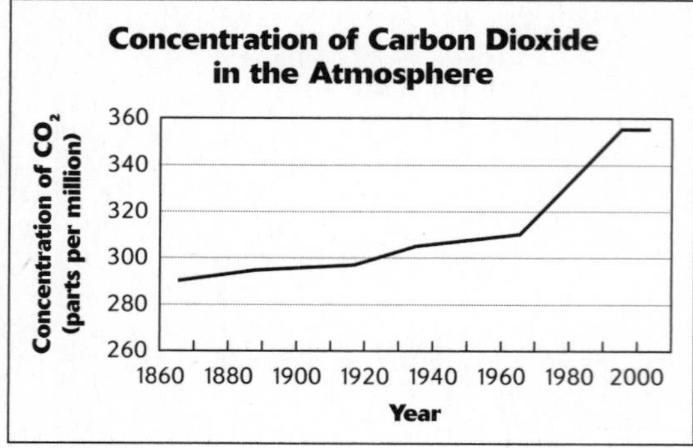


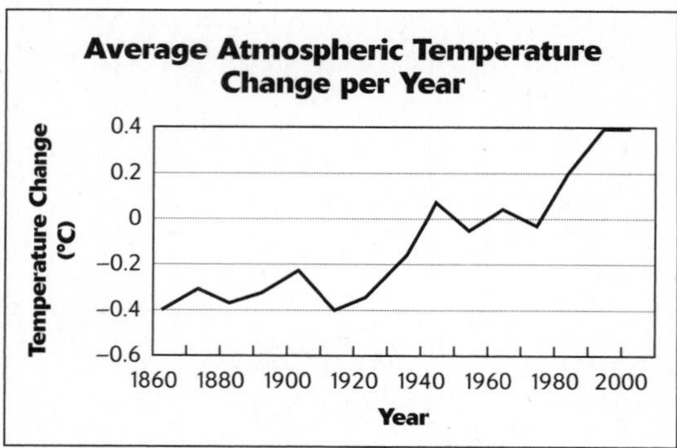


Discuss the overall relationship between carbon dioxide concentration and changes in atmospheric temperature and the effect of these factors on ecosystems. Your answer must include:

- a statement identifying the overall relationship between the concentration of carbon dioxide and changes in atmospheric temperature
- *one* way in which humans have contributed to the increase in atmospheric carbon dioxide
- *one* specific *negative* effect the continued rise in temperature would be likely to have on an ecosystem
- *one* example of how humans are trying to reduce the problem of global warming

**Correct Answer:** The first bullet asks you to identify the relationship that appears to exist between the carbon dioxide concentration and atmospheric temperature. As you look at the two graphs, you can see that, as time increases from 1880 to 2000, both of these factors increase at pretty much the same time and in the same manner. Your answer could be: "As the concentration of carbon dioxide increases, so does the atmospheric temperature."

There are several ways that humans have contributed to increasing levels of carbon dioxide in the atmosphere. They cut down trees (deforestation). Humans also drive a lot of vehicles, run a lot of engines in factories, and burn a lot of coal for electricity. Your answer should be: "Humans use a lot of combustion engines that produce carbon dioxide."

You should know the negative effects of increased atmospheric temperatures by heart and be able to say them in your sleep: Increased atmospheric temperature could cause plants and crops to die (they won't be able to tolerate the increase in temperature). The same is true for animals; an increase in temperature could cause the destruction of habitats, the melting of the polar ice caps and glaciers leading to flooding of coastal areas and islands, and it could lead to changes in weather patterns and more severe weather. Take your pick, but remember, keep it simple.

Humans can do several things to reduce global warming. First, we need to stop producing so much carbon dioxide. Second, humans can use alternative sources of energy, reduce the amount of deforestation and plant more trees, and recycle. *(Interpreting Graphs)*

Base your answers to questions 45 through 48 on the information and diagram below and on your knowledge of biology.

The diagram below shows the results of a test that was done using DNA samples from three bears of different species. Each DNA sample was cut into fragments using a specific enzyme and placed in the wells as indicated below. The DNA fragments were then separated using gel electrophoresis.

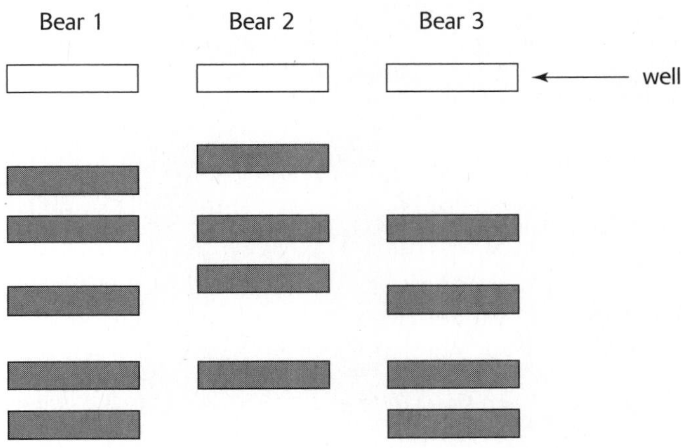


**45.** Which *two* bears are most closely related? Support your answer with data from the test results.

**Correct Answer:** The two bears that are most closely related would be those that have the most DNA fragment lengths in common. In this case, it would be Bear 1 and Bear 3. Bears 1 and 3 share four DNA fragment lengths. Bear 2 only has two fragment lengths in common with Bear 1 or 3. *(Biodiversity)*

**46.** Identify one additional way to determine the evolutionary relationship of these bears.

**Correct Answer:** Additional ways to determine the evolutionary relationship of these bears include: embryological comparison, other biochemical comparisons including different DNA fragments, antigen-antibody reactions, hormones and amino acid sequences, anatomical comparison, and any common vestigial structures. *(Biodiversity)*

**47.** Gel electrophoresis is used to separate DNA fragments on the basis of their

(1) size
(2) color
(3) functions
(4) chromosomes

**Correct Answer: (1)** Gel electrophoresis is a technique used to separate DNA fragments according to size and charge. DNA fragments, which are charged, are deposited into a well on one end of a gel plate.

An electric current is run through the gel, and the DNA fragments migrate through the pores in the gel toward the oppositely charged end of the gel. Smaller molecules, or molecules that are more highly charged, migrate faster and farther through the gel than larger, or less-charged molecules. In this way, the fragments are separated by size and charge. *(Biodiversity)*

**48.** Identify one procedure, other than electrophoresis, that is used in the laboratory to separate the different types of molecules in a liquid mixture.

**Correct Answer:** Procedures used to separate different types of molecules in a liquid mixture, other than gel electrophoresis, include paper chromatography, centrifugation, filtering, and diffusion. *(Scientific Method)*

Base your answers to questions 49 and 50 on the information and diagram below and on your knowledge of biology. The diagram illustrates an investigation carried out in a laboratory activity on diffusion. The beaker and the artificial cell contain water.

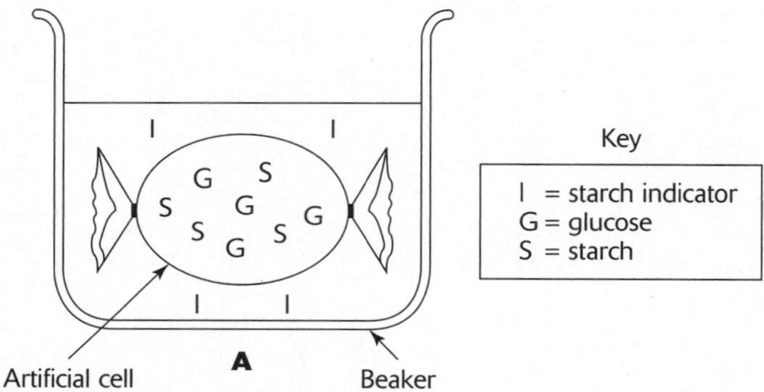


**49.** Predict what would happen over time by showing the location of molecules I, G, and S in Diagram B below.

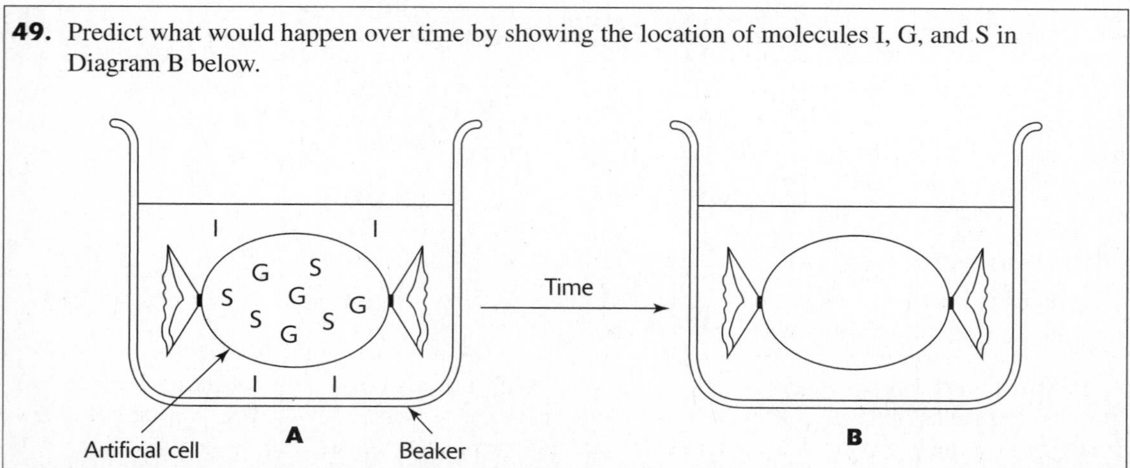

**Correct Answer:** After some time, the artificial cell in the beaker would appear as follows *(Diffusion/Osmosis)*:

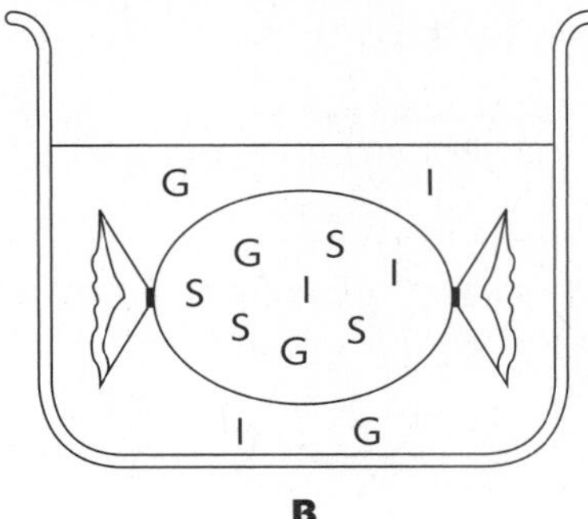


**50.** State what is observed when there is a positive test for starch using the starch indicator.

**Correct Answer:** A positive test for starch using starch indicator solution would show a color change. Specifically, the solution would change from amber to black. *(Diffusion/Osmosis)*

Base your answers to questions 51 through 53 on the following information and diagram.

A student prepared a wet-mount slide of red onion skin and observed it under high power of a compound light microscope (View A). After adding a substance to the slide and waiting one minute, the student observed that there were changes in the cells (View B).

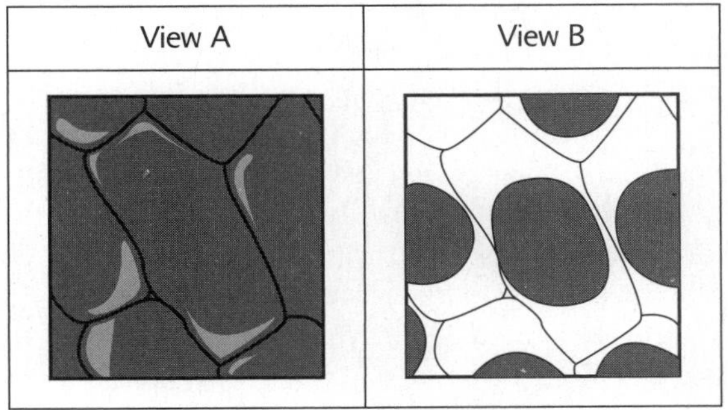


**51.** Identify *one* substance that could have been added to the cells on the slide in View A that would make them resemble the cells observed in View B.

**Correct Answer:** This question is asking about what happens to a cell when the concentration of particles on the outside of a cell is different from the concentration of particles on the inside of the cell. View A shows a "normal" view of red onion cells. The cell membrane is "regular" size because the onion cells are probably in an *isotonic* solution; this means that the concentration of particles is the same on both sides of the membrane. In View B, the cell membrane has shrunk because water has left the inside of the cell. This happens when the particles outside the cell are in greater concentration (known as *hypertonic*) than inside the cell. In order to have the concentration be the same on both sides of the cell membrane, water leaves. One substance that would do this is saltwater. That is the answer. *(Microscopes)*

**52.** Identify the specific substance that diffused to cause the change in appearance form View A to View B.

**Correct Answer:** The water has diffused out of the cell that caused the change from View A to View B. Water is the answer. *(Microscopes)*

**53.** In the box below, sketch how View B would appear when viewed under lower power of the same compound microscope.

**Correct Answer:** The question is trying to find out what happens to the field of view size, the apparent size of the object, and the number of the objects that appear when the magnification is changed from high power to low power. Do you remember doing the lab where you placed a piece of metric ruler on the stage and drew the ruler under different magnifications? Under 40X you could see 4 or 5 millimeter lines and spaces. When you switched to 100X you could only see about 2 millimeter spaces. And when you switched to high power, 400X, you could only see part of 1 millimeter space. This question is based on that lab. When you switch from high power to low power, you'll see a larger field of view; you'll see more cells, but they'll seem farther away, and you may not see all the details you saw under high power. Your drawing should have many more of the same shape and type of cells, drawn smaller. *(Microscopes)*

**54.** Molecules A and B are both organic molecules found in many cells. When tested, it is found that Molecule A cannot pass through a cell membrane, but Molecule B easily passes through. State one way the two molecules could differ that would account for the difference in the ability to pass through the cell membrane.

**Correct Answer:** Molecule A could be too large to pass through a cell membrane, while Molecule B could be small enough to pass through. One molecule may have an electric charge. The cell may have a receptor for one molecule and not the other. *(Diffusion/Osmosis)*

**55.** Plants respond to their environment in many different ways. Design a controlled experiment to test the effect of one environmental factor (such as light, acidity of precipitation, and so on) on some aspect of plant growth. In your experimental design be sure to:

- state the hypothesis
- list the steps of the procedure
- identify the control setup for the experiment
- include an appropriate data table with column headings for the collection of data
- identify the independent variable in the experiment

**Correct Answer:** A hypothesis is a prediction based on observation and prior knowledge.

- *Hypotheses:* The height (or mass) of (a particular species of) a plant is affected by the amount of light received. The height (or mass) of (a particular plant) is affected by pH level. The height (or mass) of (a particular plant) is affected by the amount of water received.
- *Steps of the procedure:* Should include all the information needed to actually set up the experiment, such as the number and species of potted plant used, the materials needed (such as growing lamps, timers, acids/bases, measuring tools, including a metric ruler, triple beam balance, and so on), variables to be kept constant (such as temperature, size of pot, species of plant, amount of water received, type of soil, timing of measurements and watering), initial measurements of the plants, and duration of the experiment.
- *Control group:* The control group is made up of the plants in which the variable is not applied and other conditions are kept constant. These are the plants left alone.
- *Data table:* The data table may include the plants in the control group and the plants in the experimental group, their original (average) height (or mass), and the final (average) height (or mass).
- *Independent variable:* The independent variable is the amount of light, the level of pH, or the amount of water the plant(s) receive. *(Scientific Method)*

**56.** If vegetables become wilted, they can often be made crisp again by soaking them in water. However, they may lose a few nutrients during this process. Using the concept of diffusion and concentration, state why some nutrients would leave the plant cell.

**Correct Answer:** Just as water can diffuse through a cell membrane from a region of high concentration to a region of low concentration, some nutrients may be able to do the same. Nutrients may diffuse from the plant to the surrounding water to reach equilibrium. *(Diffusion/Osmosis)*

**57.** *Elodea* is a plant that lives in fresh water. The diagram below represents one *Elodea* leaf cell in its normal freshwater environment.

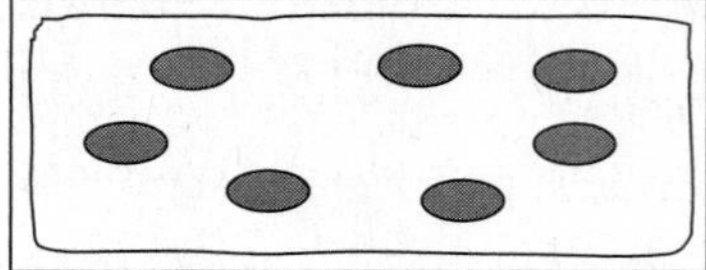

Elodea cell in freshwater

Predict how the contents of the *Elodea* cell would change if the cell were placed in saltwater for several minutes by completing the diagram, "*Elodea* cell in saltwater" below. Label the location of the cell membrane.

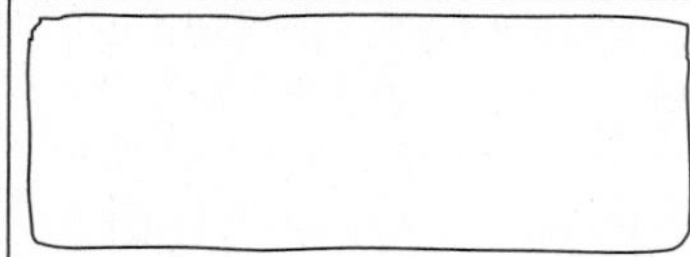

Elodea cell in saltwater

**Correct Answer:** The *Elodea* would lose water causing the cell membrane to shrink and pull away from the cell wall.

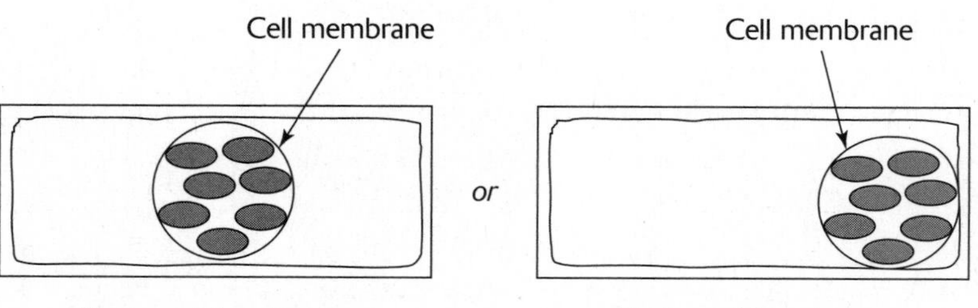


Elodea cell in saltwater    Elodea cell in saltwater

The shrunken cell may be located anywhere within the cell. *(Diffusion/Osmosis)*

Base your answers to questions 58 through 60 on the information and diagram below and on your knowledge of biology.

The DNA of three different species of birds was analyzed to help determine if there is an evolutionary relationship between these species. The diagram shows the results of this analysis.

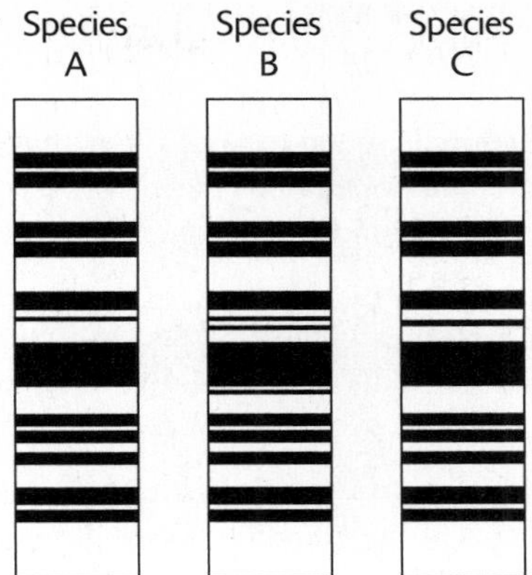


**58.** Identify the technique normally used to separate the DNA fragments to produce the patterns shown in the diagram.

**Correct Answer:** Electrophoresis. *(Biodiversity)*

**59.** The chart below contains amino acid sequences for part of a protein that is found in the feathers on each of these three species of birds.

| ***Species*** | ***Amino Acid Sequence*** |
|---|---|
| A | Arg-Leu-Glu-Gly-His-His-Pro-Lys-Arg |
| B | Arg-Gly-Glu-Gly-His-His-Pro-Lys-Arg |
| C | Arg-Leu-Glu-Gly-His-His-Pro-Lys-Arg |

State *one* way this data supports the inference that these three bird species may be closely related.

**Correct Answer:** You may say, "The three species have similar amino acid sequences, so they may be closely related," or "Because the three species have similar amino acid sequences, they have similar DNA and are closely related." *(Biodiversity)*

**60.** State *one* type of additional information that could be used to determine if these three species are closely related.

**Correct Answer:** One of the following additional pieces of data could be used to determine if the species are closely related:

- Comparing embryos
- Comparing anatomy
- Additional biochemical sequencing studies *(Biodiversity)*

Base your answers to questions 61 and 62 on the information below and on your knowledge of biology.

Gaurs, which are large ox-like animals found in South Asia, have been hunted for sport for many generations. Most recently, as human populations have increased, the gaur's habitats of forest, bamboo jungles, and grassland have dwindled. The gaur is now considered an endangered species.

Scientists have succeeded in preserving endangered species by cloning. Recently, a guar was cloned and the resulting embryo was placed inside a domestic cow, which then gave birth to a baby gaur.

**61.** State one biological benefit of preserving endangered species.

**Correct Answer:** One biological benefit of preserving endangered species is that it helps to maintain the biodiversity of ecosystems. *(Biodiversity)*

**62.** State one way, other than cloning, that gaurs might be saved from extinction.

**Correct Answer:** There are several things that can be done to save animals from extinction. Laws could be made to protect the animals and make it illegal to kill them. Preserves could be set up where the animals could live protected and not be hunted. The land where the animal lives could be protected and not be used for human projects like buildings and farming. *(Biodiversity)*

Base your answers to questions 63 through 65 on the following Universal Genetic Code Chart and on your knowledge of biology.

Universal Genetic Code Chart
Messenger RNA Cordons and the Amino Acids They Code For

| FIRST BASE | SECOND BASE: U | SECOND BASE: C | SECOND BASE: A | SECOND BASE: G | THIRD BASE |
|---|---|---|---|---|---|
| U | UUU, UUC – **Phe**<br>UUA, UUG – **Leu** | UCU, UCC, UCA, UCG – **Ser** | UAU, UAC – **Tyr**<br>UAA, UAG – Stop | UGU, UGC – **Cys**<br>UGA – Stop<br>UGG – **Trp** | U<br>C<br>A<br>G |
| C | CUU, CUC, CUA, CUG – **Leu** | CCU, CCC, CCA, CCG – **Pro** | CAU, CAC – **His**<br>CAA, CAG – **Gin** | CGU, CGC, CGA, CGG – **Arg** | U<br>C<br>A<br>G |
| A | AUU, AUC, AUA – **Ile**<br>AUG – **Met** or START | ACU, ACC, ACA, ACG – **Thr** | AAU, AAC – **Asn**<br>AAA, AAG – **Lys** | AGU, AGC – **Ser**<br>AGA, AGG – **Arg** | U<br>C<br>A<br>G |
| G | GUU, GUC, GUA, GUG – **Val** | GCU, GCC, GCA, GCG – **Ala** | GAU, GAC – **Asp**<br>GAA, GAG – **Glu** | GGU, GGC, GGA, GGG – **Gly** | U<br>C<br>A<br>G |

Some DNA, RNA, and amino acid information from four similar sequences of four plant species is shown in the chart below.

| | | | | | | |
|---|---|---|---|---|---|---|
| Species A | DNA base sequence | CCG | TGC | ATA | CAG | GTA |
| | mRNA base sequence | GGC | ACG | UAU | GUC | CAU |
| | Amino Acid sequence | **GLY** | **THR** | **TYR** | **VAL** | **HIS** |
| Species B | DNA base sequence | TGC | TGC | ATA | CAG | GTA |
| | mRNA base sequence | ____ | ____ | ____ | ____ | ____ |
| | Amino Acid sequence | **THR** | **THR** | **TYR** | **VAL** | **HIS** |
| Species C | DNA base sequence | CCG | TCG | ATA | CAG | GTT |
| | mRNA base sequence | GGC | ACG | UAU | GUC | CAA |
| | Amino Acid sequence | ____ | ____ | ____ | ____ | ____ |
| Species D | DNA base sequence | CCT | TGT | ATG | CAC | GTC |
| | mRNA base sequence | GGA | ACA | UAC | GUG | CAG |
| | Amino Acid sequence | **GLY** | **THR** | **TYR** | **VAL** | **GLN** |

**63.** Using the information given, fill in the missing mRNA base sequence for Species B in the previous chart.

**Correct Answer:** To fill in the chart, the mRNA base sequence must be derived from the DNA base sequence. When transcribing from DNA to RNA, the bases always pair in the following manner: G always pairs with C, and A always pairs with T. Using this configuration, the DNA sequence for Species B is transcribed to: ACG ACG UAU GUC CAU. *(Biodiversity)*

**64.** Using the Universal Genetic Code Chart, fill in the missing amino acid sequence for Species C in the chart.

**Correct Answer:** To find the amino acid sequence for Species C, the Universal Code Chart is read by finding the letter of the first base of the mRNA along the left side of the chart. Then, using only that single row of the chart, match the second base of the mRNA with the letters at top of the chart and read the amino acid code indicated. The mRNA base sequences for Species C are translated to GLY THR TYR VAL GLN. *(Biodiversity)*

**65.** According to these amino acid sequences, which *two* plant species are the most closely related? Support your answer.

**Correct Answer:** Species C and D are most closely related because their amino acid sequences are identical. *(Biodiversity)*

**66.** A certain plant has white flower petals and it usually grows in soil that is slightly basic. Sometimes the plant produces flowers with red petals. A company that sells the plant wants to know if soil pH affects the color of the petals in this plant. Design a controlled experiment to determine if soil pH affects petal color. In your experimental design be sure to:

- state the hypothesis to be tested in the experiment
- state *one* way the control group will be treated differently from the experimental group
- identify *two* factors that must be kept the same in both the control group and the experimental group
- identify the dependent variable in the experiment
- state *one* result of the experiment that would support the hypothesis

**Correct Answer:** Try to organize your response so that you have approximately one sentence per bullet. For each sentence, address each bullet directly.

- *Hypothesis:* Flower color is affected by soil pH.
- The control group will be planted in a soil that is slightly basic, while the experimental group will be planted in a soil that is slightly acidic.
- Every additional factor (except for soil pH) must be kept the same—for example, the amount of soil, the amount of water, the amount of light, and the type of plant used.

- The dependent variable is "flower petal color." If you make the sentence, "As soil pH changes, *then* flower petal color will change," the soil pH is the independent variable and the flower petal color is the dependent variable.
- Red flowers appear on the plants in the slightly acidic soil. *(Scientific Method)*

**67.** A student was comparing preserved specimens of three plant species, X, Y, and Z, in a classroom. Which statement is an example of an observation the student could have made and *not* an inference?

**(1)** The leaves produced by Plant X are 4 cm across and 8 cm in length.
**(2)** Plant Y has large purple flowers that open at night.
**(3)** Plant X produces many seeds that are highly attractive to finches.
**(4)** The flowers of Plant Z are poisonous to household pets.

**Correct Answer: (1)** The leaf measurements are direct observations and, therefore, not inferences. *(Biodiversity)*

**68.** On a television talk show, a guest claims that people who exercise vigorously for 15 minutes or more every day are able to solve math problems more rapidly than people who have no vigorous exercise in their daily routine.

Describe a controlled experiment that could be conducted to test this claim. In your description be sure to:

- state the purpose of the experiment
- state why the sample to be used should be large
- describe how the experimental group will be treated and how the control group will be treated
- state the specific data to be collected during the experiment
- state one way to determine if the results support the claim

**Correct Answer:** The purpose of the experiment is to determine if the claim that people who exercise vigorously for 15 minutes or more every day are able to solve math problems more rapidly than people who have no vigorous exercise in their daily routine can be supported. The sample size should be large due to variation within a population with regard to physical ability for exercise and the level of mental ability to solve math problems. There will be 2 groups of 100 people. Each group will have the same number of males and females, the same ability to solve the math problems, and the same level of physical fitness. The experimental group will exercise vigorously for 15 minutes or more every day for 30 days. The control group will not exercise for the same time period. Both groups will be given the same math problems to solve, appropriate for the level of math ability for those in the group, in a 30-minute time period at the same time and under identical conditions during each day of the experiment. The data to be collected include the day tested and the number of math problems solved for each group in the allotted time. The claim will be supported if the results indicate that the people who exercised were able to solve significantly more math problems than the people who did not exercise. *(Scientific Method)*

**69.** A student measures his pulse rate while he is watching television and records it. Next, he walks to a friend's house nearby and when he arrives, measures and records his pulse rate again. He and his friend then decide to run to the mall a few blocks away. On arriving at the mall, the student measures and records his pulse rate once again. Finally, after sitting and talking for a half-hour, the student measures and records his pulse rate for the last time.

Which graph below best illustrates the expected changes in his pulse rate according to the activities described above?

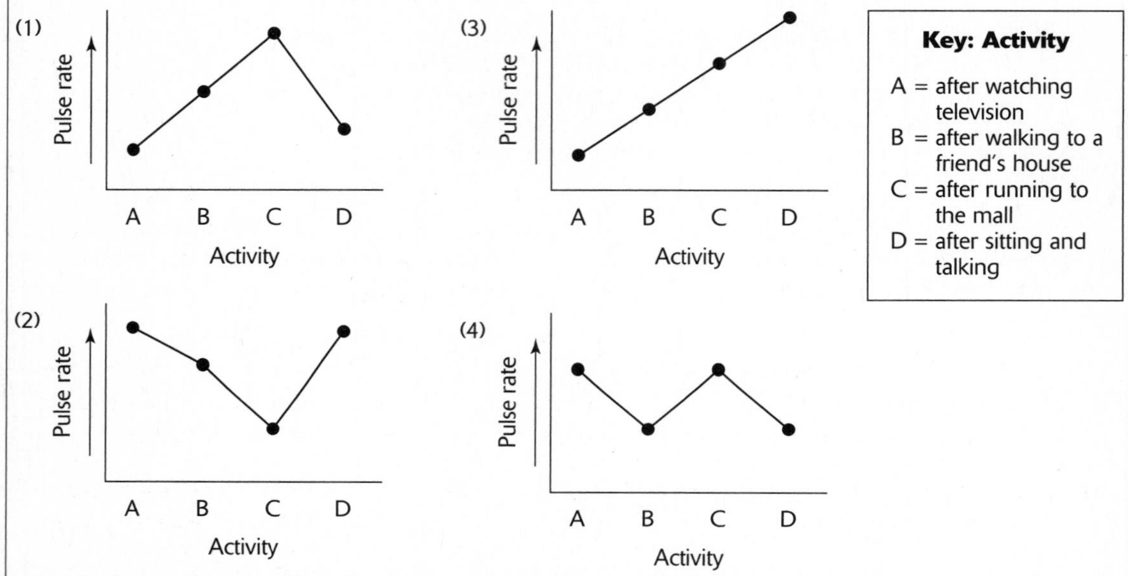


**Correct Answer: (1)** At rest, such as when a person is watching TV, the heart rate is at its lowest. During moderate activity, such as walking, the heart rate will increase because the muscles of the body require more oxygen. During intense activity, such as running, the heart rate will be even higher. At rest again after intense activity, the heart rate will decrease to nearly its initial resting rate. *(Making Connections)*

**70.** An investigation was set up to study the movement of water through a membrane. The results are shown in the diagram below.

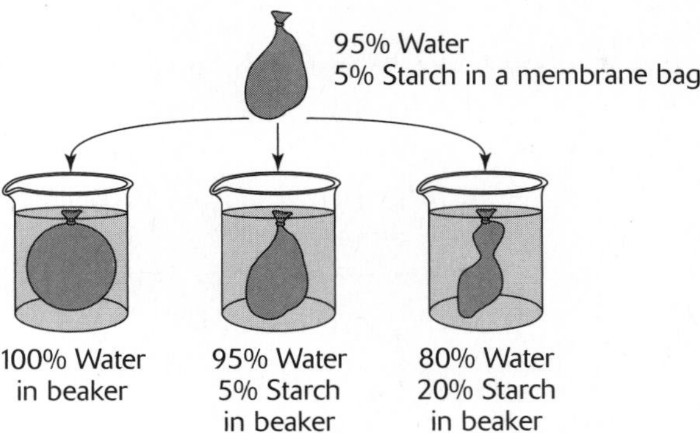


Based on these results, which statement correctly predicts what will happen to red blood cells when they are placed in a beaker containing a water solution in which the salt concentration is much higher than the salt concentration in the red blood cells?

**(1)** The red blood cells will absorb water and increase in size.
**(2)** The red blood cells will lose water and decrease in size.
**(3)** The red blood cells will first absorb water, then lose water and maintain their normal size.
**(4)** The red blood cells will first lose water, then absorb water, and finally double in size.

**Correct Answer: (2)** The diagram shows what happens to a cell when it is placed in a hypotonic, isotonic, and hypertonic solution, respectively. If a red blood cell is placed in a solution in which the water concentration is lower than that of the cell (a hypertonic solution), water will diffuse by the process of osmosis from a region of high concentration to a region of low concentration. Water will leave the red blood cell causing the cell to shrink. *(Diffusion/Osmosis)*

Base your answers to questions 71 through 73 on the information below and on your knowledge of biology.

Paper chromatography can be used to investigate evolutionary relationships.

Leaves from a plant were ground and mixed with a solvent. The mixture of ground leaves and solvent was then filtered. Using a toothpick, 20 drops of the filtrate (material that passed through the filter) were placed at one spot on a strip of chromatography paper.

This procedure was repeated using leaves from three other species of plants. A separate strip of chromatography paper was prepared for each plant species. Each of the four strips of chromatography paper was placed in a different beaker containing the same solvent for the same amount of time. One of the laboratory setups is shown below.

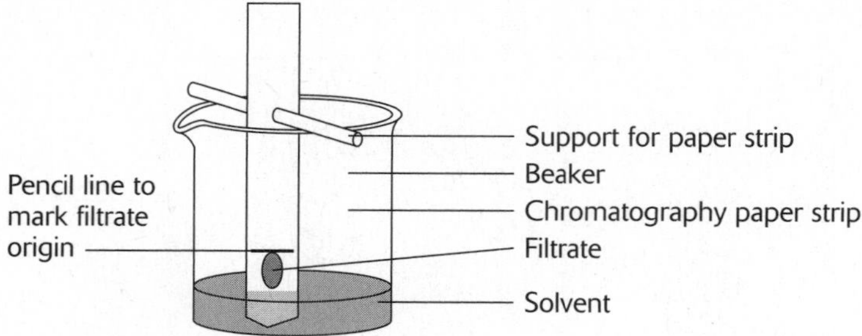


**71.** State *one* reason for using a new toothpick for the filtrate from each plant.

**Correct Answer:** The reason for using a new toothpick for the filtrate from each plant is so that there is no contamination of samples. That is your answer. If you used the same toothpick over and over to transfer drops to the paper, you would carry along drops of each filtrate, so when you went to do the chromatography, all the strips would look the same. *(Biodiversity)*

**72.** State *one* way the four strips would most likely be different from each other after being removed form the beakers.

**Correct Answer:** One way that the strips would most likely be different from each other is that the marks (colors) on the strips would be different because you were using filtrates from four different plant species. There could be different combinations and/or amounts of marks (colors). *(Scientific Method)*

**73.** State how a comparison of these resulting strips could indicate evolutionary relationships.

**Correct Answer:** One way to determine evolutionary relationships among organisms is to examine their proteins and DNA. If the patterns revealed from the chromatography are similar, than scientists could say that the organisms are related and share a common ancestor. Your answer could be: "If the strips resembled each other, then the species are probably related." *(Biodiversity)*

Base your answers to questions 74 through 76 on the information and graph below and on your knowledge of biology.

Pulse-rate data were collected from some students during their lunchtime for the lab activity, *Making Connections.* The data are represented in the histogram below.

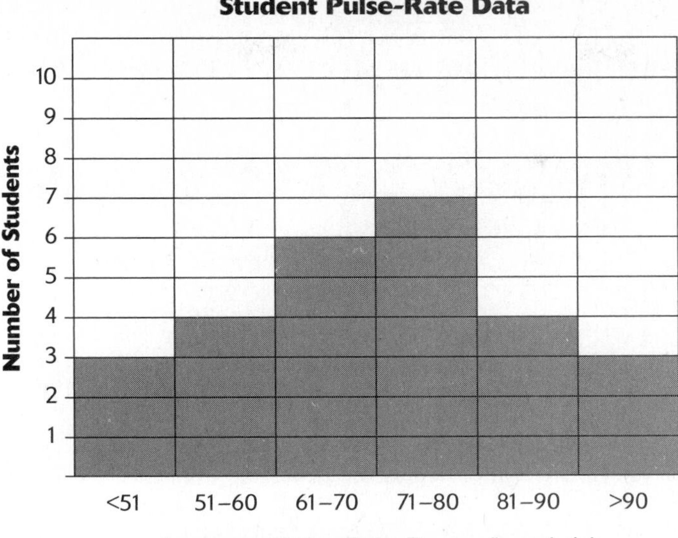


**74.** The histogram includes data from a total of how many students?

**(1)** 6
**(2)** 7
**(3)** 10
**(4)** 27

**Correct Answer: (4)** To figure out how many students were included in the study, count all the shaded boxes. The total number of shaded boxes is 27. *(Making Connections)*

**75.** Describe *one* way in which a pulse rate below 45 would disrupt homeostasis in an individual whose average resting pulse rate falls in the range of 71 to 80.

**Correct Answer:** A reduced pulse rate would disrupt homeostasis because:

- blood circulation would be reduced
- oxygen delivery would be reduced
- carbon dioxide removal would be reduced
- the body would be unable to regulate body temperature *(Making Connections)*

**76.** State *one* way the data would most likely be different if the pulse rates were collected immediately after exercising instead of during lunch.

**Correct Answer:** After exercising, the pulse rates would higher because strenuous physical activity causes an increase in pulse rate. *(Making Connections)*

Base your answers to questions 77 and 78 on the information provided and on your knowledge of biology.

A student observed the physical characteristics of seven organisms and prepared the data table below.

**Organism Comparison**

| *Organism* | *Internal Skeleton Present* | *Legs Present* | *Wings Present* | *Fur Present* | *Moist Body Covering Present* |
|---|---|---|---|---|---|
| Earthworm | no | no | no | no | yes |
| Fish | yes | no | no | no | yes |
| Fly | no | yes | yes | no | no |
| Gorilla | yes | yes | no | yes | no |
| Jellyfish | no | no | no | no | yes |
| Parrot | yes | yes | yes | no | no |
| Snake | yes | no | no | no | no |

One of the student's classmates sorted the seven organisms into two groups as shown below.

| *Group 1* | *Group 2* |
|---|---|
| Fly | |
| Parrot | Earthworm |
| Gorilla | |
| Snake | |
| Fish | |
| Jellyfish | |

**77.** Which characteristic from the data table did the student use to group the organisms?

**Correct Answer:** The characteristic used to group the organisms would be the presence of wings, or the ability to fly. *(Biodiversity)*

**78.** Another classmate suggested that the earthworm is more closely related to the jellyfish than to any other organism observed. State the evidence from the data table that the student most likely used for this suggested relationship.

**Correct Answer:** The evidence used for the suggested relationship between the jellyfish and the earthworm would be that, for every category listed, the earthworm and the jellyfish had the same characteristics. *(Biodiversity)*

**79.** Fish and snakes are very different organisms, yet they have many similarities. Provide a biological explanation for the fact that fish and snakes have so many characteristics in common.

**Correct Answer:** Fish and snakes have so many characteristics in common because they may share a common ancestor, they may have some similar environmental pressures, or they may have a large percentage of genes in common. *(Biodiversity)*

Base your answers to questions 80 and 81 on the finch diversity chart below, which contains information concerning the finches found on the Galapagos Islands.

**Finch Diversity**

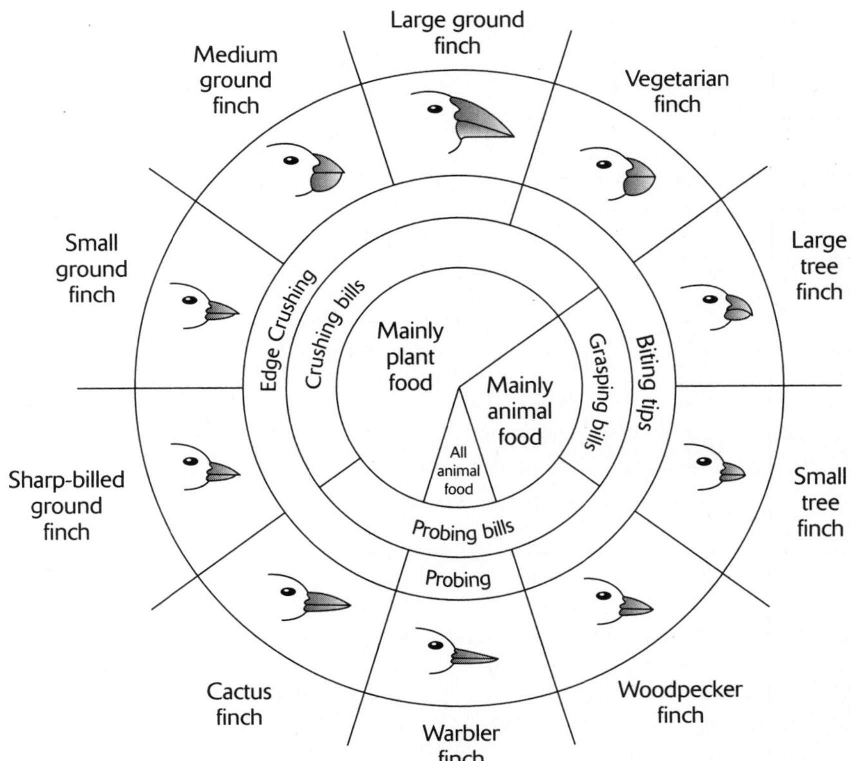

**80.** Identify *one* bird that would most likely compete for food with the large tree finch. Support your answer.

**Correct Answer:** You may answer, "The small tree finch and the large tree finch would likely compete for food because they both have grasping bills and eat mostly animal food," or "The woodpecker finch and the large tree finch would likely compete for food because they both eat the same type of food." *(Beaks of Finches)*

**81.** Identify *one* trait, other than beak characteristics, that would contribute to the survival of a finch species and state *one* way this trait contributes to the success of this species.

**Correct Answer:** Traits other than beak characteristics that would contribute to the survival of a finch and the way this trait contributes to success include the following:

- Faster or more aggressive birds get to seed faster and do not let other birds eat.
- Larger or stronger birds compete better for seeds.
- Coordination helps some birds avoid predators.

*(Beaks of Finches)*

Base your answers to questions 82 and 83 on the information below and on your knowledge of biology.

A student squeezes and releases a clothespin as often as possible for 2 minutes and then takes his pulse for 20 seconds. After a 2-minute rest, he repeats the procedure. This pattern is repeated one more time. The student's 20-second pulse counts were 23, 26, and 21.

**82.** Complete the "Pulse/Min" column in the data table below for all three trials as well as the average pulse rate per minute.

**Pulse Rate after Activity**

| *Trial* | *20-Second Pulse Counts* | *Pulse/Min* |
|---|---|---|
| 1 | 23 | |
| 2 | 26 | |
| 3 | 21 | |
| Average | | |

**Correct Answer:** The Pulse/Min for each trial is determined by multiplying the "20-Second Pulse Counts" by 3 because there are three 20-second intervals in each minute. The average "Pulse/Min" is determined by adding the "Pulse/Min" for each of the three trials, and then dividing that sum by 3. The correct data are shown in the completed table. *(Making Connections)*

| *Trial* | *20-Second Pulse Counts* | *Pulse/Min* |
|---|---|---|
| 1 | 23 | 69 |
| 2 | 26 | 78 |
| 3 | 21 | 63 |
| Average | | 70 |

**83.** What additional data should the student have collected in order to determine the effect of squeezing a clothespin on his pulse rate?

**Correct Answer:** To determine if there was an effect of squeezing a clothespin on pulse rate, the student would need the resting pulse rate for comparison. *(Making Connections)*

Base your answers to questions 84 and 85 on the information below and on your knowledge of biology.

In an investigation, 28 students in a class determined their pulse rates after performing each of three different activities. Each activity was performed there times during equal time intervals. The average results are shown in the graph below.

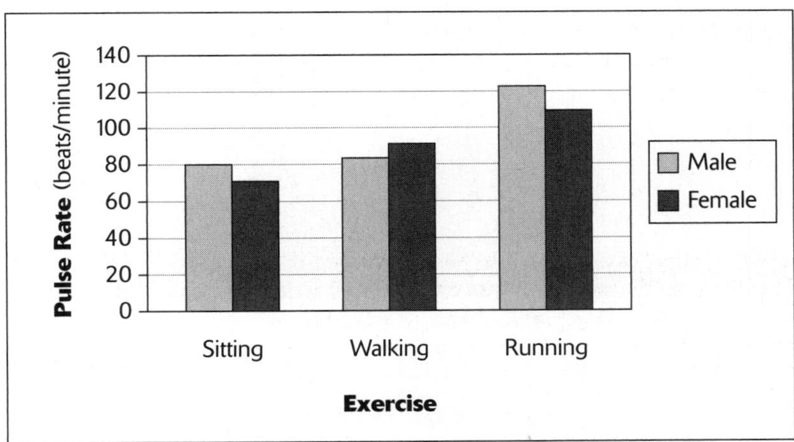


**84.** Before constructing the graph, it would have been most helpful to organize the results of the investigation in

(1) a research plan
(2) an equation
(3) a data table
(4) a generalization

**Correct Answer: (3)** Graphs are always made from data tables. *(Making Connections)*

**85.** Some students concluded that males always have a higher pulse rate than females. Does the graph support this conclusion? Justify your answer.

**Correct Answer:** Looking at the graph you see that the males' pulse rates were higher than the girls' in two of the three categories, running and sitting. Based on this evidence, the statement is false. Boys do not *always* have higher pulse rates than girls. Your answer should be: "No, the boys' pulse rate is not higher than the girls' in all activities." *(Making Connections)*

Base your answers to questions 86 through 88 on the information and diagram below.

An investigation was carried out using the two setups shown below. Other than the difference shown in the diagram, all other conditions were identical.

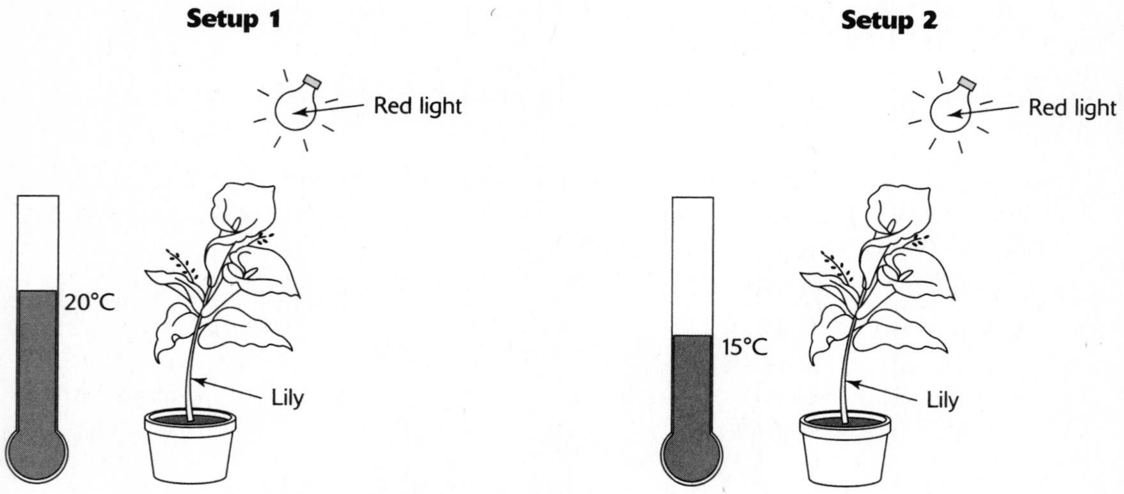


**86.** State one possible hypothesis that could be tested using these setups.

**Correct Answer:** Possible hypotheses could be the following:

- Temperature has an effect on the rate of growth of a lily grown under red light.
- Lilies grow slower at 15°C than at 20°C under red light.
- Lilies grown at 20°C bloom earlier than lilies grown at 15°C under red light.
- Lilies grown at 20°C have more flowers than lilies grown at 15°C. *(Scientific Method)*

**87.** What data should be collected in order to test the hypothesis stated in question 119?

**Correct Answer:** Data to be collected to test the hypotheses in question 119 include the following:

- height and mass of the plant
- number of leaves
- the amount of time it takes for the plants to bloom
- number of flowers on each plant *(Scientific Method)*

**88.** Describe one change that could be made in the investigation to improve it.

**Correct Answer:** Changes to improve the investigation include the following:

- use white light instead of red light
- use a range of temperatures between 15°C and 20°C
- use a larger sample size *(Scientific Method)*

Base your answers to questions 89 through 92 on the information below and on your knowledge of biology.

To demonstrate techniques used in DNA analysis, a student was given two paper strip samples of DNA. The two DNA samples are shown below.

Sample 1: ATT**CCGG**TAATCCCGTAATG**CCGG**ATAATACT**CCGG**TAATATC

Sample 2: ATTCCGG**TAAT**CCCG**TAAT**GCCGGA**TAAT**ACTCCGGTAATATC

The student cut between the C and G in each of the bold **CCGG** sequences in Sample 1 and between the As in each of the bold **TAAT** sequences in Sample 2. Both sets of fragments were then arranged on a paper model of a gel.

**89.** The action of what kind of molecules was being demonstrated when the DNA samples were cut?

**Correct Answer:** DNA can be cut by a "restriction enzyme." *(Biodiversity)*

**90.** Identify the technique that was being demonstrated when the fragments were arranged on the gel model.

**Correct Answer:** Gel electrophoresis. This lab attempts to determine which species (Sample 1 or Sample 2) was most closely related to Botana Curas. By cutting the DNA with restriction enzymes and then putting the fragments on a gel, scientists can determine which species are most closely related by the banding pattern. *(Biodiversity)*

**91.** The results of this type of DNA analysis are often used to help determine

(1) the number of DNA molecules in an organism
(2) if two species are closely related
(3) the number of mRNA molecules in DNA
(4) if two organisms contain carbohydrate molecules

**Correct Answer: (2)** This lab attempts to determine which species (Sample 1 or Sample 2) was most closely related to Botana Curas. By cutting the DNA with restriction enzymes and then putting the fragments on a gel, scientists can determine which species are most closely related by the banding pattern. *(Biodiversity)*

**92.** State *one* way that the arrangement of the two samples on the gel model would differ.

**Correct Answer:** Because a different restriction enzyme was used in each sample, the samples would be cut in different locations. As a result, the bands on the gel would form differently. The bands will likely be in different locations and in different numbers. *(Biodiversity)*

Base your answers to questions 93 through 95 on the passage below and on your knowledge of biology.

> When Charles Darwin traveled to the Galapagos Islands, he observed 14 distinct varieties of finches on the islands. Darwin also observed that each finch variety ate a different type of food and lived in a slightly different habitat from the other finches. Darwin concluded that the finches all shared a common ancestor but had developed different beak structures.

**93.** The 14 varieties of finches are most likely the result of

(1) absence of biodiversity
(2) biological evolution
(3) asexual reproduction
(4) lack of competition

**Correct Answer: (2)** Evolution is the change of species over time through survival and reproduction of the organisms that are fittest. Evolution is responsible for the diversity of life on Earth. *(Beaks of Finches)*

**94.** The second sentence best describes

(1) an ecosystem
(2) a food web
(3) a niche
(4) a predator/prey relationship

**Correct Answer: (3)** A niche is the unique role that each organism occupies in relation to all the biotic and abiotic factors. In this example, each variety of finch ate a different type of food and lived in a slightly different habitat, which describes its niche. Insufficient information is provided to describe the ecosystem, food web, or predator/prey relationship. *(Beaks of Finches)*

**95.** The different beak structures mentioned in the last sentence were most likely influenced by

**(1)** selection for favorable variations
**(2)** environmental conditions identical to those of the common ancestor
**(3)** abnormal mitotic cell division
**(4)** characteristics that are acquired during the bird's lifetime

**Correct Answer: (1)** Darwin's conclusion that all finches shared a common ancestor but had developed different beak structures was influenced by natural selection for variations that were favorable, or gave these organisms an some advantage that allowed them to survive better and reproduce more. This is the only way in which different beak structures could arise in a natural ecosystem, such as the Galapagos Islands. *(Beaks of Finches)*

**96.** Beak structures differ between individuals of one species of bird. These differences most likely indicate

**(1)** the presence of a variety of food sources
**(2)** a reduced rate of reproduction
**(3)** a large supply of one kind of food
**(4)** an abundance of predators

**Correct Answer: (1)** According to Darwin's Theory of Evolution, the presence of different beaks in a species of birds means that, over time, each bird that possessed a specific type of beak was better adapted to eat a certain kind of food. The more variety of beaks means that there is a variety of food sources.
A reduced rate of reproduction—choice (2)—would have nothing to do with differences in beaks. If there were only a large supply of only one kind of food, as in choice (3), the opposite effect would be seen: There would be fewer varieties of beaks because there would not be anything different to eat. Even if there were a lot of predators, as in choice (4), you would still see a variety of beaks, but there would be fewer birds with those beaks. *(Beaks of Finches)*

**97.** A student squeezed a clothespin as many times as possible in a 30-second time period. The student repeated this procedure nine more times in quick succession. The data obtained are in the chart below.

| *Trial* | *Number of Squeezes in 30 Seconds* |
|---|---|
| 1 | 32 |
| 2 | 29 |
| 3 | 28 |
| 4 | 27 |
| 5 | 26 |
| 6 | 25 |
| 7 | 23 |
| 8 | 21 |
| 9 | 19 |
| 10 | 17 |

State one hypothesis that this data would support concerning the relationship between number of trials and number of squeezes in 30 seconds.

**Correct Answer:** Looking at the data, you can see that, by the time the student got to the ninth trial, the number of squeezes had decreased from 32 in the first trial to just 17 in the last trial. ***Remember:*** A hypothesis is a reasonable explanation of what you expect to happen. You need to say something that relates the number of squeezes and the number of trials. Your answer could be, "As the number of trials increases, the number of squeezes decreases." Or, you could say, "The number of squeezes will decrease as the number of trials increase." *(Scientific Method)*

**98.** The diagram below shows variations in beak sizes and shapes for several birds on the Galapagos Islands.

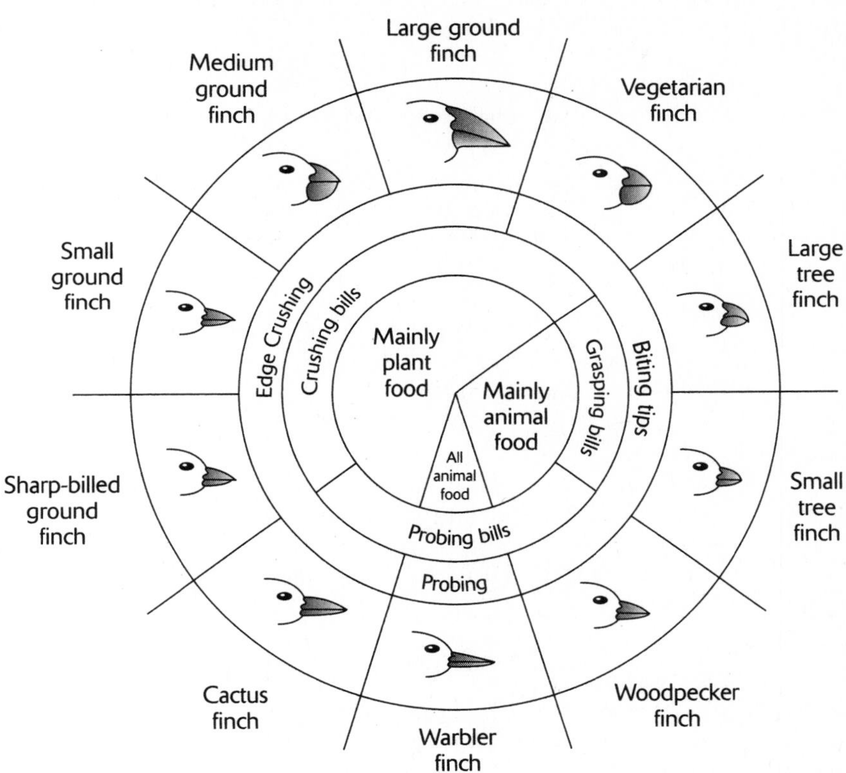


Using information provided in the chart, identify *two* birds that would most likely compete for food in times of food shortage and explain why they would compete.

**Correct Answer:** Two species that would compete for food in times of food shortage would be two birds with similar beaks feeding on similar types of food. Based on the chart, two birds that this could happen to are: medium ground finch and small ground finch. Why? Because they both have edge-crushing bills and both feed on mainly plant food. You could also pick large tree finch and small tree finch. These two birds have biting tips and grasping bills and eat mainly animal food. *(Beaks of Finches)*

**99.** Even though the finches on the various Galapagos Islands require different biotic and abiotic factors for their survival, these finches would most likely be grouped in the same

**(1)** species, but found in different habitats
**(2)** kingdom, but found in different ecological niches
**(3)** species and found in the same biosphere
**(4)** population, but found in different ecosystems

**Correct Answer: (2)** The best way to answer this question is by eliminating the other choices. It can't be choice (1), because these finches are all different species, and they all live in the same habitat. It can't be choice (3) for the same reason, but they do live in the same biosphere. It can't be choice (4), because, by definition, each species is a separate population—besides, they're all in the same ecosystem. It is choice (2), because they do all belong in the animal kingdom and, as the diagram shows, they all have different niches, or roles. Some are vegetarian feeders, while others feed on animal food. *(Beaks of Finches)*

**100.** Galapagos finches evolved partly due to

**(1)** cloning and recombination
**(2)** migration and selective breeding
**(3)** mutation and asexual reproduction
**(4)** variation and competition

**Correct Answer: (4)** Darwin's idea about variation is that some animals were born with adaptations that matched their environment. This allowed them to survive and reproduce. If the variation they possessed allowed them to better compete for food, then that also enabled them to survive more than those that lacked those adaptations.

Cloning and recombination—choice (1)—were not around when the finches evolved. The finches did migrate, but no one was involved in selectively breeding them—choice (2). The finches reproduce sexually not asexually—choice (3). *(Beaks of Finches)*

**101.** The diagram below represents a laboratory setup used by a student during an investigation of diffusion.

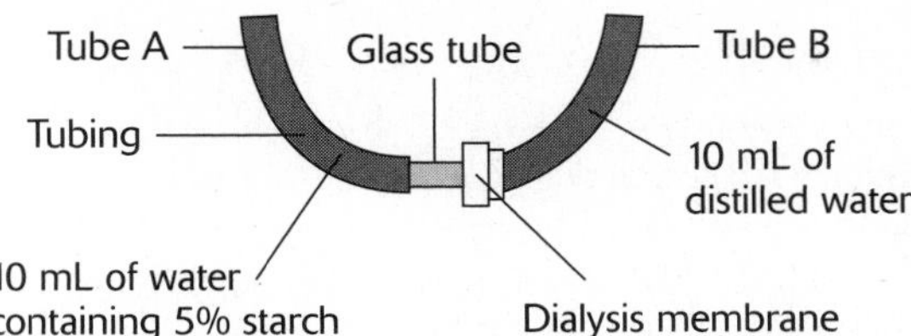


Which statement best explains why the liquid in Tube A will rise over a period of time?

(1) The starch concentrations are equal on both sides of the membrane.
(2) The water will pass from a region of lower starch concentration to one of higher starch concentration.
(3) Water and starch volumes are the same in both tubes A and B.
(4) The fluids in both tubes A and B will change from a higher temperature to a lower temperature.

**Correct Answer: (2)** Diffusion of both starch and water will occur across the dialysis membrane. Diffusion is the movement of a substance from an area of high concentration to an area of lower concentration. Starch will move from Tube A, where the concentration of starch is high (5 percent), to Tube B, where the concentration of starch is lower (0 percent). Water will move from Tube B, where the concentration of water is high (100 percent) to Tube A, where the concentration of water is lower (95 percent). The movement of water will cause the liquid in Tube A to rise over time. *(Diffusion/Osmosis)*

Base your answers to questions 102 and 103 on the information below and on your knowledge of biology.

In birds, the ability to crush and eat seeds is related to the size, shape, and thickness of the beak. Birds with larger, thicker beaks are better adapted to crush and open seeds that are larger. One species of bird found in the Galapagos Islands is the medium ground finch. It is easier for most of the medium ground finches to pick up and crack open smaller seeds rather than larger seeds. When food is scarce, some of the birds have been observed eating larger seeds.

**102.** Describe *one* change in beak characteristics that would most likely occur in the medium ground finch population after many generations when an environmental change results in a permanent shortage of small seeds.

**Correct Answer:** Beaks will get larger and stronger. If smaller seeds are scarce, the medium ground finches with larger beaks will be able to crack open seeds. They will pass on the larger beak gene to their offspring and their offspring may have larger beaks. The medium ground finches with smaller beaks that can't open seeds will die and will not pass on their genetic information. *(Beaks of Finches)*

**103.** Explain this long-term change in beak characteristics using the concepts of:

- Competition
- Survival of the fittest
- Inheritance

**Correct Answer:** When small seeds are scarce, there will be *competition* for the larger seeds. Those medium ground finches with larger beaks will be able to crack open seeds. Those finches will be *fit* for the environment, they will have a better chance of reproducing, and their offspring may *inherit* larger beaks. The medium ground finches with smaller beaks that can't open seeds will die and will not pass on their genetic information. *(Beaks of Finches)*

**104.** R, S, and T are three species of birds. Species S and T show similar coloration. The enzymes found in species R and T show similarities. Species R and T also exhibit many of the same behavioral patterns.

Show the relationship between species R, S, and T by placing the letter representing each species at the top of the appropriate branch on the diagram below.

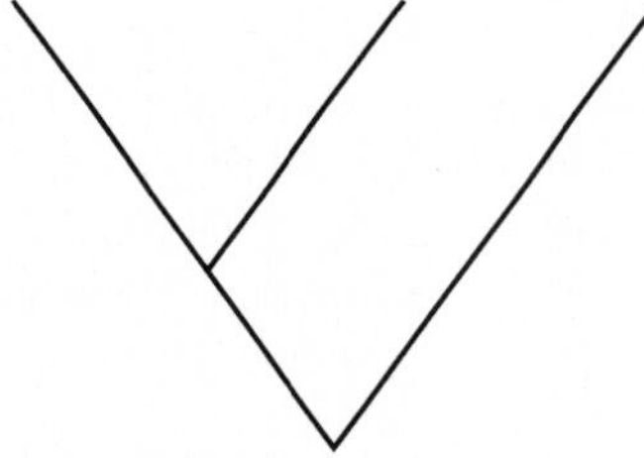

**Correct Answer:** Although species S and T show similar coloration, the enzymes (biochemical) and behavioral patterns between species R and T suggest a more recent common ancestry. Similar coloration could be due to the environment (camouflage, for example).

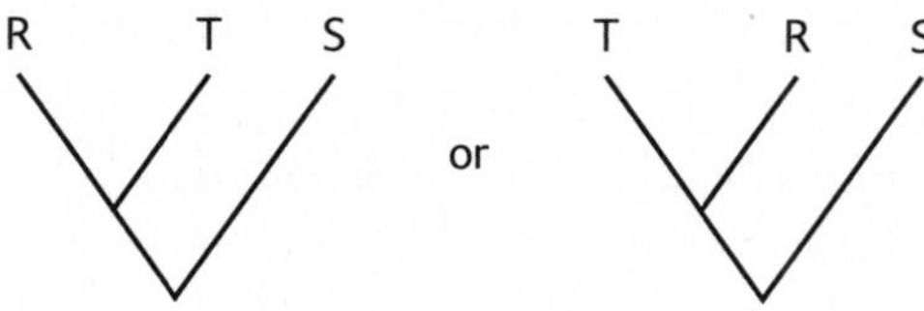


*(Biodiversity)*

**105.** An experiment was designed to see what effects ibuprofen would have on laboratory mice. Large numbers of male mice and an equal number of female mice were used in this investigation. The male mice were placed in an area with food and water. The female mice were placed in a separate area of the same size. The female mice were given additional food and water. The males were each given 100 milligrams of ibuprofen each day, mixed with their food, and the females were each given 50 milligrams of ibuprofen each day, mixed with their food.

Identify *two* errors in the design of this investigation.

**Correct Answer:** An experiment is designed to test a specific hypothesis. There is no clear hypothesis to be tested. The experimenter has not indicated exactly what it is about the mice that should be observed or measured.

In an experiment, there should be two groups—a control group that does not receive the experimental treatment, and an experimental group that does receive the treatment. There was no control group indicated in this experiment. There were two groups separated into males and females. Also, there should be equal numbers of males and females.

In an experiment, all variables must be kept the same between all subjects in the control group and all subjects in the experimental group. If the experimenter intended for the males and females to be included in the same group (the experimental group, it is assumed), the error would be that the male and female mice were not given the same amount of food and water.

In an experiment, only one variable is tested at a time so that significant differences in results between the control group and the experimental group can be owed to the experimental treatment. In this experiment, the male and female mice were not given the same dosage of ibuprofen each day. *(Scientific Method)*

**106.** Identify the substance that was used to treat the DNA to produce the fragments that were put into the wells.

**Correct Answer:** Restriction enzymes. Restriction enzymes are used to cut the DNA at specific places. The result is DNA fragments of various lengths/sizes that, when run in gel electrophoresis like this one, will separate the fragments according to their sizes. *(Interpreting Graphs)*

**107.** A student prepared a wet mount of some red onion cells and then added some saltwater to the slide. The student observed the slide using a compound light microscope. Diagram A is typical of what the student observed after adding saltwater.

Complete Diagram B to show how the contents of the red onion cells should appear if the cell were then rinsed with distilled water for several minutes.

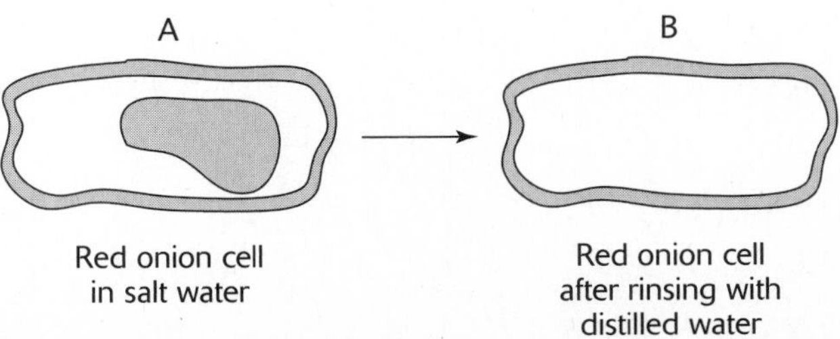

**Correct Answer:** This question is referring to the "tonics": hypotonic, hypertonic, and isotonic. It helps to know what they mean. All the terms refer to the area *outside* of the cell. In a normal red onion cell, the cell membrane should be pushed right up against the cell wall. In Diagram A, after the saltwater was added, the area outside the cell was hypertonic: The concentration of salt was greater outside the cell than inside. As a result, water left the inside of the cell and the cell membrane shrunk—it got smaller. By adding distilled water to the wet-mount slide, the reverse will happen. Now the area outside the cell is hypotonic: The concentration of salt outside the cell is less than inside the cell. Therefore, water will enter the cell and the cell will swell up, it will get larger. Your drawing should show the cell membrane expanded right up against the cell wall. *(Diffusion/Osmosis)*

**108.** In members of a bird species living on a remote island, the greatest number of beak variations in the population would most likely be found when

(1) there is a high level of competition for limited resources
(2) homeostasis is limited by a severe climate
(3) they have a large and varied food supply
(4) they are prey for a large number of predators

**Correct Answer: (3)** The more varied the food supply is, the more variety of beaks there will be. *(Beaks of Finches)*

**109.** The different tools used during the beaks of finches lab represented

(1) feeding adaptations in finches
(2) nest construction adaptations
(3) variations in seed size
(4) variations in ecosystems

**Correct Answer: (1)** This was the whole idea behind this lab: to show you what would happen to a population of birds if they had different beaks and they fed on seeds in order to survive. *(Beaks of Finches)*

Base your answer to question 110 on the portion of the mRNA codon chart and information below.

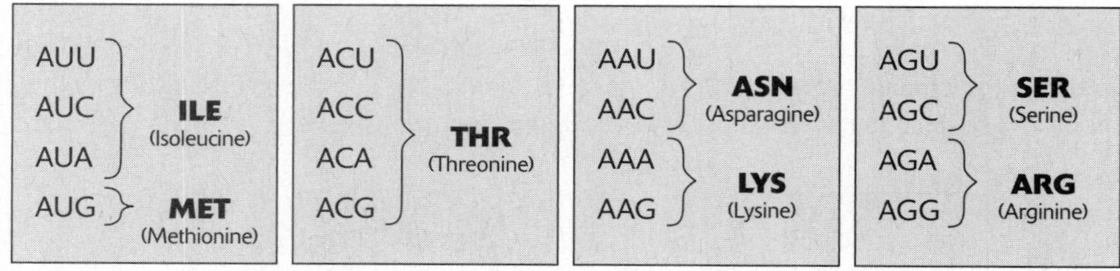


Series I represents three mRNA codons. Series II includes a mutation of Series I.

Series I AGAUCGAGU

Series II ACAUCGAGU

**110.** How would the amino acid sequence produced by the mutant strand (Series II) compare to the amino acid sequence produced by Series I?

**(1)** The amino acid sequence would be shorter.
**(2)** One amino acid in the sequence would change.
**(3)** The amino acid sequence would remain unchanged.
**(4)** More than one amino acid in the sequence would change.

**Correct Answer: (2)** If you compare the mRNA sequences, you see that, in the first codon of Series II, the codon is ACA. The first codon in Series I is AGA. AGA codes for the amino acid ARG (arginine). The first codon in Series II codes for the amino acid THR (threonine). The remainder of both sequences are the same. This excludes choices (1), (3), and (4). *(Biodiversity)*

**111.** A red onion cell has undergone a change, as represented in the diagram below.

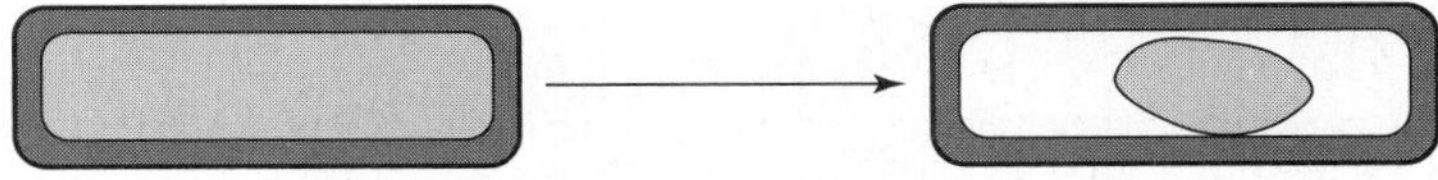

This change is most likely due to the cell being placed in

**(1)** distilled water
**(2)** light
**(3)** saltwater
**(4)** darkness

**Correct Answer: (3)** A red onion cell placed in saltwater will shrink because diffusion causes the salt to enter the cell where the concentration of salt is low compared to the surrounding solution. This movement of salt also causes water to move out of the cell where the concentration of water is lower compared to inside the cell. A cell placed in distilled water would swell, because the concentration of water would be greater outside the cell (compared to inside the cell) and water would move into the cell. Diffusion is the movement of a substance from an area of high concentration to an area of lower concentration. *(Diffusion/Osmosis)*

**112.** The photos below show two red onion cells viewed with the high power of a compound light microscope. Describe the steps that could be used to make Cell A resemble Cell B using a piece of paper towel and a eyedropper or a pipette *without removing the cover slip.*

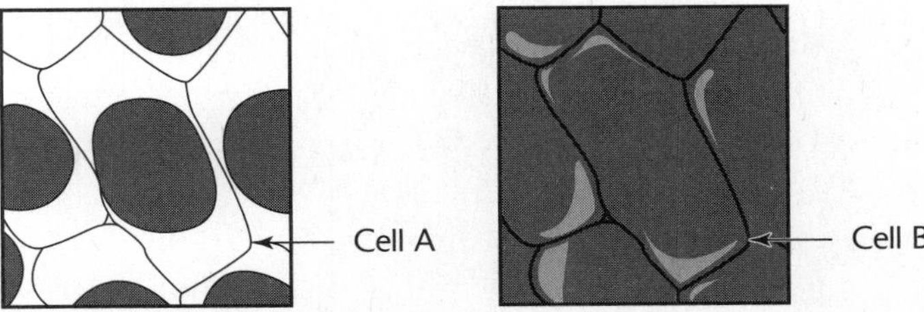

**Correct Answer:** This process is usually done in an opposite way of what is shown here: You usually start with red onion cells that look like the B cells and end up with cells that look like the A cells. The lab activity that is shown here is hypertonic concentration. The area outside the onion cells is more concentrated than the area inside the onion cells. So, to equalize the concentration, water leaves the cell and the cell shrinks. This is what is seen in the photo of Cell A. The A cells got like this because the person put saltwater on the slide and drew it through using a piece of paper towel on the other side of the cover slip from the dropper. In order to get the onion cells to like the B cells, you have to reverse the concentration. The answer you have to give is to take plain water (no salt) and, using the dropper, place several drops on one side of the cover slip. On the other side of the cover slip, place a piece of paper towel right up against the edge of it. It will start to draw out the water that's under the cover slip. The plain water that you place on the other side will now be drawn under the cover slip, replacing the saltwater. Now the process will be reversed. The concentration of salt will be less outside the cell (hypotonic) and water will enter the cell to make the concentrations equal on both sides of the cell. *(Microscopes)*

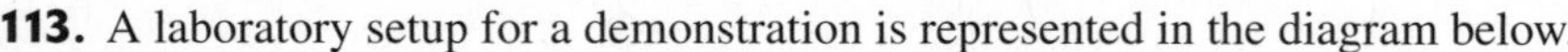

**113.** A laboratory setup for a demonstration is represented in the diagram below.

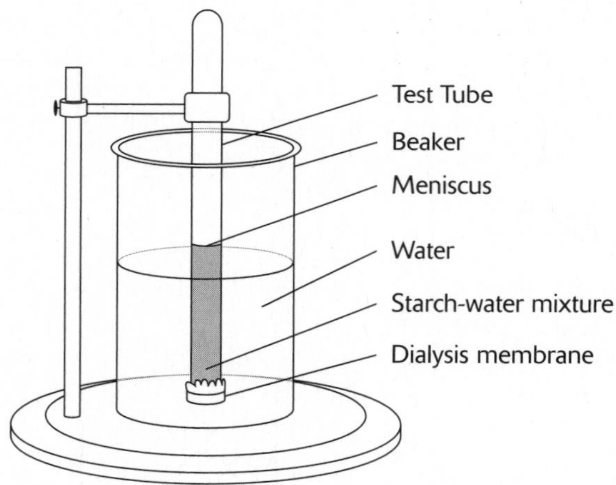


Describe how an indicator can be used to determine if starch diffuses through the membrane into the beaker. In your answer, be sure to include:

- the procedure used
- how to interpret the results

**Correct Answer:** Be sure to answer all parts of the question. To determine if starch diffused through the dialysis membrane, the starch indicator (iodine), which changes from amber black/violet in the presence of starch, would be added to the beaker. If the solution in the beaker changes color to black or violet, then starch is present and diffused through the membrane. If no color change is observed in the solution of the beaker, then starch is not present in the beaker. *(Diffusion/Osmosis)*

Base your answers to questions 114 and 115 on the information and diagram below and on your knowledge of biology. The diagram represents some cells on a microscope slide before and after a substance was added to the slide.

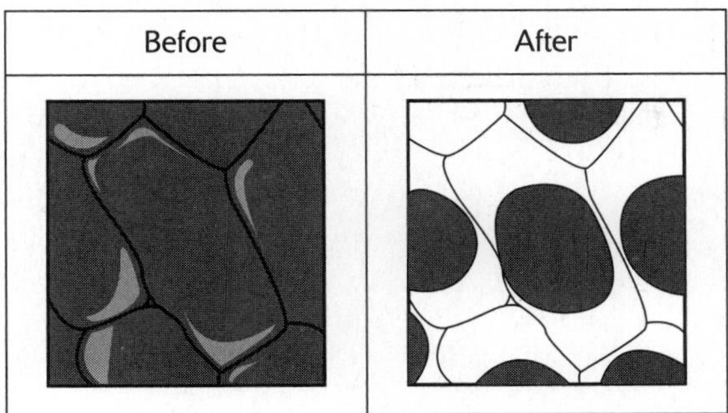


**114.** Identify a substance that was most likely added to the slide to cause the change observed.

**Correct Answer:** Saltwater. Saltwater has fewer free water molecules than the cytoplasm inside of the cell. Water will move from the more pure (inside of the cell) to the less pure (outside the cell, where there's saltwater), causing the cell to shrivel. *(Diffusion/Osmosis)*

**115.** Describe a procedure that could be used to add this substance to the cells on the slide without removing the cover slip.

**Correct Answer:** Place a drop or two of saltwater on one side of the cover slip, and put a paper towel on the other side. The paper towel will draw the water out from under the cover slip, pulling the saltwater under the cover slip to replace it. *(Diffusion/Osmosis)*

**116.** In the *Diffusion through a Membrane* lab, the model cell membranes allowed certain substances to pass through based on which characteristic of the diffusing substance?

**(1)** size
**(2)** shape
**(3)** color
**(4)** temperature

**Correct Answer: (1)** Glucose and iodine are relatively small molecules and are able to diffuse through a membrane. Starch is a relatively large molecule and is too big to diffuse through a membrane. In the human body, starch will be digested into individual glucose molecules before diffusion will occur. *(Diffusion/Osmosis)*

# Self-Evaluation Test with Answer Explanations

## Answer Sheet

| | | | |
|---|---|---|---|
| 1 ① ② ③ ④ | 21 ① ② ③ ④ | 41 ① ② ③ ④ | 61 |
| 2 ① ② ③ ④ | 22 ① ② ③ ④ | 42 ① ② ③ ④ | 62 |
| 3 ① ② ③ ④ | 23 ① ② ③ ④ | 43 ① ② ③ ④ | 63 |
| 4 ① ② ③ ④ | 24 ① ② ③ ④ | 44 ① ② ③ ④ | 64 |
| 5 ① ② ③ ④ | 25 ① ② ③ ④ | 45 ① ② ③ ④ | 65 |
| 6 ① ② ③ ④ | 26 ① ② ③ ④ | 46 | 66 |
| 7 ① ② ③ ④ | 27 ① ② ③ ④ | 47 | 67 ① ② ③ ④ |
| 8 ① ② ③ ④ | 28 ① ② ③ ④ | 48 | 68 |
| 9 ① ② ③ ④ | 29 ① ② ③ ④ | 49 | 69 |
| 10 ① ② ③ ④ | 30 ① ② ③ ④ | 50 | 70 |
| 11 ① ② ③ ④ | 31 ① ② ③ ④ | 51 | 71 |
| 12 ① ② ③ ④ | 32 ① ② ③ ④ | 52 | 72 ① ② ③ ④ |
| 13 ① ② ③ ④ | 33 ① ② ③ ④ | 53 | 73 ① ② ③ ④ |
| 14 ① ② ③ ④ | 34 ① ② ③ ④ | 54 ① ② ③ ④ | 74 ① ② ③ ④ |
| 15 ① ② ③ ④ | 35 ① ② ③ ④ | 55 | 75 |
| 16 ① ② ③ ④ | 36 ① ② ③ ④ | 56 | 76 |
| 17 ① ② ③ ④ | 37 ① ② ③ ④ | 57 | |
| 18 ① ② ③ ④ | 38 ① ② ③ ④ | 58 | |
| 19 ① ② ③ ④ | 39 ① ② ③ ④ | 59 | |
| 20 ① ② ③ ④ | 40 ① ② ③ ④ | 60 | |

# Self-Evaluation Test

## Part A

**Answer all questions in this part.**

*Directions* (1–30): For *each* statement or question, write on your separate answer sheet the *number* of the word or expression that, of those given, best completes the statement or answers the question.

**1.** The diagram below represents two single-celled organisms.

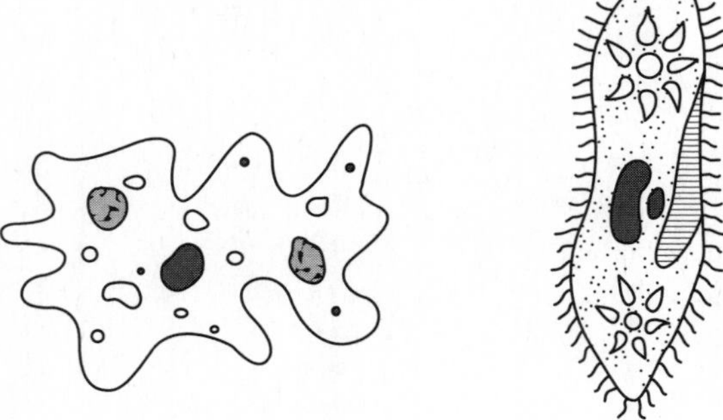

These organisms carry out the activities needed to maintain homeostasis by using specialized internal

(1) tissues
(2) organelles
(3) systems
(4) organs

**2.** Synthesis of a defective protein may result from an alteration in

(1) vacuole shape
(2) the number of mitochondria
(3) a base sequence code
(4) cellular fat concentration

**3.** Which statement is most closely related to the modern theory of evolution?

(1) Characteristics that are acquired during life are passed to offspring by sexual reproduction.
(2) Evolution is the result of mutations and recombination only.
(3) Organisms best adapted to a changed environment are more likely to reproduce and pass their genes to offspring.
(4) Asexual reproduction increases the survival of species.

**4.** Strawberries can reproduce by means of runners, which are stems that grow horizontally along the ground. At the region of the runner that touches the ground, a new plant develops. The new plant is genetically identical to the parent because

(1) it was produced sexually
(2) nuclei traveled to the new plant through the runner to fertilize it
(3) it was produced asexually
(4) there were no other strawberry plants in the area to provide fertilization

**5.** Meat tenderizer contains an enzyme that interacts with meat. If meat is coated with tenderizer and then placed in a refrigerator for a short time, how would the enzyme be affected?

(1) It would be broken down.
(2) Its activity would slow down.
(3) Its shape would change.
(4) It would no longer act as an enzyme.

**6.** An established ecosystem may remain stable over hundreds of years because

(1) species interdependence is absent
(2) there is a lack of variety in the species
(3) no competition exists between the species
(4) there are natural checks on species

**7.** Which human activity would have the most positive effect on the environment of an area?

(1) using fire to eliminate most plants in the area
(2) clearing the area to eliminate weed species
(3) protecting native flowers and grasses in the area
(4) introducing a foreign plant species to the area

**8.** The analysis of data gathered during a particular experiment is necessary in order to

(1) formulate a hypothesis for that experiment
(2) develop a research plan for that experiment
(3) design a control for that experiment
(4) draw a valid conclusion for that experiment

**9.** Which two systems are most directly involved in providing molecules needed for the synthesis of fats in human cells?

(1) digestive and circulatory
(2) excretory and digestive
(3) immune and muscular
(4) reproductive and circulatory

**10.** Which statement best describes a current understanding of natural selection?

(1) Natural selection influences the frequency of an adaptation in a population.
(2) Natural selection has been discarded as an important concept in evolution.
(3) Changes in gene frequencies due to natural selection have little effect on the evolution of species.
(4) New mutations of genetic material are due to natural selection.

**11.** What will most likely happen to wastes containing nitrogen produced as a result of the breakdown of amino acids within liver cells of a mammal?

(1) They will be digested by enzymes in the stomach.
(2) They will be removed by the excretory system.
(3) They will be destroyed by specialized blood cells.
(4) They will be absorbed by mitochondria in nearby cells.

**12.** Bacteria that are removed from the human intestine are genetically engineered to feed on organic pollutants in the environment and convert them into harmless inorganic compounds. Which row in the table below best represents the most likely negative and positive effects of this technology on the ecosystem?

| ***Row*** | ***Negative Effect*** | ***Positive Effect*** |
|---|---|---|
| (1) | Inorganic compounds interfere with cycles in the environment. | Human bacteria are added to the environment. |
| (2) | Engineered bacteria may out-compete native bacteria. | The organic pollutants are removed. |
| (3) | Only some of the pollutants are removed. | Bacteria will make more organic pollutants. |
| (4) | The bacteria will cause diseases in humans. | The inorganic compounds are buried in the soil. |

**13.** Hereditary traits are transmitted from generation to generation by means of

(1) specific sequences of bases in DNA in reproductive cells
(2) proteins in body cells
(3) carbohydrates in body cells
(4) specific starches making up DNA in reproductive cells

**14.** Meiosis and fertilization are important for the survival of many species because these two processes result in

(1) large numbers of gametes
(2) increasingly complex multicellular organisms
(3) cloning of superior offspring
(4) genetic variability of offspring

**15.** Water from nearby rivers or lakes is usually used to cool down the reactors in nuclear power plants. The release of this heated water back into the river or lake would most likely result in

(1) an increase in the sewage content in the water
(2) a change in the biodiversity in the water
(3) a change in the number of mutations in plants growing near the water
(4) a decrease in the amount of sunlight necessary for photosynthesis in the water

**16.** Which statement best describes the term *theory* as used in the gene-chromosome theory?

(1) A theory is never revised as new scientific evidence is presented.
(2) A theory is an assumption made by scientists and implies a lack of certainty.
(3) A theory refers to a scientific explanation that is strongly supported by a variety of experimental data.
(4) A theory is a hypothesis that has been supported by one experiment performed by two or more scientists.

**17.** The diagram below represents a portion of an organic molecule.

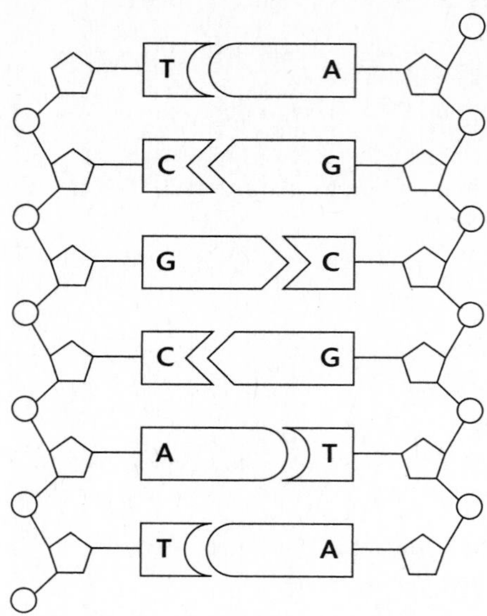


This molecule controls cellular activity by directing the synthesis of

**(1)** carbohydrates
**(2)** minerals
**(3)** fats
**(4)** proteins

**18.** The graph below shows the results of an experiment in which a container of oxygen-using bacteria and strands of green alga were exposed to light of different colors.

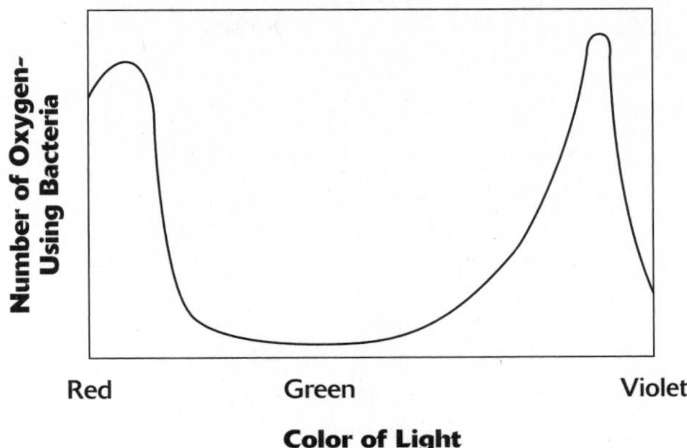


Which statement best explains the results of this experiment?

**(1)** The rate of photosynthesis is affected by variations in the light.
**(2)** In all environments, light is a vital resource.
**(3)** The activities of bacteria and algae are not related.
**(4)** Uneven numbers and types of species can upset ecosystem stability.

**19.** Steps in a reproductive process used to produce a sheep with certain traits are listed below.

**Step 1:** The nucleus was removed from an unfertilized egg taken from sheep A.

**Step 2:** The nucleus of a body cell taken from sheep B was then inserted into this unfertilized egg from sheep A.

**Step 3:** The resulting cell was then implanted into the uterus of sheep C.

**Step 4:** Sheep C gave birth to sheep D.

Which sheep would be most genetically similar to sheep D?

**(1)** sheep A only
**(2)** sheep B only
**(3)** both sheep A and B
**(4)** both sheep A and C

**20.** Which characteristics of a population would most likely indicate the lowest potential for evolutionary change in that population?

(1) sexual reproduction and few mutations
(2) sexual reproduction and many mutations
(3) asexual reproduction and few mutations
(4) asexual reproduction and many mutations

**21.** A partial food web is represented in the diagram below.

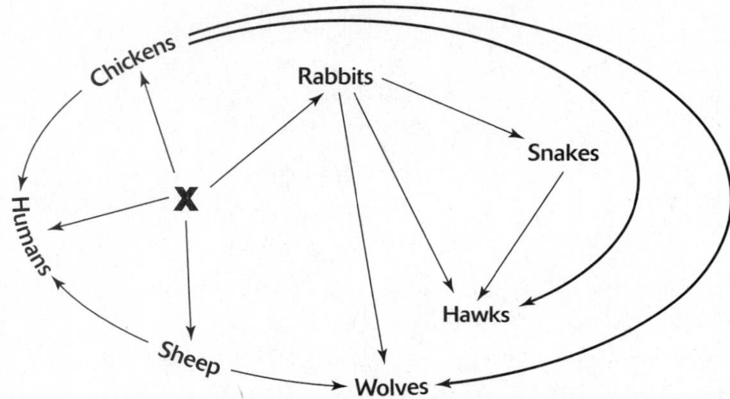


Letter X most likely represents

(1) autotrophs
(2) carnivores
(3) decomposers
(4) parasites

**22.** In the diagram of a single-celled organism shown below, the arrows indicate various activities taking place.

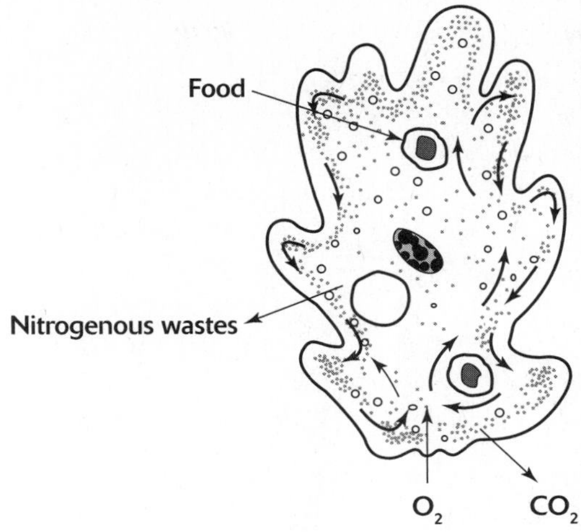


Which systems perform these same activities in humans?

**(1)** digestive, circulatory, and immune
**(2)** excretory, respiratory, and reproductive
**(3)** respiratory, excretory, and digestive
**(4)** respiratory, nervous, and endocrine

**23.** A scientist is planning to carry out an experiment on the effect of heat on the function of a certain enzyme. Which would *not* be an appropriate first step?

**(1)** doing research in a library
**(2)** having discussions with other scientists
**(3)** completing a data table of expected results
**(4)** using what is already known about the enzyme

**24.** Which row in the chart below best describes asexual reproduction?

| *Row* | *Number of Parents* | *Comparison of Offspring to Parents* |
|---|---|---|
| (1) | One | Identical |
| (2) | One | Different |
| (3) | Two | Identical |
| (4) | Two | Different |

**25.** The diagram below represents a beaker containing a solution of various molecules involved in digestion.

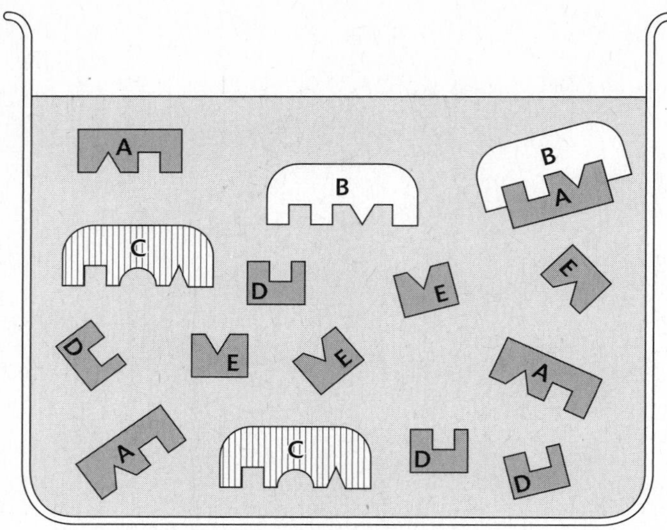


Which structures represent products of digestion?

(1) A and D
(2) B and C
(3) B and E
(4) D and E

**26.** The feeding niches of three bird species are shown in the diagram below.

Cape May warblers
feed at the top
of the tree.
Bay-breasted
warblers feed
in the middle
of the tree.
Yellow-rumped
warblers feed
in the lower part
of the tree.

What is the advantage of these different feeding niches for the birds?

**(1)** less competition for food
**(2)** fewer abiotic resources for each bird species
**(3)** fewer biotic resources for each bird species
**(4)** less energy available as the birds feed higher in the tree

**27.** Genes are inherited, but their expressions can be modified by the environment. This statement explains why

**(1)** some animals have dark fur only when the temperature is within a certain range
**(2)** offspring produced by means of sexual reproduction look exactly like their parents
**(3)** identical twins who grow up in different homes have the same characteristics
**(4)** animals can be cloned, but plants cannot

**28.** Which situation is a result of human activities?

(1) decay of leaves in a forest adds to soil fertility
(2) acid rain in an area kills fish in a lake
(3) ecological succession following volcanic activity reestablishes an ecosystem
(4) natural selection on an island changes gene frequencies

**29.** A student could best demonstrate knowledge of how energy flows throughout an ecosystem by

(1) drawing a food web using specific organisms living in a pond
(2) conducting an experiment that demonstrates the process of photosynthesis
(3) labeling a diagram that illustrates ecological succession
(4) making a chart to show the role of bacteria in the environment

**30.** In plants, simple sugars are least likely to be

(1) linked together to form proteins
(2) broken down into carbon dioxide and water
(3) used as a source of energy
(4) stored in the form of a starch molecule

# Part B-1

**Answer all questions in this part.**

*Directions* (31–40): For *each* statement or question, write on the separate answer sheet the *number* of the word or expression that, of those given, best completes the statement or answers the question.

**31.** Which substances are found on cell surfaces and respond to nerve and hormone signals?

(1) starches and simple sugars
(2) subunits of DNA
(3) vitamins and minerals
(4) receptor molecules

**32.** One variety of strawberry is resistant to a damaging fungus but produces small fruit. Another strawberry variety produces large fruit but is not resistant to the same fungus. The two desirable qualities may be combined in a new variety of strawberry plant by

(1) cloning
(2) asexual reproduction
(3) direct harvesting
(4) selective breeding

**33.** Some data concerning bird species are shown in the chart below.

| *Number of Bird Species* | *Location* |
|---|---|
| 26 | Northern Alaska |
| 153 | Southwest Texas |
| 600 | Costa Rica |

Which statement is a valid inference based on information in the chart?

(1) The different species in northern Alaska can interbreed.
(2) There are conditions in Costa Rica that account for greater biodiversity there.
(3) The different species in southwest Texas evolved from those in northern Alaska.
(4) The greater number of species in Costa Rica is due to a greater number of predators there.

**34.** The diagram below represents single-celled organism A dividing by mitosis to form cells B and C.

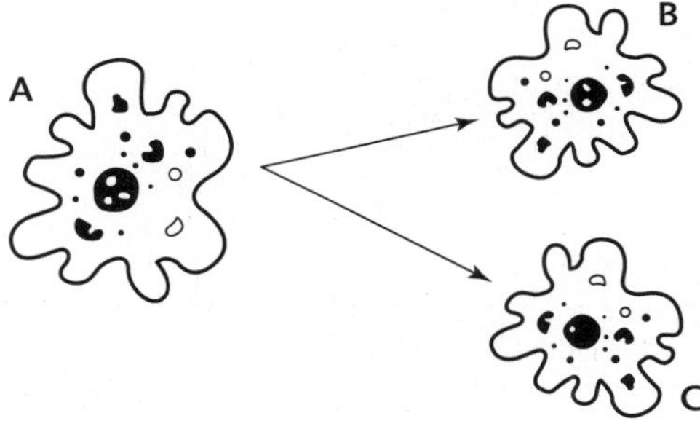


Cells A, B, and C all produced protein X. What can best be inferred from this observation?

(1) Protein X is found in all organisms.
(2) The gene for protein X is found in single-celled organisms, only.
(3) Cells A, B, and C ingested food containing the gene to produce protein X.
(4) The gene to produce protein X was passed from cell A to cells B and C.

**35.** Which row in the chart below contains correct information concerning synthesis?

| *Row* | *Building Blocks* | *Substance Synthesized Using the Building Blocks* |
|---|---|---|
| (1) | Glucose molecules | DNA |
| (2) | Simple sugars | Protein |
| (3) | Amino acids | Enzyme |
| (4) | Molecular bases | Starch |

**36.** The diagram below represents a pyramid of energy that includes both producers and consumers.

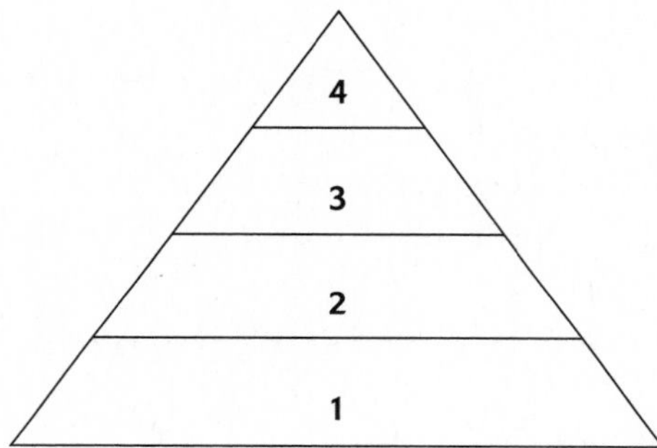


The greatest amount of available energy is found at level

**(1)** 1
**(2)** 2
**(3)** 3
**(4)** 4

**37.** Which phrase would be appropriate for area A in the chart below?

| *Technological Device* | *Positive Impact* | *Negative Impact* |
|---|---|---|
| Nuclear power plant | Provides efficient, inexpensive energy | A |

(1) produces radioactive waste
(2) results in greater biodiversity
(3) provides light from radioactive substances
(4) reduces dependence on fossil fuels

**38.** The levels of organization for structure and function in the human body from least complex to most complex are

(1) systems → organs → tissues → cells
(2) cells → organs → tissues → systems
(3) tissues → systems → cells → organs
(4) cells → tissues → organs → systems

**39.** Some farmers currently grow genetically engineered crops. An argument *against* the use of this technology is that

(1) it increases crop production
(2) it produces insect-resistant plants
(3) its long-term effects on humans are still being investigated
(4) it always results in crops that do not taste good

**40.** Which statement best describes a scientific theory?

(1) It is a collection of data designed to provide support for a prediction.
(2) It is an educated guess that can be tested by experimentation.
(3) It is a scientific fact that no longer requires any evidence to support it.
(4) It is a general statement that is supported by many scientific observations.

# Part B-2

**Answer all questions in this part.**

*Directions* (41–55): For those questions that are followed by four choices, write on your separate answer sheet the *number* of the choice that best completes the statement or answers the question. For all other questions in this part, follow the directions given in the question.

Base your answers to questions 41 through 43 on the information and chart below and on your knowledge of biology.

It has been hypothesized that a chemical known as BW prevents colds. To test this hypothesis, 20,000 volunteers were divided into four groups. Each volunteer took a white pill every morning for one year. The contents of the pill taken by the members of each group are shown in the chart below.

| *Group* | *Number of Volunteers* | *Contents of Pill* | *Percent Developing Colds* |
|---|---|---|---|
| 1 | 5,000 | 5 grams of sugar | 20 |
| 2 | 5,000 | 5 grams of sugar, 1 gram of BW | 19 |
| 3 | 5,000 | 5 grams of sugar, 3 grams of BW | 21 |
| 4 | 5,000 | 5 grams of sugar, 9 grams of BW | 15 |

**41.** Which factor most likely had the greatest influence on these experimental results?

(1) color of the pills
(2) amount of sugar added
(3) number of volunteers in each group
(4) health history of the volunteers

**42.** Which statement is a valid inference based on the results?

(1) Sugar reduced the number of colds.
(2) Sugar increased the number of colds.
(3) BW is always effective in the prevention of colds.
(4) BW may not be effective in the prevention of colds.

**43.** Which group served as the control in this investigation?

(1) 1
(2) 2
(3) 3
(4) 4

Base your answers to questions 44 through 46 on the graph below and on your knowledge of biology.

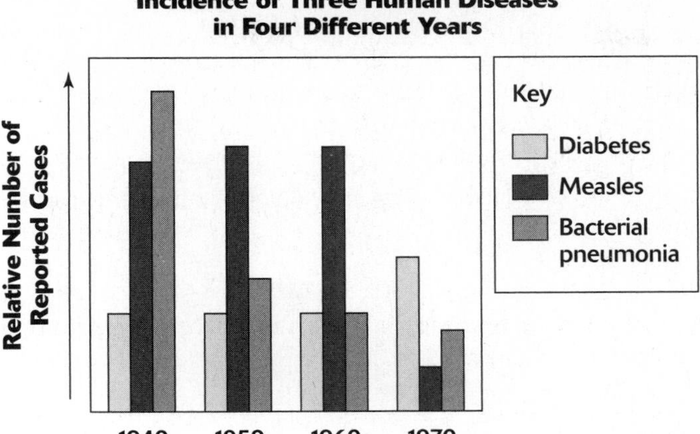


**44.** The greatest difference between the incidence of measles and the incidence of bacterial pneumonia occurred in

(1) 1940
(2) 1950
(3) 1960
(4) 1970

**45.** Which statement best explains a change in the incidence of disease in 1970?

(1) Children were vaccinated against measles.
(2) New drugs cured diabetes.
(3) The bacteria that cause pneumonia developed a resistance to the drugs.
(4) New technology helped to reduce the incidence of all three diseases.

**46.** Which statement provides the best possible reason for the decrease in number of cases of bacterial pneumonia form 1940 to 1970?

(1) As a result of genetic engineering, humans became immune to the bacteria.
(2) Antibiotics were made available for the treatment of bacterial infections.
(3) The bacteria did not respond to medical treatments.
(4) As a result of sexual reproduction, the bacteria evolved into a harmless form.

Base your answers to questions 47 through 50 on the passage below and on your knowledge of biology.

## Decline of the Salmon Population

Salmon are fish that hatch in a river and swim to the ocean where their body mass increases. When mature, they return to the river where they were hatched and swim upstream to reproduce and die. When there are large populations of salmon, the return of nutrients to the river ecosystem can be huge. It is estimated that during salmon runs in the Pacific Northwest in the 1800s, 500 million pounds of salmon returned to reproduce and die each year. Research estimates that in the Columbia River alone, salmon contributed hundreds of thousands of pounds of nitrogen and phosphorus compounds to the local ecosystem each year. Over the past 100 years, commercial ocean fishing has removed up to two-thirds of the salmon before they reach the river each year.

**47.** Identify the process that releases the nutrients from the bodies of the dead salmon, making the nutrients available for other organisms in the ecosystem.

**48.** Identify *one* organism, other than the salmon, that would be present in or near the river that would most likely be part of a food web in the river ecosystem.

**49.** Identify *two* nutrients that are returned to the ecosystem when the salmon die.

**50.** State *one* impact, other than reducing the salmon population, that commercial ocean fishing has on the river ecosystem.

Base your answers to questions 51 through 53 on the two different cells shown below. Only cell A produces substance X. Both cells A and B use substance X.

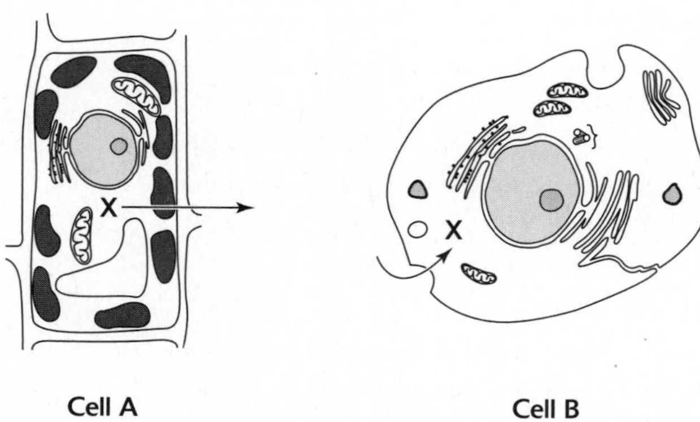

**51.** Identify substance X.

**52.** Identify the type of organelle in cell A that produces substance X.

**53.** Identify the type of organelle found in both cell A and cell B that uses substance X.

Base your answers to questions 54 and 55 on the information below and on your knowledge of biology.

Thirty grams of hay (dried grasses) were boiled in 500 milliliters of water, placed in a culture dish, and allowed to stand. The next day, a small sample of pond water was added to the mixture of boiled hay and water. The dish was then covered and its contents observed regularly. Bacteria fed on the nutrients from the boiled hay. As the populations of bacteria increased rapidly, the clear mixture soon became cloudy. One week later, microscopic examination of samples from the culture showed various types of protozoa (single-celled organisms) eating the bacteria.

**54.** The protozoa that fed on the bacteria can best be described as

(1) producers
(2) herbivores
(3) parasites
(4) consumers

**55.** Label each level of the energy pyramid below with an organism mentioned in the paragraph that belongs at that level.

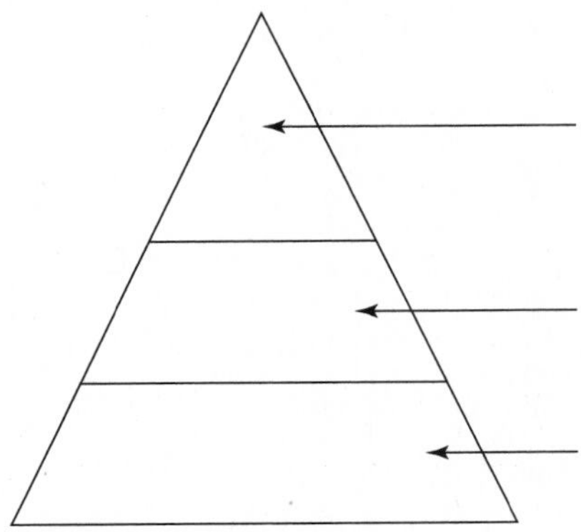

# Part C

**Answer all questions in this part.**

*Directions* (56–65): Record your answers in the spaces provided in the examination booklet.

**56.** The energy demands of a cell or an organism are met as a result of interactions between several life functions.

Identify *two* life functions involved in meeting the energy demands of a cell or an organism.

______________________

______________________

Explain how these two life functions interact to make energy available.

Base your answers to questions 57 through 59 on the information below and on your knowledge of biology.

**57.** Mutations are often referred to as the "raw materials" of evolution. State one reason that mutations are often referred to as the "raw materials" of evolution.

**58.** Use appropriate letters to write a nine-base DNA sequence that could represent a portion of a gene.

**59.** Show one example of what could happen to the nine-base DNA sequence you wrote in question 58 if a mutation occurred in that gene.

**60.** A human is a complex organism that develops from a zygote. Briefly explain some of the steps in this developmental process. In your answer be sure to:

- explain how a zygote is formed
- compare the genetic content of the zygote to that of a body cell of the parents
- identify one developmental process involved in the change from a zygote into an embryo
- identify the structure in which fetal development usually occurs
- identify *two* factors that can affect fetal development and explain how each factor affects fetal development

**61.** When living organisms obtain water and food from their environment, they may also take in toxic pesticides. Low concentrations of some pesticides may not kill animals, but they may damage reproductive organs and cause sterility. The data table below shows concentrations of a pesticide in tissues of organisms at different levels of a food chain.

**Concentration of Pesticide in Tissues**

| *Organisms* | *Pesticide Concentration (parts per million)* |
|---|---|
| Producers | 0.01–0.03 |
| Herbivores | 0.25–1.50 |
| Carnivores | 4.10–313.80 |

What does this information suggest to a person who is concerned about health and is deciding on whether to have a plant-rich or an animal-rich diet? Support your answer using the information provided.

**62.** The concentration of salt in water affects the hatching of brine shrimp eggs. Brine shrimp eggs will develop and hatch at room temperature in glass containers of salt solution. Describe a controlled experiment using three experimental groups that could be used to determine the best concentration of salt solution in which to hatch brine shrimp eggs. Your answer must include at least:

- a description of how the control group and each of the three experimental groups will be different
- *two* conditions that must be kept constant in the control group and the experimental groups
- data that should be collected
- *one* example of experimental results that would indicate the best concentration of salt solution in which to hatch brine shrimp eggs

**63.** Not all diseases are caused by pathogenic organisms. Other factors, such as inheritance, poor nutrition, and toxic substances, may also cause disease. Describe a disease or disorder that can occur as a result of one of these other factors. Your answer must include at least:

- the name of the disease
- *one* specific factor that causes this disease
- *one* major effect of this disease on the body, other than death
- *one* way this disease can be prevented, treated, or cured

**64.** State *one* specific way the removal of trees from an area has had a *negative* impact on the environment.

**65.** Many people become infected with the chicken pox virus during childhood. After recovering from chicken pox, these people are usually immune to the disease for the rest of their lives. However, they may still be infected by viruses that cause other disease, such as measles.

Discuss the immune response to the chicken pox virus. In your answer, be sure to include:

- the role of antigens in the immune response
- the role of white blood cells in the body's response to the virus
- an explanation of why recovery from an infection with the chicken pox virus will *not* protect a person form getting a different disease, such as measles
- an explanation of why a chicken pox vaccination usually does *not* cause a person to become ill with chicken pox

# Part D

**Answer all questions in this part.**

*Directions* (66–76): For those questions that are followed by four choices, circle the *number* of the choice that best completes the statement or answers the question. For all other questions in this part, follow the directions given in the question.

---

**66.** State *one* factor that influences which molecules can pass through the cell membrane of a human cell.

Base your answers to questions 67 through 69 on the information below and on your knowledge of biology.

Based on their analysis of the differences in amino acid sequences of one kind of protein, scientists prepared the following evolutionary family tree.

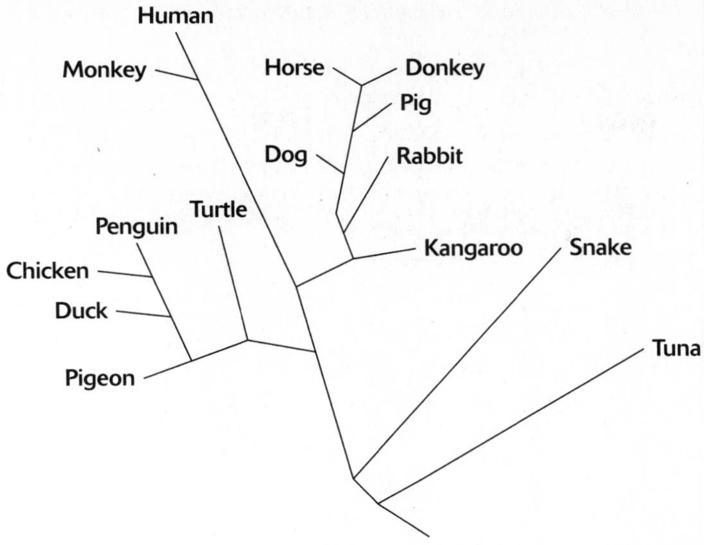


**67.** According to this diagram, the DNA of which pair of organisms would show the greatest similarity?

(1) penguin and turtle
(2) horse and donkey
(3) snake and tuna
(4) turtle and rabbit

**68.** Older systems of classification always placed penguins, chickens, ducks, and pigeons in the bird group and turtles and snakes in the reptile group. Does this diagram support the older system of classification? Explain your answer.

**69.** According to this diagram, is the pig more closely related to the dog or the kangaroo? Justify your answer.

Base your answers to questions 70 and 71 on the information and data table below and on your knowledge of biology.

Two students collected data on their pulse rates while performing different activities. Their average results are shown in the data table below.

**Data Table**

| *Activity* | *Average Pulse Rate (beats/min)* |
|---|---|
| Sitting quietly | 70 |
| Walking | 98 |
| Running | 120 |

**70.** State the relationship between activity and pulse rate.

**71.** State *one* way that this investigation could be improved.

Base your answers to questions 72 through 74 on the diagram below and on your knowledge of biology. Letters A through L represent different species of organisms; the arrows represent long periods of geologic time.

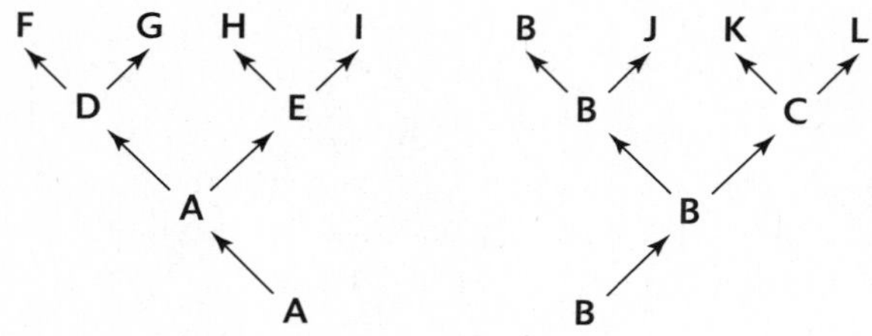


**72.** Which two species are the most closely related?

(1) J and L
(2) G and H
(3) F and H
(4) F and G

**73.** Which species was best adapted to changes that occurred in its environment over the longest period of time?

(1) A
(2) B
(3) C
(4) J

**74.** Which two species would most likely show the greatest similarity of DNA and proteins?

(1) B and J
(2) G and I
(3) J and K
(4) F and L

**75.** When a person exercises, changes occur in muscle cells as they release more energy. Explain how increased blood flow helps these muscle cells release more energy.

**76.** An indicator for a protein is added to a solution that contains protein and to a solution that does *not* contain protein. State *one* way, other than the presence or absence of protein, that the two solutions may differ after the indicator has been added to both.

# Answer Key

1. (2)
2. (3)
3. (3)
4. (3)
5. (2)
6. (4)
7. (3)
8. (4)
9. (1)
10. (1)
11. (2)
12. (2)
13. (1)
14. (4)
15. (2)
16. (3)
17. (4)
18. (1)
19. (2)
20. (3)
21. (1)
22. (3)
23. (3)
24. (1)
25. (4)
26. (1)
27. (1)
28. (2)
29. (1)
30. (1)
31. (4)
32. (4)
33. (2)
34. (4)
35. (3)
36. (1)
37. (1)
38. (4)
39. (3)
40. (4)
41. (4)
42. (4)
43. (1)
44. (3)
45. (1)
46. (2)
47. See answer explanation
48. See answer explanation
49. See answer explanation
50. See answer explanation
51. See answer explanation
52. See answer explanation
53. See answer explanation
54. (4)
55. See answer explanation
56. See answer explanation
57. See answer explanation
58. See answer explanation
59. See answer explanation
60. See answer explanation
61. See answer explanation
62. See answer explanation
63. See answer explanation
64. See answer explanation
65. See answer explanation
66. See answer explanation
67. (2)
68. See answer explanation
69. See answer explanation
70. See answer explanation
71. See answer explanation
72. (4)
73. (2)
74. (1)
75. See answer explanation
76. See answer explanation

# Answer Explanations

1. **Correct Answer: (2)** The organisms shown are the amoeba and paramecium, both single-celled protists. Protists are eukaryotic organisms that contain internal membrane-bound organelles and a membrane-bound nucleus. Organelles carry out specific functions within a cell. *(Single-Cell and Multicellular Organisms)*

2. **Correct Answer: (3)** DNA controls everything in living things including the production of proteins. If a defective protein is made, then it must be due to a change in the DNA. The only change that can happen to cause this is a change to the bases of DNA and their sequence. You have to know that DNA is made up of four bases: A, C, T, and G. If the order of these bases in DNA is changed by adding, substituting, or deleting a base, then a mutation occurs. *(Heredity)*

3. **Correct Answer: (3)** When an environment changes, organisms better equipped to handle the changes will live, reproduce, and have offspring that may have the same traits that helped their parents survive. Organisms that are not well equipped will be more likely to die and be less likely to produce offspring. Therefore, the traits that are well suited for the new environment get passed on and the traits that are not well suited for the environment don't get passed on. *(The Theory of Evolution)*

4. **Correct Answer: (3)** Whenever anything reproduces asexually, the offspring, in this case a strawberry plant, will be genetically identical to the thing it came from. It could be a bacteria, a skin cell, or a strawberry plant. If it came from asexual reproduction, it will be identical to the "parent." Sexual reproduction, on the other hand, results in new combinations of traits; the offspring will look different because it came from two "parents" that each gave some of their traits to the new offspring. *(Types of Reproduction)*

5. **Correct Answer: (2)** Enzyme activity slows down at low temperatures, such as those found in a refrigerator. Enzymes are proteins that speed up reactions, but they aren't changed or used up by that reaction. Because of this, they can be used over and over again. *(Biochemistry)*

6. **Correct Answer: (4)** Imagine that mice live in the ecosystem and that they are the prey of owls. If owls (a form of natural check) did not exist or did not do their jobs as predators, the population of mice might be out of control. Therefore, natural checks are needed in an ecosystem to ensure stability. *(The Structure of Ecosystems)*

7. **Correct Answer: (3)** A positive impact on the environment involves some activity that has some beneficial effect on the environment. Setting a fire, clearing an area, and introducing a foreign plant species all impact the natural environment in a negative way. Protection of native plant species has a positive effect on the environment. *(Negative Effects of Humans on the Environment)*

8. **Correct Answer: (4)** After data is obtained from an experiment, it needs to be analyzed to show patterns or relationships that may not be readily apparent. Analyzing data allows results to be interpreted so a conclusion may be drawn. *(Interpreting Graphs)*

9. **Correct Answer: (1)** The synthesis of fats requires its building blocks—glycerol and fatty acids. These building blocks come from the food we eat in the form of complex molecules that are broken down into simple molecules during the process of digestion. The products of digestion are absorbed into the bloodstream and circulated throughout the body where they can be used by cells to synthesize specific compounds. *(The Characteristics of Life)*

**10. Correct Answer: (1)** Natural selection is a process whereby organisms with favorable adaptations are better able to survive and reproduce than organisms with less-favorable adaptations. Those organisms with favorable adaptations will be able to pass their genes on to the next generation, increasing the frequency of those genes (alleles) in the population. Organisms with unfavorable adaptations are less likely to pass their genes on to the next generation, thereby decreasing the frequency of the unfavorable genes in the population. *(The Theory of Evolution)*

**11. Correct Answer: (2)** Mammals remove waste products from their circulatory system through their excretory system. The excretory system filters the blood for cellular or metabolic wastes and removes the wastes as urine. *(Human Body Systems)*

**12. Correct Answer: (2)** The genetically engineered bacteria would remove organic pollutants. This is the stated reason that the bacteria were added into the environment and is the positive effect of adding the bacteria. Simply adding human bacteria to the environment is not a positive effect, although it may *cause* a positive effect. If the added bacteria cause more pollution, this is a negative, not a positive, effect. *(Positive and Negative Effects of Humans on the Environment)*

**13. Correct Answer: (1)** Inherited traits are transmitted from one generation to the next only through reproduction. Reproductive cells contain genetic information that determines the traits of the offspring. These traits are controlled by genes, which are made up of DNA. DNA is made up of many nucleotides. Each nucleotide has one base. Many nucleotides together in a specific sequence determine a specific trait, such as eye color or hair texture. *(The Structure of DNA/RNA)*

**14. Correct Answer: (4)** Through the processes of meiosis and fertilization, genetic variation occurs within species. This is because, during meiosis, certain events happen that give new combinations of genes and chromosomes. This is called *crossing over.* In addition, fertilization can bring together a sperm and an egg (gametes) that have gone through crossing over and have new combinations of genetic traits that are not seen in either parent. With these new traits, offspring may possess the necessary adaptations that will enable them to exist and survive in their environment. *(Types of Reproduction)*

**15. Correct Answer: (2)** As bad as the other choices are in terms of the environment, a change in biodiversity has much more far-reaching negative consequences for the environment in general, and for the river and lake ecosystems in specific. *(The Structure of Ecosystems)*

**16. Correct Answer: (3)** A scientific theory is a comprehensive explanation of some phenomena, formed after several hypotheses surrounding the theory have been scientifically tested and supported by the data collected. The gene-chromosome theory states that chromosomes are found in homologous pairs and are made of DNA, and segments of DNA on a chromosome are called genes, which code for a specific trait. This theory has been supported by scientific data and may be revised or discarded if new scientific evidence is found to dispute the theory. *(Scientific Method)*

**17. Correct Answer: (4)** You should know that this is a diagram of DNA. Whenever you see the word *control,* connect it to DNA. The primary function or job of DNA is to code for, or direct the production or synthesis of, proteins. The other substances—carbohydrates, minerals, and fats—are not coded for by DNA. *(The Structure of DNA/RNA)*

**18. Correct Answer: (1)** Algae are photosynthetic. They require light to survive, and in the process of that survival, they produce oxygen that the bacteria need so that they can survive. Because the bacteria are photosynthetic, just like plants, they grow best under red and blue or violet colors of light, and grow poorly under green light. *(Interpreting Graphs)*

**19. Correct Answer: (2)** Sheep D is the genetic offspring of sheep B. The nucleus of sheep B (which contains the DNA) was inserted into the unfertilized egg from sheep A, but the nucleus (which contained the DNA from sheep A) had been removed. Sheep C gave birth to sheep D but served only as the surrogate mother and did not contribute any genetic information to sheep D. *(Technology of Reproduction)*

**20. Correct Answer: (3)** Evolutionary change requires variation in DNA. Variation results from sexual reproduction and mutation. There is little variation in the process of asexual reproduction because the offspring is genetically identical to the parent. Few mutations would limit the potential for variation. *(Mechanisms of Evolution)*

**21. Correct Answer: (1)** Letter X is something eaten by rabbits and sheep. Rabbits and sheep are herbivores, so X must be a plant (autotroph). *(Energy Flow in Ecosystems)*

**22. Correct Answer: (3)** The diagram shows a food vacuole, nitrogenous wastes exiting the cell, oxygen entering the cell, and carbon dioxide leaving the cell. A food vacuole is similar to a human digestive system, which takes in and breaks down food; nitrogenous waste is leaving the cell similar to the human excretory system, which excretes liquid nitrogenous wastes like urea; and the gases entering and leaving the cell is similar to a human respiratory system, which takes in oxygen from the environment and releases carbon dioxide. *(Single-Cell and Multicellular Organisms)*

**23. Correct Answer: (3)** The data table must show results from the experiment performed—not fabricated or expected results. *(Scientific Method)*

**24. Correct Answer: (1)** Asexual reproduction starts with one "parent" organism or cell and produces two identical offspring. Asexual reproduction can be found in plants as well as animals and includes such types as binary fission, budding, and sporulation in such organisms as *Paramecium, Hydra,* yeast, and bacteria. *(Types of Reproduction)*

**25. Correct Answer: (4)** Digestion is the process of breaking down food mechanically and chemically. Mechanical digestion physically breaks food into smaller pieces (increasing surface area) using the teeth, tongue, and stomach. Chemical digestion uses the action of enzymes to break complex food molecules into simple molecules. This diagram shows the chemical digestion of particle A by enzyme B into particles D and E. As you can see, particles D and E together form the shape of particle A. *(Human Body Systems)*

**26. Correct Answer: (1)** A niche is the role an organism plays in an ecosystem. In this case, the role of the Cape May warblers is one of the feeders at the tops of the trees. The other bird species can be thought of in the same way. So, if you have three different species of birds feeding in three different areas of trees, there will be less competition for food. *(The Structure of Ecosystems)*

**27. Correct Answer: (1)** If the environment modifies the expression of genes, it means that the environment can change the way an organism looks, even though the way an organism looks is determined by genes. For example, if your skin is exposed to the sun, it turns darker (tans). Your skin color is determined by your genes, but exposure to the sun can change that. The same is true for some animals, such as foxes: New fur grows in dark if the temperature is high, but new fur grows in white if the temperature is low. *(Heredity)*

**28. Correct Answer: (2)** Acid rain is caused by human pollution. Humans burn fossil fuels, which release sulfuric and nitrogen compounds into the atmosphere. These gases are converted into acids and lower the pH of the water in the atmosphere. *(Negative Effects of Humans on the Environment)*

**29. Correct Answer: (1)** An ecosystem includes a community and its physical environment (both abiotic and biotic factors). Ecosystems can be thought of in terms of energy flow. In an ecosystem, the flow of energy begins with the producers—mainly, photosynthetic plants (autotrophs). Producers convert solar energy into chemical energy to make organic compounds. Energy stored in organic nutrients is transferred to consumers when the plants are eaten. Because consumers can be herbivores, carnivores, or omnivores, many feeding relationships can exist, forming a food chain. An ecosystem is made up of many types of organisms and many different food chains. The food chains are ultimately connected, forming a food web. *(Energy Flow in Ecosystems)*

**30. Correct Answer: (1)** There are no simple sugars in proteins. The building blocks of starch and complex sugars are simple sugars, like glucose. The building blocks of proteins are amino acids. *(The Characteristics of Life)*

**31. Correct Answer: (4)** Receptors in the cell membrane allow cells to communicate with each other. The structure of the cell membrane is a lipid bi-layer with membrane proteins stuck in the bi-layer. These membrane proteins may have carbohydrate side chains attached to them. The ability of cells to communicate with each other for cell recognition is probably the most important functions of these membrane proteins. *(Cell Structure)*

**32. Correct Answer: (4)** Selective breeding is an old and very reliable way to breed animals and grow plants by selecting the best ones (those that have the best qualities) and mating them (if they are animals) or cross-pollinating them (if they are plants). The breeder or grower selects the animal or plant that possesses the desired trait and breeds it or crosses it with another animal or plant that possesses a different but also desired trait. The result will be an organism that possesses *both* desired traits. *(Heredity)*

**33. Correct Answer: (2)** Nothing can explain the greater number of bird species in Costa Rica other than the fact that the conditions for survival are much better than the conditions in the other locations. Costa Rica probably has an abundance of food, niches, and habitats, as well as fewer predators. *(Patterns of Evolution)*

**34. Correct Answer: (4)** Becase all cells shown have produced protein X, and instruction for production of proteins is heritable, cells B and C must have received the genetic instructions for protein X from cell A during mitosis. *(Heredity)*

**35. Correct Answer: (3)** Enzymes are proteins. Proteins are made up of amino acids. *(Biochemistry)*

**36. Correct Answer: (1)** Level 1 is at the bottom of the pyramid. It represents the producers. The producers contain the greatest amount of available energy because they receive energy directly from the sun. A producer will use some of the energy for metabolic processes. As a result, any organism that consumes a producer will receive less energy. *(Energy Flow in Ecosystems)*

**37. Correct Answer: (1)** Waste from nuclear power plants is hazardous to human health and to the environment. Nuclear waste causes radiation sickness, which damages body tissues such as bone marrow, the spleen, and lymph nodes. Radiation sickness can be mild and temporary (such as weakness, loss of appetite, vomiting, diarrhea, and reduced resistance against infection) or more severe (such as anemia, hemorrhage, dehydration, or even death). There is no cure for radiation sickness. Nuclear waste must also be specially stored to prevent contamination of the environment, becoming the burden of future generations. *(Negative Effects of Humans on the Environment)*

**38. Correct Answer: (4)** Cells are the basic unit of life; they are the building blocks of all body structures in complex organisms. Tissues are a specialized group of cells that have the same basic structure and perform the same function. Organs are a group of tissues that work together to perform a function. Systems are groups of organs that work together to perform a function. For example, cells make up heart tissue, heart tissue makes up the heart (an organ), the heart is part of the circulatory system along with veins, arteries, and so on. Cells are the least complex, because they make up all the others. Systems are the most complex because they are composed of all the others. *(Single-Cell and Multicellular Organisms)*

**39. Correct Answer: (3)** Genetically engineered crops are relatively new and possible long-term effects on humans is still being investigated. *(Genetic Engineering)*

**40. Correct Answer: (4)** This is a basic definition of a theory. A theory is not a collection of data designed to provide support for a prediction; that's an experiment. It is not an educated guess that can be tested by experimentation; that's a hypothesis. And it is not a scientific fact that no longer requires any evidence to support it; that's a law. *(Scientific Method)*

**41. Correct Answer: (4)** The amount of sugar was the same for each group. Aside from the amount of BW in each pill, the health history of the volunteers had the greatest influence on the results. Age, gender, lifestyle, and many other factors were not accounted for and could have had an effect on the results. *(Scientific Method)*

**42. Correct Answer: (4)** Based on the results, you can infer that BW may not be effective in preventing colds. The results are about the same between the control group and the groups that had 1 gram and 3 grams of BW, respectively, in their pill. Only at the 9-gram level did it seem that BW had an effect on the number of colds that the volunteers developed. *(Scientific Method)*

**43. Correct Answer: (1)** A control group is one that does not receive the experimental treatment. *(Scientific Method)*

**44. Correct Answer: (3)** Examining the graph, compare the first three bars for measles; they are all the same. Now compare the bars for bacterial pneumonia; in 1960, it is the greatest difference from measles. *(Interpreting Graphs)*

**45. Correct Answer: (1)** As more children became vaccinated against measles, the incidence will decrease. *(Disease)*

46. **Correct Answer: (2)** Probably the single biggest advance in the treatment of bacterial diseases is the use of antibiotics. Many lives have been saved and people's health has improved because of them. *(Disease)*

47. **Correct Answer: Decomposition** Decomposers break down the remains of dead organisms and waste products to return the nutrients to the environment. This way the nutrients are available for other organisms in the ecosystem. *(Energy Flow in Ecosystems)*

48. **Correct Answer:** Choose any organism found in a river. Examples include decomposer/bacteria, small fish, seagulls, green plant, and so on. *(The Structure of Ecosystems)*

49. **Correct Answer: Nitrogen and phosphorous** The answer can be taken directly from the passage: "Research estimates that in the Columbia River alone, salmon contributed hundreds of thousands of pounds of nitrogen and phosphorus compounds to the local ecosystem each year." *(Energy Flow in Ecosystems)*

50. **Correct Answer:** Any of the following apply: Fishing deprives upstream ecosystems of nutrients; consumers in the ecosystem are deprived of food; decomposer populations decrease; fishing disrupts food webs. *(Negative Effects of Humans on the Environment)*

51. **Correct Answer: Oxygen.** *(Cells and Their Environment)*

52. **Correct Answer: Chloroplast.** *(Cell Structure)*

53. **Correct Answer: Mitochondria.** *(Cell Structure)*

54. **Correct Answer: (4)** Protozoa are unable to make their own food and must obtain their nutrients from consuming other organisms. *(Organisms in Their Environment)*

55. **Correct Answer:**

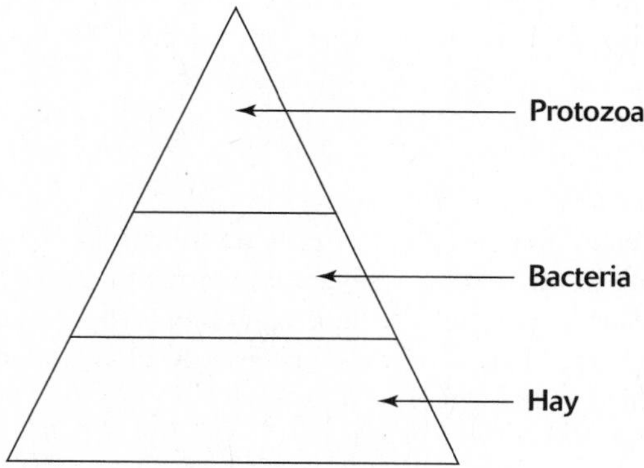


Hay is a producer and makes up the lowest and largest level of the energy pyramid. The bacteria represent herbivores, the middle level of the pyramid. The highest and smallest level of the pyramid represents protozoa, the consumers that feed on other heterotrophic organisms. The amount of energy decreases as the level in the pyramid increases because very little energy is transferred from one level to another. Energy is lost as heat and used for cellular processes. *(Energy Flow in Ecosystems)*

**56. Correct Answer:** There are several life functions to choose from, including digestion, transport, respiration, and photosynthesis. Digestion is the process that breaks down food particles into smaller molecules; the digestive system then interacts with the blood vessels of the transport or circulatory system to bring the molecules to the cells. Another possible answer is to combine photosynthesis and respiration. Photosynthesis is the process in plants that converts the energy of the sun into the chemical energy of glucose. The glucose then becomes one of the main ingredients for respiration to combine it with oxygen to produce energy. *(The Characteristics of Life)*

**57. Correct Answer:** Evolution is change over time. Change in organisms occurs through mutations in the genes and chromosomes. These changes lead to variation in the organism. Variations can be a difference in size, shape, speed, resistance to disease, and so on. Some of these variations will allow organisms to survive and pass on these new variations or traits to their offspring. This passing on of new traits is how evolution occurs. Your answer should read something like this: Mutations cause variations in the organism, which can then be passed on to the offspring. *(Mechanisms of Evolution)*

**58. Correct Answer:** The four letters that represent the four bases of DNA are A, T, C, and G. Simply write nine letters in a row using these four letters. Letters can be used more than once. For example, you could write: ATAGGCTCG. *(The Structure of DNA/RNA)*

**59. Correct Answer:** There are a few ways to make a mutation in a sequence of DNA. One letter (or base) can be left out—a deletion. For example, from the sequence ATAGGCTCG, you could leave out one letter—say, the second A. The resulting sequence would be: ATGGCTCG. Another mutation could be to add a letter (or base). You could add a T in between the two Gs: ATAGTGCTCG. The third kind of mutation could be a substitution, where one letter (or base) is switched for another letter (or base). For example, switch the last T with an A. This would give you: ATAGGCACG. *(The Structure of DNA/RNA)*

**60. Correct Answer:** When a haploid sperm nucleus fertilizes a haploid egg nucleus, a diploid zygote is formed. The genetic content of the zygote is different from the body cell of either parent, but the amount of genetic information is the same (46 chromosomes). The zygote contains half of the genetic information from each parent; each parent contributes 23 chromosomes. After fertilization, the zygote begins to divide by the process of mitosis in a series of divisions called cleavage. As the cells continue to divide and grow, they begin to differentiate into specialized cells that will make up the tissues and organs of the embryo. Development of the fetus occurs in the mother's uterus. Factors that can affect fetal development include smoking, which can result in low birth weight and premature birth; alcoholism, resulting in fetal alcohol syndrome (FAS), which can cause brain damage, hyperactivity, learning disabilities, and depression; drug addiction, which can result in the child becoming addicted; age of the mother, which may result in Down syndrome; exposure to viruses such as HIV, which causes AIDS; and health and nutrition of the mother (poor diet can cause low birth weight). *(Human Reproduction)*

**61. Correct Answer:** If you look at the data, it shows that plants have lower concentrations of pesticides in them than the other two. Herbivores are animals that eat those plants. Carnivores are animals that eat other animals. If you're concerned about your health and diet, you would choose the food with the least amount of pesticides possible. Your answer could be: "This information suggests that if a person has an animal-rich diet, he will ingest (or eat) the highest amount of pesticides." Or, you could say, "This information suggests that if a person has a plant-rich diet, she will ingest (or eat) the least amount of pesticides." *(Organisms in Their Environment)*

62. **Correct Answer:** Be sure to answer all parts of the question:

- The experimental groups are those that have changes to the variable of interest in the experiment. In this case, the salt concentration is being tested and three different levels of this variable are called for. For example, 2 percent, 4 percent, and 6 percent salt concentrations (or any three concentrations) could be used. A control group is the one used for comparison that has not had changes in the experimental variable. In this case, seawater or water with no added salt (0 percent salt concentration) could be used.
- In order for the experiment to be valid, as many conditions as possible must be kept constant for all groups. These conditions include: the temperature, the amount of liquid in each container, the size and type of container, the amount of food that the shrimp receive and the feeding frequency, the species of brine shrimp, and the number of eggs placed in each container.
- The data that should be collected is the number of brine shrimp that have hatched after a consistent time in each of the different salt concentrations.
- Experimental results that indicate the best concentration of salt in which to hatch brine shrimp eggs would be the concentration in which the most eggs hatched or the concentration in which eggs hatched soonest.

*(Scientific Method)*

63. **Correct Answer:** Be sure to answer all the parts of the question:

- Many different diseases would fit into the description provided in the question. It is important to follow the direction provided and choose a disease that is caused by a factor other than bacteria or virus. Diabetes and cancer are two possibilities. Cancer will be used as an example for the remainder of this question.
- Cancer can be caused by exposure to harmful UV radiation from the sun.
- Cancer can cause tumors to grow in the body.
- Cancer can be treated by chemotherapy.

*(Disease)*

64. **Correct Answer:** The following answers apply:

- Less oxygen is produced.
- Less carbon dioxide is removed from the atmosphere.
- Habitats are destroyed.
- Biodiversity is diminished.
- Plant species valued for medicines are lost.
- Global temperatures are affected.
- Erosion increases.

*(Negative Effects of Humans on the Environment)*

**65. Correct Answer:** Be sure to answer all the parts of the question:

- Antigens can be virus particles, bacteria, fungi, pollen, or even animal dander. Your answer should be: "Antigens are proteins that stimulate the immune system to respond." Or, you could respond: "Chicken pox virus are antigens that cause the immune system to produce antibodies."
- There are all kinds of white blood cells and all of them play important roles in an immune response. Some white blood cells produce antibodies, others engulf foreign particles, and others "remember" exposure to an antigen. Your answer should be: "White blood cells produce antibodies that are specific for the chicken pox virus." Or, you could respond: "White blood cells attack and destroy the chicken pox virus." (This answer covers both the white blood cells that produce antibodies and those white blood cells that will engulf the virus antigens.)
- Every foreign particle or antigen causes the immune system to respond with an antibody that is uniquely *specific* to each antigen. So, every cold and flu virus, every pollen grain, and every bit of pet dander you have ever been exposed to will cause your immune system to make separate and specific antibodies for each individual antigen it's exposed to. Your answer should be: "These antibodies are specific for the chicken pox virus." Or, you could say: "When you are exposed to the chicken pox virus, the immune system will make antibodies against that particular virus only."
- Vaccines to chicken pox and most other diseases are made with weakened forms of the disease. This way, the vaccine presents the body with an antigen that is just strong enough to stimulate the immune system, yet not strong enough to make someone sick with the disease. Your answer should be: "Chicken pox vaccine contains a weakened form of the disease that will stimulate the immune system but not make you sick."

*(Disease)*

**66. Correct Answer:** One quality of the cell membrane is that it is *selectively permeable.* This means that only some molecules may pass through it, but not all particles. Factors that affect whether they will pass through are: size of the molecule and size of the opening in the membrane; concentration of the molecules (if the concentration of a molecule is greater on one side of the membrane than on the other side); charge of the molecule; and shape of the molecule. *(Cell Structure)*

**67. Correct Answer: (2)** The closer together two organisms are to each other on the "tree," the more closely related they are. Go through each pair of animals and compare their position on the tree. Penguin and turtle are on separate branches, horse and donkey are very close together, snake and tuna are on separate branches, and turtle and rabbit are the farthest apart. The answer is choice (2), horse and donkey, because they are the closest to each other on the tree. *(Mechanisms of Evolution)*

**68. Correct Answer:** This diagram does not support the older system of classification because turtles are in the same branch as birds. You could also say that the diagram does not support the old system because the turtles and snakes are in different groups. *(Patterns of Evolution)*

**69. Correct Answer:** Based on the diagram, the pig is closer on the tree to the dog than to the kangaroo. *Remember:* The closer together on the tree the animals are, the more closely related they are. *(Patterns of Evolution)*

**70. Correct Answer:** Relationships should describe how the independent variable affects the dependent variable. As your activity increases (independent variable), the pulse rate (dependent variable) increases. *(Making Connections)*

**71. Correct Answer:** Two safe answers to this question are to increase the numbers of participants (two students aren't enough) and to increase the numbers of trials (repeat the experiment multiple times). *(Making Connections)*

**72. Correct Answer: (4)** Letters A and B represent common ancestors for each group of organisms. As you go up the diagram from either A or B, the species evolve into new species (represented by the other letters). ***Remember:*** The closer together two letters or organisms are, the more closely they are related. Therefore, F and G are most closely related; they are only separated by letter D. J and L are on two separate branches, one from B and the other from C. G and L are really separated from each other—there's no way they are closely related. F and H are also on two separate branches as are J and L. *(Patterns of Evolution)*

**73. Correct Answer: (2)** The species that possesses the best adaptations for its environment will survive the longest. Looking at the diagram, you can see that species B started as the common ancestor for species C, J, K, and L. Species B also survived on its own for four generations (each generation is a level on the diagram). Species A only lasted for two generations. Species C and J only lasted for one generation. *(Patterns of Evolution)*

**74. Correct Answer: (1)** The closer two organisms are on the diagram, the more closely related they are. And, the more closely related they are, the greater will be the similarity in DNA and proteins. Species B and J are the closest on the diagram. *(Patterns of Evolution)*

**75. Correct Answer:** The function of blood is to carry things like dissolved gases, oxygen, and carbon dioxide; nutrients (carbohydrates, lipids, and proteins); and wastes. If more blood is flowing, then more of these substances are being carried. Your answer should be: "The increased blood flow will carry more oxygen to cells and get rid of more wastes." *(Feedback)*

**76. Correct Answer:** Indicators change color in the presence of a specific substance. All you need to say is: "The solution with the indicator and protein will change color; the other one will not." *(Scientific Method)*